MOHAMMAD

THE APOSTLE OF MERCY

Also, by Qazi Fazl Ullah

Sharia & Politics

Science of Hadith

Jesus in the Quran

Jihad: Why, How, & When

Sayyidah Aaisha: Age & Marriage

Ramadan: Components of the Holy Month

MOHAMMAD

THE APOSTLE OF MERCY

WRITTEN BY **QAZI FAZL ULLAH**

HUND INTERNATIONAL PUBLISHING

LOS ANGELES, CALIFORNIA

2023

COPYRIGHT © 2023 BY QAZI FAZL ULLAH

All rights reserved. This book or any portion thereof may not be reproduced or used in any manner whatsoever without the express written permission of the publisher except for the use of brief quotations in a book review or scholarly journal.

EDITED BY EVELYN THOMPSON

SECOND PRINTING: 2023

ISBN: 978-1-970049-31-2

HUND INTERNATIONAL PUBLISHING

LOS ANGELES, CALIFORNIA

PRINTED IN THE UNITED STATES OF AMERICA

TABLE OF CONTENTS

PREFACE	24
ARABIA (IN GENERAL) BEFORE ISLAM	41
ALEXANDER AND ROMANS	42
MESOPOTAMIA	42
AKKADIANS AND AMORITES	43
BABYLONIAN RELIGION	43
ASSYRIANS	44
HEBREWS	44
BYZANTINE	45
SASANIAN EMPIRE	45
"JAZEERAT UL - ARAB" OR ARABIAN PENINSULA BEFORE ISLAM	47
"Jazeeratul Arab" or "Shibh – al - Jazeera"	47
ARAB TRIBES	49
PROPHET IBRAHIM	49
PROPHET ISMAIL (ISHMAIL) BORN	50
HAGAR AND ISMAIL IN MAKKAH	51
PROPHET ISMAIL (THE SLAUGHTERED ONE)	53
PROPHET IBRAHIM VISITS MAKKAH	58
SECOND VISIT OF IBRAHIM	59
CONSTRUCTION OF KABAH	60
CONDITIONS OF ARABIA AT THE ADVENT OF ISLAM	61
POLITICAL CONDITION	61
CULTURAL CONDITION	62
ECONOMIC CONDITIONS	64
SOCIAL CONDITIONS OF ARABIA	65
ETHICAL CONDITIONS	68
RELIGIOUS CONDITION	69
JEWISH TRIBES AND JUDAISM	70
CHRISTIANS AND CHRISTIANITY	74
THE POLYTHEISTS	77
SIGNS AND PROPHECIES OF THE PROPHET MOHAMMAD	78
THE PROPHECIES ABOUT PROPHET MOHAMMAD	79
ZOROASTRIAN'S PROPHECY	80
BUDDHA'S PROPHECY	80
HINDUISM PROPHECY	81
JUDAISM PROPHECY	82

CHRISTIANITY'S PROPHECY 83
PROPHET MOHAMMAD IN THE EYES OF NON-MUSLIM NOTABLES 86
SIGNS AT THE BIRTH OF THE PROPHET 90
THE PROPHET'S FAMILY 95
    ISMAIL (ISHAMEL) 96
    AID 97
    ADNAN 98
    THE FAMILY OF THE PROPHET 100
    QUSAI BIN KILAB 101
    ABD MANAF 102
    HASHIM BIN ABD MANAF (646CE) 103
    AL MUTTALIB 104
    WHY WAS MAKKAH ATTACKED? 105
    ABDULLAH BIN ABDUL MUTTALIB 107
    ABDULLAH AND HIS MARRIAGE TO A'AMINAH 108
PROPHET MOHAMMAD FROM BIRTH TO PROPHETHOOD 109
    HALEEMAH SADIA'S NURSING 110
    "SHAQQUS SAD'R" OR THE SPLIT OF THE CHEST 110
    MOHAMMAD'S TRIP TO MADINA (575) 111
    MOHAMMAD IN THE CUSTODY OF HIS GRANDFATHER: 111
    THE FIRST TRIP TO SHAM 112
    THE BATTLE OF FIJAR OR FUJJAR (580-590 CE) 113
    HILFUL FUDOOL (THE FUDOOL TREATY) 114
    THE PROPHET'S SECOND TRIP TO SHAM (595 CE) 115
    THE RECONSTRUCTION OF THE KABA 116
THE FIRST *WAHI* 119
    THE SECOND *WAHI* 122
    CALL TOWARDS ALLAH 123
    THE PROPHET USED TO PRAY IN SECRET 123
    QURAISH AS DELEGATION TO ABU TALIB 128
    ABU LAHAB 130
    SOME NOTABLE ENEMIES AND THEIR IGNOMINIOUS ACTS ... 131
    DARI ARQAM 131
    THE FIRST MIGRATION TO HASHAH 132
    THE STORY OF *SAJDAH* 132
    THE SECOND HIJRA TO HABSHAH 133
    CONVERSION OF HAMZAH IBNI ABDUL MUTTALIB 139
    CONVERSION OF UMAR IBNUL KHATTAB 139

QURAISH AND THEIR TACTICS **143**
   SOCIAL BOYCOTT 150
THE DELEGATION OF MAKKANS **151**
   AAMUL HUZ'N (THE YEAR OF GRIEF) 152
   MARRIAGE WITH SAUDAH BINT ZAMAAH 153
   TRIP TO TAIF 154
TRIBES CALLED BY THE PROPHET **160**
   SUWAID IBNI SAMIT 161
   IYAS IBNI MU'AAZ 162
   ABUZAR AL GHIFARI 163
   ZIMAD AL AZDI 165
   TUFAIL IBNI AMR ADDAUSI 165
   SIX PEOPLE FORM YATHRIB (MADINAH) 166
MARRIAGE TO AAISHA **168**
AL ISRA WAL MERAJ (ASCENSION) **169**
BAI'AT AQABA (THE AQABA PLEDGE) **180**
BAI'AT AQABAH THANIA (THE SECOND PLEDGE OF AQABAH) **183**
DARUN NADWAH'S MEETING **189**
"HIJRAH" (MIGRATION) TO MADINA **191**
   THE PROPHET'S STRATEGY 193
   THE STRUGGLE TO FIND THE CLUE 194
   DEPARTURE FROM THE CAVE 195
   SURAQAH IBN MALIK 195
   UMM MA' BAD AL KHUZA'IYAH 196
   BURAIDAH IBN AL-HASEEB 197
THE PROPHET'S ARRIVAL IN QUBA **198**
   ALI AND OTHERS ARRIVED IN QUBA 199
   MASJID QUBA 200
   DEPARTURE TO MADINA 200
   KHALID IBNI ZAID IBNI KULAIB (ABU AYUB) 202
   MASJIDI-NABAWI 203
MADINA **204**
ABDULLAH IBNI SALAM **205**
SALMAN AL FARSI **206**

THALABAH AND ASAD IBNI OBAID 209

AWS AND KHAZRAJ TRIBES 210

THE PROPHET AT MADINA 211

    THE TREATY OF MADINAH 212
    THE PACT AND THE JEWISH TRIBES 213
    BROTHERHOOD TREATY 215
    MARRIAGE TO AAISHAH 219

TAHWEELI QIBLAH 220

START OF AZAN FOR PRAYER 222

FASTING AND *ZAKAT* 223

    ZAKAT 223

***GHAZAWAT* AND *SARAYA* (EXPEDITIONS)** 224

DAWAT AND JIHAD 225

    SEIFUL BAH'R 227
    RABIGH 228
    SARIYAH KHARRARS 228
    GHAZWATUL ABAWA (GHAZWAT WADDAN) 229
    GHAZWAH BUWAT 229
    GHAZWAT SAFWAN 230
    GHAZWATUL USHAIRAH 230
    SARIYAH ABDULLAH IBNI JAHSH AL ASADI 231

GHAZWA-I-BADR 234

    CARAVAN COMING BACK 235
    QURAISH AND KINANAH 236
    QURAISH AND THEIR NUMBER 236
    THE MUSLIM ARMY 238
    INSPIRING RESPONSE OF SAHABAH 238
    NUMBER OF ANSAR AND MUHAJIREEN 240
    SAHABAH WHO WERE REGISTERED, BUT GIVEN DIFFERENT DUTIES
    241
    ARRANGEMENTS 242
    BADR 242
    QURAISH ARRIVED IN BADR BEFORE MUSLIMS 245
    THE PROPHET ACCEPTED KHABBAB'S OPINION 246
    SA'D'S SUGGESTION 246
    HAKEEM ASKED OTBAH TO AVOID WAR 248
    THE ARMY FACE TO FACE 250

QURAISH VS. QURAISH	250
THE BATTLE	252
THE SPIRIT OF MUSLIMS	254
ABUL BUKHTARI	255
UMAYYAH IBNI KHALAF AL JUMAHI	256
MU'AAZ AND MU'AWWAZ	256
IBNI MASUD FOUND ABU JAHL	257
ABBAS IBNI ABDUL MUTTALIB	259
THE MARTYRED	261
MUSHRIKEEN KILLED	262
THE CAPTIVES (PRISONERS OF WAR)	263
OBAIDA IBNUL HARITHA	265
THE SPOILS OF WAR	267
THE CAPTIVES/PRISONERS OF WAR	268
RELEASE FOR RANSOM AND FOR FREE	270
ABBAS, THE UNCLE OF THE PROPHET	271
ABUL AAS	272
WAHAB IBNI OMAIR	273
THE REASONS FOR VICTORY	275

THE DEATH OF RUQAYYAH, THE DAUGHTER OF THE PROPHET .. 278

THE MARRIAGE OF FATIMA, THE DAUGHTER OF THE PROPHET 279

EXPEDITIONS BETWEEN BADR AND UHUD 281

GHAZWAH BANI SULAIM 282

GHAZWAH BANU QAINUQA 283

GHAZWAH-I-SAWEEQ 286

GHAZWAH-I-ZEE AMAR 287

THE MARRIAGE OF UMMI KULTHUM 287

THE MARRIAGE OF HAFSAH 289

KA'B IBNI ASHRAF (A VILLAIN) 289

IBNI SUNAINAH 294

ABU AFAK AND ASMA 295

THE BATTLE OF NAJRAN 296

SARIYAH OF ZAID IBN HARITHA 296

GHAZWA-I-UHUD (THE BATTLE OF UHUD) 297

ABU AZZA 298

SAFWAN AND JUBAIR 299

THE QURAISH ARMY 300
QURAISH'S DEPARTURE 300
EMERGENCY DECLARED 301
QURAISH ARRIVAL 301
THE PROPHET AND HIS COMPANIONS 302
THE PROPHET PREPARED 304
THE PROPHET MADE THREE FLAGS 305
IBNI UBAI RETURNED 306
WAR SKETCH AND PLAN 307
THE PROPHET'S SWORD 308
THE STRATEGY OF QURAISH 309
ABU DUJANAH AND THE PROPHET'S SWORD 311
THE BRAVERY OF MUSLIMS 312
HAMZA WAS KILLED 312
HANZALAH IBNI AAMIR 315
THE ATTACK OF MAKKANS 315
ANAS IBNI NADR 317
THABIT IBNI DAHDAH 318
THE PROPHET WAS INJURED 318
TALHAH IBN OBAIDULLAH 322
OTBAH IBN ABI WAQQAS WAS KILLED 324
UMMI AMMARAH 324
MUS'AB IBNI OMAIR 325
THE MUSLIMS AND DROWSINESS 326
THE BRAVERY OF MUSLIM WOMEN 329
ABU SUFYAN REJOICED 330
THE MARTYRED AND THE WOUNDED 332
SA'D IBN RABEE 334
THE MARTYRS 334
EMERGENCY DECLARED MADINA 339

GHAZWAH, HAMRA-UL ASAD 348

A BELIEVER IS NOT TO GET BITTEN TWICE FROM THE SAME HOLE 350

MU'AAWIAH IBNI MUGHEERA IBNI ABIL AAS 351

MISSIONS AFTER UHUD 352

SARIYAH ABU SALAMAH 352
SARIYYAH ABDULLAH IBNI ONAIS 353
SARIYATUR RAJEE 353
AASIM IBNI THABIT 357

SARIYYAH-I-BEER-I-MA'OONAH 357
THE GHAZWAH OF BANU NADEER 360
CONSPIRACY 361
THE PROPHET'S WARNING 361
THE SIEGE 362
THE "FAY" 363
GHAZWA-I-ZATUR RUQA 367
GHAZWA-I- BADR AS-SAGHRA 370
GHAZWAH DOOMATUL JUNDAL 372
MARRIAGE WITH ZAINAB BINT JAHSH 373

GHAZWA-I-AHZAB 376

A RESERVATION AND ITS ANSWER 377
THE BACKGROUND OF GHAZWA-I-AHZAB 377
THE INVADERS MARCH 378
THE SHURA 378
THE INCIDENTS 380

BANU QURAIZAH 381

THE QADA PRAYERS 383

A STRATEGY TO CREATE A DISUNITY 383

THE PROPHET PRAYED AND INVOKED ALLAH 385

GHAZWA-I-BANU QURAIZAH 388

THE ADVICE OF KA'B IBNI ASAD 390
ABU LUBABAH 391

SA'D IBNI MU'AAZ AND ARBITRATION 393

PLOTS OF THE BANU QURAIZAH 395

EXEMPTIONS 396
DISTRIBUTION OF SPOILS OF WAR (BOOTY) 397

EXPEDITIONS AFTER AHZAB 398

KILLING OF SALLAM IBNI ABUL HUQAIQ 398
SARIYAH-I-QARTA 399
GHAZWA BANU LAHYAN 401
RAID OF OYAINAH IBNI HISN 402
SARIYYAH-I-GHAMR 402
SARRIYAH MOHAMMAD IBNI MASLAMAH 403
SARRIYAH ABU OBAIDAH IBNUL JARRAH 403
SARRIYAH ZAID IBNI HARITHA 404

SARRIYAH EIS	404
SARRIYYAH ZAID IBNI HARITHA	405
SARRIYYAH ZAID IBNI HARITHAH	405
SARRIYATUL-KHABT	405
SARRIYAH ABDUR RAHMAN IBNI AWF	406
SARRIYAH ALI IBNI ABI TALIB	407

GHAZWAH - BANI-MUSTALAQ 407

THE BACKGROUND	409
THE CONSPIRACY OF ABDULLAH IBN UBAI	410

THE STORY OF "IFK" OR FALSE ACCUSATION 414

THE SON OF ABDULLAH IBNI UBAI 415

THE PROPHET ASKED ABOUT	416
AAISHA GOT THE NEWS	418

SARAYA AND MISSIONS AFTER BANI-MUSTALAQ 422

SARIYYAH ZAID IBNI HARITHA	422
THE MISSION OF IBNI RAWAHAH	423
UKAL AND ORAINAH TRIBES, AND KURAZ'S MISSION	424

PACT OF HUDAIBIYAH 426

THE PROPHET PUT ON HIS IHRAM	426
THE DELEGATIONS TO THE PROPHET	428
UTHMAN ON MISSION	432
BAI'AT-I-AQABAH	433
THE PACT OF HUDAIBIA	434
THE PACT	436
THE WISDOM IN TREATY	438
ABU JUNDAL	440
THE PROPHET CAME OUT OF IHRAM	441

ABU BASEER ARRIVED IN MADINA 447

THE WOMEN AND THE RETURN	449
GHAZWAT UL GHABAH	450

LETTERS TO THE KINGS AND LEADERS 451

LETTER TO CAESAR THE KING OF ROME	452
JUZAM ROBBED DIHYAH	455
LETTER TO "KISRA" (KHOSROW) THE PERSIAN EMPEROR	455
LETTER TO NEGUS THE ABYSSINIAN KING	458
THE MARRIAGE OF UMMI HABIBA	460

LETTER TO MUQAUQAS THE KING OF MISR (EGYPT) 461
MARIA QIBTIA (COPTS) 465
LETTER TO HARITH IBNI ABI SHAMIRR' AL GASSANI 465
LETTER TO HAUDAH IBNI ALI, THE RULER OF YAMAMAH 466
LETTER TO MUNZIR IBNI SAWA GOVERNOR OF BAHRAIN 467
LETTER TO THE KING OF OMAN JAIFER AND HIS BROTHER ABD S/O JALANDI 469

THE BATTLE OF KHYBER 471

THE FORTS IN KHYBER 472
THE PROPHET AND HIS ARMY 473
THE PROPHET ON HIS WAY TO KHAYBER 475
THE MUSLIM ARMY AT THE BORDERS OF KHYBER 476
THE BATTLE 477

ALI ON MISSION 478

THE MUSLIMS TOOK OVER A FEW FORTS 480
THE CATAPULT AND THE CONQUEST OF NAZAR FORT 482
THE KATEEBA ZONE 482
THE SURRENDER AND THE PEACE TREATY 483
THE *NIKAH* OF SAFIA 484
THE POISONOUS LAMB 485
JAFAR AND ABU MUSA JOINED THE PROPHET 486
THE FADAK 487

GHAZWAT WADIL QIRA 487

SARIYAH OF ABAN IBNI SAEED 489

MISSIONS AFTER KHYBER 490

UMRAT UL QADA 492

THE MARRIAGE OF MAIMUNAH BINT UL HARITH 495

KHALID AND AMR 495

THE ISLAM OF KHALID 497

THE BATTLE OF MUTA 499

THE PROPHECIES ABOUT MARTYRDOM 500
THE ARMY DEPARTED 501
THE NEW LEADERSHIP 503

SARIYYAH ZATUS SALASIL 505

SARIYYAH ABU OBAIDAH IBNUL JARRAH 506

THE CONQUEST OF MAKKAH 508

KHUZA'A AND BANU BAKR 508
QURAISH WERE AFRAID 509
AMR IBNI SALIM FROM KHUZA'E 510
ABU SUFYAN IN MADINA 512
THE PROPHET WAS GETTING READY 514
THE STORY OF HATIB'S LETTER 514
THE ARMY MARCHED TOWARDS MAKKAH 517
THE MUSLIM ARMY AT MARUZ – ZAHRAN 521
THE MARCH TO MAKKAH 524
THE PROPHET'S ENTRANCE TO MAKKAH 528
KHALID WAS ATTACKED 528
ENTERING MASJID UL HARAM AND BAITULLAH 530
THE PROPHET MOHAMMAD INSIDE KABAH 531
THE PROPHET'S ADDRESS 532

GENERAL AMNESTY ANNOUNCED 535

THE WANTED PEOPLE 535
ABDULLAH IBNI ABI SARAH AL AAMIR 535
ABDULLAH IBNI KHATAL 536
FARTANA 537
QAREEBAH OR FAREEBAH 537
IKRAMAH IBNI ABU JAHL 537
HUWAIRITH IBNI NAQEEZ 538
HABBAR IBNUL ASWAD 538
MIQYAS IBNI DUBABAH 538
HARITH IBNI HISHAM 539
ZUBAIR IBNI UMAYYAH 539
KA'B IBNI ZUHAIR 539
SAFWAN IBNI UMAYYAH 540
WAHSHI IBNI HARB 541
SARAH 542
HIND BINT-I-OTBAH 543

THE IDOLS AND STATUES 544

ABU QUHAFAH ACCEPTED ISLAM 546

MISSIONS AFTER THE CONQUEST OF MAKKAH 546

MISSION OF KHALID 546
MISSION OF AMR IBNUL AAS 547
IDOL MANAT 548
KHALID TOWARDS BANU JUZAIMAH 549

THE BATTLE OF HUNAIN 551
THE PROPHET MARCHED 552
MUSLIMS FOLLOWED THE ENEMY 556
THE PROPHET PROCEEDED TOWARDS TA'IF 557
THE PROPHET ESTABLISHED A CATAPULT 558

THE BOOTY (SPOILS OF WAR) AND ITS DISTRIBUTION 559

THE NEWCOMERS TO THE FOLD OF ISLAM 563

THE PROPHET AND THE ANSAR 565
THE UMRAH 566
THE MISSION OF TUFAIL IBNI AMR ADDAUSI 566
THE MISSION OF QAIS IBNI SA'D 567
THE MISSION OF OYAINAH IBNI HISN 568
THE MISSION OF WALEED IBNI OQBAH 570
THE MISSION OF QUTBAH IBNI AAMIR 572
THE MISSION OF ZAHHAK IBNI SUFYAN 573
THE MISSION OF ALQAMAH 573
SARIYYAH OF ALI TO "QALS" 574

BATTLE OF TABUK 578
THE TENSION 579
DONATION AND CONTRIBUTION 580
THE DEPARTURE 583
THE PROPHET WROTE A DOCUMENT FOR THE PEOPLE OF AILAH 588
THE MISSION OF KHALID IBNI WALEED 588
COMING BACK TO MADINA 589
THE STAYED BEHIND AND THEIR CASE 590
THE BATTLE OF TABUK AS MENTIONED IN QURAN 592

MASJID-I-ZIRAR 600
THE DEATH OF ABDULLAH IBNI OBAI 604

THE HAJJ OF ABU BAKR 606

CAN NON-MUSLIM ENTER HARAM? 609

THE ATTACK OF KHALID IBN UL WALEED ON THE BANU KA'B 615

THE DEATH OF IBRAHIM, THE SON OF THE PROPHET 619

THE MISSIONS AND THE DELEGATES 619
ABU MUSA AND MU'AAZ WERE SENT TO YEMEN AREA 620
THE MISSION OF ALI 620

THE DELEGATES 621

- ABDUL QAIS DELEGATIONS 622
- DAUS DELEGATION 622
- FARWAH IBNI AMR AL JUZAMI 623
- SADA DELEGATION 623
- THE DELEGATION OF UZARAH 623
- THE DELEGATION OF BALI 624
- THE DELEGATE OF THAQEEF 625
- THE HAMDAN DELEGATION 626
- THE DELEGATION OF BANU FAZARAH 626
- THE KINGS OF YEMEN 627
- THE DELEGATION OF NAJRAN 627
- THE MUBAHALAH 632
- BANU HANEEFAH DELEGATION 632
- THE DELEGATION OF BANU AAMIR IBNI SA'SAA 635
- THE DELEGATION OF TUJEEB 635
- THE TA'I DELEGATION 636

HAJJATUL WIDA 636

- ARAFAT'S SERMON 638
- 10TH OF ZUL HIJJAH 642
- KHUTBAH AT MINA 643

SARIYAH OF OSAMAH AND THE NUMBER OF GHAZAWAT AND SARAYA 644

- SARIYAH USAMA IBNI ZAID 645
- THE NUMBER OF GHAZAWAT AND SARAYA 646

THE SICKNESS AND DEATH OF THE PROPHET 646

- SAHABAH AND THEIR FEELINGS 652
- THE PROPHET'S DEATH AND ABU BAKR 653
- SAQEEFAH BANU-SA'IDAH 654
- THE BURIAL OF THE PROPHET 655

WHAT WAS THE PROPHET'S PERSONALITY? 656

- THE NOBLE CHARACTER OF THE PROPHET 659

THE FAMILY OF THE PROPHET 660

- KHADIJA BINTI KHUWALID 661
- SAWDAH BINT-I-ZAMA'AAH 663
- AAISHA THE DAUGHTER OF ABU BAKR 664
- HAFSAH BINTI-I-UMAR 665

ZAINAB BINT-I-KHUZAIMAH 666
UMMI SALMAH 667
ZAINAB BINT-I-JAHSH AL ASADIA 669
JAWARIA BINTUL HARITHA 672
UMMI HABEEBAH RAMLAH BINTI ABU SUFYAN 672
SAFIYA BINTI HUYAY IBNI AKTAB 673
MAIMUNAH BINTUL HARITH 675
MARIA QIBTIA 675
THE CHILDREN OF THE PROPHET 678

JIHAD AND THE PROPHET 683

THE PROPHET'S SWORDS 687

ZUL FIQAR 687
MAATHUR 687
AS SAMSAMAH 687
AL QAL'E 687
AL-ADB 688
HAT'F 689
QAZEEB 689
AL MUHZIM 689
GHALAS 690
RASOOB 690
AL BATTAR 690
AL-URJUN 691
AL FAQR UL HADR 691

THE BOWS OF THE PROPHET 691

AS SAFRAA 691
AL BAIDAA 692
AZ ZORA 692

THE SPEARS AND LANCES OF THE PROPHET 692

AL MATHWA 692
AL MUTHANNA 693

THE SHIELDS OF THE PROPHET 693

FANAQ 693
AZ ZALUQ 693

THE ARMOR COATS OF THE PROPHET 694

ZATUL FUZUL 694
ZATUL WISHAH 694

ZATUL HAWASHI 694
AS SAFRIA 694
AL BATRA 695
AL HAZEEQ 695

THE HELMETS OF THE PROPHET: 695

AL MUWASHSHAH 695
AL SABOO 695

THE MOUNTS OF THE PROPHET 695

THE CAMELS OF THE PROPHET 696
AL QASWAA 696
CAMELS 696
JAD'AA 696
ADBAA 696

HORSES OF THE PROPHET 697

AL MURTAJIZ 697
AS SAKB 697
YAASUB 697
AZ ZARF 697
AL LAHEEF 698
SAB'HA 698
AL WARD 698
AL LAZAZ 698

THE MULES OF THE PROPHET 698

DULDUL 698
FIDDAH 699
THE GUARDS OF THE PROPHET 699

BOOKS BY *QAZI FAZL ULLAH* 702

ABOUT THE AUTHOR 720

PREFACE

Praise be to Allah the lord of all worlds and peace, and blessings of Allah may be upon his last prophet, whom he sent as a great mercy for all worlds. Also, peace be upon his followers until the day of judgment, and his family as well. Peace and blessing on all the prophets and messengers (i.e., Moses, Jesus, Noah…) sent by the Lord of all the worlds.

1. <u>MANKIND AN HONORABLE CREATION</u>

Allah (SWT) the sole creator of the universe has honored mankind with his special bounty. He created the angels and put in their nature the element of "AQL" (intellect). So, they obey the commandment and perform their duties in full. They do not even know disobedience.

> *"They do not disobey what Allah has ordered them and do what they have been ordered." (66:6)*

He created the animals and put in their nature desires and lusts, so they fulfill their desires. And He created mankind as a special creature and put in their nature, both intellect and lust to test them so that they may be honored more and more if they kept balance in their actions and deeds. It means he has created them balanced creatures as he has said in the Holy Quran,

> *"And (I swear) by "Nafs" (human nature) and its perfection in proportion, that he has inspired it, its evils and its piety." (91:7-8)*

And as we know that mostly human desires and lusts overtake his intellect, which is a failure in the sight of Allah, but purification of his nature by keeping up with balance is success.

As Allah said,

> "Indeed, succeeded one who purified (sanctified) it and lost one who corrupted it." (91: 9-10)

His physical structure is unique as He said,

> "Then we originated him (mankind) as another (unique) creation. So blessed (who blesses also) is Allah the best creator." (23:14)

Also, Allah said,

> "Indeed, we have created mankind in the best stature (Mold)." (95:4)

Allah has given them this talent which is actually the result of the combination of these two elements, the intellect, and the desire. They use their intellect to use the things in the universe to the best of their talent to fulfill their desires, while angels do not need it as they do not have desires, and animals are incapable because they don't have intellect.

Allah (SWT) has made the world and the things therein, subject and subservient to mankind. Mankind is searching, researching constantly, and continuously to approach all these things and to use it for his good and needs.

Allah *Said,*

> "See you not that Allah has subjected to you what is there in the heavens and what is there in the earth, and he has completed (with perfection) his favors on you, the open one and the hidden one." (31:20)

Allah said,

> *"He has subjected to you the ships that they (ships) may sail through the sea by his command, and he has made rivers (also) to be subject to you. And he has made the sun and the moon, both constantly pursuing their courses, to be subject to you and he made the night and the day to be of service to you. And he gave you all that you asked for (need it) and if you count the blessings of Allah, never will you be able to count them." (14:32-34)*

Allah (SWT) not only gave them the right to utilize all these, but he ordered them to do that.

He said,

> *"He (Allah) is one who made the earth subservient to you so go into its shoulders and eat of his provision and to him is the resurrection." (67:15)*

He also said,

> *"O group of Jinn and mankind! If you can get into the diameters of the heavens and the earth, then get into (it) you can't do it, but with power." (55:33)*

This exploitation and utilization is a great honor given to them. Allah said,

> *"Indeed, we have honored the children of Adam and given them charge in land and sea and provided them the pure lawful things and we have preferred them above many of those we have created with a marked (great) preferment." (17:70)*

2. ALLAH WANTS MANKIND TO GO NEAR TO HIM

As we said, mankind has mostly disregarded and forgotten the other aspect of his life which is intellectual and spiritual, because of the things here in this world and its use for his worldly life. Even though, this is a need and not an object. The actual object of human life is to establish a connection with Allah, his creator who has honored him to utilize all his creatures, but to grow closer to him and to have a prosperous life in the hereafter, so, he has to seek means of going close to him, as He said,

> "O you who believe! Fear Allah (fulfill your obligations) and seek means (sources to go close to him) and strive hard in his path (cause). So, you may become successful." (5:35)

But they are doing otherwise so they are losers.

> "Say (O Mohammad) shall we tell you the biggest losers in respect of deeds? Those whose efforts are wasted (lost) in the life of this world and they think that they are doing something good." (18:103-104)

To get them out of this big loss to put them in a balanced life, to take them closer to Allah, so they may get into success in the hereafter, Allah has sent to them messengers to guide them in this regard so they may not have any excuse.

Allah said,

> "(Allah sent these) Messengers as givers of glad tidings and warnings, so there may not be (any) excuse after these messengers." (4:165)

So, sending messengers was a great mercy of Allah (SWT).

3. <u>MESSAGE OF THE MESSENGERS, IS THE MERCY OF ALLAH</u>

Allah (SWT) sent all these messengers with one and the same message and "Deen" (religion) proceeding towards further perfection through different ages and messengers.

1) MESSAGE

The message is, as Allah said,

> "And we haven't sent before you any messenger, but we had been revealing to him that there is no God but only me (Allah), so worship me (alone)." (21:25)

2) DEEN OF ALL MESSENGERS

They were given the same "Deen" Islam, as He said,

> "He (Allah) has ordained for you the same religion (Islam) which he ordained for Noah (Nuh) and that which we have revealed to you (o Mohammad!) and that which we have ordained to Ibrahim, Musa (Moses), Isa (Jesus) so you may establish that religion and make no division there in it." (42:13)

3) COMPLETION OF DEEN

Allah completed this "Deen" in the time of Mohammad (SAS).

> "This day I have completed for you your "Deen" (religion) and perfected on you my favor and chose for you "Islam" as "Deen" (system of life)." (5:3)

4) FINALITY OF THE PROPHET HOOD

All messengers had this "Deen" as their mission but in a specific area, for a specific people of their respective times. That's why they address using the word "Ya Quami" O my people, but prophet Mohammad (SAS) was not a messenger of a specific people, specific time and specific area. That's why his address starts with the words "Ya Ayyuhannas "O mankind. He is the messenger for all mankind, as Allah said,

> "Say (O Mohammad!) O Mankind! Verily I am the messenger of Allah to you all." (7:158)

He is the messenger for all coming generations. Allah said,

> "He (Allah) is the one who sent in illiterate people (Makkans and people of peninsula) (a great) messengers from amongst them, reciting to them his verses sanctifying them and teaching them the book and wisdom (how to dispose of affairs) even though they were before (this) in a plain error.

> "And (he has sent him to) others of them who have not yet joined them (the coming generation until the last day) and he is all mighty, the all wise. That is the grace of Allah, which he bestows on whom he wills. And that Allah is the owner of mighty grace," (62:2-4)

His grace is a message, and making Prophet Mohammad as the last and final prophet till the last day is his mighty grace. The word "mighty" embodies greatness as well as a decisive power, that he has completed the message and decided to stop sending any further messenger and this is his power which no one can challenge. Also, he is all-wise, knowing the wisdom therein, so, no one can ask, "why."

Allah said,

> "Mohammad is not the father of any of your men, but he is the messenger of Allah and the last (and seal) of the

prophets. And Allah is ever all aware of everything." (33:40)

So, Allah has sent him as the final prophet. If someone asks 'why?' Allah has answered himself that he is the all, aware of everything. So, when he is all aware of, he is almighty and all wise, then, no one has any right to say that message and prophethood is the mercy of Allah so it could not be stopped. Yes, the message of Mohammad is going on continuously, so his mercy never stopped. But if someone says that, no, we mean messenger and prophets are mercy, we say yes, but till Allah says so and when he says otherwise, then, that is no more mercy. That's why, Allah (SWT) very clearly said,

"And indeed we had written in (all, written books after "zikr"(reminder, admonition, remembrance of Allah, zikr and statement about Mohammad) that my righteous servants shall inherit the earth verily in this (zikr which is mentioned before or in this Quran or in this information which I have given you here about that "zikr") there is "Balagh" (message, qualifying statement which makes satisfied or approach to final destination/goal) for a people who worship (listen, obey, believe, understand and practice) and we have not sent you but a great mercy to "Al-Alamin"(All words)." (21:105-107)

Now when Allah said that Mohammad is the great mercy/grace to all worlds, then there is no room for questioning how and why, as the wise people said,

"Don't put a question mark where Allah has put a period."

Then, the message basically has two aspects: "Bashara," giving glad tidings to those who believed in and "Inzar," giving warning of ultimate consequences to those who disbelieved.

Allah said,

> *"And we have not sent you but a giver of glad tidings and a warner to all mankind. But most men know not."* *(34:28)*

The last portion of this verse indicates that this especially important point must be understood by all mankind. But most of them do not as the word "Kaaffah" includes time, place, and kind which means all humans at all times anywhere in the world.

Also, Allah ordered the prophet to say,

> *"And this Quran has been revealed to me, so I may warn you therewith this (Quran and whomsoever it may reach." (6:19)*

"Whoever it may reach" means human beings everywhere and in every time.

As this Deen is the same one started with Adam, processed, and proceeded through all the Messengers and completed with Mohammad, that's why it is must for everyone to believe in all Messengers and their Message as well.

For example, we can say that Message and Messengers are just like a course processing through various steps toward completion like one who is a PhD in a subject and one believes in his degree, it means he believed in his all-dependent diplomas and degrees.

5) DEEN IS ONE, BUT LAWS ARE DIFFERENT

Yes, message and religion is one and the same, but details were different in different times, areas and for different people.

> *"For each one of you we have prescribed a (specific) law and a clear way." (5:48)*

This difference was due to circumstances in various times, even though the basic concept was the same.

Allah said to the Prophet (SAS),

> *"Then we have put you on a (plain) way (given you a specific set of laws and rules) so follow that and follow not the desires of those who know not." (45:18)*

Allah had given to every people a specific way of actions, as he said,

> *"For every "Ummah" (people/followers of a specific messenger) we have ordained (a specific) "Mansak" (Religious ceremonies/ways rules etc.) which they used to follow, so let them not dispute you on this matter (Religious ceremonies or ways in your "Shariah") and invite to your Lord verily you are on the straight guidance." (22:67)*

Also, Allah said,

> *"And for every Ummah (people/nation) we have ordained "Mansak" (Religious ceremonies/Ways/Rules etc.) so that they may mention the name of Allah over the beast of cattle (when slaughtering them)." (22:34)*

These verses mean that different ways in different times were revealed from Allah. But aim and object was one and the same which is belief in Allah and to invite others towards Allah and straight guidance.

6) WAHI (REVELATION IS MUST)

Messengers and Wahi is important for guidance as for seeking knowledge there are three means:

1) Sensation /Senses and these are commonly found even in animals and birds.

2) Aql and intellect which human beings have, but mostly they use it for their physical, material and worldly attachments. Then, this Aql or intellect is different in different individuals. It could never be decided that which one of the human beings is perfect in his intellectual approach to be followed by others, so, Aql is not a sufficient means of knowledge because:

   a) Aql and intellect is affected by diseases like the human body and organs when it cannot approach even, rather than proper approach.

   b) Aql or intellect gets confused very often.

   c) Aql or intellect gets affected by superstitions.

   d) Aql or intellect gets affected by customs, even if these customs are illogical, unreasonable, and even destructive.

   e) A very sound and safe Aql and intellect has a limited approach to its bounds and limits. It cannot go beyond those limits, while there are facts and realities, beyond that which has to be known, especially human's spiritual needs.

Now, this is a fact that the human body is created by Allah from dust,

> "And indeed, we have created mankind from extract (Nucleus) of dust." (23:12)

Then, Allah has sent down soul and spirit from "Hazeeratul-Quds" (Enclosure of Sanctity), a place upon the seven Heavens. The soul and spirit is immaterial element of life.

"And they ask you (O Mohammad*) about "Ruh" (spirit); say: "Ruh" (spirit) is the 'Amr' (Matter/affair/command) of my Lord. And you have not been given knowledge, but a little." (17:85)*

Now, all the requirements of the human body are fulfilled from the earth from which is the origin of his body, but as "Ruh" (spirit) is from upon the seven Heavens, its requirements and needs are to be fulfilled from there and that is in shape of "Wahi" (revelation). That's why Wahi is also called "Ruh" which gives actual life.

Allah said,

"He sends "Ruh" (revelation) by his command to whom he wills of his slaves, that he (the servant) may warn (people) of the day of mutual meeting (with their Lord)." (40:15)

Also, He said,

"And the same way we revealed to you "Ruh" (Revelation) of our command." (43:52)

Then, Allah (SWT) has sent more or less than 124,000 messengers and Prophets. Three hundred and thirteen out of them are messengers or "Rasul" and the rest are Prophets or "Nabi." A messenger is one who received a revealed book or scripture in written or in verbal shape or received a "Shariah" (set of Rules and Laws), while a Prophet is one who followed the Shariah of another messenger. Both of them were bound to convey that and try to establish and implement that in words and spirit.

7) <u>TO UNDERSTAND A BOOK, A TEACHER IS A MUST.</u>

Allah has sent many Messengers without a written book. But he never sent a book without Messenger which means that a Qualified Scholar or Teacher of any field can teach and train without a book. But none can learn from a book if that is beyond his scope and approach. To learn a book, one needs to have it from a knowledgeable person of that field. Messengers got brought up under the eyes of Allah, then, a Messenger is a perfect person developed by Allah as regarding prophet Musa.

Allah said,

> "In order that you may be brought up under My Eye." (20:39)

Also, Allah said to Musa,

> "And I have made you for myself (my job, the Message)." (20:41)

No Messenger of Allah has ever learnt from anyone. But he received the Message from Allah through revelation and inspiration. Most of them were brought up without the supervision of his father, even.

Prophet Ibrahim's father never taught him anything as he was an idol worshiper and Ibrahim by nature disliked that. Prophet Musa's bringing up took place in the house of Pharaoh (Firaun). Prophet Isa was born without having a father, Prophet Ismael was left as a baby there in Makkah valley, Prophet Yusuf was thrown in a well as a teenager and was taken to Egypt where his upbringing took place. And Prophet Mohammad was born as an orphan. But all of them were given a pious and pure nature. As Allah said, regarding Ibrahim,

> "And indeed, we had given Ibrahim maturity/rectitude before (attaining the age of puberty or before receiving Message) and we were well aware of him." (21:51)

Because of that God-given pure nature, nobody had any objection on the character of any Messenger, but even they presented their pre-message time as evidence and proof to their people as Prophet Mohammad said,

> "I have spent (big) life (40 years) amongst you before this so you do not use your intellect." (10:16)

Meaning no one had blamed him for any misbehavior.

He also asked before conveying to them the message for the first time,

> "Have you found me a truthful one or a liar?"

They said we have found in you nothing but truth only.

And because of that, the prophet is the perfect role-model for his people, and that's why Allah blessed human beings by sending them the messengers from amongst them whose life was known to them, so, they may follow them in their physical and material fields as well as they have the same basic human requirements.

Allah said,

> "Say (O Mohammad!) I am but a man like you (but), have been inspired that your God is only one God so who so ever hopes (believe) the meeting with his Lord (life after death) so he may practice righteousness and associate none as a partner in the worship of his Lord." (18:110)

h. PROPHET IS A ROLE MODEL

This righteousness or righteous virtuous deeds could be known through prophets and their teachings and practice.

> "Indeed, in the messengers of Allah there is the best example (role model) for you, those who hope (believes) for (the meeting with) Allah and the last day and remember Allah a lot." (33:21)

And that's why Sahabah used to watch the Prophet (SAS) and follow him in words, practice and spirit as they knew that the prophet of Allah is the practical interpretation of the Holy Quran.

Aaisha said,

> "His character (daily behavior) was Quran."

i. PROPHET'S TEACHINGS ARE PRESERVED:

The Sahabah carefully have collected and memorized his teachings which are called Sunnah and Hadith and the forthcoming generations of Ulama(scholars) have very carefully compiled those which exceed the number of 700,000 Ahadith. Not only that, but these Ulama also put on record the Biography of all those who narrated the Ahadith. This is also a miracle of Mohammad and a confirmation of the promise of Allah where He said,

> "Verily, we, we, we have sent down "Zikr" and verily we are for it the Guards." (15:9)

"Zikr" in the Holy Quran is used in different meanings. It means remembrance, reminder, admonition, advice, knowledge, wisdom and skill, mentioning advice, Holy Quran (itself) and also the saying and practice of the Prophet.

j. PROPHET'S TEACHINGS EXPLAINED THE HOLY BOOK:

To mean Holy Quran by word "Zikr" here in the aforementioned verse is clear as Allah said, "verily we have sent down 'Zikr'." But it includes the saying and the practice of the prophet as well. Because that has also been sent down, revealed and inspired. Also, that is called "Zikr" as Allah said,

> "And we have not sent down to you the Book, but to explain to them, things they differed therein and a guidance and a mercy for people who believe." (16:64)

Now, how, and where from The Prophet will explain the Book? He received the same from Allah as well either in a revealed shape or in an inspired shape.

> "And we have sent down to you the "Zikr" so you may explain to people what has been revealed to them and that they may think." (16:44)

Here in this verse, there is "Zikr" which with the prophet will explain and there is "which is revealed to them" so the "Zikr" is the sayings and practices of the Prophet, (SAS) and the "revealed to them" is the Holy Quran. Prophet (SAS) was given two things from Allah (1) The Quran and (2) His Hadith and Sunnah as Allah said,

> "Move not with this (Quran) your tongue to make haste there with. It is for us to collect it (in your heart) and to (make you able for) its recital. So, when we (our messenger Gabriel) recite it then follow its recital (with concentration and due attention). Then it is for us to explain it." (75:16-19)

Here in these verses Allah made it truly clear that he revealed the explanation of the Quran as well and that is the Hadith and Sunnah.

Also, He said,

> "This is (the) Book, its verses are filled with wisdom, then explained (in detail) from one (Allah) who is all-wise, well acquainted." (11:1)

Again, Allah made it clear that after the Book is revealed in parts it was explained from him as well, and that explanation is in the form of sayings and practices of the Prophet (SAS).

Prophet's sayings and practices were made safe by Allah.

Allah said,

> "Neither your companion (Mohammad) wandered from the right path/erred (ignorantly) nor he seduced (arrogantly) nor does he speak of his own desire. This is, but a revelation revealed." (53:2-4)

Here, in these verses Allah has totally negated any intentional error or seduction in his actions and also negated any talk of his based on evil desire which means he was watched and guarded by Allah, inspiring him with all these words and acts.

Allah said,

> "And put your trust (O Mohammad!) in the All-Mighty, The Merciful, the one who looks at you (see you/watch you/guard) when you stand up (to call towards Allah or to pray alone) and (look at) your movements (changing forms) among those who prostrate. Verily he is the all-hearer, the all knower." (26:217-220)

It means every time you are safe guarded by Allah to keep you in the proper way in your saying and practices as well, that's why that is followed by,

> "Verily he is the all hearer (hears your words) the all-knower (knows your actions)."

In Islamic literature one can find the Prophet, his sayings and practices everywhere, but Muhaditheen (compilers of Hadith) have collected and compiled his teachings, words, and practices. Historians preserved his life and history in different ways while other scholars wrote Books in his "Seerah," which is also his biography. One can very easily find out ways of life from his biography. To write a Book in "Seeratun-Nabi" is actually seeking a way to have a connection with the Prophet (sas). This is also a Book like that even though we cannot aid more to this field, but to our best we will try to have a moral written wherever and whenever we can deduce it from His Seerah.

May Allah (SWT) enable us to do what is good in this regard and to make this effort a useful and beneficial one. Amen.

ARABIA (IN GENERAL) BEFORE ISLAM

As we all know, Allah (SWT) has sent more than a hundred thousand messengers to human beings. They might have been sent to various regions and nations, where the life was in progress in various times, but the messengers who are mentioned in the Holy Quran by names and their stories are stated there in, their region message was alongside the Mediterranean, which is now today occupied by Palestine, Israel, Syria, Iraq, Egypt and Saudi Arabia. As we see that Nuh, Hud, Saleh, Yunus, Ibrahim, his descendants, Musa, his followers then all messengers of Bani Israel and Issa were sent in that region. Let us see why this region was chosen for the message and especially for the Message of these known Messengers?

Here one can say either a messenger is or was to be sent to an uncivilized, unsocial and an illiterate region or to be sent to a social and civilized region to teach them and to give them some spiritual knowledge, because ultimately a civilization is to be exported by the said nation to others or to be imported by other nations from them, with all this the message requires civilization of the territory in Toto.

Historians say that Egypt was the cradle of human civilization some six thousand years ago. Archeologists are busy discovering whether Iraq and Syria were prior to it, as these were the base for Mesopotamian and Phoenician civilization. Whatever the results may be, one thing is recognized that the civilization was connected to the Mediterranean Sea, and Egypt was the one who exported its civilization to Greece and Rome. As far as the far cast civilization is concerned, we do not discuss that as Islam first influenced the near east's civilization and then that mixed civilization influenced the far east and the rest of the globe as well.

The Semitic race is one of the famous ancient civilizations. This race occupied a special place in mankind history. In this region, religion always influenced civilization, though the people most of the time either rejected it or got rid of it. The most famous religions of this race are Judaism, Christianity and Islam.

These Semitic people sometimes immigrated to different parts of fertile land known as Babylonian, attributed to Babyl the birth city of Ibrahim their great grandfather, while some other time they were named as Assyrians, the Phoenicians, and the Hebrews. Around 3500 B.C. these people settled in the Tigris Euphrates valley of the civilized Samarian people.

ALEXANDER AND ROMANS

Alexander the Greek hero conquered Persia, then, the eastern civilization was introduced into Europe and a new civilization from the mixture grew up, which was called Helixes civilization. In 146 B.C Romans conquered Greece, and then in 7th century, Islam conquered Persia and Rome both, and a new civilization arose up in the Region.

MESOPOTAMIA

The Region between Tigris and Euphrates rivers is called Mesopotamia. The northern part of the region was named as Assyria and the southern part as Babylonia. This second part was fertile. Before Isa, this part had several states, and each had its own god and king as well. There were fights and wars amongst them.

AKKADIANS AND AMORITES

Akkadu was the capital and Akkad was the Ruler from this Semitic Race. Akkad or Sargon 1 united the southern valley in 2800 B.C and conquered Syria.

Amorites, the second group of the Semitic people, came from Syria and dominated the Euphrates valley under the leadership of Hammurabi (2123 -2081 B.C). He united the whole valley divided into two parts Sumeru and Akkad and renamed it as Babylon. He collected and codified the ancient laws of Babylonia.

BABYLONIAN RELIGION

These people were the idolaters with gods and goddesses, they had faith in evil spirits and foretelling of events by stars and planets' movement.

The Holy prophet (PBUH) said in this regard that there is no "Safar" an evil spirit in a specific lunar month between Muharram and Rabi-Ul-Awal and also said,

> *"Whenever there is mentioned some stars so keep silent."*

Means do not attribute to them the events. In another Hadith it is said that Allah says,

> *"Son of Adam makes partner to me by saying that such and such star or because of it we been rained."*

They developed some words for writing. They had proficiency in astrology more than Egyptians. They divided the year into twelve months as nature is. Allah (SWT) says,

> *"The number of the months (of a year) is twelve in the book (natural system is record) of Allah (SWT)." (9:36)*

In mathematics, they invented the decimal system.

ASSYRIANS

They were in the northern part. They conquered the countries by cruelty. Sargon 2 was the cruelest king (722-705B.C), he captured Samaria, Israel's capital, and carried ten tribes of them as captives which were lost forever. His son Sanacherib was also of such nature (705-68 B.C) He subjugated Egypt and Palestine. Asher Banipal (668- 626 B.C) was recognized as an authority of Western Asia. After his death, Assyrians declined and later on they got sacked by the Aryan of Persia (612.B.C). Assyrians with all their cruelty were knowledgeable, builders and imitated none. They had developed a centralized system; the governors were directly responsible to the emperor.

HEBREWS

These people called Jews were claiming Ibrahim to be their Ancestor. They were nomads of the desert and later on settled in Palestine the Cannan. They had established their kingdom under Dawood S/o Jesse of the Juda tribe and after him his son Soloman was the king (961-922 B.C) as in Holy Quran, Allah said,

"And Dawood killed Jalut and Allah (SWT) gave him the rule." (2:251)

Also, He said,

"And Soliman inherited Dawood." (27:16)

Soliman made Jerusalem as capital. He was keen of learning, building and commerce. After his death the Jews divided the kingdom in two parts namely Juda in the south and Israel in the north. Assyrian conquered Israelia in 722 B.C and Chaldean king Nebuchadnezzar conquered Juda in 568 B.C.

Jews were religious people having belief in Tawheed.

BYZANTINE

Sasanians and Byzantine were two powers in the Middle East – Byzantian was the capital. This Roman Empire consisted of Egypt, Syria, Palestine and some parts of Europe. This Greek city Byzantium was made the capital in 327 AD by Constantine the Great, later on named it as Constantinople. After him there were some 70 Rulers; it fell in 1204 AD. Theodosius 1 (379-395) made Christianity as state religion. Justinian 1 (527-565 AD) had collected the Roman laws. He built a university and also the church of St. Sophia which was first built by Constantine the Great. Heraclius (610-641) had freed Syria and Egypt from Sasanian and fought Iranians as well, but he could not control the recovered provinces against Muslims. He was the one who gave respect to the messenger of the Holy prophet.

SASANIAN EMPIRE

In 1500 B.C some Aryan tribes settled in western Iran. In the southern parts they were called Persian while in the mountains Medes. In 539 B.C. king Cyrus with the help of his people Medes and Persians dethroned Chaldean king. Power passed from Babylonians to Aryans. Cyrus' son Cambyses after him captured Egypt. In 334 B.C Alexander the Great invaded Persia and the Empire finished. In 226 AD Ardsher led a revolt against the Greek rule Sasanian came to power. Ardsher the son of Papak of Faris captured Karman, so Ardawn (Greek) invaded Faris. The final fight was fought in Hormuz. Ardawn was killed and later on Sasanian ruled Persia for four centuries. Under them the old religion of Zoroaster renewed. His son Shahpur (309 AD-329 AD) also ruled bravely, but after him the decline started. Shahpur fought Romans and regained the five lost provinces by his grandfather. Nowsherwan ascended the throne in 531 AD. He was keen of learning and was a great builder and best administrator known for his justice.

Khosrow Pervez (590 AD) the grandson of Nowsherwan was the last powerful king of this dynasty. He was the one who had torn the letter of the Holy prophet calling him to Islam. He was brave and courageous in his early life, but tyrannical in old age. In the days of Yazda Gard (634) this Empire was overthrown by Muslims.

Christianity brought by Romans to Persia was supported by India and the Far East, and it was face to face with the Zoroastrianism.

Isa appeared in Nazareth in Palestine and in the days of Tiberius they passed a decree of his crucifixion in Syria where his teaching was first preached by St. Paul.

Allah said,

"They have not killed him nor crucified him." (4:157)

This whole history and mixing up developed new civilizations and also one religion influenced the other.

Because of the Birth and rescue story of Isa (Jesus), Christianity is divided into sects and actual religion could not remain.

"JAZEERAT UL - ARAB" OR ARABIAN PENINSULA BEFORE ISLAM

"Arab" The word "Arab" means deserts and a vast barren land which is almost treeless and waterless. Also "Arab" means one who speaks clearly and eloquently and can express what is there in his heart and mind. When it is said, "Aaraba" it means, He spoke and expressed clearly. People living in deserts speak their pure language without mixing and also, they are simple and close to nature and for bearing, having no reservations, so, they speak clearly what is there in their mind.

"JAZEERATUL ARAB" OR "SHIBH – AL - JAZEERA" is a peninsula. It is surrounded by the Indian Ocean on the south, Syrian ocean, Tigris and Euphrates rivers or that is enclosed in the west by the red sea and Sinai, in the east by the Arabian Gulf, in the South by the Arabian sea, which is an extension of the Indian ocean, and in the north by old Syria and part of Iraq – the area is estimated between a million and a quarter square miles.

Mostly that area is desert and life is a tough sort of life, that's why the people there had been enjoying a complete sort of liberty and independence through the ages, even though two empires, Byzantine and Persian, used to fight each other to grab as much land as they could. However, in the case of the peninsula, they never tried to control it directly, as materially there was no attraction for them, and its people, due to their tribal nature, were tough and hard to be controlled by outsiders. Its geographical situation, as it was surrounded by seas almost completely from three sides made it difficult to be invaded. But as this area had a strategic position, providing links through sea and land, it remained the center of the world and also it was the center of trade, culture, and religion as well. Due to the desert nature of the area and tough nature of its people, being custodians of the House of God, it was a link for nations through sea and land. Its people were freely moving all over and conducting business as well.

Allah said,

> *"And Allah puts forward (states) the example of a township (Makkah as it was the city where the House of Allah situated and was the center for trade etc. as a route) which was secure and content (satisfied), its provision was coming to it in abundance from every place. But it (its people) denied/ rejected the favours of Allah (the message of Mohammad and Holy Quran) so Allah made it taste extreme of hunger (Famine and also their business trips were no safer) and fear, because of what they used to do." (16:112)*

They had their safe trips in winter and summer both as Allah said,

> *"(Because of) taming of Quraish, their taming of trips in winter and summer, so they may worship the Lord of this House (Kabah) who has fed them against hunger and made them safe from fear." (106:1-4)*

These trips became their nature-like habits that had been made safe by Allah, and they were bringing their needs from everywhere and they were safe as well.

Allah said,

> *"So have we not established for them a secure sanctuary (Makkah) to which are brought fruits of all kinds, a provision from our side, but most of them know not."* (28:57)

Allah also said,

> *"Have they not seen that we have made (Makkah) a secure sanctuary, while men are being snatched away from all around them? Then do they believe in false and deny the graces of Allah."* (29:67)

ARAB TRIBES

1) Ancient Arabs about whom a little bit in history is preserved like Ad, Thamud, Emlaq etc. They are called Arab-Ba'idah.

2) "ARAB-AL'ARIBAH" OR PURE ARABS

They are the progeny of Ya'rub bin Yash Jub bin Qahtan-They are known as "Qahtanid."

3) "ARABI MUSTARABAH" OR ARABIZED ARABS

They are from the offspring of Ismael bin Ibrahim. They are called "Adnanid." Pure Arabs used to live in Yemen while the Arabized Arabs from the children of Ismael mostly lived in the peninsula.

PROPHET IBRAHIM

Ibrahim was born in "Ar" near Kufa on the west Bank of Euphrates River. The people of that area used to worship heavenly bodies and idols of different types. It is known clearly from the story of Ibrahim in the Holy Quran. For details, see Surat Ul An'am verses 74-81, Surat Ul Anbiya verses 51-70 Surah As - Saffat verses 83-99.

Ibrahim strongly opposed their beliefs; he broke their idols, and they threw him into blazing fire.

Allah said,

> *"So, they plotted a plot against him, but we made them the lowest." (37:98)*

Allah ordered the fire to be cool and safe for him.

We (Allah) said,

> *"O fire be cool and safe for Ibrahim and they wanted to harm him but we made them the worst losers." (21:69)*

After that he left for Palestine as Allah relates,

> *"And he (Ibrahim) said verily I am going to my Lord. He will guide me." (37:99)*

PROPHET ISMAIL (ISHMAIL) BORN

Ibrahim made Palestine the center of his message. He went all over the area till he went to Egypt. There the Heksus or Emalekite kings had been ruling that area. They had a bad habit of taking any beautiful woman by force. Sarah, the wife of Ibrahim, was also a beautiful lady. The king tried to take her by force but every time he was stopped by Allah, and he felt that this lady is not only beautiful but also has a connection to God.

To acknowledge both her beauty and attachment to Allah, he gave his daughter, or niece who he had adopted as his daughter, Hagar (Hajar) to Sarah for her services. As Sarah had no child, she gave Hagar to Ibrahim as wife. When they returned to Palestine, Hagar gave birth to a beautiful son who was named Ismail (Ishmael).

HAGAR AND ISMAIL IN MAKKAH

It is but natural that Sarah became jealous of Hagar and forced Ibrahim in one way or another to take Hagar and her son to a faraway valley in "Hijaz" by the sacred House of Allah (SWT). That area was very much exposed to floods. Also Ibrahim was inspired by Allah to take them both there. He placed them under a tree, which was later on the site of "Zam Zam" (The Holy water). At that time there was no life at all. Nobody was living there, nor was there any water available. Ibrahim put a leather bag with some dates and another one with water near them. When Ibrahim departed, Hagar asked him,

"Where are you going, leaving us here?"

He neither turned his face nor answered. She repeated the same question several times but in vain. Then, Hagar asked him,

"Have you been ordered by Allah to do so?"

Ibrahim said,

"Yes."

Hagar said,

"So now he will never neglect us."

When Ibrahim came to such a place where they could not see each other, he faced the "Holy Kabah" and said,

> "O our Lord! I dwelt my offspring in an uncultivable valley near your sacred House. Our Lord! in order to perform prayer to make the hearts of some people inclined towards them and provide them with fruits (material and spiritual as well) so they may pay thanks (to Allah)." (14:37)

Hagar was eating dates, suckling her son, and using the water. The water being used up, she and her son both became thirsty. Ismail was crying because of thirst. She couldn't endure looking at him. She went to the top of the nearest mountain "Safa" and looked all around the valley to try to see someone but she couldn't find anyone. She came down off the hill, in the lowest part of the valley she started running. She went to the other side of the valley to another mountain "Marwah" to try to see someone, but again, nobody was there. She did the same practice seven times. This is the source of "Sa'i" between Safa and Marwah in Hajj and Umrah which is "Fard" (mandatory) according to three imams and "Wajib" (compulsory) according to Imam Abu Hanifa, but the running in the specific part in between Safa and Marwah is not allowed for women and is for men only.

For the last time when she was on Marwah, she heard a voice twice.

> "O! You have made me hear your voice; have you got something to help me? And Behold! She saw an Angel at the place of Zamzam digging the earth with his heel (or wing), till water flowed from that place. She started to make something like a basin around it using her hands in this way and started filling her water bag with water, and the water was flowing out after she had scooped some of it."

The prophet said,

> "May Allah Bestow mercy on the mother of Ismael! Had she let Zamzam, it would have been a stream flowing on the surface of the earth."

The Angel further said, don't be afraid for this is the House of Allah which will be built by this boy and his father. She lived there till some people from Jurhum tribe of Yemen passed. They landed in the lower part of Makkah where they saw a bird that had the habit of flying around water. They sent one or two messengers who discovered that there was water, so those people came to Hagar sitting near the water. They asked her if they could stay there. She said yes, but they will have no right to possess the water. They agreed to it. Also, they invited other people from their tribe, and some of them settled there – The prophet said, the mother of Ismael was happy to have their company. Ismael later on learnt Arabic from them.

PROPHET ISMAIL (THE SLAUGHTERED ONE)

Once Ibrahim saw a dream as this is mentioned in the Holy Quran,

> "So they plotted a plot against him (put him on fire) but we made them the lowest (losers) and he said (after his rescue) verily I am going to my Lord. He will guide me. My Lord! Grant me (offspring) from the righteous. So we gave him the glad tidings of a for bearing boy. And when he (his son) was old enough to walk with him, he said, 'O my Son I have seen in a dream that I am slaughtering you. So look what you think? He said, O my Father! Do that which you are commanded. If Allah wills you shall find me of the patients."

"Then when they both surrendered to (the will of) Allah and he laid him prostrate on his forehead (or on the side of his fore head) we called unto him O Ibrahim!"

"You have fulfilled the dream verily in such a way we reward the good doers verily this indeed was a manifest Trial. And we ransomed him with a great sacrifice (Ram), and we left for him (a goodly remembrance) among the later generations. Peace be upon Ibrahim. Thus, indeed we reward the good doers verily he was one of our believing slaves." (37:98:111)

The dream of a Messenger is a sort of Wahi, that's why Ibrahim took it literally and tried to slaughter his son, and actually he did.

That's why Allah said;

"You confirmed/fulfilled your dream."

Now who was the slaughtered son of Ibrahim, Ismail, or Ishaq (Isaac)?

Jews claim that it was Ishaq, their great-grandfather, and he tried to slaughter him on the Rock in Jerusalem. They claimed the same to have this honor.

Christians say the same, while some Muslim scholars also expressed the same that this was Ishaq.

Not at all! It was Ismael.

1. It is mentioned in ancient books that Ibrahim tried to slaughter his lonely son, and this is understood that Ismael was born of Hagar, the first ever son of Ibrahim, when Ibrahim's age was 86 years, and Sarah became jealous of Hagar as she did not have a child. Ishaq was born almost 14 years after Ismail, and Ishaq was not the only son of Ibrahim as Ismail was already there.

2. Holy Quran itself when narrating the story of slaughtering said after that.

> "And we gave him glad tidings, a prophet from pious people." (37:112)

It means that this glad tiding was after that trial, another reward, as the first one was that Ismail was ransomed by a ram, and Ibrahim's remembrance with good words and peace by people of coming generations lasted, while this glad tiding is the second one and Allah (SWT) has mentioned the word reward twice in above said verses, once in verse 105 and for twice in verse 110.

3. In Holy Quran it is mentioned that Ibrahim left "Ar" for Palestine, he made "Dua" (invoked Allah) and Allah accepted that,

> "O my lord, grant me (offspring) from the righteous, so we gave him the glad tidings of a forbearing boy." (37:100-101)

For this boy Allah used the quality "Forbearing" while for the other son Allah said,

> "(The angels said) verily we give you glad tidings of a boy having much knowledge." (15:53)

Also, Allah said,

> "And they (the angels) gave him happy tidings of a son having knowledge." (51:28)

Now, these are two different qualities of two different sons. The second quality is related in the story of the glad tidings about Ishaq (Isaac), so the first one "forbearing" quality is for his other son Ismael, and he showed that quality in his life-long history by facing the hardship there in valley alone and later on showed his free consent for sacrifice as well. But it doesn't mean that either of them did not have the other quality, but in the said one, he was the example.

4. Regarding glad tidings about Ishaq, Allah said:

   "So we gave glad tidings to her (Sarah) of Ishaq and after Ishaq of Yaqoob (Jacob)." (11:71)

   Now it is understood that the dream was taken literally by Ibrahim, and the son concerned was "when he reached the age of working with him" meaning early teenager. He received another message about Ishaq as well. He will have his son Jacob, which means Ishaq will still remain to beget children and will not be slaughtered in his early age. Now, if it was Ishaq to be slaughtered for sure Ibrahim would have been confused considering the glad tidings of Ishaq's future children.

5. Then, throughout history, the followers of Ibrahim have been celebrating that sacrifice in Hajj in Mina where Ismael lived. Ishaq was living in Palestine, which means Ismael was slaughtered.

6. The Arabs from generation-to-generation have been transferring this story about Ismael's slaughter.

7. When the ransomed ram was slaughtered, its horns were preserved there in Kabah for centuries until Hajjaj bin Yusuf attacked Abdullah bin Zubair in Makkah and Kabah was demolished, and these horns were lost as well. Ibni Abbas and Aamir Ash Shabi both said they had seen these horns in Kabah.

Now the Jewish thought was otherwise to have higher status. The Christian's own narrations are confused. Their narrations said that he was ordered to sacrifice his lonely son Ishaq, while other narration said that Ibrahim's wife Sarah did not have any child, and Hagar delivered the first son, it also said that when Ismael was born, Ibrahim was 86 and Allah told him and his wife Sarah that they will also have a son. When he was born, Ibrahim was 100 years old. Also, Ibrahim circumcised Ismael when he was 13 years of age, one year before the birth of Ishaq. This was also a type of sacrifice cutting a piece of his body.

Those Muslims who said it was Ishaq Ibni Kathir related that Ka'b Ul Ahbar, a Jew who became a Muslim in the time of Umar, even though he was a good Muslim and a scholar as well, would sometimes narrate something from the ancient books as well. Umar used to listen to him and others.

The Prophet said,

> *"Take (knowledge) from me, that is not sin and take (it) from people of the Book and that is not a sin. Now taking from them has a condition and that is if it does not contradict Quran and Sunnah as most of their books and narrations are perverted,"*

And one perverted narration is this one.

8. Also, the Prophet said.

> *"I am the offspring of two slaughtered."*

Meaning Ismael and Abdullah.

The story of Abdullah goes as follows: Abdul Muttalib gave a pledge to God that if he is given ten sons, he will sacrifice one of them. He had ten sons. When they all reached their manhood; he told them about his vow. They gave their consent that whoever he wants to slaughter, he is ready. He wrote their names on divination arrows and gave it to the guardian of their powerful and beloved goddesses Hubal. The arrows were shuffled and drawn. It showed the name of Abdullah on it. Abdul-Muttalib took him to Ka'ba to slaughter him. The Quraish tribe Bani Makhzum, the maternal uncles of Abdullah and his brother Abu Talib, tried to convince Abdul-Muttalib not to do so and to seek a substitute. He asked them for advice. They said to bring the she-diviner. She advised to draw the divination arrow with respect to Abdullah as well as ten camels. She said to repeat the same for another ten added to the first ten, if the name of Abdullah came out, then, do the same until the Camel's arrow comes out. They did the same 10 times. In the end when the number of camels was 100 it came out. So, 100 camels were slaughtered and Abdullah was spared. The same number later on was counted as the capital for blood money and the same was adopted by Islam as well. A custom that has been kept intact. Referring to the story of Ismael and the story of Abdullah, the prophet said as Ibni Hisham related;

> "I am the son of two slaughtered."

It is also said that Abdul Muttalib had forgotten the vow. Then, he was reminded of that in a dream.

PROPHET IBRAHIM VISITS MAKKAH

Once Ibrahim came to Makkah to visit his wife and son. This time his wife Hagar had passed away. Ismail had married Mamid, a woman from Jurhum tribe, those who were dwelling there in Makkah. Ismail was not home and his wife was there. Ibrahim asked her about Ismail, she said, he has gone for livelihood. He asked her about their way of living. She said,

> "We are living in misery." We are living in "hardship and destitution,"

complaining of their life. When Ibrahim was leaving, he told her,

> "When your husband comes back, convey my salutation to him, and tell him to change the threshold of the gate of the house."

When Ismael came back, she told him the entire story and the complexion of the old man. He said that was my father, and he ordered me to divorce you as you are not a content and grateful woman. So he divorced her. After that he married the daughter of Mudad bin Amr, the chief of the Jurhum tribe living there.

SECOND VISIT OF IBRAHIM

Once again Ibrahim came to see him. This time also he was not at home. Ibrahim asked his wife about him. She told him he had gone hunting. He asked her about their way of living. She said, we are well off and prosperous and thankful to Allah. Ibrahim asked her,

> "What are you people eating and drinking?"

She said,

> "We eat meat and drink water."

Ibrahim said,

> "O Allah bless their meat and water."

The prophet of Allah said,

> "At that time, they did not have grain there. And if they would have it, he would have invoked Allah also to bless their grain. The prophet also said, if someone will take only meat and water and nothing else, his health and disposition will be badly affected, unless he lives in Makkah, and drinks Zamzam."

Then he said to her, when your husband comes back, give my regards to him and tell him to keep firm the threshold of his gate. When Ismael came, his wife told him the story. He said,

"This was my father Ibrahim, and he ordered me to keep you with me."

CONSTRUCTION OF KABAH

"And (remember) when Ibrahim was raising up the foundations (walls) of the house of Allah and Ismael (as well) saying, our lord, accept (it) from us verily you are the all hearer, all knower. Our lord! And make us submissive unto you and from our offspring (also make) a nation submissive unto you and show us our "Manasik" (Rituals/ Ceremonies/ Laws and rules) and accept our repentance. Verily you are the one who accepts repentance, the most merciful.

Our Lord! send amongst them (the people of this valley (the great) messenger of their own, who shall recite unto them your verses and shall teach them the book and "Hikmat" (wisdom) and purify them, verily you are the all mighty, the all wise." (2:127-129)

Ibrahim also made a "Dua" for Kabah and those who will dwell there in.

"And (remember) when we made the house (Kabah) a place of resort for mankind and a place of safety and take you people the "Maqam" (stone whereupon Ibrahim used to stand when building the house of Allah and his feet are curved therein like one in mud or "Maqam" Means the house itself) of Ibrahim a place of prayer. And we commanded Ibrahim and Ismael to purify my house (Kabah) for those who circumambulate it, or retreat, or who bow down and prostrate themselves.

And (remember) when Ibrahim said, "My Lord! Make this city (Makkah) a place of security and provide its people with fruits (material and spiritual benefits) for those who believe in Allah and the last day." He (Allah) answered. "As for him who disbelieves, I shall leave him in contentment for a while, then I shall compel him to torment of the fire and worst indeed is that return place." (2:125-127)

Then he was ordered to proclaim "Hajj":

"And proclaim to mankind the Hajj (pilgrimage) they will come to you (to Kabah the place of your call to) on foot and on every lean camel from every deep and distant mountain highway. So that they may witness things that are of benefits to them (materially and spiritually both) and mention the name of Allah on appointed days over the beast of cattle that he (Allah) has provided for them (when sacrificing) then eat thereof and feed therewith the poor who have a very hard time." (22:27,28)

He invoked Allah with all these requests and Allah accepted all these supplications.

Studying thoroughly this history the historians found out that Ibrahim made at least four trips to Makkah to visit his son.

CONDITIONS OF ARABIA AT THE ADVENT OF ISLAM

POLITICAL CONDITION

As we have mentioned earlier that originally the existing Arabs for so many centuries were of two kinds.

A. Arabi- Aariba or pure Arabs who are called Qahtanids as well.

B. Arabi - Musta'rabah or Arabized Arabs who are also called Adnanids.

Both of these Arabs were dispersed and spread almost all over Arabia, those who were settled in a little bit more fertile and cultivated area had compromised a bit on their freedom due to settling there. And those who were moving as nomads were committed to their natural freedom and never compromised on it. In other words, it is said that except certain portions in the north which was subjugated to some rulers, and they were subjugated either to the Roman or Persian Empires, the rest of the area did not have a central government. On one hand, the members of one tribe were very much loyal and obedient to their tribal chiefs and very friendly to their own tribe members, but they were hostile to other tribes. Battles amongst tribes were the practice of every day. Most of the time the battles started for no reason, and sometimes it was because of a very petty issue, which lasted for decades. This led to hundreds of people's lives being deprived; they never hesitated to go to any extent for their ego, honor, and prestige. However, others gave the people of Makkah and Hijaz a due respect because of their custodianship of the Holy sanctuary as we have mentioned before.

CULTURAL CONDITION

The time prior to Islam is called "Ayyam - Ul - Jahiliya" or "The Time of Ignorance," but it doesn't mean that they did not have any literacy or education. Rather, they were poets, writers, experts in business, warriors etc. That's why when they refused the message of Mohammad (SAS), saying that he has invented this Quran,

Allah Said,

> "And those who disbelieved said this is but a lie, he (Mohammad) has invented it."(25:4)

Then, Allah (SWT) challenged them to compete with it by inventing ten surahs (chapters) or even a one small surah (chapter) like this.

> "Or they say, He (Mohammad) forged it, say then you bring ten surahs like this forged, and call whomsoever you can, other than Allah. If you speak the truth. If then they responded to you not, then, know that it is sent down with the knowledge of Allah."(11:13-14)

> "Or they say that he (Mohammad) has forged it, say then bring one surah like this and call upon whomsoever you can besides Allah if you are truthful."(10:38)

> "And if you are in doubt about what we have sent down to our slave, then bring you a surah like that of it and call upon your witnesses (scholars) against Allah if you are truthful. So, if you did not do and you could never do, then fear the fire, which fuel is mankind and stones (of sulfur) and that is prepared for disbelievers."(2:23-24)

These verses clearly mention that they were writers, poets etc., otherwise to challenge people who do not know the field concerned, doesn't make sense. Yes, they are called "Ummiyeen."

Allah Said;

> "He (Allah is the one who has sent amongst "Ummiyeen" a messenger."(62:2)

"Ummiyeen" has two meanings here:

A. Attributed to "Umm - Al - Qura" another name for Makkah, so it means amongst the people of Makkah.

B. Illiterate- who had no knowledge of revealed religion as they had never seen a messenger after Ismael from amongst them. Prophet Mohammad was the first ever messenger in the offspring of Ismael. So, they were illiterate in this regard. As for the knowledge of worldly things is concerned, they were literate. That's why when prisoners of war in "Badr" were brought to Madinah, some of them were released for free, some others for ransom, while some of them were set free after they taught writing to ten people each from the people of Madinah. There was no educational system there.

Their poetry, words, and proverbs are used as a source to find out the meaning of the Holy Quran as well. They used to arrange gatherings for their poetry and its correction and criticism as well. Also, they used to put their poems on the wall of the Kabah as a challenge to others, if they could say some poem like this. That's why the Quran is a Mo'jizah (miracle), which rendered them unable to compete with it even though they were very eloquent people.

ECONOMIC CONDITIONS

Most of their land was barren desert. There were no agricultural or mineral products which could have fulfilled their needs. And as no raw materials were available, therefore they were alien to industries. Most of their livelihood was upon trade, and trade was also in need of security, which was available in the sacred months, as they were not harming each other in these months. These months were Muharram, Rajab, Zil - Qadah, and Zil - Hajjah (1st, 7th, 11th, and 12th months of Islamic calendar).

"And they ask you regarding sacred months, about

> *fighting therein. Say, fighting therein a big (violation)."(2:217)*

Also, Allah said:

> *"Verily, the number of months with Allah is twelve months (in a year). In the book of Allah (His record) from the day he created the heavens and the earth, of these, four are sacred, that is the Deen (natural laws) which manages (everything)."(9:36)*

But the people of Makkah in particular were very much protected in their lives, wealth, and businesses as well. Because people of other areas used to give them due respect as their custodianship of the house of Allah, which was a big honor and people from all around used to go for Hajj. The people in Makkah had been very hospitable to them. Also, the four sons of Abd - Manaf had treaties of peace with different authorities and government to have their businesses safeguarded.

Allah (SWT) reminded them in the Holy Quran of this honor and protection in a few places.

a) *"Have we not established for them a secure sanctuary to which are brought fruits of all kinds, a provision from our side, but most of them know not."(28:57)*

b) *"Have they not seen that we have made (Makkah) a secure sanctuary, while men are being snatched away from all around them."(29:67)*

c) *"And Allah puts forward (brings forth) the example of a township (Makkah) which was secure and content, its provision was coming to it from all around." (16:112)*

SOCIAL CONDITIONS OF ARABIA

As they did not have an established government, but tribal system, that's why their social system had different customs, some good and some bad as well.

Women, on one hand were honored so much that blood would be shed easily in defense of their honor. Women were the most decisive key to a bloody fight or friendly peace. But on the other hand, some tribes used to bury their daughters alive as she would be an economical burden, she cannot help in battles and also to defend her honor, there could be bloodshed.

Allah said;

> *"And when any one of them is given the news of (the birth of) a daughter, his face becomes dark, and he is filled with inward grief. He hides himself from the people because of the evil of that whereof he has been informed. (Thinking) shall he keep her with dishonor or bury her in the earth? Certainly, evil is their decision."(16:58-59)*

> *"And when one of them is given the news of (the birth of) that which he set for as a parable (attribute) to the Most Beneficent, his face becomes dark, gloomy, and he is filled with grief. A creature that is brought up in adornments and in dispute she cannot make herself clear (cannot combat in a battle)." (43:17-18)*

In marriage, there was no need for the consent of the woman but she was forced to do what the guardian decides. Even after the death of her husband someone from the family of the deceased would put a cloak on her head, which meant she had been claimed. So later on, either the same guy had the right to marry her or with his approval, consent, terms, and conditions, she could marry someone else. This was called "Adzal," which literally means restrictions/restricted.

Allah said:

> *"O you who believe, this is not lawful for you to inherit women by force (unwillingly) and to put her in difficult situation (when marrying another one) so you may take a part of what you (the deceased one) have given her (as bridal money or gifted her something)."(4:19)*

So women had no social or economic rights, but men had all the right to keep as many women as they wished. Later on, Islam decreased that number to four and that is also a case of permissibility not of recommendation. Allah Says,

> *"If you have the fear that you cannot be able to deal justly with orphans, then marry from (lawful) women of your choice, two, three, or four, but if you fear that you shall not be able to deal justly with them, then (marry) only one."(4:3)*

This verse needs a little bit of analysis.

1. *"If you fear that you will not be able to deal justly with the orphans"* means that they used to marry widows having a lot of wealth to grab their wealth. But at the same time these widows had their orphaned children with them, whom the new husband would not deal justly with. These husbands used to take a plea that marriage with a few women is permissible, so Allah said but unjust dealing of orphans is a major sin. So, to avoid that sin you should marry other lawful women of your choice having no child with, so you may not be in a test.

2. Allah decreased the number to four at most but also said *"if you have fear that you will not be able to deal with them justly then (do marry) one only"* means yet you have not experienced that injustice, but you have a fear then do marry only one.

Also, there were prostitute women. Whenever they delivered a child a seer would have to tell whose child this is. Or, sometimes someone made a claim to a child even from a married woman. The Prophet said in such a case "no claim in Islam for pre-Islamic affairs, the child is to be attributed to one on whose bed he is born, and stoning is the lot of an adulterer (Abu Dawud). It means he will be stoned to death if that is proven on him and if "Aahir" means fornicator then the Last Part of Hadith means that his lot is stone means nothing.

Another social norm of that time was *"support your brother (tribesman) an oppressor maybe or an oppressed."* So they used to support their tribe in any way if they were right or even if they were wrong. Later on, this was called tribal prejudice; Islam prohibited this and said that to support the oppressor means to deter him from transgressing as The Prophet said, *"To seize his hands."*

In brief, one can say that their life was a gloomy picture of contrast, it was a paradoxical life, or an animal-like life as they were shedding blood for years for no reason. The wars of Aws and Khazraj, and of others are some examples.

ETHICAL CONDITIONS

Like all other fields, this field was also a contrast. As all evils and vices were rampant in every aspect of life, but still there were some virtues and norms that they were committed to. For example, keeping up with covenants, firm will and determination to honor, repudiation of injustice, hospitality, simple life, and mildness was also seen obviously.

That's why the Prophet when he came, he classified customs into three categories:

A. Good customs- he kept them as is.

B. Bad customs- he abolished and nullified it.

C. Partially good and partially bad- he reformed these customs.

But at the same time, they had some bad ethics as well, like depriving the weak and the orphans of their due rights, as Allah said,

> *"And they (those who eat up the property of orphans) should have (the same) fear (in their minds). If they would have left weak offspring behind (they would have fear about them) so they may fear Allah (regarding the weak offspring of others) and may speak the right words (in its time when it is needed and required)." (4:9-10)*

RELIGIOUS CONDITION

Some people there were atheist, who did not believe in Allah or God or an entity who runs this system, but they were of the view that this system is auto dynamic. People are born and they die, and this will be going on forever, and that world in its running is not subject to any invisible entity.

Allah Says,

> *"And they say, there is nothing but our life in this world, we die, and we live and nothing destroys us but time, and they have no knowledge of it, but only presumption." (45:24)*

But anyhow most people living in that part of the world at the advent of Islam were in three groups. Either they were Jews, Christians, or polytheists. And all of them used to claim that they are the true followers of Prophet Ibrahim.

Allah said:

> *"Ibrahim was neither a Jew, nor a Christian, but he was a true Muslim, and he was not from the polytheists as well."(3:67)*

JEWISH TRIBES AND JUDAISM

The followers of Musa (Moses) are called Jews or "Yahud." In the time of Musa, they used to do reasoning with him in the commandments of Allah. As they did in the case of the Cow, when Allah ordered them to slaughter a cow as they were in love with cows, as a goddess was worshiped in Egypt. They were ordered to slaughter a cow to take that love off their mind.

And when Musa said to his people,

> *"Verily Allah orders you to slaughter a cow." They said, "Do you make fun of us?" He said, "I seek Allah's refuge from being amongst "Al - Jahileen" (the ignorant stubborn people)." They said, "call upon your Lord for us that he may make plain to us what it is." He said, "He says, verily it is a cow neither too old nor too young, but (it is) between the two conditions so do what you are commanded."*
>
> *They said, "Call upon your Lord for us to make plain to us its color." He said, "he says, it is a yellow cow, bright in its color pleasing the beholders. They said, "call upon your Lord for us to make plain to us what it is. Verily, to us all cows are alike. And surely, if Allah wills, we will be guided." He said, "He says, it is a cow neither trained to till the soil nor water the fields, sound having no other color except bright yellow. They said, "now you have brought the truth. So, they slaughtered it though they were near to not doing it." (2:67-72)*

They were refusing clear orders of Allah (SWT). When Musa was ordered to take them to the Holy Land, they refused to go as they were used to cowardice and slavery and were very much afraid of various tribes living in the holy land.

Allah says;

> *"And (remember) when Musa said to his people, O my people! Remember the favor of Allah to you as he made Prophets among you, made you kings, and gave you what he had not given to any other among the "Alamin" (Jinn and mankind before you). O my people! Enter the Holy Land, which Allah has assigned to you and turn not back, for then you will be returned as losers."*
>
> *They said, "O, Musa! In that (land) there are people of great strength, and we shall never enter it till they leave it, when they leave, then we will enter.*
>
> *Two men of those who feared (Allah) on whom Allah has bestowed His grace said, "Enter on (assault) them through the gate, for when you are in, victory will be yours and put your trust in Allah if you are believers indeed."*
>
> *They said, "O, Musa! We shall never enter it as long as they are there. So go you and your Lord (big brother) and fight you two; we are sitting right here.*
>
> *He said, "O my Lord! I have no power but only my own self and my brother, so separate us from the disobedient people. He (Allah) said, "Therefore, it is forbidden to them for forty years, in distraction they will wander through the land, so be not sorrowful over the people, who are the "Fasiqeen" (rebellious)."(5:20-26)*

They used to make and craft unlawful stratagems and to have lame excuses when violating a rule. As they did in the case of fishing on Saturday which was prohibited to them. As a test for them, the fish on Saturday were coming in abundance. So, they could not control themselves and they established water channels from sea towards ponds and reservoirs for the said purpose.

So, on Saturday, they used to bring water to these ponds carrying fish and the next day they used to catch it. Allah Says,

> "And indeed, you knew those amongst you who transgressed in the matter of the "Sabbath."(2:65)

Also, he said,

> "When they used to transgress in "Sabbath" when their fish came to them openly on their Sabbath day and did not come to them on the day, they had no Sabbath."(7:163)

They worshiped a calf made of gold as a god when Musa went to Mount "Tur". Allah says,

> "And (remember) when we appointed Musa forty nights, and you took the calf (for worship) after him (Musa) and you were wrong doers."(2:51)

Their Rabbis used to pervert, change, and distort "Taurat (the book), mixing truth with falsehood and hiding the truth.

Allah said,

> "Then woe to those who write the book with their own hands and then say, "This is from Allah to gain with it a little price."(2:79)

Allah said,

> "And mix not truth with falsehood and conceal not the truth and you know."(2:42)

In brief, we can say that they used to torture Musa mentally. As Holy Quran says,

> "And (remember) when Musa said to his people, O my people! Why do you annoy me while you know certainly

> *that I am the messenger of Allah to you? So, when they deviated (listening not), Allah caused their hearts to deviate and Allah guides not the rebellious."(61:5)*

After Musa, they started to reject their Prophets and even to kill some of them, as they had become the slaves of their vain desires.

Allah said,

> *"It is that whenever there came to you a Messenger with what you do not want (against your desires), you became arrogant (thought of yourself very high)? Some of these (Prophets) you disbelieved and some (of them) you killed"(2:87)*

On the other hand, they made their religious leaders as their Lords as Allah says,

> *"They took their rabbis and their monks as lords besides Allah." (9:31)*

They claimed to be the beloved of Allah so he will never punish them, doesn't make difference whatever violations they commit.

Allah said,

> *"And Jews and Christians say we are the children of Allah and his beloved"(5:18)*

But they both disregard each other and degrade each other. Holy Quran said,

> *"And Jews said that Christians are not on any (right or valuable) thing (religion) and Christians said, that Jews are not on any (right or valuable) thing (religion)."(2:113)*

While both of them claim that only they will enter paradise.

> "And they (Jews and Christians) said, "none shall enter paradise except one who is a Jew or a Christian."(2:111)

Each group was claiming the same for them only.

CHRISTIANS AND CHRISTIANITY

As we mentioned, the Jews used to reject their Prophets and even killed some of them. In the same way Prophet Jesus came. He was born of his mother only without having a father.

Allah said:

> "Remember when the angels said, O Maryam! Verily Allah gives you the glad tidings of a word (be) from him, his name will be the Messiah Isa (Jesus) the son of Maryam (Mary), held in honor in this world and in the hereafter, and will be one of those who are near to Allah."(3:45)

As Jesus was born of his mother only without a father, by the process of self-pollination (parthenogenesis) as Prophet Adam was created by Allah without father and mother both.

Allah said:

> "Verily the example of Isa is like that of Adam. He (Allah) created him (Adam) from clay, then he said to him be, and he was."(3:59)

Then the Jews to whom Jesus was sent, they first said that he is the son of Yusuf-an-Najjar (Mason) who was a relative of Mary. And not only that, but later on when he started giving the message and tried to bring them back to the right track, they were not ready to sacrifice their evil desires and vested interests, so they got a decree against him to execute and crucify him. In this regard one of Isa's close associates conspired, but Allah protected him.

Allah said:

> "Then when Isa came to know of their disbelief, he said, "Who will be my helpers in Allah's cause?" The disciples said, "We are the helpers (of the Deen) of Allah. We believe in Allah and bear witness that we are Muslims."
>
> "Our Lord we believe in what you sent down, and we follow the Messenger so write us down among those who bear witness (to belief)."
>
> "And they plotted (to kill Isa) and Allah planned too, and Allah is the best of planners."
>
> And when Allah said, "O Isa (Jesus)! I will take you and raise you to myself and clear you (of the forged statement that Jesus is the son of God, or he is Lord, or he was crucified) of those who disbelieve and I will make those who follow you (properly) superior to those who disbelieve (in the proper way of monotheism of Allah and your message) till the day of resurrection, then you will return to me and I will judge between you in the matters in which you used to dispute."(3:52-55)

Now the Jews are of the belief that Jesus was crucified and we got rid of him, while the Christians believe that Jesus is the son of God, he is Lord, he was crucified as an expiation for the sins of his followers, so anyone of his followers may commit sins and they are pardoned.

Allah said:

> "Surely, they have become disbelievers who say, "Allah is the messiah son of Mary." (5:72)

Also, Allah said:

> *"Surely they have become disbelievers who said that Allah is the third of three (belief in trinity)." (5:73)*

Also, Allah said:

> *"They have neither killed him nor crucified him." (4:157)*

In other words, we can say they both had created an access towards sins in the name of Deen (religion), the Jews said, *"we are the children of Allah"* so he will never punish us, and the Christians said, "for our sins Isa was already crucified by his enemies, so we are pardoned."

THE POLYTHEISTS

1. They believed in Allah but with so many partners and associates.

   "Then those who disbelieve, hold others equal to their Lord (Allah)." (6:1)

2. They were of the belief that a human cannot be the messenger.

Allah says;

   "So, they said, (Amazing) a human will guide us (as a messenger), so they disbelieved."(64:6)

3. Regarding life after death, they were rejecting it totally.

   "There is nothing but our life in this world." (45:24)

   "Who will give life to bones, become rotten and dust."(36:78)

They were superstitious.

But with all these three groups, Jews, Christians, and Polytheists claimed to be the followers of Ibrahim.

Allah said:

"Ibrahim was neither a Jew nor a Christian but he was a sincere Muslim, and he was not of the polytheists. Verily among mankind, the best to claim to Ibrahim are those who followed him, and this Prophet and those who have believed with him. And Allah is the protector/friend of the believers."(3:67-68)

SIGNS AND PROPHECIES OF THE PROPHET MOHAMMAD

As we said before, Allah (SWT) has established this universe for the purpose of wisdom and philosophy. He subjugated it to humans so they may exploit it for their good, but at the same time He made them bound to obey His commandments and to live as law-abiding servants to Him. This is for their benefit, in order to get in touch with Him, get close to Him and to have a satisfied life here and a happy one in the hereafter.

For this purpose, He sent the Prophets, inspired them to spread His commandments, and gave them books and scriptures to guide people towards Him. He gave them the same message of *Tauheed* and the same *Deen* of Islam. This message started with Adam, and this *Deen* progressed toward completion and perfection through all the messengers in their respective times and areas. They conveyed this message to the people they were sent to and later on the global universal and final Prophet of Allah, Mohammad came in the end and conveyed this message to the entire world.

Almost every Messenger of Allah informed his followers about the Prophets to come and ordered them to follow, and more specifically, they informed them about the last and final Prophet of Allah.

Allah said:

> *And remember when Allah took the covenant of the prophets, [saying], take whatever I gave you [the book, wisdom, laws, and rules] and afterward there will come to you a messenger confirming what is with you, you must then believe in him and help him. He [Allah] said, "do you agree and take up my covenant?" They said, "we agree." He said then bear witness and I am with you of*

the witnesses."(3:81)

THE PROPHECIES ABOUT PROPHET MOHAMMAD

THE FORM OF PROPHECIES

1. Prophecies are like dreams they need explanation and interpretation. These prophecies do not always look clear to the general public and sometimes not even to the special people. Sometimes it only becomes clear when the relevant messenger is sent.

   Christian scholars said that sometimes it is not clear for the said Prophet as well as it was in the case of Elias (Elijah), that Issa (Jesus) said about him that he was Elias (Elijah), while he himself said "I am not."

2. Prophecies are mostly given by mentioning the qualities or actions and sometimes the appearance of the person concerned. Very rarely is the person mentioned by name.

3. In prophecies the names of the places are also Qualities' name.

4. If any time or days are mentioned in the prophecies, it does not mean our own time (universal timeline).

5. If in the prophecies there is some fictional, illogical, or unreasonable concept given then it is not meant literally, and it requires interpretation.

6. If the second coming of a messenger is mentioned in a prophecy, then it means a messenger like him, except in the case of Jesus.

7. If in the revealed book there is mention of some contradictory statement to that of the known one, there for sure that part is corrupted as most of the divine books have been corrupted except the Holy Quran, so Quranic concept is considered a criterion in this regard.

THE PROPHECIES

ZOROASTRIAN'S PROPHECY

In Zoroastrian religious book, 28:129, it is said to Zaratasht (per the translation of James Darator), " His name is the kind conqueror, and his name is "Astut Arina" as he is the mercy for the whole world. He is the collector of people. As a perfect and spiritual human, he will correct the believers and the polytheists.

"Astut Arina" means "the praised one" and that is the meaning of the name Mohammad as well. His kindness as a conquering leader is clearly seen at the time of the conquest of Makkah.

BUDDHA'S PROPHECY

Buddha has given a prophecy about "Metteyya" (Maitreya) as Chakawati Sungnad wrote in Tantadi 3:76. A great personality would be sent in this world; his name is holy "Metteyya." With a perfect wisdom, piety, a unique scholar of the world, a guide looking for the guidance of the people, the teacher of the angels and the humans.

Regarding Mohammad's book (Quran), he said,

"Like a great Buddha as I am now. He knows perfectly

and sees as I see and know. Truth will be in its adornment and the knowledge about real life in its clean and perfect sense would be seen in its word and spirit, as I show it now. With him there will be thousands of companions as I have a few hundred" (Buddha's Holy book Vol 4 page 73-74).

This word "Metteyya" (I) pronounced in Sanskrit as "Metriyya" which means compassionate and kind, as does *Rauf* and *Rahim* in Arabic (Sanskrit Dictionary, Munir William, pg. 181)

In Holy Quran, Allah named him as Compassionate, Kind in Surah 9:128.

(II) This is the name of the coming Buddha who will be the fifth one of this stage.

(III) This word is "Matry" in its origin which means the giver of mercy and love, meaning mercy for the entire world. And in Pali, the sacred language of Theravada Buddhism, it means, "friendship," "kindness," "mercy," "compassion," and "sympathy."

Now these concepts could not be applied but only to Prophet Mohammad. Buddha never wrote book nor ever received a divine one. But what he taught was written in Pali language in the first century B.C. His name was Siddhartha Gautama, born in in Lumbini (now known as Nepal) in 563 B.C. and raised in Kapilavaustu, where his father was king. He died in 483 B.C. in Kashinagar, India. Buddha means "the awakened one," and in the aforesaid prophecy he indicated towards the Holy Quran that truth is there in its full beauty in words and spirit.

HINDUISM PROPHECY

In Hinduism holy books, the Pati Sarg para III: 335-338. A

"Malechha" or a spiritual teacher from a strange country and language will come with his companions. His name is Mohammad. Also, in "Kantap Sokat" it is said, "O people listen to it, a praiseworthy would be praised, the Koram (king of peace on earth) we find the uprooters of 60,000 and 90,000 enemies."

In the prophecy it is mentioned that:

I. His name is Mohammad (praiseworthy).

II. He is for peace on earth.

III. Allah will protect him amongst his enemies.

In Sam Ved it is said,

> *"Ahmad received from his Lord a shariah full of wisdom, getting light from him like sun." (Paryatic)*

In this prophecy, his name is Ahmad and a *shariah* full of wisdom is given to him where the guides get light, like the sun. In Sanskrit, "shloka pandit" Raja Ram's translation, he is mentioned as a camel rider from desert land, which sounds very much true for Mohammad.

JUDAISM PROPHECY

In Judaism's Holy book in Istisna, chapter 18 verse 17-22, it is mentioned,

> *I will send to them from their brothers a prophet like you, and put my word in his mouth and whatever I will tell him, he will say it to them, he will tell them in my name, I will put them to accountability, but a Prophet if says something in my name which I have not commanded to him to convey it and will say something in the*

name of Gods, he would be killed.

Now, in all the prophets of Bani Israel, no one has ever claimed that Isa is the like of Musa. Even when people asked John, "are you that one?" he said "no." Isa also never claimed that he was that promised one. And with him this process of Prophethood finished.

Allah said in the Holy Quran,

> *"We have sent to you a messenger like the one we sent to Firaun (Pharaoh)." (73:15)*

And to *Firaun* Allah sent Musa. Also, in "Istisna" it is said,

> *"God came from Sinai, and rose up from Shaeer over them, showed up his light in full from Faran came with 10,000 godly people and in his right hand there was a shariah for them."*

Now from Sinai, Musa came from "Shaeer". And where Baitul Lahm and Nasirah are situated is where Isa came from, but what is "Faran"? It is Jabal - Un - Nur, where from the Prophet Mohammad came with Shariah, and later on he was the one who entered Makkah (Mecca) with 10,000 companions at the time of its conquest.

CHRISTIANITY'S PROPHECY

Prophet Isa (Jesus) spoke a lot about Mohammad, as he was coming after him without any other prophet in between. In Matthew 21:33 it is mentioned:

> *Listen to a parable: an owner of a house planted a grape garden, and he protected it from all four sides, he made a pond therein and he gave it to the contractors. He went outside the country then when that was the time of the*

outcome, then, these contractors killed some of his workers, beat others, and stoned some others. He then sent some other workers more in number. These people did the same to them as well. Eventually he sent his son so they said, this the heir we should kill him; they brought him out and killed him now when the owner of the garden will come then what he will do to them? They said he will destroy these bad people and give the garden to others to give him the fruits in its season.

These grapes are the children of Israel, as that is in "Yas'iya". The one who plants it is the God of Israel. Now, "son" means the beloved one and "killed him" means beat him severely and "owner of the garden comes" means Prophet Mohammad as the attributes of Allah reflected in him in a perfect way.

He will "give the garden to others" means that prophethood will go to the children of Ismail".

In another parable he said,

"Then what is that? What is written that the stone, which the masons rejected, became the corner stone, so anyone who falls on this stone will get smashed and on whom it will fall it will grind them (Luke 20:17-18)."

In this parable, the masons are Israel, who used to reject the children of Ismael, and the Prophet Mohammad was from the children of Ismael. Who was the corner stone of the building of the prophethood as this process got completed with him? For sure, it was Mohammad.

Isa addressed his followers and said:

1. "If you love me then look at my orders.

2. I will invoke father, he will give another Paraclitus, he will stay with you forever.

3. I tell you the truth, if I will not go, then Paraclitus will not come to you, if I go, I will send him to you people."

Paraclitus is a Greek word that means *Ahmad*. Whatever signs about this Paraclitus are mentioned in the book of John. Those are applicable only to the Prophet Mohammad.

And in the aforesaid prophecy, the words "he will stay with you forever" refer to the finality of the prophethood of Prophet Mohammad.

This prophecy of Jesus with the name Ahmad is mentioned in the Holy Quran:

> *"And (mention) when Jesus the son of Mary said, O children of Israel, indeed I am the messenger of Allah to you confirming what came before me of the Taurat and bringing good tidings of a messenger to come after me, whose name is Ahmad." (61:6)*

PROPHET MOHAMMAD IN THE EYES OF NON-MUSLIM NOTABLES

In his book *the 100: A Ranking of the Most Influential Persons in History*, Michael Hart included religious leaders like Moses, Jesus, and Buddha; great philosophers like Plato, Aristotle, and Confucius; great scientists like Isaac Newton, Albert Einstein, and Charles Darwin. He described the greatest kings, like Alexander the Great, Ashoka, and Julius Caesar. He found that an illiterate man named Mohammad (PBUH) ibn Abdullah ibn Abdul Muttalib from the desert town of Makkah in the Arabian Peninsula take the topmost position in this lengthy list of great personalities from all around the world. First, he picked great personalities in history in different fields, then he made his research on every one of these 100 influential people and after that he made a comparison and put Prophet Mohammad in as number one in ranking. He did not put Jesus there nor Karl Marx, even though he is a Christian by faith and a communist by ideology. As in his writings, he said that Mohammad influenced not only his followers but others as well; he did not influence religious people only, but also non-believers.

He not only influenced people of his time only, but the generations to come also. He said very rightly that,

> "*Mohammad was the only man in history who was supremely successful on both the religious and secular levels and this led the list of the most influential personalities in the world.*"

This ranking of his came after his extensive study of history and historically great personalities and showed that Mohammad was such a supremely successful and influential personality that he influenced not only the people of his time, but he is still influencing people and will influence the future generations.

Thomas Carlyle, in his book *On Heroes: Hero Worship, and Heroic in History*, wrote,

> *A poor shepherd people roaming unnoticed in the deserts since the creation of the world, a hero prophet was sent down to them with the word they could believe, the see the unnoticed become noticeable, the small has grown the world great, within one century afterwards, Arabia is a Granada on this hand, and Delhi on that glancing with valor and splendor and the light of genius. Arabia shines through long ages over the section of the world."*

So, Mohammad's personality was such that all excellences were blended in that one personality He was a perfect teacher, a perfect guide, and a perfect role model in every field and aspect of human life. He was a man of great status, a military genius, a perfect legislator, an exemplary judge, and a compassionate teacher.

He himself first practiced what he taught and ordered. He established not only an ideal society, but a civilization with no incompleteness or deficiency. He commanded people towards rational, understanding, and sound reasoning on the basis of learning theories, observations, experiments, and research. He insisted upon faith, knowledge, character, good deeds with full sincerity.

His teachings covered every aspect of human life from habits of everyday life, up to establishment of a state and also inter states relation. In history no other such person is ever found. Jesus was a great prophet, but never a statesman or warrior. Plato was a great philosopher, but never a religious leader. Einstein was a great scientist, but never a political leader. Alexander was a great king and warrior, but never a spiritual luminary. But Mohammad had (and still has) the utmost exalted position in each and every field.

In the West, Thomas Carlyle is the first one who unveiled the truth and showed the truth and the true picture.

From John the Apostle to Voltaire, Westerners have tried to defame this great personality either out of ignorance or because of their prejudice towards him and his religion, Islam. In other words, we can say that those past prejudicial authors showed our Prophet to the west, as an imposter (may God forgive and forbid), but Carlyle's work showed him as a reformer and a great man in human history.

Carlyle said,

> *"How one man singlehandedly could weld warring tribes and wandering Bedouins into a most powerful and civilized nation in less than two decades."*

British historian Edward Gibbon said,

> *The great success of Mohammad's life was affected by sheer moral force without the stroke of a sword. His memory was capacious and retentive, his wit easy and social, his imagination sublime, his judgment clear, rapid, and decisive. He possessed the courage of both thought and action.*

George Bernard Shaw, an Irish playwright and ardent socialist in his book, wrote *The Genuine Islam* that,

> *Mohammad was by far the most remarkable man that ever-set foot on the earth. He preached a religion, founded a state, built a nation, laid down a moral code, initiated numerous social and political reforms, established a powerful and dynamic society to practice and represent his teachings. And completely revolutionized the worlds of human thought and behaviors for all times to come. He must be called the savior of humanity. I believe that if a man like him were to assume the dictatorship of the modern world, he would succeed in solving its problems in a way that would bring it much needed peace and happiness. During the short period*

> *of twenty-three years of his prophethood, he changed the complete Arabian Peninsula from paganism and idolatry to the worship of one God, from tribal quarrels and wars to national solidarity and cohesion, from drunkenness and debauchery to sobriety and piety, from lawlessness and anarchy to disciplined living, from utter bankruptcy to highest standards of moral excellence. Human history has never known such a complete transformation of people, or a place before or since, and imagine all these unbelievable wonders in just over two decades. Europe in the beginning to be enamored of the creed of Mohammad. In the next century it may go further in recognizing the utility of that creed in solving its problems if any religion has the chance of ruling over England, nay Europe within the next hundred years it could be Islam.*

Alphonso De Lamartine, a great French poet, and historian said in his book *Historia de la Turqe,*

> *If greatness of purpose, smallness of means, and astounding results are the three criterions of human genius who could dare to compare any great man in modern history with Mohammad. The most famous men created arms, laws of empires only. They founded if anything at all no more than material powers which often crumbled away before their eyes. This man not only moved armies, legislation, empires, people, and dynasties, but millions of men in one-third of the then inhabited world and more than that, he moved the altars, the gods, the religions, the ideas, the beliefs, and souls on the basis of a book, every little of which has become law. He created a spiritual nationality of every tongue and every race. His endless prayers, his mystic conversations with God, his death, and his triumph after death, all these attests to an imposture but to a firm*

> *conviction which gave him the power to restore a dogma. This dogma was twofold, the unity of Allah and the immateriality of Allah, the former telling what Allah is, and the latter telling what Allah is not. The one overthrowing false gods with the sword, the other starting an idea with the words.*

He continued,

> *Philosopher, orator, apostle, legislator, warrior, conqueror of ideas, restorer of rational dogmas, of a cult without images, the founder of twenty terrestrial empires and of one spiritual empire that is Mohammad. As regards all the standards by which human greatness may be measured, we may well ask, is there any man greater than he.*

Mahatma Gandhi, the Indian liberator, and thinker said,

> *I became more than ever convinced that it was not the sword, that won a place for Islam in those days in the scheme of life. It was the rigid simplicity, the utter self-effacement of the Prophet, the scrupulous regard for his pledges, his intense devotion to his friends and followers, his intrepidity his fearlessness, his absolute trust in God and in his own mission. These and not the sword carried everything before and surmounted every obstacle.*

SIGNS AT THE BIRTH OF THE PROPHET

1. Prophet Mohammad's father was married to a woman from Bani Zuhrah named Aaminah, daughter of Wahab. Abdullah left for a

business trip to Syria after his marriage to Aaminah. One morning, Aaminah told her servant Barakah that she had a dream that light-like rays came out of her womb. They went up until it lightened all the mountains, the hills, the valleys, and deserts all around Makkah. It spread at the space and lightened the world. Barakah asked her if she thought she was pregnant. She said she was but did not feel any discomfort as women often do, so she did not reveal it. Barakah told her she would give birth to a child who would bless the entire world. In another dream she heard a voice that she was carrying the chief of the people.

2. When Mohammad's grandfather summoned people for the naming ceremony, as was the custom at the time, told them that he was inspired to name this child Mohammad as he would be praised a lot, and this was a name not known to Arabia before.

3. Back then, city dwellers used to send their newborn babies to wet nurses in the desert as it was believed to be beneficial to them. Halima from Banu Sa'd said that when she was given Mohammad to nurse, her breasts filled with milk, as did the udders of her cows. Even the donkey she was riding was weak and could not join the group when they were going to Makkah, but when she was given Mohammad, it was amazing, they joined the group even though they had left before us and not only that, but they took them over and left them far behind.

Later on, we will mention a lot in this regard Insha'Allah. These prophecies and these signs are proof that he is the Messenger of Allah.

This is also a sufficient proof that not only is his biography preserved, his words and actions are saved and those who saved it, the transmitters, and narrator's biographies, have also been saved. Dr. Springer has asserted that no nation has ever saved all the words and actions of their leader as the followers of Mohammad did. And for the said purpose, they have saved the biographies of the savers as well and they are 500,000 in count.

Urwah ibn Zubair Ibn Ul Awwam wrote his biography of Mohammad in Arabic in 92 A.H. Urwah was the nephew of Aaisha (Mohammad's wife), the son of her sister Asma. He lived with his aunt and preserved her knowledge. Then Aban Ibn Uthman wrote the Prophet's biography in 105 AH, but these complete biographies are no longer extant. Different parts of these books are found scattered in books of history, Seerah, and Hadith, even though certain others also wrote the Prophet's biography in the following years. A piece of the book of Wahab ibn Munnabih is preserved in Heidelberg, Germany.

In 152 AH (After Hijra), Ibn Ishaq wrote the Prophet's biography, which is considered perfect. Later on, Ibn Hisham summarized it, as Ibn Ishaq's opus was very lengthy. He wrote it almost fifty years after Ibn Ishaq and in later times this was considered a proper reference in Seerah of the Prophet. Later on, the great Muhaditheen compiled the Ahadith of the Prophet: his words, actions, and sanctions that we can say that are the primary interpretation of the Holy Book.

As Aaisha said,

"The Prophet's daily life was the Quran."

Which means he used to utter and practice what the Quran said, so we can say that Sunnah is the Seerah and Seerah is the Sunnah of the Prophet. Following the Seerah is following the Sunnah.

We are sorry to say that many Muslims do not know much more about the Seerah, so we must learn more.

Allah said,

"Say that I am not a new thing among the messengers." (46:9)

Allah used to send the messengers to different nations, as He said,

> *"Indeed, we have sent you with the truth, a bearer of glad tidings and a warner and there never was a nation but a warner has passed among them." (35:24)*

The message of all these messengers was one and the same as Allah said,

> *"And we have not sent before you any messenger, but we used to reveal to him, that there is no god but Me so worship Me alone." (21:25)*

They all were bearers of the same *Deen* Islam as Allah said,

> *"He has ordained for you the same Deen, which we ordained for Nuh (Noah) and that which we have inspired in you and that which we ordained for Ibrahim (Abraham), Musa (Moses) and Isa (Jesus) to establish (keep straight and right/implement) the Deen and make no divisions therein." (42:13)*

The distinction is that all the messengers were sent to their specific nations, in a specific area and specific time, as this is apparently seen in their addresses when they said "Ya Quami" which mean "O my nation" while Prophet Mohammad is sent to the whole world until the last day, as Allah said,

> *"Say! O mankind I am the messenger of Allah to all of you." (8:158)*

Also, Allah said,

> *"Mohammad is not the father of any man among you but, he is the messenger of Allah and the "seal" of the Prophets." (33:40)*

Sufficient a proof for this finality and universality of him and his message is the Holy Book. He is given it intact and safe, down to its commas and colons, all over the world, and the same is true of his biography, his words, and actions.

He revived Islam in its true sense and transformed one of the worst societies of the time, possibly even in history, and raised it to one of the utmost progressive societies in norms, values, and character.

THE PROPHET'S FAMILY

Genealogists have established three parts of the prophet's lineage up to Adam.

1: The first, most recent part starts with the prophet's father Abdullah and goes to Adnan, the 21st grandfather of the prophet to whom the "Adnanian" (Adnanid) Arabs are attributed in lineage, and who are called Al-Arab-Al Musta'rabah" (Arabized Arabs). The Prophet himself used to mention his lineage up to Adnan stops there and say, "Genealogists tells lies" Means they are wrong about this. But certain genealogists do not give any significance to this hadith, so they go beyond that as well.

2: The second part is from Adnan up to the Prophet Ibrahim. In that part Adnan has forty grandfathers.

3: The 3rd part is from Ibrahim up to Adam. In that part of lineage prophet Ibrahim has nineteen grandfathers.

So altogether the Prophet Mohammad (sas) has eighty grandfathers between him and the first human being Adam. This number includes his father Abdullah.

1- Adam – 81

2- Sheith – 80

3- Anusha -79

4- Qaiman – 78

5- Mahla'il – 77

6- Yarid – 76

7- Akhnukhh (Enoch, who is said to be a prophet) - 75.

8- Mutwashlack – 74

9- Lamik – 73

10- Noah – (prophet Nuh) - 72

11- Sam – 71

12- Arfakhshad – 70

13- Salikh – 69

14- Abir – 68

15- Falik – 67

16- Ra'u – 66

17- Sam – 65

18- Nahur – 64

19- Iarih (who is called Azar/Aazar) – 63

20- Abraham (prophet Ibrahim) – 62

21- Ismael (prophet Isma'ili) – 61

ISMAIL (ISHAMEL)

22- Qaidar – 60

23- Aram – 59

24- Awda – 58

25- Mazzi – 57

26- Sami – 56

27- Zarih – 55

28- Nahith – 54

29- Muksar- 53

30- Aiham – 52

31- Afnad- 51

32- Aisar – 50

33- Deshan – 49

34- Aid – 48

35- Ar'awi – 47

36- Yalham – 46

37- Yahzir – 45

38- Yathrabi – 44

39- Sanbir – 43

40- Hamdan – 42

41- Ad - Da'a – 41

42- Ubaid – 40

43- Abqar – 39

44- Aid – 38

45- Makhi- 37

46- Nahish – 36

47- Jahim – 35

48- Tabikh – 34

49- Yadlaf – 33

50- Bildas – 32

51- Haza – 31

52- Nashid – 30

53- Awwam – 29

54- Obai – 28

55- Qamwal – 27

56- Buz – 26

57- Aws – 25

58- Salaman -24

59- Humaisi – 23

60- Add – 22

61- Adnan -21

ADNAN

62- Ma'ad – 20

63- Nizar – 19

64- Mudar – 18

65- Elias – 17

66- Mudrikah (who is called Amir) - 16

67- Khuzaiman – 15

68- Kinana – 14

69- Nadr (who is called Qais) – 13

70- Malik – 12

71- Fahr (who is called Quaish, and a tribe was named after him) – 11.

72- Ghalib – 10

73- Loai – 9

74- Ka'b – 8

75- Murrah – 7

76- Kilab – 6

77- Qusai (also called Zaid) - 5

78- Abd Manaf (called Al-Mughirah) - 4

79- Hashim (named Amr) – 3

80- Abdul Muttalib (called Shaiba) – 2

81- Abdullah - 1

82- Mohammad (the Prophet sas)

THE FAMILY OF THE PROPHET

The Prophet of Allah said that Allah selected Ismael from the sons of Ibrahim, Kinanah from the children of Ismael, Quraish from the sons of Kinanah, Hashim from the sons of Quraish and he selected me from the sons of Hashim. (Muslim)

Imam Tirmizi narrated a hadith:

> *Verily Allah has created the creation and he created me the best of them from the best group of them and best of the two groups. Then he chose the tribes, so he put (created) me in the best of tribe, then he selected families and selected me from the best thereof. I am the very best in person and family. The children of Adnan were spread out to various parts of Arabia.*

The Quraish tribe dwelt mostly in Makkah but were totally disunited until Qusai Bin Kelab succeeded in uniting them.

The Prophet Ismael had twelve children/sons from the daughter of Mudad bin Amr. Their names were Nabet, Qaidar, Edbael, Mebsham, Mishma, Duma, Micha, Hudud, Yetma, Yetour, Nafis, and Qidman. The twelve tribes of Arabized Arabs were formed from these sons who spread all over Arabia. The offspring of Ismael included Egyptian blood from their grandmother Hagar's side, Hebrew blood from Ibrahim's side, and Arab blood from their mother's side, the Jurhum tribe.

After the death of Ismael at the age of 137, his sons Nabet and Qaidar succeeded him, but soon their maternal grandfather Mudad Jurhami got hold of it. But he left some responsibilities in the hands of the offspring of Ismael. Jurhum used to take care of the House of Allah and to serve the pilgrims. They held control for almost 20 centuries.

Later, because of destination and difficult living conditions, Jurhum mistreated the pilgrims' extorted funds from them. The Adnanids from the offspring of Ismael, with the help of the Khuza'a tribe, turned them out of Makkah, but then Khuza'a controlled Makkah, although the Mudar tribes enjoyed some special privileges.

Khuza'a ruled the area for 300 years and Adnanids spread all over Najd and the sides of Iraq and Bahrain. Some small groups from the Quraish remained in Makkah. The Quraish did not have any role in Makkah until the appearance of Qusai bin Kilab.

QUSAI BIN KILAB

Qusai Bin Kilab (480CE) He was the great-grandfather of Abdul Muttalib, the grandfather of the Prophet (sas) when his father Kilab bin Murrah died, Qusai was a baby. His mother Fatima daughter of Sa'd married Rabiah bin Haram who took her with Qusai to a Border town near Syria. Qusai was of the view that Rabiah is his father but later his mother told him that your father was Kilab, and his family is the nobler one.

Qusai came to Makkah. As he was a wise man, very soon the Quraish tribe assembled around him. The Khuza'a king, Hulail Bin Hubshiyya, married to him his daughter Hubbah. On his death, Hulail tried to give the keys of the Holy Kabah to his daughter Hubbah, but she refused. So, he gave them to one Abu Ghibshan Jurhami, who was a drunkard and soon he exchanged the keys for jug of wine to Qusai. The Khuza'a tribe tried to dispose of him, but with the help of Quraish and other Tribes Qusai was judged the wise man having the right to keep it.

Qusai, once he had established himself, asked the Quraish to build up their Houses around the Holy Kabah, which no one had done before. He also established *An - Nadwah* (Assembly), a house for meetings where the Quraish elders used to meet and to dispose up their affairs.

This House brought unity to Quraish. However, Qusai had the privileges of leadership:

1: He presided over meetings.

2: He controlled the issues of war and peace.

3: He held the keys of the Ka'ba and was responsible for its service and protection.

4: He provided sweetened water to pilgrims and fed them. To cover expenses, he imposed a land tax upon Quraish tribe. They had to pay that in pilgrimage.

As Khuza'a demolished the Zamzam well and filled it with the treasuries of Kabah and mud. So, Qusai used to bring water from outside, put it in the reservations he made and later, at Hajj time, put it in pitchers sweetened with dates and raisins.

ABD MANAF

The grandfather of Abdul Muttalib and son of Qusai was a wise man. Qusai had another son, Abdul Uzza R Abd-ad-Dar. Abd Manaf was not the older one, but his father loved him so much and, in his lifetime, he trained him for leadership. But when he became old, he gave the *Hijabah*, the keys of the Holy House, to Abda – Ad - Dar, his eldest son. He also gave him the *Siqayah* to provide water, to the Pilgrims, the *Liwa*, the flag with which to lead wars if necessary, and the *Rifadah*, the tax Qusai imposed upon the Quraish to provide food to the pilgrims. Abd-Manaf never objected to this; rather, he helped him. After Abd – Ad - Dar and his sons tried to do the same, but they were not as honored in the eyes of the people as the four sons of Abd-Manaf, whose names were Hashim, Muttalib, Naufal and Abd-Shams. Because of the poor conditions of the services resolved to take over the privileges, the Quraish tribe was divided. The sons of Abd-Manaf entered a treaty amongst them called "Hilf-al-Mutayyibeen," named for the fact that they dipped their hands in perfume to mark the agreement.

The sons of Abd-ad-Dar entered another treaty called "Hilf-al-Ahlaf," or "treaty of the allies." The ultimate result was a civil war between two cousins, although it was eventually resolved. Based on that, the children of Abd- Manaf were given *Siqayah* and *Rifadah* and the children of Abd-ad-Dar were given *Hijabah*, *Liwa* and *Nadwah*. Until the advent of Islam, they lived in peace under these terms and conditions.

HASHIM BIN ABD MANAF (646CE)

When different duties were distributed amongst the sons of Abd-ad-Dar and Abd-Manaf and later on received *Siqayah* and *Rifadah*, they cast their lot for Hashim, and he took on these responsibilities. He was a rich, honest, and hospitable man as well as a very experienced merchant and noble politician.

He went personally to Byzantium and the Ghassan tribes to establish a treaty of good relation and friendship with them both. He also got permission from Byzantine for Quraish to move freely in Syria and to do business. His brother Abd-Shams had a treaty of trade with Negus of Abyssinia, other brothers Nawfal and Muttalib both had a treaty of trade with Persia and Himyar tribe from Yemen. Referring to that blessing of Allah holy Quran mentioned:

> "And Allah puts forward the example of a town (Makah) which was a secure and content one, its provision was coming to it from all sides in abundance, but it denied the blessings of Allah, so Allah made it taste extreme of

> *hunger and fear, Because of what they used to do."*
> *(16:112)*

Also, Allah said,

> *"Because of taming of Quraish, their taming of winter and summer (to different areas for business). So, they may worship the lord of this house (Kabah) (who has blessed them with this respect and security) who fed them against hunger and made them safe from fear."*
> *(106:1-4)*

In chapter 28 verse 57, Allah said,

> *"So have we not established for them a secure sanctuary to which are brought fruits of all kinds, a provision from our side. But most of them don't know." (28:57)*

So, Makkah was prosperous due to their widespread business. Once Hashim was on a trip to Sham, when he saw the lady Salma, daughter of Amr from Bani Adi Ibnan Najjar Al Khazraji, who was known for her beauty and business acumen in Yathrib (Madina). He asked about her marital status and learned she was divorced. He proposed to her, and she accepted. He stayed for some time there, and then he left for Sham and passed away in Gazza. Later on, that lady delivered a son of Hashim named "Shaibah" because he had white hair. Later he was known by his nickname Abdul Muttalib.

AL MUTTALIB

After the death of Hashim, Al Muttalib took over as he was well respected. He thought of his nephew, Shaibah bin Hashim. He went to Yathrib to ask his sister-in-law, Salma. She agreed to and handed over Shaibah to his uncle Al Muttalib. Shaibah was riding ahead of him on his camel when coming to Makkah, so the Quraish thought that he was a slave of Muttalib and called him "Abdul Muttalib" (slave of Muttalib). This nickname became so popular that his actual name was forgotten. Muttalib told people,

> *"He is my nephew, son of Hashim."*

Hashim left a lot of wealth and Muttalib wanted to give it to Abdul Muttalib, but another uncle of Abdul Muttalib named Nawfal objected to this. When Abdul Muttalib grew up, he asked for the support of his maternal uncle from Yathrib and some eighty Khazraj horsemen came to Makkah. Nawfal gave up and returned the wealth of Hashim and "Siqayah" and Rifadah" offices to Abdal Muttalib after Muttalib's death.

<u>Abdul Muttalib</u>: Upon leaving Makkah, the Jurhum tribe demolished the Zamzam well and filled it up with dust and mud. They also buried two deer made of gold, some swords, and the black stone as well. Abdul Muttalib, being responsible for *Siqayah*, used to arrange drinking water from outside of Makkah. He had at that time only one of his sons, Harith, to help, and thus he was totally exhausted. Then he dreamt of reopening the well of Zamzam. No one was aware of the proper place of Zamzam. He was inspired to dig a place in between the two idols of Isaf and Naila. He started digging that place with the help of his second son, Mughirah, until the water gushed forth. He found the swords, the black stone, and the two golden deer. Quraish asked for their share in that wealth. After a lengthy reasoning they came to an agreement to draw lots among Abdul Muttalib, the Quraish, and the Kabah. They drew lots inside Kabah near their extra powerful goddess Hubal. The Quraish lost. The swords went to Abdul Muttalib and the two golden deer to the Kabah. He ordered the swords to be reforged as a door for Kabah and placed the two deer inside Kabah.

WHY WAS MAKKAH ATTACKED?

Throughout history societies have often gone to war over trade and commerce. A Jewish king of Yemen Dzu-Nawas who brutalized the Christians in Najran is mentioned in "Surat Ul Buruj".

> *"Cursed be the fellows of the trench who fed the fire with fuel, when they sat by it and witnessed what they were doing against the believers, they had no fault except that they believed in Allah all mighty, ever praised." (85:4-8)*

The Christian government of Abyssinia retaliated and destroyed his government. They were supported by the Romans, who were trying to get control of the businesses run by Arabs for the last few centuries, since the time they occupied Egypt and Syria. So, they put a big army on the western coast of Arabia to control that ocean route for business, but due to geographic situation they could not do that. Then they brought their navy to the Red Sea and blocked Arab trade. Now the Arabs had only their land route for business. To get control of this route they helped the Abyssinian government and gained control of Yemen. Abraha became the assistant of the Abyssinia king in Yemen and later he became almost an autonomous king of Yemen. For the said purpose of obtaining control of that business route he plotted to cut off the Arabs, but as Arabs were respected as custodians of Kabah, he built a church in "Sana'a". He declared that the Hajj must be done here. By doing so he was trying to provoke Arabs into retaliating so he would have a reason to attack the Kabah. And eventually some Arabs tried to burn that church. It is also possible that the Abraha (Abranees) plotted this. So, he arranged an army of 60,000 along with several elephants (who were well trained to demolish buildings). On his way to Makkah, he was capturing all the cattle of Quraish where he caught some 200 camels belonging to Abdul Muttalib. Abdul Muttalib came to him and asked for his camels. He said, "oh! I thought you are here to request me not to demolish Kabah." Abdul Muttalib said, "Kabah has its own lord who will protect and defend it."

The economical object was motivated by the desire to build a church. But Allah destroyed that big army in Muhassab Valley near Muhassar (Mash'aral-Haram, Muzdalafah).

Allah said,

> "Have you not seen how your lord dealt with the owners of the elephant? Did he not make their plot go awry? And he sent against them birds in flocks. Striking them with stones of Sijjil [baked clay). And he made them like an empty field of stalks [i.e., the leavings after harvest]." (105:1-5)

ABDULLAH BIN ABDUL MUTTALIB

He was the father of the Prophet (SAS). He was a very handsome man and beloved of his father.

Because of *Siqayah*, once Abdul Muttalib made a pledge to Allah that if he fathered 12 sons, he would sacrifice one of them. Later on, he had 12 sons besides Abdullah, but he had forgotten his pledge, so he was reminded in a dream to sacrifice Abdullah the beloved son. (In some books it is said that he did not forget but he asked all his sons to draw arrows to see who would be sacrificed.) Now he took Abdullah towards *Isaf* and Naila, the idols, to slaughter him. When the Quraish found out they rushed to him and asked him not to do it, otherwise they would sacrifice their sons as well. Mughirah, son of Abdullah al Makhzoomi said, "let us go to the soothsayer in Khyber and tell her everything." They went there. She said, "today you should go back and come tomorrow." The next day she asked them, "how much is the blood money in your culture?" They replied that it was 10 camels. She said, "go and make a draw between Abdullah and 10 camels. If it comes out for camels, then slaughter them and if it came out in the name of Abdullah then aid to it another 10 and do the same until the draw comes for camels." They started the procedure and when the number was 100 camels then the draw came for camels. He slaughtered these camels and Abdullah was ransomed. Referring to this the prophet said, "I am the sons of two sacrifices, Ismael and Abdullah." Subsequently, one hundred camels were fixed as blood money in Makkah and later the prophet also approved that by the leave of Allah, and it became the part of Shariah.

ABDULLAH AND HIS MARRIAGE TO A'AMINAH

Abdul Muttalib the father of Abdullah approached the family of Wahab Ibni Manaf Azzuhari for Aaminah. Before this a few women and certain families had approached Abdullah for marriage. Some of them offered him great wealth as well, as he was a handsome and wise young man from a noble family. But as he was a cultured man as well, he refused. When his father asked for Aaminah, they were more than happy, and the marriage was solemnized. The same day Abdul Muttalib married a cousin of Aaminah, Halah, who later gave birth to Hamzah, the uncle of the prophet.

Later, when Abdullah was going on a business trip to Gaza, on his way back to Makkah he stayed in Madinah, fell sick, and died. Aaminah was pregnant. The death of Abdullah was a shock for his father, his wife and entire family as well.

Abdullah was born in 545 CE to a noble lady, Fatima binti Amr Ibni Aa'iz. His original name was Abdud Dar. But it was changed to Abdullah after his would-be sacrifice.

PROPHET MOHAMMAD FROM BIRTH TO PROPHETHOOD

THE BIRTH OF THE PROPHET (570CE)

Prophet Mohammad was born on Monday, Rabi Ul Awal 9th or 12th. It was the same year Allah protected the Kabah from the elephants and the Arabs started their calendar from this year. So, this was the first year of elephant's event.

At the time of his birth, a noble lady, Shifa, the mother of Abdur Rahman Ibn Awf, served as a midwife.

Aaminah informed Abdul Muttalib about his grandson. He was at Kaba at that time. He came and took him to Kabah to get blessings. He named him Mohammad ("the praised one"). This name was not very familiar in the area and when people asked Abdul Muttalib why he chose it, he said, "he will be praised forever".

Several historians have mentioned a few unusual events at that time, but the great one that is mentioned in holy Quran is that the demons (*Jinn*) ceased to approach heaven,

> "And we have sought to reach the heaven, but found it filled with stern guards and flaming fires. And verily we used to sit there in stations to have a hearing. But anyone who [tries to) listen now he will find for himself a flaming fire ready [to shoot him]." (72:8,9)

Ibni Sad narrates that his mother saw in her dream that a light came out of her that illuminated the castles of Sham.

Besides his own mother Aaminah, a few other ladies suckled him. Amongst them these are named Thuwaibah, a slave of his uncle Abu

Lahab, who also suckled before him, his uncle Hamzah, and also her Abu Salmah al Makhzoomi. She was suckling her own son Masruh also. Ummi Aiman also suckled him. Khawlah Binti Munzir suckled him as well, but the lucky lady who suckled him for a long time was Halima Sadia the daughter of Abu Zuwaib. Her nickname is Ummi Kabshah.

HALEEMAH SADIA'S NURSING

This was a tradition to send their children to desert for their growth in a natural atmosphere. Some tribes were known for their extra care specially the Baua Sa'd tribe. The ladies of these tribes used to make a trip to Makkah for the purpose, but as Mohammad who was an orphan and thus, he was not an attractive choice, as the wet nurse would not be compensated well for orphans. Each lady visited but they did not show interest in this infant. Halima also visited the house but when she could not find any other infant, then eventually she took Mohammad.

She relates that thanks to this blessed child they enjoyed every type of blessings: even her own child became fat.

Halima had her son, Abdullah Ibn Ul Harith, Aneesah Bint Ul Harith and Shaima whose name was Juzamah or Huzafah. She had nursed Abu Sufyan Ibn Ul Harith, the first cousin of the prophet also. Mohammad was growing there and after two years they brought him back to his mother as per contract. But still they wanted him for another term and ultimately, they got him.

"SHAQQUS SAD'R" OR THE SPLIT OF THE CHEST

After a few months, as narrated by Imam Muslim from Anas, the archangel Jibril (Gabriel), along with another angel, came to Mohammad when he was there with his brother and other children. They put him on the ground or over a rock, opened his chest, brought out his heart, washed it in a golden tray, and put it back in its place.

The children rushed to Halima, crying that Mohammad had been killed. The family rushed to him, finding him alive but a little pale. He related this story as well.

MOHAMMAD'S TRIP TO MADINA (575)

After four years in Banu Sad, he was brought back to his mother. As the mother of his grandfather Abdul Muttalib was from Madina, that family wanted Abdul Muttalib and Aaminah to bring the child to Madina. Also, Aaminah wanted to visit the grave of her husband. They went to Madina but on their way back to Makkah Aaminah died at a place named Abwa. She was buried there. Mohammad was brought back by Ummi Aiman the wet nurse, to his grandfather.

MOHAMMAD IN THE CUSTODY OF HIS GRANDFATHER:

As the chief of Makkah and custodian of Kabah, Abdul Muttalib used to sit to the wall of Kabah on a cushion and his sons sat around him, but he put Mohammad with him on the cushion.

When the prophet was only 8 years, two months, and 10 days old, Abdul Muttalib passed away. At the time of his death, he extracted a pledge from his son Abu Talib to take extra care of Mohammad. Abdul Muttalib died in 578 CE.

Abu Talib, even though he was not rich, still took care of *Rifadah,* the hospitality to the visitors of the holy house, while Abbas was taking care of *Siqayah.*

Abu Talib was devoted to the Prophet. He used to keep him close every time. He was the respected man. Once, the people came to him asking him to make *Dua* for rain. Ibni Asakir narrates that he brought Mohammad to kabab and made *Dua* and ultimately there was a shower. Abu Talib said a *Qaseedah* (poem).

And the shining face with his face the clouds are asked for rain, he is a support for orphans and protection for widows.

The Perishing Bani Hashim takes shelter by him, and they are in graces and virtues because of him.

This *Qaseed* is comprised of 80 verses (Ibni Ishaq): Even in the time of Abdul Muttalib once he put him on his shoulders and asked for rain while standing over Mount Abu Qubais, and the rain fell. Abu Talib claimed he had observed that (*Khattabi*)

THE FIRST TRIP TO SHAM

In 582, when he was 12, Abu Talib was going to Sham on a business trip, so he took Mohammad with him. The caravan was passing by the monastery of a monk named Buhira. He came to the caravan and invited them for food, which he had never done before. He asked about Mohammad's father. Abu Talib said, "I am his father." Buhira did not believe him. He was sure Mohammad was an orphan. Abu Talib said "Yes, He is." Then he asked Mohammad a few questions and he answered them. Buhira also asked him to show his shoulders, where he saw the natural seal of the prophethood. He told them that I was standing on the terrace looking at you people, the cloud was shadowing this young man and the stones and trees were saluting him, and these are the signs of a prophet. Buhira asked Abu Talib not to take a risk taking him to Sham as if the Jews recognize him, they will bother you, and thus Abu Talib sent him back with some youngsters. How Allah protected this orphan, as Allah says,

> "Have we not found you an orphan, so we sheltered you?" (93:6)

THE BATTLE OF FIJAR OR FUJJAR (580-590 CE)

These are actually four battles that took place in the same period. The first one was between the Kinana, and Hawazin tribes. The second one between Quraish, Kinanah, the 3rd was between Kinana and Banu Nadr. The fourth and the last one was between Quraish and all tribes of Kinanah and Hawazin. This happened because of the wrongdoing of one person. The king of Heirah, Numan Ibni Munzir, sent his loaded camels to the national annual market of Okaz, located between Taif and Makkah. There were two other similar markets, Majannah, and Dzul Majaz, in the proximity of Arafat. These bazaars had been taking place in the holy months when all tribes, even the Jews and Christians, were bound not to harm each other. All people used to get together in these markets for trade, poetry competitions, and even talking freely about their faiths.

The caravan of Noman was staying with Urwah from the Hawazin tribe. In his shelter, a man from Kinana tribe Barrad Ibni Qais killed Urwah and then, he ran away towards Khaybar. He asked Bisher Ibni Hazim Al Asadi, a poet, to inform Abdullah Ibni Jad'aan, Hisham Ibni Mughirah, Harb Ibni Umayyah, Naufal Ibni Muaa'wiyah, and Bal'aa Ibni Qais, so they would not be harmed. He came to Okaz and warned them. These people left for the safety of Haram. The tribe of Hawazin refused to avenge Barrad Ibni Qais as Urwah was chief of Hawazin, so for him they wanted to avenge a big man from Kinanah or Quraish. The Hawazin chief Abu Bara said that Quraish had cheated them, as they killed Urwah in a holy month. So, the Hawazin tribe came after the people of Quraish, but they had already entered the Haram limits, which is why a man from Abu Aamir, Auram Ibni Shuaib, challenged them to a war next year. The next year, because of the war preparation on both sides, the Okaz market did not take place. In the battlefield on the Quraish and Kinanah side came to the field Abdullah Ibni Jad'aan, Hisham Ibni Mughirah, Harb Ibni Umayyah, Abu Uhaiha Saeed Ibn Ul Aas, Utba Ibni Rabia, Aas Ibni Wa'il, Mamar Ibni Habib Jumahi, Ikramah Ibni Aamir Ibni Hashim, and others, On one side of this group, Kinanah's Abdullah Ibni Jad'aan was in command, while on the other side there was Kuraiz Ibni Rabia and in the middle there was Harb Ibni Umayyah. From the Hawazin tribe, there were Abu Bara Aamir Ibni Malik Ibni Jafar, Subai, Rabia Ibni Muaa'wiyah Nadri, Dareed Ibni Shammah, Masud Ibni Mutab, Abu Urwah Ibni Masud, Auf Ibni Abi Harittah Muri, Abbas Ibni Ra'l Sullami. It is said that this army was led by Abu Bara. In this battle, the Quraish and Kinanah were defeated and Utbah Ibni Rabi'a, who was a young man of 30 years, asked for peace. Now based on a peace treaty the Quraish were made bound to pay the blood money of the deaths of Qais and Hawazin and not vice versa.

The Prophet joined one of these battles with his uncles, picking up the arrows shot at Quraish by Hawazin and Qais to be reused.

HILFUL FUDOOL (THE FUDOOL TREATY)

After these battles, when the Quraish came back, someone from Zubaidah city brought some goods to Makkah and Aas Ibni Wa'il bought them but refused to pay their price. The seller asked help from his allies, Banu Abdul Dar, Banu Makhzum, Banu Sah'm, and Banu Jumah, but they refused. So, Zubeidi went to the Abu Qubais Mountain and asked for help. The Quraish sitting in the yards of Kaba heard his plea. Zubair Ibni Abdul Muttalib stood up and he gathered Banu Hashim, Banu Zuhrah, Banu Taim and Banu Asad in the house of Abdullah Ibni Jad'aan, where after debate and discussion they agreed to help and support the oppressed, whosoever they may be, and they would try to establish peace. The prophet was a young man at that time, but he attended that meeting and later referring to that, he said that I loved that agreement more than the fleet of Red Cattle (camels, the Arabs' greatest treasure of the time). He also said that if I were invited to such a treaty now, he would attend, which means he was a peace-loving person.

THE PROPHET'S SECOND TRIP TO SHAM (595 CE)

As the prophet gained fame as a trustworthy person in Arabia, wealthy people were sometimes looking for such a person to work for them. A wealthy noblewoman, lady Khadija Bint Khuwaylid, sent a message to him asking if he would go on a business trip for her and she offered him a big part of the profit. With the approval of his uncle Abu Talib, he agreed to it. She sent her slave Maisarah with him. In Busra city they stayed close to the monastery of a monk named Nastura under a tree. Nastura came to Maisarah and asked him, "who is this young man?" He said, "he is from Quraish." Nastura said, "Do his eyes remain Red all the time?" He said, "yes." Nastura said, "this is the last and final prophet of Allah. I wish I will be there when he will receive the message." He said to Maisarah, "keep close to him." The prophet accomplished his job and returned to Makkah. Khadija saw that he was shadowed. Maisarah told her the same and also about the popularity of the prophet in the bazaar.

Khadija was a widow of two husbands, one after the other. The first one was Attiq Ibni Aa'iz and from him she had one daughter, Hind.

The second husband was Abu Halah. She had one daughter, Hind, and one son, Halah, from him. She sent a message to the prophet through her sister or her friend Nafeesah for marriage. Before this, some well-off men had proposed her, but she had refused. The prophet, as a cultured man said, "I will ask my uncle." They agreed to it. Abu Talib solemnized this marriage and recited its *Khutbah*, in which he praised Allah and mentioned the virtues of his people and the qualities of Mohammed. After that a cousin of Khadija named Warqa Ibni Naufal also recited a *Khutbah* and proposed to Khadija. It is said that Khadija's uncle Amer Ibni Asad or her brother Amer Ibni Khuwaylid acted as male guardian. The prophet slaughtered one or two she-camels and arranged *Waleemah*. It is also related that amongst other Abu Bakr the prophet's close friend also attended the marriage. Khadija's father Khuwaylid got dead before battle of Fijjar / Fijjar.

Khadijah was 40 at the time of the marriage and the prophet was 25. This was the prophet's first and only marriage. All children of the prophet were from Khadija except Ibrahim; he was born to Mariyah Qibtiyya. The Prophet had two sons from Khadija named Qasim and Abdullah. His other sons were called Tayyib and Tahir. Also, the prophet had four daughters. They are Zainab, Ruqayyah, Ummi Kulthum and Fatima.

THE RECONSTRUCTION OF THE KABA

The Kaba is situated in the valley of Makkah, almost right in the middle of the globe. The date line and magnetic line both pass right beneath Kaba. That part of the earth is the center of gravity as well, and Allah has made His house as His sign and the spiritual center of the world. Makkah is called "Umm Ul Qura" (the mother of the city). In Western world, the word "mecca" (Makkah) is used to describe a place that attracts many people.

> *"And (remember) as we made this house a returning place for human beings and a place of safety." (2:125)*

This house is situated in such a place where the floodwater comes from the mountain. So, the walls got broken. The Quraish tribe agreed to fund its reconstruction by asking for donations. At that time, they also arranged to repair a broken ship at Jeddah seaport. Waleed Ibn Ul Mughirah and a few others went there and brought it to put the roof on the Kaba. This was the first time the Kaba got a roof, but due to a lack of funds, they built it square instead of rectangular like before. They left a part of it outside, which is called *Hateem* (broken part). If someone enters the *Hateem* in a round of *tawaf,* that round is not counted as *tawaf* as it must be around the Kaba.

Baqoom, a slave of Saeed Ibn Ul Aas, was a good carpenter. They asked him to do that job of construction and roof. He is the same man who made the *minbar* (pulpit) of the prophet in Madina later. In this construction all the four tribes of Makkah took part, and each tribe was given one wall to demolish and rebuild. But due to superstition, no one wanted to start until Wahid Ibn Ul Mughirah started; when nothing happened to him, the others also started.

The Prophet also took part in this work, with his tribe placing stones. When the time came to place the sacred black stone in its place, every tribe wished to have this privilege. Bani Abdad Dar and Bani Adi put a bowl full of blood and dipped the tips of their fingers in it as pledge to go to any extent of bloodshed for the honor. Because of this action of them, they were called blood mongers.

Abu Umayyah al Makhzoomi, the father of Ummi Salma, when he saw that this was leading to another civil war, said, "let's see who enters Kaba the first tomorrow; he will arbitrate." Everyone agreed to it and the first one who entered the next day was Mohammad. All of them said, "here is Assadiq Ul Amin." Mohammad said, "give me a robe." He put the stone in it and said, "let the elder of each one of the four tribes, hold one edge of the robe and lift it to the appointed place."

When they did so, Mohammad picked up the stone there from and put it in its place and thus bloodshed was averted.

For further protection, the Quraish put the door above the ground on the height of tall person and put in only one door. They modified it,

- (i) leaving *Hateem* outside,
- (ii) putting one door instead of two, and
- (iii) putting the door on a height and
- (iv) putting the roof

It is also mentioned in *"Tehzeeb Ul Asma"* that once Abbas Ibni Abdul Muttalib got lost, his mother, Nateela Binti Khabbab al Khazrajeyah, vowed to make a *Ghilaf* (cover) for the Kaba if he was found and eventually, she did it. It is said that this was the first ever *Ghilaf* of Kaba.

THE FIRST *WAHI*

It was a custom in Arabia to retreat to a desert or cave once a year to disconnect oneself from all worldly things as much as possible to provide rest for the mind and brain. Mohammad did this but for him there was another reason also and that was to find out the truth and the reality. But in these solitary retreats in Hera the law, of whom he followed? Scholars have different opinions about whether he followed the laws of Nuh or Ibrahim or Moses or Isa. But the real answer to this question is that he followed every right deed of whichever law he found in the light of his pure nature to find the truth.

Through this he was granted transparency, which he began to see in his dream and visions of truth. He was satisfied with his job. The series of these dreams remained for six months, and they told him that his people had gone astray, even the Jews and Christians as well. He spent these six months in the cave going forth and back. At that time, he was scared and intimated to his wife the fear that he might be possessed by an evil spirit. She reassured him not to be afraid, as honest, truthful and Amin, so, nothing will happen to him.

First *Wahi*: Once he was in the cave an angel (Gabriel) came to him saying "Iqra," which means" Read," as he has not been at school or seen a teacher never and he was illiterate; therefore, he was called "Ummi," as a person born illiterate of his mother. No messenger of Allah who has brought Shariah from Allah has been a student of anyone, but rather got knowledge directly from revelation. So, one may not say,

> *"He is not a prophet from Allah, but a literate person and can speak so from his own,"*

And therefore Allah (swt) challenged the pagans when they rejected holy Quran as revelation, saying that,

> *"If you are in doubt about what he have revealed to our servant (Mohammad), bring a [short) sura [chapter) by someone like him [illiterate] and call your witness [scholars/literati as well]."*

But even a literate one or an assembly of literates cannot say so. The angel said so for three times, squeezed him thrice and he answered the same every time, that I am illiterate. For the third time the angel started reciting:

> *"Read in the name of your lord who created [everything]. He created the mankind from clot. Read and your lord is the most generous/respect giver, the one who taught by the pen. Taught to human being which he knew not." (96:1-5)*

Some points: The angel said, "Iqra", which means "read" or "recite;" he might have asked him to follow him in recitation of word "Iqra" as a student follows the pronunciation of his teacher. Then, as the first word that touched his ear was "Iqra", it indicates the importance of reading and knowledge and expresses how much importance Islam places on seeking knowledge, because it was in the first *Wahi,* and it was said twice. The second thing that Allah has not mentioned the object of "Iqra:" it means that one can read whatever one can, but in the name of one's lord, anything to be read in the name of Allah must be at least permissible one and then there is the word *Rabb,* which means an entity taking a thing towards its completion very kindly. So, whatever you will read must be with good intention and kindness towards all creatures. The third thing is that he first mentioned creation in general and then the mankind as a special type of creature. Then he stated that he has been created from a clot so he is a sort of animal originally, but he can get respect and attain priority only by knowledge, and therefore the word "Iqra" is repeated followed by the attribute of your lord that "Al - Akram." *Karamat* means honor, dignity, and generosity. It means that respect is found by seeking knowledge and that is generosity as well. Humans are a type of creation that can use a pen, a small tool that can do very big jobs. and fields. This allows his knowledge to be extendible and deductive. So, he will learn more and more until his last day. This was actually a road map for his message and teachings. Rasulullah, (sws) as narrated by Imam Bukhari, declared that Gabriel squeezed him three times whenever he said that he was illiterate, and the third time he squeezed him so hard that he was afraid of death. Then, he came to his house in a frightened position asking Khadija (ra) to cover him with blanket as he was feeling cold. But Khadija, his wife who was knowing him very well, asked him if something unexpected might have frightened him He told her the whole story and expressed fear that it could happen again. But she encouraged him by saying,

> *"Not at all by Allah, Allah will never disgrace you. Indeed, you keep intact the relation with relatives, and you take the responsibility of one who is a burden on his own self, you give work to the unemployed, you are hospitable to the guest and help the calamity affected one."*

This means that noble character is noble, and Allah does not let down people of noble character in such a situation.

No wife can console her husband in a more beautiful way than this.

After this consolation, Khadija took heir to her cousin Waraqah Ibin Nawfal a blind man who converted to Christianity in the time of ignorance and was known for his knowledge of Taura and Injeel. He had gone blind. She said,

> *"Cousin, listen to your nephew."*

The prophet related his story. Waraqah said,

> *"This is the secret keeper came to Musa. I wish if I was young and wish that if I was alive when your people will take you out of your city."*

The prophet said,

"They will turn me out?"

Waraqah said,

"Yes! Never there came a man like you with the same message but he has been treated with enmity and if that day happened and I was there I shall help you to the utmost."

Then the prophet was in a situation of hope and fear, hoping for mercy but afraid of being squeezed again if the angel reappeared. Sometimes he thought of throwing himself from a hilltop. But whenever he intended this, the archangel called on him and said,

"O Mohammad you are the messenger of Allah."

And thus, he was getting satisfied.

THE SECOND *WAHI*

The prophet used to go for a few days every month to Hira after this. And after 6 months, once he was on his way back to Makkah, and he was close to Hira as Imam Bukhari narrates from Jabir that Rasulullah told us that, he was called by same one from the sky, so he looked at and that was the same angel who came to him in Hira sitting on a chair between the sky and the earth. So, he rushed to his family, asked them to cover him in a mantle and then the angel came with these verses:

"O you who covered himself in a mantle! Stand up and warn. And magnify your lord. And purify your cloth. And shun the filth. And do not favor to acquire more. And for your lord so be patient." (74:1-7)

This second message made it clear when warning people, one's first ever duty is to stop them and later put them on the right track and put the greatness of Allah in their mind. "Cleaning cloth" means to improve the character and to promote it, as the prophet said: "I have been sent to promote character and to take people out of the filth of faith and to do good to people expecting no reciprocation of them and for sure you will face difficulties in this regard so be patient, stable and steadfast."

CALL TOWARDS ALLAH

The prophet of Allah started his *Dawat* towards Allah, but secretly, for almost 3 years.

The first one who accepted his *Dawat* was Khadijah, Zaid Ibni Haritha and he was 23 at that time; Ali was 12 years of age. But all these three were in the house of the prophet while outside the house the first one who accepted the message without any if and but, that was Abu Bakr, his lifelong friend and he accepted, as he knew him better than anybody else. Abu Bakr not only accepted Islam, but he convinced his close associates Uthman Ibni Affan, Zubair Ibn Ul Awwam, Abdur Rahman Ibni Awf, Sa'd Ibni Abi Waqas and Talha Ibni Ubaid Ullah to accept Islam as well. Also, Abu Bakr exchanged his slave for Bilal as Bilal was from those who accepted Islam. This was a little bit later.

THE PROPHET USED TO PRAY IN SECRET

The prophet and his followers used to pray secretly and individually somewhere in the canyons. Once Sa'd Ibni Abi Waqas and a few others were praying in a canyon, some Makkans saw them and cursed them. Sa'd hit one of them and he was injured. This was the first blood of an enemy of Islam. After some time, the prophet made the house of Arqam Ibni Abil - Arqam as his secret base for *Dawat* and prayer. They used to pray two prayers, one before sunrise and one before sunset, i.e., Fajr and Asr at that time. Five prayers became mandatory at Meraj (ascension time). In this time more people accepted Islam: Aamir Ibni Abdullah Ibni Jarrah (Abu Ubaidah Ibn Ul Jarrah), Abu Salamah, Abdullah Ibn Ul Asad, Arqam Ibni Abil Arqam, Uthman, Qudamah and Abdullah, sons of Maz'oon, Ubaidah Ibn Ul Harith, Saeed Ibni Zaid, His wife Fatemeh Bint Ul Khattab, Asmah Bint Abi Bakr, Aaisha Bint Abi Bakr, Sa'd and Umar, sons of Abu Waqas, Abdullah Ibni Masud, Masud Ibn Ul Qari (known as Ibni Rabee'a), Saleet and Hatib, sons of Umar, Ayyash Ibni Abi Rabee'a, his wife Asma Bint Salamah, Khunais Ibni Huzafah Ibni Qais, Aamir Ibni Rabee'a, Abdullah and Abu Ahmad, the sons of Jah'sh, Hatib Ibn Ul Harith, Jafar Ibni Abi Talib, his wife Asmah Binti Omais and the ally of Banu Zahrah Khabbab Ibn Ul Aratt.

In the meantime, Abu Bakr insisted on starting worship openly even though the prophet disagreed, as the number of Muslims was still small, but he insisted, so they came out and Abu Bakr made speech. This was the first ever speech by someone regarding Islam in the presence of the prophet. The Makkans jumped on him and threw him to the ground, kicking and beating him, especially Utbah Ibni Rabee'a, who did his utmost until Abu Bakr became unconscious. His tribe, the Banu Tameem, came and took him home, making an announcement that if anything happened to him, then for sure they would kill Utbah. In the evening he came around and the first thing he asked was,

"How is the prophet?"

He asked his mother if she could go to Umm Ul Fazl, the wife of Abbas, and ask her. She came with his mother and told him,

"He is ok and he is in Dari Arqam."

He said,

> "I want to go and see him,"

But they told him the situation was still very tense. The next day they brought him to the prophet when the prophet saw him that he could walk, albeit with the support of others, he burst into tears and started kissing Abu Bakr. He said,

> "There is no problem as long as you are all right."

Also, he said,

> "This is my mother who takes such good care of me."

The prophet made a *Dua* for her and she accepted Islam.

The prophet received the first *Wahi* on August 6th 610 and started open call in 613 as Allah ordered him.

> "Declare what you are commanded and turn away from the polytheists." (15:94)

Also, Allah said,

> "And warn your nearest kindred." (26:214)

The prophet invited Banu Hashim, so they came along with a few persons from Banu Muttalib, about 45 people in total. But before the prophet started, Abu Lahab said,

> "These are your uncles and cousins, so speak, but not childishly, as we cannot counter all tribes. If you stand on what you say that is the worst thing you will do."

So, the prophet did not speak. Then after some days he insisted, and he spoke about *Tauheed*. Abu Lahab said,

> "Stop him before others jump on him, but Abu Talib said, by God, we will defend him as long as we are alive. He said to The Prophet go ahead for what you have been ordered, but I cannot desert the Deen of Abdul Muttalib."

Then one day the prophet came to Safa and shouted,

> "Ya Sabahaa",

A known call for gathering. So, the people rushed to him. Ibni Abbas said he called on different tribes of Quraysh by name as Bukhari narrated. He said to them,

> "Have you found me truthful or a liar?"

They said,

> "We have never seen but only truth in your personality."

Then he said,

> "If I said that an enemy of yours is coming now but has come from beyond this mountain, will you believe me?"

They said yes. Then, he said,

> "Say there is no God, but Allah. You will succeed by saying so."

Abu Lahab threw a stone towards him or some pebbles and sand. He disheartens that that when my real uncle did so, what will be the case of others? Allah (SWT) encouraged him and gave him fortitude,

> "Perish the two hands of Abu Lahab and perish he. His wealth and his children will not benefit him. He will be burnt in a fire of blazing flame and his wife too, the career of woods (thorns throwing it in the path of The

> *Prophet, or it means that, she used to slander Rasulullah (SWS). In her neck is twisted rope of palm fiber."*

Some of the scholars said that all this denotes the torment of the hellfire, while some others said that Abu Lahab actually fell sick with the plague or smallpox, which damaged his hands and whole body as well, while his wife died because of a rope of palm fiber fell on her neck and she was choked and died. And one of his sons when he was on his way to Syria and with Caravan, he was resting in a rest area, a wild dog picked him up from amongst the people and threw him against a tree, crushing him to pieces. He and his brother both divorced the daughters of The Prophet as after this call of the prophet Abu Lahab ordered them to do so. This one used bad language to the prophet and the prophet said,

> *"O Allah, put on him a dog from your dogs."*

Abu Lahab used to frighten people coming to Makkah so they would not meet The Prophet.

Tariq Moharibi said,

> *"I saw the prophet in the bazaar calling people to Allah and an old man was saying behind him, this is a liar. I asked who is this man? They said, 'Abu Lahab his uncle.'"*

His wife who is mentioned in the Surah, Ummi Jamil, was the sister of Abu Sufyan, an archenemy of the prophet at that time.

Those who accepted Islam started to convince more people. Many of the elites started opposing and countering this *Dawat*, including Abu Lahab and Abu Jahl. Oqbah Ibni Abi Mo'eet used to attack him and his followers.

QURAISH AS DELEGATION TO ABU TALIB

As Abu Talib was his staunch supporter, so the Quraish as a delegate came to him either to stop him or to leave him alone, and they were able to handle him. But he turned them down politely and the prophet continued on his mission. Sometimes they came again and said to Abu Talib,

> *"You are a respectable man and we requested you to stop your nephew, but you didn't so again we say, stop him or face us."*

Abu Talib called the prophet and told him about the situation. The prophet thought that now he was too much for his uncle who is too old, so he said,

> *"Uncle! "If they put the sun in one of my hands and the moon in the other, I am not going to leave my mission until I die,"*

and with that he stood up and burst in tears. Abu Talib said,

> *"Nephew! Go ahead and carry on your mission, I am not going to leave you alone."*

As the prophet was conveying the message wholeheartedly and people were taking it to heart, the Makkans came once again and brought with them a very handsome wise young man named Ammarah Ibn Ul Waleed and offered Abu Talib to adopt this wise young man and give them your nephew.

> *"We may get rid of him as he curses ours and your gods and Deen,"*

They said.

Abu Talib said,

> "You are giving me your son to feed and raise and want me to give you my son to kill him? What a terrible deal is this, I will never ever agree."

Mutim Ibni Adi said,

> "Your people brought forth a just solution, but you did not accept it."

Abu Talib said,

> "You did not do justice to me, and you plotted for my humiliation today, so do whatever you want to do."

Then Abu Talib told this whole story to Banu Hashim and ask them to protect Mohammad and they said they would.

Now the Makkans were angry, so they plotted to harm the prophet mentally and his followers physically, especially the slaves who accepted Islam. Bilal, for example, was tortured by his master Umayyah Ibni Khalaf, who used to put him on hot sand, and put a huge rock on his chest. But Bilal used to say "Ahad" "Ahad" in that situation also. Abu Bakr said to Umayyah,

> "Look! The whole day you have engaged him in this, and he cannot serve you, so let's make a deal: I have a slave who is healthier than Bilal, so take him and give me Bilal."

This Umayyah was killed by Bilal on the occasion of Badr with the help of Muaz Ibni Afra, Kharijah Ibni Zaid, and Habib Ibni Asaf, while Ummayah's son Ali was killed.

Ammar Ibni Yasir and Habib Ibni Asaf, as well as Ammar's father Yasir and his mother Sumayyah accepted Islam. The Makkans killed Yasir. Sumayyah exchanged hot words with Abu Jahl, and he stabbed her genitals with spear and she died. She was the first martyr of Islam. They used to put Ammar not only on hot sand but on burning coals as well. Once the prophet was passing by and he saw it, he covered his face with his garment and said,

> "O Fire! Be cold and peaceful for Ammar as you had been for Ibrahim."

These brutalities were going on against the companions, but their stability, patience, and loyalty are worthy of mention.

ABU LAHAB

Amongst others, this uncle of the prophet (whose name was Abu Lahab due to his red complexion) was his archenemy. He used to go after him everywhere to slander him even, to Okaz, the annual bazaar of Arabs. He and his wife Ummi Jameel both worked hard to put the prophet down, even though two of his daughters, Ruqayyah, and Ummi Kulthum, were engaged to their sons. Abu Lahab asked his sons to divorce their wives and they did it. When Surat Ul Lahab was revealed, Ummi Jameel came to the yard of the Kabah where the prophet was sitting with Abu Bakr. She was to throw some pebbles on the face of the prophet, but Allah caused her not to see the prophet. She said,

> "The cursed we disobeyed, refused his message, and hated his Deen."

Abu Bakr asked the prophet, who responded,

> "Allah took away her sight at that time, so she couldn't see me."

SOME NOTABLE ENEMIES AND THEIR IGNOMINIOUS ACTS

Ibni Ishaq said,

Abu Lahab, Hakim Ibni Abil Aas, Oqbah Ibni Abi Moeet, Adi Ibni Hamra, and Ibn Ul Asda were the prophet's neighbors harming him a lot, throwing filth on him and into his house as well, and sometimes the prophet used to say, 'What kind of neighbor and neighborhood is this? Once Oqbah Ibni Abi Moeet put the aborted fetus of a she-camel on the prophet's back when he was in sajdah, others started laughing and enjoying this until Fatima came and pulled it off the prophet's back. The prophet made a Dua on Abu Jahl, Oqbah, Shaibah Waleed, Umayyah Ibni Khalaf and Ammarah Ibn Ul Waleed. Ibni Masud says I saw all of them their dirty bodies were thrown in the trench at Badr (Bukhari).

DARI ARQAM

This house of Arqam was the first center or Madrasah of "Deen" as the companions had to gather together somewhere in the canyons, so Arqam offered this house of him close to "Safa". The Muslims used to gather there, while the prophet used to give his call openly and was meeting the Muslims there in Dar Ul Arqam, so they may not be harmed by the disbelievers. This center was started in 4th year.

In this situation Banu Hashim and Banu Muttalib, the two cousin tribes used to support the prophet even though most of them have not accepted Islam but due to their relation they used to do this. A few of them were still against the prophet and his message.

THE FIRST MIGRATION TO HASHAH

In the month of Rajab 5th year of the prophethood, 12 men and 4 women migrated to Abyssinia (Habshah) Uthman Ibni Affan and his wife Ruqayyah were amongst them. Uthman was their group leader. The prophet said regarding this couple,

> *"The first family after Ibrahim and Lut migrated in the cause of Allah."*

This group got into two trade boats. The Quraish followed them to catch them, but they had already fled. In this group were: Uthman, his wife Ruqayyah, Abu Huzaifah, his wife Sahlah Bint Suhail, Musab Ibni Omair, Zubair Ibn Ul Awwam, Abdur Rahman Ibni Awf, Abu Salamah Ibn Ul Aswad, his wife Ummi Salamah, Uthman Ibni Maz'oon, Abdullah Ibni Masud, Aamir Ibni Rabee'a, Abu Sabra, his wife Laila binti Abi Haithamah, Hatib Ibni Amer, and Suhail Ibni Baida (also called Ibni Wahab). This was a small group in number but a great one in value and cause as this mission opened the way of Hijrah.

THE STORY OF *SAJDAH*

The prophet was praying in the yard of the Kabah and reciting "Sura - An - Najm". Some disbelievers were also sitting there. The prophet recited the last verse of the surah that says,

> *"So prostrate to Allah and worship." (53:62)*

And this verse is the verse of *sajdah* also when someone recites it or listen to it, he is bound to make *sajdah*. So, the prophet did *sajdah* and Allah also caused the rest of them to prostrate. It is also said that Allah blessed those who did it later with Islam. Now the news that all the Makkans had accepted Islam went all the way to Abyssinia, so these immigrants came back, but when they came, they found that this news was wrong. But they told others that we are doing good there. In Makkah, these immigrants were tortured and harmed by their own people, so the prophet ordered them to go back.

THE SECOND HIJRA TO HABSHAH

This time 82 or 83 men and 18 or 19 women planned Hijrah. Of these women, eleven were from Quraish. The king of Habshah kindly sheltered them. Later, 33 men and 8 women returned when they heard of the migration of the prophet to Madinah. They came through Makkah so two men died in Makkah and 7 of them were stopped at Makkah.

The people of Makkah thought that if they stayed in Habshah, they would not only spread their *dawah* there (Habshah), but maybe they will be threat for us (in Makkah). So, they sent Amr Ibn Ul Aas and Labeed Ibni Abi Rabee'a with gifts to the king, As'hamah an Najjashi, to ask him for these wanted people. They asked there for a meeting with the king. They told him that these were same foolish young people who deserted their own religion and accepted a new one that neither he nor they know. They came to him on behalf of all the elders of their tribes to hand them over to them so they may take them back. Their priest agreed to do but Najjashi said,

> *"This is only one side of the story. They have come here as refugees asking for asylum as they don't feel safe there, so without listening to other side of the story it is*

wrong to hand them over because they might be killed or tortured."

He invited these Muslims to ask them for their story. The first cousin of the prophet Jafar Ibni Abi Talib stood up as their spokesperson and said,

"O king, we were in state of ignorance and immorality, worshiping idols committing all types of inequity. We neither honored our relatives nor assisted our neighbors. The strong used to exploit the weak. Then, God sent us a prophet. His lineage, truthfulness, and honesty are well known. He asked us to worship Allah alone and to shun idol worship. He asked us to be truthful and honest, to keep our trust and promises, to help our relatives, to be kind to neighbors and to abstain from evils and blood shedding, to avoid fornication, perjury, and false testament. He ordered us not to eat up the properties of the orphans and not to put false charges against chaste women. He said to worship Allah alone to pray to fast and to pay charity, so we followed him, and our people tried to sway us away from our religion. They persecuted us and inflicted upon us great suffering. So, when they went to their utmost, then, we have chosen you and your country and came to have your protection in peace and justice."

Negus asked him if they had anything of what he brought to them. So, he recited the verses of Surah Maryam (19) 1-36:

Surah Maryam (Mary)

In the Name of Allah, the Most Gracious, the Most Merciful.

1. *"Kaf- Ha-Ya- 'Ain-Sad."*

2. *"(This is) a mention of the mercy of your Lord to His servant Zachariah.*

3. **"***When he called to his Lord a private call [i.e., supplication].***"**

4. *"He said, "My Lord, indeed my bones have weakened, and my head has filled with white, and never I been in my supplication to you, my Lord, unhappy [i.e., disappointed].*

5. *And indeed I fear the successors after me, and my wife has been barren, so give me from Yourself an heir.*

6. *Who will inherit me and inherit from the family of Jacob. And make him, my Lord, pleasing [to you]."*

7. *[He was told], "O Zachariah, indeed, we give you good tidings of a boy, whose name will be John. We have not assigned to any before [this] name."*

8. *He said, "My Lord, how will I have a boy when my wife has been barren, and I have reached extreme old age?"*

9. *[An angel] said: "Thus [it will be]; your Lord Says, 'It is easy for Me, for I created you before, when you were Nothing.'"*

10. *[Zachariah] said: "My Lord, make for me a sign." He said: "Your sign is that you will not speak to the people for three nights, [being] sound." [(or you will not be able to speak]*

11. *So he came out to his people from prayer chamber and signaled to them to exalt [Allah] in the morning and afternoon.*

12. *[Allah said], "O John, take the Scripture [i.e., adhere to it] with determination." And We gave him judgement [while yet] a boy.*

13. *And affection from Us and purity, and he was fearing of Allah.*

14. *And dutiful to his parents, and he was not a disobedient tyrant.*

15. *And peace be upon him the day he was born, and the day he dies, and the day he is raised alive.*

16. *And mention, [O Mohammad] in the Book [the story of] Mary, when she withdrew from her family to a place towards the east.*

17. And *she took, in seclusion from them, a screen. Then We sent to her Our angel [Gabriel], and he represented himself to her as a well-proportioned man.*

18. *She said, "Indeed, I seek refuge in the Most Merciful from you, [so leave me], if you should be fearing of Allah."*

19. *He said: "I am only the messenger of your Lord to give you [news of] a pure boy [i.e., son]."*

20. *She said, "How can I have a son when no man has touched me, and I have not been unchaste?"*

21. *He said, "Thus [it will be], your Lord says: 'It is easy for Me, and We will make him a sign to the people and a mercy from Us. And it is a matter [already] decreed.'"*

22. *So she conceived him, and she withdrew with him to a remote place.*

23. *And the pains of childbirth drove her to the trunk of a palm tree. She said, "Oh, I wish I had died before this and was in oblivion, forgotten."*

24. *But he called her from below her, "Do not grieve; your Lord has provided beneath you a stream.*

25. *And shake toward you the trunk of palm tree; it will drop upon you ripe, fresh dates.*

26. *So eat and drink and be contented. And if you see from among humanity anyone, say, 'Indeed, I have vowed to the Most Merciful abstention, so I will not speak today to [any] man.'"*

27. Then she brought him to her people, carrying him. They said, "O Mary, you have certainly done a thing unprecedented.

28. *O sister of Aaron, your father was not a man of evil, nor was your mother unchaste."*

29. *So she pointed to him. They said, "How can we speak to one who is in the cradle a child?"*

30. [Jesus] said, "Indeed. I am the servant of Allah. He has given me the Scripture and made me a Prophet.

31. *And He has made me blessed wherever I am and has enjoined upon me prayer and Zakah as long as I remain alive.*

32. *And [made me] dutiful to my mother, and He has not made me a wretched tyrant.*

33. *And peace is on me the day I was born and the day I will die and the day I am raised alive."*

34. This is Jesus, the son of Mary: the word of truth about which they are in dispute.

35. It is not [befitting] for Allah to take a son; exalted is He! When he decrees an affair, He only says to it, "Be," and it is.

36. [Jesus said], "And indeed, Allah is my Lord and your Lord, so worship him. That is a straight Path."

Negus and his religious leaders broke in tears. Negus said what Jesus brought, came from the same source, and told Amr Ibn Ul Aas and Abdullah Ibni Rabee'a to leave. Negus said,

> *"I will never hand them over to you."* Amr Ibn Ul Aas told Abdullah, *"We will go now and tomorrow we will come to him once again."* They came the next day and said to Negus to ask the Muslims what they say regarding Jesus. Negus called the Muslims and asked them about Jesus. Jafar said, *"Our belief about Jesus is what our Prophet told us that he is the slave servant of Allah, His Messenger, His spirit, and his Kalimah (word) with which He inspired the virgin Mary (Mariam)."*

Negus picked up a straw and said that Jesus was not more than what he himself said even to the extent of this straw. Then he said to the Muslims to go and that they were the *Shuyum* (secured) in his land.

> *"I will not like to have even a mountain of gold to harm one of you."*

Negus also ordered his people to give back the gifts of the Makkans to them.

CONVERSION OF HAMZAH IBNI ABDUL MUTTALIB

Hamzah was the uncle of The Prophet Mohammad and his friend. He was also the fostering brother of the Prophet. Both of them had suckled the breast of Thuwaibah, who was the slave of Abu Lahab. He also is the cousin of the Prophet (sas) because Abdul Muttalib married Halah and she was from the family of the Prophet's mother.

Once Abu Jahl came across the Prophet (sas) and insulted him. It is said that he hit the Prophet with a stone and the Prophet's head started bleeding. At that time a slave girl of Abdullah Ibni Jad'aan was in her house on the top of the hill of Safa hill and saw the incident. Abu Jahl came to the elders sitting in the yard of "Kabah" and in the meantime Hamzah was coming from hunting, holding his bow. This lady told him about the incident, so Hamzah came to Abu Jahl and hit him with the bow and injured him. His people stood up to Hamzah saying,

"Does this mean you have changed your faith?"

Hamzah said,

"Yes, I believe in Mohammad."

With this the Quraish felt that Mohammad gained further strength. Hamza was one of the three people who came out to accept the challenge against the three Makkans in the battle of Badr later alongside Ali and Ubaidah. Hamzah fought wholeheartedly and killed 31 enemies, and as Wahshi Ibni Harb was trained for the purpose of killing Hamzah with a spear, and after doing so will be freed, so he hit Hamzah from far and then dismembered him in Uhud. Hamzah accepted Islam in the 6th year.

CONVERSION OF UMAR IBNUL KHATTAB

It is narrated that the Makkans fixed a price of 100 camels to anyone who would assassinate the Prophet (sas). So, Umar picked up his sword and volunteered. He was by nature a brave man, ready to accept any challenge. On his way towards the Prophet, Nuaim Ibni Abdullah Al Adawi met him and asked him that where he was going. Umar said he was going to take care of Mohammad. Nuaim,

> "Said if you kill Mohammad, his tribe Banu Hashem will not let you live."

Nuaim said,

> "First you must take care of your sister Fatima and her husband Saeed Ibni Zaid. They have both accepted the message of Mohammad."

So, Umar went to their house where Khabbab Ibn Ul Aratt was teaching them the Quran. Umar knocked at the door, calling Saeed. They hid Khabbab and opened the door. Umar entered in rage and tried to hit Saeed, but his sister came in between and was injured. She also got angry and said,

> "Do whatever you want to, but we will never desert Islam."

Umar calmed down when he saw blood on his sister. He sat down and said,

> "What was this recitation I heard when I was at the door?"

His sister said,

> "That was the holy Quran."

He said,

> "I want to see it."

So, she brought it, but when he tried to touch it, his sister said,

> "You cannot touch it because you are not pure."

So, his sister started reciting from Surah Taha. She said Bismillahir Rahmaanir Raheem. Umar said pure names and then she recited verses 1-14, "Taha:"

> *We have not sent down to you the Quran that you be distressed but only as a reminder [admonition] for one who fears [Allah]. A revelation from one who created the earth and the high heavens. The beneficent who rose over the throne. To Him belongs what is in the heavens, what is on earth, and what is in between them both, and what is under the soil. And if you speak loudly, then indeed He knows the secret and what is more hidden. There is no deity but Him. To Him belongs the beautiful names. And indeed, the story of Musa [Moses] has reached you when he saw a fire and said to his family stay here, I have perceived a fire, maybe I will bring you a torch or find at fire (place) a guidance. And when he came to it, he was called, "Moses, indeed, I am your lord so take off your shoes indeed you are in the sacred valley of Tuwa. And I have chosen you so listen to what is revealed (to you). Indeed, I am Allah, there is no deity but Me, so worship Me and perform the prayer for my remembrance.*

When Khabbab heard Umar, he came out and said,

> *"Umar! Have glad tidings. Maybe Allah has accepted the invocation of the Prophet this past Thursday night, when he asked Allah for one of you, either Umar Ibn Ul Khattab or Amr Ibn Ul Hisham (Abu Jahl)."*

Tirmizi narrated from Ibni Umar and Tabrani from Ibni Masood and Anas that the Prophet (sas) made this *Dua* to have one of these two.

Afterwards Umar went to Dari Arqam where the Prophet was with his companions. Since Umar's sword was hanging at his side when he knocked on the door and said,

> *"Open the door,"*

Sahabah said,

"It's Umar with his sword."

Hamzah said,

"Open the door! If he is coming for something good, he is welcomed, and if not, we will cut him."

The Prophet said,

"Open the door for him."

Omar entered and said,

"I am the son of Khattab."

The Prophet took hold of Umar's garment and scabbard and asked Umar,

"Will you not stop until Allah causes you humiliation like Waled Ibn Ul Mughirah?"

So, Umar said,

"I testify that there is no deity but Allah and I testify that Mohammad is the messenger of Allah."

Then the Muslims chanted

"Allahu Akbar."

Imam Bukhari narrated that Aas Bini Wa'il Sahami came to Umar. Umar said to him,

"Do your people have a plot to kill me?"

He said,

"No, because Banu Sah'm were the allies of Banu Adi."

Aas saw people coming towards Umar's house. He asked them,

"Where?"

They said to Umar,

> *"He said no."*

And they then went back.

Mujahid related from Ibni Abbas, that Umar was asked,

> *"How you are named Farooq?" He said, 'I accepted Islam 3 days after Hamzah.' I asked the Prophet, 'Are we not right and true?' He said, 'Yes, we are.' So, I said, 'Then why this hiding?' So, we came out of Dari Arqam in two lines and I was in one line and Hamzah was in the other one. We came to the house of Allah and Quraish saw us so they fell to grief. The Prophet saw that, so he named me Farooq, which means the 'one who separated right from wrong.'*

Sohaib Ibni Sinan says after Umar's conversion they started praying in the yard of Kabah, sitting there in their own circles.

QURAISH AND THEIR TACTICS

REPRESENTATIVE OF QURAISH TO THE PROPHET

Utbah Ibni Rabee'a, a leader of Quraish from Banu Umayyah, once said in the meeting of Quraish,

> *"If you can officially delegate me to Mohammad, he is there in the yard of Kabah."*

They said,

> *"Yes, just go."*

He came to him and said,

> "O nephew! You for sure enjoy among us a great eminence and noble lineage and you have brought about a great issue and divided your people. Listen! I am going to offer you a few things maybe one of these will satisfy you and will resolve this problem. If you have brought this thing to the community to get wealth, we can make you the richest amongst us. If you are looking for power, we can make you our chief with such power that nothing could be done without your consent. We can even crown you as our king if you want. If you are suffering from some sickness and you do what you do, we can treat you at our expense until you recover."

When he stopped, then the Prophet asked him if he can listen? So, he started reciting Surah Hamim Sajdah (41:1-13):

> *Hamim (is) a revelation from The Beneficent, The Merciful. A Book which's verses have been detailed as an Arabic Quran for people who know. As a giver of glad tiding and a warner, but most of them turn away so they do not hear. And they say our hearts are in coverings from that to which you invite us and in our ears is deafness and between us and you there is cover so do [what you want] and we do [what we want]. Say I am Only a man like you to whom it has been revealed that your God is, but one God, so, take a straight path to Him and ask Him for forgiveness and woe to those who associate others with Allah. Those who do not give zakat and in the hereafter, they are disbelievers. Indeed, those who believe and do righteous deeds, for them, there is an uninterrupted reward. Say, do you, indeed, disbelieve in one who created the earth in two days, and you make for him equals. He is the Lord of the worlds. And he placed on it firmly set mountains over its surface and he blessed and determined there in it sustenance in four days, equally for those who ask (need). Then he directed himself to the heaven while it was smoke and said to it and to the earth, come (work/function) willingly or unwillingly. They said we come willingly. So, he completed it seven heavens in two days and inspired in each heaven its affair (function) and we adorned the nearest heaven*

> with lamps and as protection. That is the decree of the Almighty, All-Knowing. Then, if they turn away, then, say, I have warned you of a thunderbolt like the thunderbolt of Ad and Thamud.

It is narrated that with this Utbah put his hand on the mouth of the Prophet and said,

> "Please make no bad Dua on your own people." "The Prophet said, Abul Walid, now you know and your business."

Then, Utbah went to the Quraish and said to them,

> "By God, neither this is poetry, nor sorcery, nor soothsaying, so, you may leave him alone, so, if some other people caught him, then you got rid of him and if he overtook, then, His honor is your honor, and his kingship is yours."

They said,

> "He has bewitched you."

Abu Jahl came close to him and said,

> "These people will get you, so say I was testing you. He is but a sorcerer."

It is also said that when the Prophet recited the last verse Utbah stood up and put his hand on the mouth of the Prophet asking him not to make any bad *Dua* on his people.

After this Abu Jahl told people,

> "I have to take care of him so watch me tomorrow at Kabah."

He came having a very huge rock in his hand to throw it on the Prophet, when he would be making *sajdah*. As he tried to go through with it, suddenly he stopped and started running in reverse. The Quraish rushed and asked him,

> "What happened? Why couldn't you throw the rock? You started running away."

He said,

> "When I went close to him a healthy young camel with such a huge head that I had never seen before nor such teeth came in between us. The camel then tried to eat me. Ibni Ishaq said the Prophet said this was the angel who came in between."

Also, in these times the Quraish tried every tactic to stop the Prophet i.e., offering him things and intimidating him as well. Once Aas Ibni Wa'il, Umayyah Ibni Khalaf, Waleed Ibn Ul Mughirah, and Aswad Ibni Muttalib came across the Prophet at Kabah and said,

> "Let's make a deal. You worship our gods with us and we will worship your God with you."

So, Allah said,

> 109:1-6 "Say! O disbelievers, I will not worship what you worship, nor you are worshippers of what I worship. Nor I am the worshipper of what you worship, nor are you the worshippers of what I worship. For you is your Deen and for me is mine." (Ibni Ishaq, Abd Ibni Humaid)

Ibni Jareer said that the Quraish asked him to worship their gods one year and they will worship his god one year.

So, Allah said (39:64)

> "Say! So other besides Allah you order me to worship O the ignorant."

Once they asked him (10:15)

> "Bring us a Quran other than this one or change this one. Say it is not for me to change it on my own accord. I only follow what is revealed to me. Actually, I fear if I will disobey my Lord, the punishment of a tremendous

day."

They also used to propagate against the Prophet that he is a sorcerer, a soothsayer, a poet, a liar, a fabricator, insane, and bewitched, which was a psychological campaign against him.

> *"But they said [This Quran] is a mixture of false dreams [confused and disturbed dreams] but he invented it, and he is a poet." (21:5)*

> *"The disbelievers said indeed this is an obvious sorcerer." (10:2)*

> *"And they said, o the one to whom the zikr (Quran/Wahi) has been (sent down)! Indeed, you are mad." (15:6)*

They said (44:14)

> *"(Oh!) He is a learned madman!"*

They also said (16:103)

> *"And indeed, we know that they say verily a human teaches him."*

This was a Christian blacksmith known as Balaam. The Prophet used to sit with him sometimes, so they attributed to him. So, Allah answered (16:103)

> *"The language of the one they refer to is not Arabic, while this [Quran] is clearly [literary] Arabic."*

So, how can one who does not know this type of language teach it? Then they said (25:5)

> *"And they said [this is] the fiction of former people. He asked for its writing, and it is dictated to him in morning and in the afternoon."*

Then they used to say that if Allah was to send a messenger, then why not an angel? So, Allah said (17:95)

> "Say if there were on the earth angels walking [living] securely [permanently], then for sure we would have sent down to them from the heaven an angel as a messenger."

They said (25:7)

> "And they said what is [wrong] with this messenger that he eats food and walks in markets."

Allah said (25:20)

> "And we have not sent before you messengers, but they used to eat food and walk in markets."

Meaning that they have been sent to humans as role models, so it was a must for them to be human as well. That's why Allah said, (6:9)

> "And if we should have made him an angel, we for sure would have changed him to man, and we would have caused them the same confusion they confuse themselves with."

They also used to ask him for miracles, while showing that miracles are not a part of Prophethood. Yes, sometimes Allah gives some miracles to a Prophet, so Allah said, (17:90-93)

> "And they said we will not believe you until you cause to flow for us a spring from the earth or until you have a garden of palm trees and grapes and make rivers gush forth within them in abundance or you make the heaven fall upon us in fragments, as you said, or you bring Allah and angels before us, or you may have a house of gold or you ascend into the sky, but we will not believe in your ascension until you bring down to us a book (a letter) we may read. Say glory be to my Lord, I am but a human messenger."

All this they were doing to avert him from his mission, as Allah said,

> "And indeed they had plotted to tempt you away of what

we have revealed to you in order to [make] you to fabricate about us something else and then they will take you as a friend and if we would not have strengthened you, you would have almost inclined to them little by little, then we would have made you taste a double [severe] punishment in life and a double [severe] punishment at death [after death], then you would not find for yourself against us a helper. And indeed, they have plotted to incite you from this land [Makkah] to turn you out of it and then they will not remain [in peace] after you but a little, as an established way for those whom we sent before you mean our messengers and you will not find in our way any alteration [change]." (17:73-77)

Now when nothing stopped the Prophet, Abu Talib felt a fear that they would try to assassinate him. So, he invited Banu Hashim, his tribe, and Banu Muttalib, his cousin's tribe, and asked them to stand by Mohammad for protection. All of them responded positively except Abu Lahab. It was unheard of in their culture that a tribesman would not stand by his tribe. This degraded Abu Lahab in the eyes of the people.

SOCIAL BOYCOTT

Now when new people and even some known people like Umar and Hamzah accepted Islam through which the Muslims were getting courage, they used to be tortured and endured it stoically. Also, they had found a safe haven in Abyssinia for those who wanted to go there. So, the Quraish and their various tribes plotted to boycott Banu Hashim and the cousin tribe Banu Muttalib socially and economically, in order to cut them off from people and halt the spread of the call. For them it was now or never, as later they did not think they would be able to stop it. They got together in Muhassab valley in mina in Kheif of Banu Kinanah and agreed to a treaty not to have any relation nor any passion or compassion towards these two tribes, not to sit with them in any way, no reconciliation with them, no trade with them; but if they hand over Mohammad to them, they will kill him. Hafiz Ibn Ul Qayyim said that Mansoor Ibni Ikramah Ibni Aamir inscribed the treaty. Also, it is said that Nadr Ibn Ul Harith wrote it, but the authentic saying is that Bagheez Ibni Aamir Ibni Hashim wrote it. The Prophet made a *Dua* against this writer, and his hand was paralyzed and later on, he was unable to write. They kept it hanging inside on the wall of the holy Kabah. This took place in Muharram 7th year of the message (617 years after Jesus).

Based on this treaty, these two tribes of the Prophet were confined to Abu Talib's apartments called Shabi Abi Talib. They used to come out to mingle with people only in Hajj season, and they used to buy their necessities from traders coming to Makkah in sacred months. Sometimes children crying from hunger used to be heard outside the quarters.

Hakeem Ibni Hizam sometimes used to take some wheat to his aunt Khadijah. Once Abu Jahl got him engaged in arguments and even caught him not to take it to her house, But Abul Bukhtari got involved and let him go to take it. In this pull and push Abul Bukhtari hit Abu Jahl with the jawbone of a camel and injured him. Then the Quraish blamed each other for this cruel move.

Hisham Ibni Amr also used to take some food and grain on his camel and let him enter the apartments area. Once he went to Zubair Ibni Abi Umayyah, a cousin of the Prophet i.e., the son of Atikah Bint Abdul Muttalib and said,

> *"How bad is that you eat and dress and your maternal uncles and aunts are blocked. If they were the uncles of Abu Jahl and you would have asked him to do that to his uncles, he would never had done it. So, how did you have done it for him to your uncles. So, let's go to some elders to take away this blockade."*

They went to Mut'im Ibni Adi Abul – Bukhtari, Zama'ah Ibn Ul Aswad, and Adi Ibni Qais. All of them agreed over the issue. So, once after *tawaf* Zubair addressed people saying,

> *"What is this unjust pact? We have revoked it."*

Abu Jahl said this is a sacred pact and is inviolable, thus these other elders also stood up in support of Zubair and countered Abu Jahl. Here he also realized that already it has been agreed upon by them.

On the other side the Prophet told his uncle Abu Talib that Allah informed me that the document hanging on the wall had been entirely eaten by termites except the name of Allah. Abu Talib told that to the elders sitting there in the vicinity of Kabah and told them that if this was the case, they should stop it. Mut'im went inside the Kabah to tear up the pact and he found it as Abu Talib told them. So, these elders came to the apartments and told Banu Hashim and Banu Muttalib to go to their own houses and this was the end of this unjust action by the people of Makkah.

THE DELEGATION OF MAKKANS

Abu Talib, the supporter of his nephew, grew old, more than eighty years, but still he used to be around his nephew. When he fell sick the Quraish decided to go to him once again as Islam was spreading and he was the only channel they can use to stop it. So Utbah, Shaibah, sons of Rabee'a, Umayyah, Abu Sufyan, Abu Jahl and altogether some 25 elders and chiefs came to him pretending that they wanted to inquire about his health but really, they just wanted to ask him if he could make a deal with his nephew on their behalf. He called the Prophet and said that these are the elders of your nation, they wanted him to give them something and they would give him something as well, and then he told him what they said. The Prophet said,

> "Should I give you people a Kalimah (word)? If you say it, you will own Arabs, and the non-Arabs will become subject to you."

Abu Jahl said,

> "And what is that word?"

He said,

> "La Ilaha Illallah."

They said,

> "So you change all gods to one only, this is strange.: And then they said to one another (38:6) "Carry on and be stuck to your gods, verily this is the thing meant of you [we want it]."

AAMUL HUZ'N (THE YEAR OF GRIEF)

In the month of Ramadan 620, the Prophet's uncle Abu Talib passed away, and 3 days later his wife Khadija passed away. They were his supporters, consolers, and consultants. For the Prophet (saws), this year was a year of grief.

Imam Ahmad narrated what the prophet (saw) said to Aisha when she asked him about Khadija (ra). He said,

> "She believed in me when people disbelieved; she trusted me when people belied me; she shared her wealth with me when people despaired me and Allah gave me from her only, the children."

Note: this he said when he did not have Mariyah Qibteya's hand having a son Ibrahim from this lady. He also died at the age of nine months.

Now after the death of these two staunch supporters of the prophet his mental torture by the Makkans increased. It is related that once the prophet was coming home when some outlaws put dust on his head. He came home and his daughter washed his head and started to cry. The prophet said,

> "Cry not, Allah will protect your father."

It is also narrated that this was the time that even Abu Bakr - intended to Migrate to Abyssinia, but Ibn Ul Daghinah brought him back (Ibni Hashim).

MARRIAGE WITH SAUDAH BINT ZAMAAH

In Shawal, the 10th year of prophethood, the prophet married Saudah. This noble lady accepted Islam early on and she also migrated to Habshah. Later on, her husband Sakran Ibni Amr died either in Habshahor at Makkah, when they came back.

TRIP TO TAIF

When the tease and torture increased by the day, in Shawal 10th year the prophet planned to go to Taif, a very fertile city 60 miles away from Makkah, to get settled there and make it his base of *dawah*. For that purpose, he took Zaid Ibni Harithah with him. He tried to convert the tribespeople he met on the way, but nobody accepted his call.

In Taif, he went to three sons of Amir Ibni Umair Thaqafi: Abdi Yaleel, Masud, and Haseeb. They were the elders of the city. Their reaction was very rude; one of them said,

> *"Sending you as a messenger Allah is going to tear the 'Ghilaf' [cover] of the Kabah. The other one jeered, "What? Allah couldn't find anyone else to appoint as a prophet?" while the third one sneered, "I don't want to talk to you as if you are a prophet then, that is a disrespect and if you are not, then you aren't worth it."*

For ten days, the prophet asked various elders for help, but they told him to leave the city. They also incited their young people to take Mohammad and Zaid Ibni Harithah out of their city and hit them with stones on the lower parts of their legs. They started bleeding. A few times the prophet had to sit down because of blood was filling his shoes and he was in great pain, until they came out of city and sheltered themselves in a wall of a grape garden which belonged to Utbah and Shaibah, son of Rabee'a. When the prophet was stoned, Zaid tried to take the blows for him, but how many could he endure? This garden was some three miles out of that town. The prophet raised his hands and said,

"O Allah to you alone I make complaint of my helplessness the paucity of my resources and my little esteem before mankind. You are the most merciful of the merciful. You are the lord of the helpless and the weak. O Lord! Into whose hands you abandon me? Into the hands of an unsympathetic distant relative who will sullenly frown at me, or at an enemy who will dominate my affairs? But if your wrath does not fall on me there is nothing for me to be worried about. I seek protection in the light of your countenance which illuminates the heaven and dispel darkness and which controls all affairs in this world and the affaires of the hereafter as well. May it never be that you should incur your wrath or that you should be wrathful to me, and there is no power nor resource, but yours alone."

After leaving Taif the prophet leaned against the wall of the garden of Utbah and Shaibah, son of Rabee'a. When they saw him, they sent their servant Idas to him with some grapes by. The prophet said,

"Bismillahir Rahmaanir Raheem."

Idas said,

"This practice is not known here, but it is in our area."

The prophet asked him,

"Where do you come from?"

He said,

"I come from Nainwa, and I am a Christian."

The prophet said,

"Oh! That is where my brother Yunus Ibni Matta live." Idas said, *"How do you know him?"*

Mohammad said,

> "He was a prophet, and I am a prophet."

Idas kissed his head, hands, and feet. Utbah and Shaibah said,

> "Oh! he has misled our servant,"

And when he came back, they told him,

> "Your religion is better than his religion. He said that he told me a thing which only a prophet knows, and his religion is the true religion."

Imam Bukhari narrates from Urwah that Aaisha told him,

> "I asked the prophet, 'was any day in your life harder than that of Uhud when he was injured very badly?" He said, "Yes, the day of Aqabah when I asked shelter and help of Ibni Abdi Yaleel Ibni Abdi Kulal, but they refused and when I was in Qarnuth - Tha'aalib. Then I looked up at the heaven and a piece of cloud shadowed me and I saw Jibril therein. He told me that Allah heard what your people said to you and how they repulsed you, so Allah has sent the angel of mountains to you. Then that angel paid gratitude to me and said, 'O Mohammad! what you want? If you want, I can crush them in between the two mountains, Abu Qubais and Qai Qaaan to the opposite side of Abu Qubais at Makkah.' The Prophet said, 'I want from their offspring to be those who will not make associates with Allah.'"

The Prophet was satisfied, and he proceeded to Nakhleh Valley and stayed for a few days there, where there was water. Once at night the prophet was praying and some Jinns listened to him as Allah said 46: 29-32

> *"And when we turned towards you a group (3 to ten) of Jinn listening to Quran, when they attended to it, they said, keep quiet and when it was finished, they returned to their people to warn them. They said, "O our people! Verily we have learned a book sent down after Musa confirming what came before it. It guides to the truth and to the straight path. O our people! respond [positively] to the caller of Allah and believe in him. He [Allah] will forgive your sins and He will save you from a painful torment. And whoever will not respond the caller of Allah, then he is not a defeater [to Allah to escape] on earth and there are no Auliya [saviors] for him against Allah and they are in plain error".*

Note: There is a story of jinn mentioned in chapter 72;-1-15 also. Some scholars are of the view that is also regarding this event, but we say that in this event there was only Zaid Ibni Hantha with the prophet and they were coming from Ta'if back to Makkah, while the event mentioned in Chapter 72, Bukhari and Muslim relate from Ibn Abbas that the prophet was going to the market in Okaz between Makkah and Ta'if in sacred months, where Arabs used to get together peacefully. A few companions were accompanying him, and he stayed for rest and *Fajr* prayer in Nakhleh. He led the prayer and the Jinn listened to him.

Now the event mentioned in chapter 46 is that of the 10th year of the prophethood when the prophet was coming back from Ta'if while Ibni Abbas did not mention when the story mentioned in chapter 72 happened. Yes, we can say maybe either in early years of *dawah* when the prophet was going there to call people towards Allah and Abu Lahab used to follow him telling people not to listen to him because he was a liar. But there is one reservation: historians said that the event of Ta'if was the first ever event of Jinn, and this is also not clearly mentioned in both events that whether the Jinn met the prophet, or they listened to him and went back to their people to inform them of what they saw and what they heard. So it may be that the prophet was going there after the tenth year also, as he was more eager in *dawah* after the

Ta'if event as this is related that he used to go to Mina in the time of Hajj to convey the message and there the two pledges of Aqabah took place. But these are two events, as the contents are also different. But to mention the difference in the content we want to mention the verses of chapter 72 first:

> *(72:1-15) Say, O Mohammad it is revealed to me that a group [3-ten] of jinn listened to this Qur'an and they said, "Indeed we have heard a wonderful Qur'an which guides towards guidance/maturity [sense] so we believed in it and we will never associate with Lord anyone. And that exalted is the majesty of our Lord who has neither taken a wife not [begotten] a child. And that the foolish among us used to say an enormous falsehood against Allah. And verily we had thought that human and Jinn will never tell any lie against Allah [but they did]. And verily, there were people from mankind seeking protection with male persons of Jinn so they increased them in transgression. And they also believed as you believed that Allah will never send anyone (as prophet after Jesus) (or he will never resurrect anyone). And we sought to reach the heaven so we found it filled with stern guards and fire flames (comets). And we used to sit for it in places of learning but whoever will now try to listen, he finds for himself a blazing fire flame watching him in ambush. And we did not know whether an evil is intended for those on earth or their lord intended for them a guidance. And among us there were some good people and some others on the contrary we were different types. And we know that we cannot defeat Allah on earth nor we came defeat him by flight. And indeed, when we heard the guidance, we believed in it, so whosoever will believe in his lord shall have no fear of decrease (in reward) nor any increase (in punishment). And of us there are Muslims and of us there are deviated people so whosoever submitted (to Allah) then such like people*

have sought guidance. And as for the deviated people, so, they will be fuel of hellfire.

Now let us understand the difference in the Jinn mentioned in chapter 46,

1) They were not looking for something but Allah brought them to the prophet while those who are mentioned in chapter 72, they were amazed by the guarding of heaven so they were looking for the reasons that why it happened.

2) The Jinn in chapter 46 referred to Musa, which means they were Jews, while the Jinn in chapter 72 mentioned the wrong concepts of wife and child or son of Allah, which means they were Christians.

3) The Jinn in chapter 46 did not expressly mention whether they accepted Islam or came first to tell their people to accept it together. Yes, the implicit word of they went back to warn them can mean either way i.e., warning before acceptance or after.

That is why we say, these are two different events.

So, coming back from Ta'if these Jinns are coming and listening to the prophet and telling of Allah to the prophet about that was a source of satisfaction and solace for The Prophet and also it was a message to the disbelievers that even if they do not believe in him, the Jinn believed in him. This was also a threat to his enemies that not only the angel asked his permission to handle his enemies but even if he wants, he can tell the Jinn to handle them.

Then, Zaid asked him,

"Where are we going now?"

The Prophet said,

"To Makkah."

Zaid was amazed and said,

"To Makkah, when they drove us out of Makkah?"

Then, the Prophet came to a cave called Hira and sent someone to Akhnas Ibni Shuraiq if he can give him protection. He refused and said,

> "I have made a pact with the Quraish. Then he asked Suhail Ibni Amr. He also said that Banu Aamir cannot go against Banu Kab."

Later, he sent that man from Khuza'a to Mut'im Ibni Adi. He agreed. He asked his sons and his tribe as well to take position around Kaba having their weapons as he promised shelter to Mohammad and then, he asked the prophet to come, so he came. Mut'im stood up and declared his shelter to the prophet. The prophet did Istilam, made *tawaf*, and prayed two *Rakat* and went home.

Ibni Hesham narrated that Abu Jahl came to Mut'im and asked him whether he has sheltered him only or accepted him? He said,

> "I sheltered him."

Abu Jahl said,

> "We do what you did."

Imam Bukhari narrated that regarding the prisoners of Badr the prophet said,

> "If Mut'im was alive and had asked me for their release, I would have released them."

TRIBES CALLED BY THE PROPHET

After that the prophet came back to Makkah, he started inviting different tribes to Islam in Hajj time. In the 10th year he invited:

1) <u>Banu Abdullah</u> – This is a subtribe of Banu Kalb. The Prophet said to them, *"What a beautiful name Allah has given to your father, so accept His message,"* but they didn't.

2) <u>Banu Hanifah</u> – He came to their tents, but they refused him very bluntly.

3) <u>Banu Aamir Ibni Sa'sa</u> – He invited them to Islam.

One man by the name of Buhaira Ibni Faras said if we supported you and you rose to power, can we inherit that power after you? The prophet said that power belongs to Allah. He gives that to whom He wills. They said,

> *"Then why should we sacrifice ourselves for others to gain power?"*

But when these people went back, they told this story to one elder. He put his hand over his head and said,

> *"What that Ishmaelite said is the truth but what can I do if you have missed the opportunity and misjudged him?"*

Still from outside Makkah a few known people accepted Islam, and these are:

SUWAID IBNI SAMIT

He was from Madinah, the then-Yathrib from a well-known tribe and family, a known poet, and a learned person who came to Makkah for Hajj or Umrah. The prophet called him towards Islam. He said,

"Maybe you have the same life wisdom I have."

The Prophet asked him,

"What do you have?"

He said,

"The wisdom of Luqman."

The prophet said,

"Then bring it forth."

He said a few things. The prophet said,

"This is good but what I have is much better than that: I have the Quran; Allah has sent it. It is a perfect guidance and a light as well,"

And then he recited to Suwaid and asked him to accept Islam, so, Suwaid did it and said,

"Indeed, this is the best one."

But when he came back to Madinah, he was killed in the battle of Bu'aath between the Aus and the Khazraj. He had accepted Islam in the beginning of the eleventh year of the prophethood.

IYAS IBNI MU'AAZ

A young man came from Madinah looking for a treaty with Quraish against Khazraj. He himself was from Aus. He came with a delegation of Aus, and this was in the beginning of eleventh year, before the battle of Bu'aath. Khazraj was a big tribe. When the prophet came to know about this delegation, he approached them and asked them,

> *"Are you looking for a Khair (good)? I have it."*

They said,

> *"What is that?"*

The prophet told them,

> *"I am the messenger of Allah,"*

And he recited to them some verses of the Quran. Iyas said By God O people!

> *"This is the good we are looking for."* One man from the delegation named Abul Haisar Anas Ibni Rafi picked up some dust and threw it on Iyas' face and said, *"Get away from us, we have come for something else."*

Iyas was young so he didn't say anything. However, no treaty took place, and they went back but after going back to Madinah, Iyas did not live long, and at his death he was saying.

> *"La Ilaha Illallah, Allahu Akbar, Subhan Allah, Alhamdulillah (Ahmad, Ibni Hesham)."*

ABUZAR AL GHIFARI

In this regard Imam Bukhari related from Ibni Abbas that Abu Zar said,

> *"I was from Ghifar, and we heard that a man has appeared at Makkah saying that he was the prophet of Allah. So, I asked my brother to go and speak to this man and then tell me. He told me, 'I saw him, he enjoins good and forbids evil.' I said, 'You couldn't bring me*

enough,' so I took my bag and stick, and I came to Makkah. I did not know him but didn't like to ask someone about him. I was drinking at Zamzam and staying at masjid, so Ali passed by and said I looked like a traveler [stranger]. I said yes. He took me with him. He neither asked me anything nor did I tell him anything. The next day early in the morning I came back to the masjid. Ali again passed by and took me with him again. This time he asked me. I said, 'Will you keep my secret?' He said, 'Of course.' I told him that I was there to see the one who says he is the prophet of Allah. He said, 'I am going to him so follow me and if I feel any fear of someone, I will lean against a wall pretending that I am fixing my shoe, but you should proceed.' So, I did and entered where the prophet was. I asked him to tell me how to accept Islam and I did. The Prophet said to me, 'Go back to your people and when our work is more open them come.' I said, 'I will announce this in front of people here. So, I went to the sitting place of the Quraish, and I repeated my Shahadah. They jumped on me, beating me until Abbas covered me and told them, 'You don't know beating a man from Ghifar while they are on your way to Sham for trade' so they left me.

ZIMAD AL AZDI

He was from Azd Shanoo'ah from Yemen and was known for *Ruqya* from magic, Jinn, and insanity. He came to Makkah and people told him the prophet was an insane man. He said,

> "I must meet him if I can treat him."

So, I met him and told him that I do this treatment. He said,

> "Innal Hamda Lillahi Ahmaduhu wa astaeenuhu munyahdehillahu fala mudilla lahu wa mun yudlil fala hadiya lah wa ashhadu al la ilaha illalahu wahdahu la shareeka lahu wa ashhadu anna Mohammadan abduhu wa rasuluh"

I said,

> "Wait please, repeat it."

and he repeated the same I told him,

> "By God I have heard the soothsayers, the magicians, the poets, but never heard the like of this from anyone. Give me hand to give you a pledge so I accepted Islam."

TUFAIL IBNI AMR ADDAUSI

He was a cultured man and a poet who came from Yemen in the 11th year of Prophethood. The people of Makkah welcomed him and told him that this man had caused them disputes but his words had sorcery. So, they advised him not to meet or listen to him. Tufail said,

> "They told me so much that when I was coming to

masjid, I put cotton in my ears so as not to hear any word from him. I saw him close to the Kabah, while he was praying. I came close to him and heard some wonderful words so I said my mother may bereaved me he is a learned poet. So, I made my mind to listen to him when he was going back, I followed him. I told him all about myself and what the people told me and what I did. Then I asked him about his message. He told me about that and recited some verses of the Quran to me. I came to know that there is no better word than his word, no better message than his message. So, I accepted Islam, and I asked him to ask Allah to give me some sign to call my people towards this message. Then when I came close to my people, Allah created a light in my face like a lamp. I asked Allah, not in face or body, for maybe they think that is because of that you have deserted the <u>Deen</u> of your forefathers, so the light went to my staff [stick]. He called his father and his wife to Islam, and they accepted that."

His people were getting it but slowly until he migrated after the battle of Ahzab with 70+ people. He was a good Muslim and was martyred in the battle of Yamamah in the time of Abu Bakr. The prophet after conquest of Makkah sent him to Zul Kaffain, an idol from Amr Ibni Humamah. Tufail himself had asked for this mission. He went and broke it.

SIX PEOPLE FORM YATHRIB (MADINAH)

In Hajj season, the prophet went to Mina to meet people and to call them towards Allah. This was in year 11. The lunar month is not known as the people of Arabia used to change the time for Hajj to their own convenience. But it is said that it was July 620.

In this trip to Mina Abu Bakr and Ali were with the prophet. They passed by the people from Zuhal and Banu Shaibah Ibni Thalabah. The prophet talked to them, but they neither accepted not rejected Islam. Then in Mina he met six young people from Yathrib, from the tribe of Khazraj. They are:

1. Asad Ibni Zuraraiah,
2. Auf Ibn Ul Harith Ibni Rifa'a Ibni Afra. They were both from Banu Najjar.
3. Rafi Ibni Malik Ibni Ijlan from Banu Zuraiq
4. Qutbah Ibni Aamir Ibni Hadeedah from Banu Salamah
5. Oqbah Ibni Aamir Ibni Nabi from Banu Haram Ibni Kab
6. Jabir Ibni Abdullah Ibni Ri'aab from Banu Ubaid Ibni Ghanem.

Jews used to live in Madinah and had a treaty with Khazraj and Aus. The prophet asked them,

"Where do you come from?"

They said,

"From Yathrib."

The prophet said,

"Oh! The allies of Jews."

They said,

"Yes."

The prophet said,

"Should I not talk to you?"

They said,

"Yes, you can."

The prophet talked to them and recited to them some verses. They looked at each other and said,

> "Maybe you are the messenger the Jews used to talk about so they may not precede you. Let us accept his call,"

and they did. They said to the prophet,

> "We are fed up with our disputes, fights, and bloodshed. Maybe Allah will help us patch it up through you."

So, they went and talked to people there. Talking about this prophet became a daily subject in every house.

MARRIAGE TO AAISHA

Khadijah passed away and the prophet was all alone. Khawlah Binti Hakim, the wife of Uthman Ibni Maz'oon, the prophet's fostering brother, said to the prophet,

> "You should remarry. The prophet said, "But to whom? She said, "Either Aaisha binti Abu Bakr or Sawdah Bint Zama'ah."

When the prophet gave his approval, she first went to Aaisha and Abu Bakr, but Abu Bakr had given his word to Jubair Ibni Mut'im, so he said,

> "Let me ask them if they are still interested."

Aaisha was at that time, of marriageable age. Later, she was engaged to The Prophet in year 11th as Riwayat said, but in a hadith narrated by Bukhari in Kitab Ul Adab from Aaisha that she got engaged to the prophet a little before *Hijra* to Madina.

It shows that in year 13 her age was 17 years. Wali Ud Din Al-Khatib said in his book al Ikmal that she was younger than her sister Asma by 10 years. Asma passed in year 73 in the age of 100 years, 10 days after the martyrdom of her son Ibni Zubair, which means her age at the time of Hijrah was 27 years so then Aaisha was 17 years of age. Now the Riwayah of 7 could be a *Musamaha* where sometimes people drop words in casual conversation, so, instead of "Sab'ata Ashara" they say "Sab'atash", but the last abbreviated word is not heard of this is "Naskh" means a dropping in writing.

AL ISRA WAL MERAJ (ASCENSION)

Allah is the creator and the whole world is his creation. Of this creation human beings are the most honored creatures as Allah has given them *Aql* (intellect). He subjected to them the world and the things therein, but on the other hand he made them bound to obey his orders and commandments. His orders to be conveyed to human beings, he sent to them Prophets and Messengers, giving them the rules, shariah, books and scriptures. He sent different Prophets and Messengers in different times, different areas, and to different people, but their original Message was one and the same. The base of this Message is *Tawheed*, the oneness of Allah, which means subjugation only to him and worshipping him only, and their conveying his Deen. They worked in their respective time in the people of the specific area they were sent to, and then, he sent his last and final Prophet to the whole world i.e., to all human beings until the last day of this world and completed His *Deen* with the Message of Mohammad.

In other words, we can say that this Message and Deen started with Prophet Adam processed through all the Messengers towards its completion and completed with the Message of Mohammad. It looks like that this whole process was done for the universal and final Message of Mohammad.

We clearly see in the address of all these Messengers, that they say,

> *"O My People!",*

But we do see in the Message of Mohammad that he says,

> *"O human beings!",*

And the Message of all of them was,

> *"Worship Allah as for you there is no other Ilah" (deity to be worshipped or any ruler of the world),*

And thus, when Mohammad called towards the same faith, then, their objection to it was not just and reasonable, as this was not a new thing.

Allah said,

> *"And we have not sent any Messenger before you, but we used to reveal to him that there is no god, but only Me, so, worship Me alone" (21:25)*

Also, he said,

> *"Say (O Mohammad!) I am not an innovation among the Messengers." (46:9)*

This means the Message itself, its subject and Me, too, are not new or unknown and strange things.

So, this *Deen* is:

1) The *Deen* of Allah

2) The *Deen* of all the Messengers

3) The *Deen* of all human beings

And then, Prophet Mohammad is a mercy for all worlds, so, Allah is *"Rabbul Aalameen"* i.e., Lord of the Worlds, and Mohammad is *"Rahmatul Lil Aalameen"* i.e., Mercy for all Worlds.

He was tortured physically and mentally, as well, to a great extent, so, when he was feeling alone after the death of Abu Talib and Khadijah and was stoned out of Ta'if, on his way back to Makkah, Allah sent to him the mountain angel, if he wants these people of Ta if to get destroyed, then he brought towards him a few Jinn who listened to the Quran and believed in him and now Allah took him to upon the seven heavens to show to his enemies that he is a man of high status in the eyes of Allah, but he is taking all these suffering for Allah and for the good of humanity to be guided. So, Prophet Mohammad was a perfect human being, a perfect believer, and a perfect prophet, that is how he earned the title of the final prophet.

As the last, final, global, and universal Messenger and a big mercy of Allah for all worlds Allah willed to show him all these worlds in totality, not totally, as that is the quality and attribute of Allah that he knows his creature and all worlds totally, i.e., each and every single atom therein, whether it was in past or is now or will be in the future. So, Allah took him beyond space and time and for the said purpose, an electromagnetic ride known as "Buraq" or "Barraq" was used from Makkah to Jerusalem and therefrom up to upon the seven heavens. This ride was going on light speed or more as the prophet said, its every step fell where his eyesight could reach. Now, how keen was its eyesight? It is known to Allah. Barraq or Buraq is derived from "Barq" which means "light" and "electricity."

From Sidrat Ul Muntaha he took "Ruf Ruf', a fluttering or flying cushion. For our purposes, we can say it was like space shuttle, but one was made by Allah and not bound by space or time. Humans' approach is to the limits of their senses, and to the extent of the science of their times.

Let's see that Allah created all living entities from water,

"And we created from water every living entity."(21:30)

Also, it is known from Quran and science both that Allah created the heavens, the earth, the heavenly bodies, and his *Arsh* (throne) was over water before that and in living entities, human beings are the perfect and honored creature/ So, the degree of freedom of man is beyond the reach of archangel Gabriel, that's why he stopped at "Sidrat Ul Muntaha" (The Lotus tree of utmost boundaries). The prophet said that from all around, it was covered by butterflies of light.

Now, it became clear that human being as kind is the perfect creature and Prophet Mohammad is the most perfect individual ever, so he reached at the utmost high altitude and he had to, to have a look of that world he has been sent to as a Messenger and he is a mercy for that - yes, this look was in totality, not totally. His personality is the utmost transcending personality and this transcendent position could not be availed, but only when that personality is not subjected to physical rules in times - Men, in general, how high is their wisdom and approach is subject to limits, but the Prophet, in that event, was beyond space and time and beyond limitation.

This celestial journey was by body and soul, both, and this was not a dream nor that of soul only.

When did it take place?

There are a few narrations in this regard.

1. It took place in the same year he received the Message for the first time.
2. After five years of Prophethood.
3. In the month of Rajab 10th year.
4. In Ramadan 12th year.
5. In Muharram 13th year.
6. In Rabi Ul Awwal 13th year.

But the majority of scholars and historians say it was in 11th year after the death of Abu Talib and Khadijah and after the trip to Ta'if. Abu Talib and Khadijah both passed away in Ramadan year 10th.

Here we can add another point also, that the Prophet was full of grief upon the death of Abu Talib and Khadijah and he was shocked by what the people in Ta'if did to him, so, this journey was a relief and relaxation for him also.

THIS EVENT HAS TWO PARTS

I. Isra, i.e., traveling on ground from Makkah to Jerusalem.

II. Meraj, i.e., ascension to the heavens and upon the seven heavens.

The first part is mentioned in Surah Bani Israel, verse one:

> "Glory be to Allah, the one who took his slave on a journey at night from Masjid Ul Haram to Masjid Ul Aqsa, the one we have blessed the area around it to show him our signs, indeed, he is the All-Hearer, All-Seer."

The second part is mentioned in Surat An Najm:

> *Indeed he (Mohammad) saw him (Gabriel) at a second time. Near "Sidrat Ul Muntaha" i.e., a Lote tree of the utmost boundary. Near that is the paradise of abode when that thing covered the Lote tree which did cover it. The sight (of Mohammad) turned not aside nor it transgressed beyond the limits. Indeed, he saw the great signs of his Lord." (53:13-18)*

Then, there are *Riwayat* (narrations) from so many *Sahabahs*; amongst them, there are:

Umar, Ali, Ibni Masud, Ibni Abbas, Abu Saeed Al Khudri, Huzaifah, and Aaisha. But the very detailed narrations are that of:

Anas Ibni Malik, Malik Ibni Sa'sa 'a, Abu Zar Ghifari, and Abu Hurairah.

Almost 25 *Sahabahs* narrated this event.

Note: Allah, the sole creator, has established this physical world and laid down some natural rules and laws for its functions and smooth running. Scientists look for these rules and laws. Their field is matter and materials. They do not want to get involved in things that are not material or not connected and related to matter, and they can do what is possible regarding matter, material world, and natural laws, but the concept of possible and impossible is for creature and human and not for the creator.

Now, how did the Prophet accomplish this in one night? That is not their subject to affirm or to deny and should not be. The rules and laws of nature are laid down by Allah, but he himself is not subjected to nor subjugated to these rules and laws because he is the source of law. This is a known fact and rule, just like how the United Kingdom is a constitutional monarchy where the throne is considered the very source of law as laws are promulgated in the name of the Crown, even though the throne has nothing to do with law practically.

So, the crown is not subject to law while Allah is not the king of the world only, but its creator, owner, and master as well. So, usually things happen in accordance with those laws and rules and that is sometimes called the *Tadbeer* (planning) of Allah and sometimes the *Taqdeer* (decree and pre-ordained law) of Allah, but sometimes he demeans that rule in specific cases for some reasons known to him only, and he can do that as he is *Qadir* and *Qadeer*, having irresistible power over everything and that is how he took the Prophet up to upon the seven heavens and brought him back in a part of night.

Because of short of understanding this basic point or that people's sight and knowledge cannot go and does not beyond matter, material world, science, and technology of the time, a specific people are living therein, they either deny such things or at least they get confused = and say,

> *"But say how this is possible?"*

Possibility is a condition for creature not for the creator.

> *"Is the one who creates the like of one who cannot create? Will you not think [about this]?" (16:17)*

He is the only creator and He is the planner who is behind the function of each and every single atom, and therefore the smooth running of this worldly system.

> "Behold! To him belongs the creation and the planning [as well]." (7:54)

So, he has the power to determine the function of any atom or anything. This journey was of both his body and soul, and not a dream or a journey by soul only, because if that was a dream, then anybody can dream and then there would be no distinction of a Prophet and a Messenger. Also, we knew that before receiving the Message the Prophet had dreams for six months and its *Tabeer* (happening) was taking place as immediately as dawn breaks after night. But now if he had the dream, then, did it happen after that or not? If not, then if it happened later on, instead of going up, his dreams came down. Also, when it comes to dreams the person concerned must have actually seen such things before, so the dream is a replay or reflection of that, even though there might be a small difference, as the Prophet related later on, most of it is not imagined. As for those who say that it was by soul only, the soul came out of body or it was inside the body. Then, if it was inside the body, then, that is imagination and anyone can imagine that; and if the soul were to leave the body and go up to the seven heavens, then, the body would be dead.

In the verse of Surah Bani Israel, when the word *Roya* is mentioned, one meaning is "dream," but it has another meaning and that is "scene," especially a unique one. This event was like that and was beyond the approach of human beings, even, beyond their imagination, like the growing of the *Zaqqum* tree in the burning fires of Hell.

So, Allah said,

> "And we have not made the [unique] scene which we have shown you in the night [of ascension], but a test for people and the tree which is mentioned in Quran cursed (is its eater and is a test as well)." (17:1)

This means as they apply their senses and say,

> "A tree in burning fire? the same way they say one night and travelling to heavens and coming back? No way!"

And that is why when the Prophet said it to people, then, Mut'im Ibni Adi said,

> *"You were saying strange things, but this one is the strangest, so this is too much."*

That's why the *Mushrikeen*" made a fun of the Prophet when he described the ascension of both his body and soul. Also, Allah said the *Kalimah* "Subhana" in verse (17:1), which literally means "glory," but technically it is used for something that happens in an astonishing and wonderful way Then, he said he took his slave, which means a living person, not just his soul. Also, he said,

> *"'So we may show him our signs."*

And showing is to the eyes of a living person and this was the actual wisdom to show him the wonderful signs of other worlds and not to show him his own self as that does not need any ascension, as Allah could not be enclosed or surrounded by space and time. Allah spoke to Musa from behind the veil and Musa was on the ground.

Then, there are narrations that he was taken:

1. From his house
2. From the house of Ummi Hani
3. From Abu Talib's apartments
4. From Hateem
5. From Bait Ullah (House of Allah)

This is not a contradiction, as that house of Ummi Hani was the apartments of Abu Talib and the Prophet ascribed that to himself as sometimes, he used to stay therein, then, he was brought to the house of Allah and prayed and then, he took his ride from Hateem. This also proves that this ascension was that of a living body, otherwise, for soul there is no need of any ride as that flies itself like light or even, swifter.

Here, we will quote a brief from a Hadith narrated by Imam Ahmad from Anas. Ibni Malik narrated that the Prophet said,

Buraq' was brought to me, it was a white animal bigger than a donkey and smaller than a mule. One stride of it covered a distance of its sight. I rode on it and it took me to Bait Ul Maqdis, where I tethered it at the hitching post of the prophets. Then, I prayed two Rakat there and Jibril brought me a vessel of wine and another one of milk. I picked up the one with the milk and Jibril said, "You have chosen the fitrah (nature or natural instinct as milk is the natural food of infants)." Then, I was taken up to the first heaven and Jibril asked for it to be opened. He was asked about himself and about the one who was with him and the same practice took place at every heaven. In the first heaven, I saw Adam, I said "Salam" to him. He answered and welcomed me in the second heaven, I saw the maternal cousins Yahya and Isa (John and Jesus). They answered my greetings and welcomed me. In the third heaven, I saw Yusuf (Joseph), he answered my Salam and welcomed me. He was given a considerable part of beauty. In the fourth heaven, there was Idris [Enoch]. We exchanged greetings, and he welcomed me. In the fifth heaven, I said "Salam" to Harun [Aaron]; he answered me and welcomed me. In sixth heaven, I saw Musa, I said "Salam" and he answered it and welcomed me. Then, I was taken to the seventh heaven and there I saw Ibrahim [Abraham]. He was leaning on the most frequented house [Al Baitul Mamoor], where every day 70,000 angels make tawaf of it, but they can never come there again. After that, I was taken up to" Sidrat Ul Muntaha" (the Lote tree of utmost boundaries). Its leaves were like an elephant's ears and its fruits were like the pitchers of Hajar. It was veiled with that great [thing]. It changed [its colors changed] so, no creature can describe its beauty.

Then, Allah revealed that which he revealed to me. He enjoined on me 50 prayers every day and night. I came down until I reached Musa. He asked me what Allah enjoined on my ummah. I told him 50 prayers. He said, "Go back and ask your Lord to reduce it, as your ummah will not be able to manage that. I tested the children of Israel and I found how they were, so I went back and

Allah reduced it by five prayers." Musa sent me back nine times, so, altogether 45 prayers got were waived and only five remained. Once again, Musa told me to go and ask for more to be reduced, I told him, "Now, I feel shy about going back. When only five prayers remained, Allah told me these are five in number, but 50 in reward.

In a Hadith of Qatada, it is said that

"Before mounting to depart, He [Jibril] brought out my heart and brought a golden vessel filled with faith and wisdom. He washed it and filled it up [with faith and wisdom] and put it back."

In a Hadith of Abu Hurairah, it is said that the Prophet was brought a vessel of milk and another one of honey. Now, this wash was like preparing him for ascension just like nowadays, astronauts who are going to space do different types of preparations. Maybe he was brought three cups as at Bait Ul Maqdis, he was brought milk and wine and, in the heavens, he was offered honey and milk, but in both places, he picked up milk because of his very clean and neat nature.

Then, as to whether He saw Allah there: Abu Zar said, I asked the Prophet and he said,

"I saw light [Muslim]."

Also, he said,

"Light! How could I see him?"

This is like the one who says,

"I saw the sun."

And at another time, he says,

"Light, how can I see it as its light is seen?"

As the very body of sun is not seen due to its flash.

The Prophet had was also shown some scenes of Paradise and Hellfire. He saw in hellfire those who had taken away the properties of orphans; their bellies were filled up with pieces of fire. He saw those who used to be involved in usury; they were being crushed under the feet of "Aali Firaun". He saw those who used to commit *zina* (adultery and fornication); in front of them was some fresh meat and rotten meat, and they were eating the rotten meat. He also saw those women who attributed their illegitimate children to their husbands; they were hanging from their breasts.

The Prophet left the house of Ummi Hani and came back there in the morning. He told Ummi Hani about what happened, and as he was going out, Ummi Hani said,

> *"Don't tell this to your people, they will belie you."*

She held onto his cloak to tell him this. The Prophet pulled on the cloak to get it free. She later said that at that place where he pulled, a flash happened, and her sight was dazzled, so she made a *sajdah* at the moment and then, he was gone. She sent Nab'a, her servant, to find out where the Prophet has gone. She reported that he was in Hateem; where Abu Jahl, Mut'im was, among others. The Prophet told them about this event at night and that was the time when Mut'im said,

> *"Up until now your case was easy, but now this is way too much."*

Then he said,

> *"Let me ask you a few questions if you have really gone."*

He asked him about Masjid-I-Aqsa. Allah through Jibril presented to him a full picture of it and he answered them correctly. He even told them about a caravan of them that in such and such time, it was in such and such place and after sunrise tomorrow, it will cross over that hilltop and the next, all of which was entirely accurate. It is said that someone told Abu Bakr about this story, that do you believe this? He said,

> *"If he has said it, then it is true, for he has never told a lie, nor will he ever tell a lie."*

BAI'AT AQABA (THE AQABA PLEDGE)

There are two famous pledges of Aqabah in the books of Seerah, but the basis of these two are those six people who were in Mina for Hajj. The Prophet came to Mina. Abu Bakr and Ali were both with the Prophet. The Prophet asked them where they were from, and they said they were from Yathrib.

The Prophet said,

> *"Oh! The Allies of Jews."*

They confirmed this. The Prophet talked to them and they said,

> *"We accept your Message. Let us go back to our people if we can convince them."*

These six people were:

1. As' ad Ibni Zurarah
2. Auf Ibn Ul Harith
3. Rafi Ibni Malik
4. Qutbah Ibni Aamir
5. Oqbah Ibni Aamir
6. Jabir Ibni Abdullah

They all were from Khazraj tribe and this event took place before the ascension event.

Now, in year 12, five out of these six (except Jabir) came for Hajj along with seven more people:

1. Muaz Ibn Ul Harith

2. Zakwan Ibni Abdul Qaisr

3. Obadah Ibni Samit

4. Yazid Ibni Thalabah

5. Abbas Ibni Ubadah

They all were from Khazraj and

6. Abul Haitham Ibni Taihan and

7. Owaim Ibni Sa'idah

They were from the Aus tribe.

The Prophet talked to them and they gave their pledge to the Prophet that

> *They will not associate anything with Allah, nor they will steal, or commit zina or kill their newborn babies, nor will they slander. The Prophet also told them, and you will not disobey me in any good thing (Bukhari).*

After Hajj, when they were going back the Prophet sent with them his envoy (Emissary), a famous Sehabi, Mus'ab Ibni Omair.

He stayed with Asad Ibni Zurarah. Mus'ab was called Al Qari and Al Muqri there. One day Asad took him to Banu Abdul Ash'hal, where they saw Sa'd Ibni Muaz and Osaid Ibni Hudair. Sa'd said to Osaid,

> *"Go and stop them both, they do befool our youth, but Asad is my cousin, so I can't do it."*

When Osaid was approaching them, Asad told Mus'ab,

> *"Look! This is the elder of the tribe coming to you, so, give him the Message in a good way."*

Osaid came with a harsh and a hard tone. Mus'ab said to him more gently,

"Can you sit with us for a while to listen to what we say?"

The elder agreed, so, Mus'ab spoke a little bit about Islam and recited some Quran to him. Asad said,

"By Allah, we saw Islam in his face before he spoke and also said, what a wonderful word?"

He asked the procedure how to accept Islam. They told him to bathe, have dress in clean clothes, and then take *Shahadah*. He did it and also, they made him to pray 2 *Rakat* prayer and said,

"Look there is Sa'd. If he accepts it, then, nobody from Banu Abdul Ash'hal will stay behind."

He went there. Sa'd told his colleagues,

"By Allah, Osaid's face is changed. He asked him what he had done."

He said, "I talked to them and I think that Banu Haritha are talking about killing of your cousin Asad."

Sa'd became angry, came to Mus'ab and Asad, and used some hard words to them. To Asad he said,

"You are my cousin and I will never allow anyone to touch you."

Mus'ab said,

"You are a noble man. Can you please sit to listen to what we say as we cannot force anyone to accept? So, if you liked it, then, that is up to you and if not, then, you can go."

He said,

"All right! Carry on."

Mus'ab said a little about Islam and then recited the Quran. He also said,

> "What a wonderful word. What do you have to do to accept Islam?"

They told him and he accepted Islam. Then, he came back to his people and they saw him changed. He told them,

> "Look! You have to accept Islam, otherwise, nobody may try to speak to me,"

So, all of them accepted Islam except Osairim. But later on, when Uhud came to the battle, he too accepted Islam, fought with bravery, and was martyred. He is the one about whom the Prophet said,

> "This man did a little and was rewarded a lot."

He had not yet prayed a single prayer nor fasted a single fast but he went to paradise since he accepted Islam and had not committed a single sin. In his last moments, people asked him,

> "Did you come to fight for your people and ego or for Islam?"

He said,

> "For Islam."

BAI'AT AQABAH THANIA (THE SECOND PLEDGE OF AQABAH)

In Hajj season of the 13th year, the Madinites came for Hajj, some 73 men and two women. Amongst them were those also who made the pledge. These two women were Ummi Ammarah Naseebah binti Ka'b Al Mazinia from Banu Mazin and Ummi Manee Asma Binti Amr from Banu Salamah. These people contacted the Prophet and agreed to meet at Mina at night.

They said,

> *"One of our elders, Abu Jabir Abdullah Ibni Amr Ibni Hiram, was with us and had not accepted Islam yet. We convinced him to accept Islam and he did, then, we informed him about our appointment with the Prophet."*

The Prophet came along with his Uncle Abbas, who had not accepted Islam yet, but he came to make for his nephew a strong word of support and protection from these Madinites. He was the first to speak and said, Mohammad is protected among us, though we face a lot of hardships, and you people want him to get settled in Madina, so, think about that as this is not an easy job, but a challenge to Arabia. Then, Kab Ibni Malik said, now, you speak o Mohammad as we listened to what Abbas said and we picked up the bottom line, i.e., protection, at any cost. The Prophet recited the Quran and then asked them for Bai'at. The contents of Bai'at were:

1. To listen and obey in both prosperity and adversity.

2. To spend as much as one can, whether one is rich or poor.

3. To enjoin good and forbid evil.

4. To stand firmly for Allah and not to fear the censure of anyone.

5. To defend me in case I ask your help at any cost.

Bara Ibni Maroor said,

> *"We are good in a fight; we will protect you the way we protect our children, and our belts and trousers [i.e., our honor]."*

Abul Haitham Ibni Taihan said,

> *"We have alliances with these Jews, but we are going to cut them, but if Allah grants you power and victory, then you are not going to leave us and take your own people Quraish." The Prophet said, "Nay, it would never be, your blood is my blood, I am from you and you are from me, I will fight who you will fight and make peace whom you will make peace with."*

When they were ready for Bai'at, Abbas Ibni Obadah Ibni Nadlah said,

> *"You people know what you say that you are ready to fight, black and white, but later on, when you will face it and then you turned around, so, turn now as that will be a shame of this world and of the hereafter and if you are ready, then, don't delay as this is the ultimate good of both worlds."*

They said,

> *"Yes, we will do that at any cost."*

Jabir said,

> *"We jumped to do Bai at, but As' ad Ibni Zurarah grabbed the hand of the Prophet and said, "Look people! We are here because we know that he is the Prophet of Allah, we are going to separate him from his own people, so, if you will show stability when the swords of people are cutting you, then, do that and if not, then, leave him as that is sufficient an excuse for you people."*

They said,

> *"Asad! Let us have it,"*

So Asad was the first one who did Bai'at, and then, all others did it.

The Prophet, after Bai'at appointed, 12 leaders for them, nine were from Khazraj and they were:

1. Asad Ibni Zurarah

2. Sad Ibni Rabee Ibni Amr

3. Abdullah Ibni Rawaha Ibni Thalabah

4. Rafi Ibni Malik

5. Bara Ibni Maroor

6. Abdullah Ibni Amr Ibni Hiram

7. Obadah Ibni Samit

8. Sa'd Ibni Obadah

9. Munzir Ibni Amr

And three from Aus were:

1. Osaid Ibni Hudair

2. Sa'd Ibni Khaithamah

3. Rifa' ah Ibni Abdul Munzir

He told them,

> "You for your people are like the Hawariyyun of Isa."

The Prophet appointed Asad as their chief.

The Quraish were on high alert and someone got the news, so, he shouted on Quraish saying that Mohammad and people of Yathrib agreed to fight them. Abbas Ibni Obadah said,

> "O, Messenger of Allah, maybe we will be facing these people with our swords tomorrow."

The Prophet said,

> "No, just go back and get some rest."

The next morning, a delegation of Makkans came to Mina and spoke to the Madinites, who were not aware of that treaty and pledge and Abdullah Ibni Obai, the chief hypocrite, was amongst them, he said,

> "How is that possible without taking me in confidence."

So, the Makkans went back. The Muslims kept quiet.

Later on, the Quraish confirmed the news. The Hujjaj already had left, but they got Munzir Ibni Amr and Sa'd Ibni Obadah. Munzir escaped, but they caught Sa'd and brought him to Makkah. They beat him, but Mut'im Ibni Adi and Harith Ibni Harb made them release him because provided protection to their caravans in his area.

By the Bai'at, we can say Islam found a place and founded it is a base.

The Prophet then asked the Muslims to migrate to Madinah, so, they started that and their relatives were trying to stop them. The first one who planned to migrate was Abu Salamah along with his wife Ummi Salamah and his small son Salamah, and this was before the second pledge. When the in-laws of Abu Salamah learned about this, they came and told him that he could not take their daughter with him, so, they stopped Ummi Salamah and her son, but later on, the tribe of Abu Salamah came and said,

> "As you people did not allow your daughter to go with her husband, we will not leave our child with you."

Both families started pulling the baby so hard, that they dislocated his shoulder his arm was dislocated, but the in-laws took him in the end. Then, every day, Ummi Salamah used to come out to the outskirt of Makkah, sitting on the road, and crying for her son as she didn't know for his condition. Then, one day one of her relatives felt sorry for her and she said to her family,

> "Why do you people not show some mercy to this poor lady? Let her join her husband,"

And they agreed. She asked her in-laws for her son. She took off for Madinah, but she was all alone with her baby son not knowing where to go. In Tan'eem, Uthman Ibni Talha Ibni Abi-Talha saw her and when she found that she doesn't know how to go, he took her all the way to Qaba. He told her,

> "I know your husband is in this village, so, go and join him."

When Suhaib Ibni Sinan Arrumi planned to leave, the Makkans told him,

> "You came to Makkah a destitute with nothing, so now, if you want to go you cannot take all that wealth you made here."

He said,

> "That is fine with me. You have it, but I have to go." When the Prophet came to know, He said, "Suhaib won."

The Makkans used to torture those who were leaving. When Umar planned to leave, he came to Kabah when these Mushrikeen were sitting. He announced,

> "Tomorrow, I am leaving for Madinah, so anyone who wants his mother to grieve him, his wife to become a widow, and his children to be orphans, he should stop me."

The people kept quiet. With Umar, two other people, Ayyash Ibni Abi Rabee'a and Hisham Ibn Ul Aas, also, were to go, but Hisham was stopped by his people and couldn't join them. They both got into Qaba. A few days after, Abu Jahl along with his brother, Harith, and said to Ayyash,

> "Your mother has made a pledge that she will never come out of the sun or comb her hair until she sees you."

Umar said to Ayyash,

> "Look, this is a trap. When the sun of Makkah burns the body of your mother, she will rush out to shade, and when the lice bother her, she will comb for sure, but he said, "But mom." Then, Umar gave him his own she-camel, that if you feel any fear, then, have it, it will help you escape."

On their way to Makkah, Abu Jahl said,

> "Ayyash! This camel of mine bothered me a lot, can I ride your she-camel behind you?"

And when they made their camels sit, they both jumped on him. They tied his hands and legs and brought him to Makkah and said to people,

"Do to your fools what we did to ours."

After this pledge of Aqabah, in a few months, the Muslims migrated to Madina, even, most of those who had migrated to Abyssinia already, and in Makkah there remained only a few of them.

DARUN NADWAH'S MEETING

Qusai, the great great-grandfather of the Prophet, took over the custody of the House of Allah and asked the Quraish as they had dispersed to come to Makkah.

He allotted them land to make their houses and to pay a specific amount to the treasury to host the guests of Allah. He also established a proper social and political system for them. So, he built an assembly hall to the north of the Kaba, with its door opening towards the Kabah. They used to have their meetings there.

Now, when the Makkans came to know that some Muslims migrated to Habshah while a big number of them settled in Madinah and sooner or later, they will be a threat to us. They summoned a meeting on 26th Safar-Ul-Muzaffar year 14, September 12th, 622. This was Thursday. All tribes took place therein. Some elders were:

1) Amr Ibni Hisham (Abu Jahl) from Banu Makhzoom

2,3,4) Jubair Ibni Mut'im, Tu Aimah Ibni Adi, and Harith Ibni Aamir from Banu Naufal Ibni Abdi Manaf

5,6,7) Shaiba, Utbah, and Abu Sufyan from Banu Abd Shams

8) Nadr Ibn Ul Harith from Banu Abd-Dar

9,10,11) Abul Bukhtari, Zama'ah, Hakeem Ibni Hizam from Banu Asad

12,13) Nabeeh and Munnabih from Banu Sah'm

14) Umayyah Ibni Khalaf from Banu-Jumah.

It is said that at the meeting time, "Iblis" (Satan) was standing at the entrance pretending to be a sheikh (elder) from Najd to take part in that meeting and to give his opinion.

In the meeting Abdul Aswad said,

> "We should turn Mohammad out of Makkah to some far-flung area."

Iblis said,

> "He is eloquent in speech, he can gather people outside, and can attack you."

Abul Bukhtari said,

> "We should chain him and put him in a lonely place until he dies."

Iblis again said,

> "This is not doable as Banu Hashim and others can get him released.

Then Abu Jahl said,

> "The proper way is to take people from every tribe, to surround his house at night, and when he comes out of his house in the morning, then all these people may attack him at once, and kill him and in the same way Banu Hashim will not fight all these tribes, so, we will pay them the blood money."

Iblis said,

> "This is the right course of action," and so it was approved. (Ibni Hisham).

Holy Quran said,

> "And remember when the disbelievers were plotting against you to imprison you, or to kill you, or to get you out (of Makkah). They were plotting and Allah was planning (to rescue you) and Allah is the Best Planner."(8:30)

"HIJRAH" (MIGRATION) TO MADINA

HIJRAH TO MADINAH (622 AFTER JESUS)

This was the month of Safar when the aforesaid session of Makkans was held, wherein this plot to kill the Prophet was finalized. After this the archangel Jibril came to the Prophet and told him not to stay in his bed that night (Ibn Hisham). Imam Bukhari narrated from Aaisha that

> "We were sitting at home and this was midday when the Prophet came to our house. He told Abu Bakr to get everyone out. Abu Bakr said that only Aaisha is here. Then the Prophet said, 'I have been ordered from Allah to go out of Makkah tonight so you will be in my company.'"

Abu Bakr showed the Prophet two young she-camels and said,

> *"Some time back you told me about this and since then I got these camels, raising them with care for our ride, so which one would you like?"*

The Prophet chose one and asked for the price. Abu Bakr said,

> *"Price?"*

The Prophet said

> *"For this mission, I have to spend my own money."*

After that the Prophet went his home back waiting for the night, while Quraish were working on their plot.

The Prophet used to go to Haram in the last part of the night. The *Mushrikeen* were around his house waiting for him to come out. He had already called Ali to lie on his bed and cover himself with a blanket. The Prophet came out with sand or small pebbles in his hand reciting Surah Yasin

> *"Yasin! By the Quran full of wisdom. Truly you are one of the messengers on the straight path, the Tanzeel (sending down) of the Almighty, the Merciful, in order to warn those whose forefathers were not warned, so they are heedless indeed the word (decree of punishment) has proved against most of them so they will not believe. Verily We have put a barrier in front of them and a barrier behind them and we have covered them with barriers from all around so they cannot see."*
> (36:1-9)

He threw that sand on these people and everyone who got even one grain of it on themselves fell asleep, including Iblis, the Devil. The Prophet came therefrom to the House of Abu Bakr.

THE PROPHET'S STRATEGY

As we said that the people of Makkah were aware of that when he will leave Makkah, will go to Madina and Madina is situated to the north of Makkah. But the Prophet took Abu Bakr with and started going towards south, i.e., towards Yemen. This was the 27th of Safar. Then when they woke up a little bit later, they tried to look through the cracks of the door inside the house whether the Prophet is still in his bed and as Ali was therein so they were thinking this is him.

They went to a cave in Mount of Thaur. They bound their feet to cover their tracks. Abu Bakr picked up the Prophet on his back halfway there and carried him until they arrived. Abu Bakr said to the Prophet,

> *"Please wait outside and let me check the cave and clean it."*

As Abu Bakr cleaned, he saw holes all around so he ripped his cloak into pieces to plug them, but still one hole remained open. He asked the Prophet to come in. He put his foot over the open hole and bade the Prophet sleep. The Prophet put his head on Abu Bakr's thigh and slept. While he slept, Abu Bakr was bitten by some poisonous insect. He tried to keep still but his eyes watered and the tears fell on the Prophet's face. The Prophet opened his eyes and asked him a what/who has put you in tears?

He said,

> *"Some insect bit me,"*

But still he was holding his foot there so the insect may not harm the Prophet. The Prophet asked Abu Bakr to show him the bite and he put his saliva on and Abu Bakr was healed.

Razeen narrated from Umar that every year on the same day Abu Bakr used to feel that pain from the bite and later on he died of that.

Amir Ibn Fuhairah, the servant of Abu Bakr, used to graze his goats in the same mountain the whole day and in the evening, he used to bring it close to the cave to give some milk to them to drink. Abdullah, the son of Abu Bakr, used to come at that time to update them about the Quraish.

The Quraish were waiting his coming out of house but as he didn't then they entered the house. They found Ali there. They asked him about the Prophet. He said,

"I know where he is gone but I will never tell you."

Then they came to the house of Abu Bakr. They asked Asma Binti Abu Bakr,

"Where is your father?"

She said,

"Why should I tell you where he is?"

Abu Jahl slapped her so hard that her ear was broken.

THE STRUGGLE TO FIND THE CLUE

The Quraish got an expert to find the clue. He brought them to the cave but as a miracle Allah sent a pigeon to lay eggs right in the entrance of the cave and it was sitting over and a spider wove its web there so he told them,

"They have come here for sure but not entered the cave, otherwise these two things would not have been there."

From inside Abu Bakr saw them so he told the Prophet if they will look at the level of their feet, they will see us. The Prophet said as Quran related (9:40) when they both were in the cave, when he was saying to his companion,

> "Worry not Allah is with us, then Allah sent His peace to his heart."

DEPARTURE FROM THE CAVE

When Abdullah told them that now the Quraish got cooled down as they think now you are way too much far from their approach, Then, they on first Rabi Ul-Awwal started their journey towards Madina. Abu Bakr got a guide Abdullah Ibni Araiqat a non-Muslim to guide them through some unknown route. Here from this guide and Aamir in Fuhairah accompanied them. The guide took them towards the ocean to take them alongside the shore.

Imam Bukhari narrated from Abu Bakr:

> "On our first day we were travelling until midday and then we were resting under the shade of a big rock. I levelled the place for the Prophet so he may take some rest. I saw a herdsman with his goats. I asked him if I could milk one of them. This was the culture at that time that they used to allow this. He said, yes, go ahead. So, I milked a goat and brought milk for the Prophet. I cooled the milk by sprinkling water on the pot. I woke up the Prophet. He drank the milk and said, now let us start. On the way at night someone came across Abu Bakr and asked him who was with him. He said only, 'My guide,' and so he kept the secret."

SURAQAH IBN MALIK

Suraqah said,

> "I was sitting in a group of my tribe Banu Mudlij. One man said I saw from far some people were going along with the shore and I think it was Mohammad and his colleagues."

Suraqah continued,

> "I thought the same, but only to divert their attention from this I said, 'I saw them these were some other people' and I just named a few random names. After some time, I came home and told my servant girl to prepare my horse and travel things and bring it to me from the back door. I mounted my horse and spurred it until I approached them. My horse stumbled repeatedly and I realized that that was a warning of Allah so I begged the Prophet penitently and asked for forgiveness."

It is said that every time after the horse stumbled, he did it, but every time he changed his mind and contemplated his evil design. In any case, the Prophet forgave him. He asked for a written token of forgiveness and Aamir in Fuhairah wrote it for him on a piece of skin [parchment]. The group carried on their journey towards Madina while Suraqah returned to Makkah. On his way to Makkah, whosoever he saw in pursuit of the Prophet, he told him, this way I have checked for you to very far, to foil their attempts. He was not adding to it that I could find Mohammad.

UMM MA' BAD AL KHUZA'IYAH

Umm Ma'bad, Atikah Bint Khalid was a lady living in a tent. She was poor but generous. Outside her tent she had put a mat for travelers to rest and drink water. If she had anything to offer to the traveler, she would do so.

The Prophet and his companions also wanted to take some rest and some food if she had any, but she told them that that day unfortunately she did not have anything, and even not even any milk at home or any milking goats, except one lean one that could not go to pasture. The Prophet asked her permission to milk it and she said yes. He touched its udder and the milk flowed. He milked it and he offered the milk to the lady to drink, then he milked it for a second time and he and his companions drank. Then he milked it for a third time and gave it to the lady to keep. Later on, when her husband came home, he saw the milk and asked Umm Ma' bad wherefrom she got it and she related the story to him. He asked her very eagerly about the appearance, character, and behavior of this traveler. He said,

> "This is the Prophet from Quraish. We heard about him."

He expressed his wish and joy in a few verses of poetry that became famous in the whole area later on. Eventually this man joined the Prophet and accepted Islam.

BURAIDAH IBN AL-HASEEB

As it is narrated that the chiefs of Makkah announced a bounty of 100 camels for whoever would either kill the Prophet or bring him in alive. Buraidah Al Aslami, along with 70 people, came after him. The Prophet talked to him. He asked him his name. Buraidah told him. The Prophet said.

> "Baradal Amr" (The issue cooled down).

He asked Buraidah about his tribe. He replied,

"Aslam."

The Prophet said.

"Salamna" (we were safe).

He further asked,

"Which subtribe do you belong to?"

Buraidah said,

"Banu Sahm."

The Prophet said,

"Kharaja Sahmuk" (your draw came out).

All these the Prophet said as a good omen. Buraidah and his people accepted Islam. This happened in between Rabigh and Juhfah. Buraidah said,

"When you are entering Madina, we should have a symbol."

So, he made his white turban a flag and he carried that. On his way toward Madina, Zubair Ibn Ul Awwam (and in some narrations Talha Ibn Ubaid Ullah and maybe both but separately coming back from a business trip) met the Prophet and gave the Prophet and Abu Bakr new white robes to wear.

THE PROPHET'S ARRIVAL IN QUBA

Quba was a town outside Madina. The Prophet arrived in Rabi Ul Awwal on September 23rd, 622 AJ. Urwah ibn Zubair said that on the day the people of Madina heard about the departure of the Prophet from

Makkah, they came out early in the morning to Harrah to wait for the Prophet, and then went back when he did not arrive. One day when they went back at midday to rest, a Jew saw that the Prophet is coming so he went over an elevated place and called the people:

> "O people! Here is the grandfather you were waiting for."

The people came out of their houses saying *Tabeer* in loud voices.

The Prophet was staying in Quba with Kulthum Ibn Ul Haddam. People used to come to see him. Abu Bakr was standing for the people and the Prophet was sitting. Those who couldn't recognized the Prophet saluted Abu Bakr, but when the sun's heat came on the Prophet and Abu Bakr started to shadow him, then they knew which one is the Prophet.

ALI AND OTHERS ARRIVED IN QUBA

Even though they refused the message often spoke out against the Prophet, The Makkans entrusted him with their valuables and the Prophet ordered Ali to stay behind to return those valuables to their owners. After three days he also arrived Quba along with Umm-I-Aiman, the Prophet's two daughters Ummi Kulthum and Fatima, his wife Sawdah and Usamah Ibn Zaid, Abdullah, son of Abu Bakr, Aaisha and others also arrived.

Zainab, the daughter of the Prophet, was unable to come, because she was in Makkah until Badr. Abu Bakr and Bilal fell sick. The Prophet made a *Dua*,

> "O Allah, engrave in our hearts the love with Madina as it was for Makkah."

MASJID QUBA

The Prophet stayed in Quba for a few days. In some narrations, fourteen days are mentioned, and it is the famous one that he stayed for four days, as he arrived on Monday and left for Madina on Friday. There he built up a simple masjid in a piece of land gifted by a lady cousin of his host named Leena. This is the first ever masjid built by the Prophet. The Prophet said,

> *"Whoever made wudu at home and came to masjid Quba and prayed two Rakat will have there a reward of a complete umrah."*

The Prophet himself used to go there almost every week, sometimes on foot and sometimes riding. Allah said regarding this masjid (9:108):

> *"The masjid whose foundation is laid from day one on Taqwa is more worthy that you stand therein. In it there are men who love purity and Allah loves those who are pure?"*

DEPARTURE TO MADINA

The day he was going to Madina, the Prophet informed the ancestors of his grandfather Abdul Muttalib from his mother's side Banu Najjar to come and to take him to Madina. They came with their swords with, kept him company.

On his way towards Madina, when he was there in the cone of Banu Salim Ibni Auf, Jibril came and told him to *pray salat-Ul-Jumah*. This was the first ever *Jumah* prayer he prayed. Almost 100 people were with him.

After *Salat - Ul - Jumua* he mounted his she-camel Qaswa and proceeded towards Madina. Every household he passed asked him if he would stay with them but he said, regarding his she-camel,

"Let it be as she is inspired."

So, the she-camel came to an open field and sat there. The Prophet did not come down and the she-camel once again stood up and proceeded further, but then she made a U-turn and came back to the same place and sat there again. The prophet wished to stay in Banu Najjar and this place was that of Banu Najjar. Close to this piece of land was the house chosen by Allah through the double sitting of the she-camel. It belonged to Abu Ayyub Ansari of Banu Najjar.

Tubba The King of Yemen: -

The piece of land was a selection by Allah for the Prophet's masjid. Hafiz Ibni Asakir related those 1000 years before the Prophet, a king of Yemen Tubba al Himyari, along with 132,000 cavalry, 113,000 infantry, and 12,000 scholars, philosophers and thinkers was going on a tour. He was looking for the people to come out and to salute him and he was blessing them with gifts. When he arrived at Makkah and stayed in its outskirts, nobody came out to salute him. He was outraged and asked his retinue,

"Why did these people not come?"

They told him as they were considered religious leaders of the world and custodians of a holy house it was against their protocol. In himself he took an oath that he would demolish this house and at that moment, very bad, foul-smelling blood started coming out of his mouth and nose. His doctors tried a lot but every treatment was in vain. Then he asked the scholars and they said that it was heavenly disease so physical treatment would never work. So, if he intended any bad thoughts or deeds regarding anything heavenly, he should repent sincerely and change his intention. He did that and recovered. As a thanks he covered the Holy Kabah with a silky cover and gifted everyone in Makkah seven silk dresses and 7 dinars each. Then he continued until he arrived in Madina. There the scholars started smelling the dirt and looking at the stones and rocks. They came to know that this is the place, where the last and final prophet of Allah will get settled. They asked the king if they could stay here. The king not only allowed them to stay but he also built-up hundreds of houses for them and in the middle, he built one for the grand scholar and one two-story house for that prophet to come as the scholars told him. The king wrote a letter in the name of the prophet to be kept for in the hands of the offspring of the grand scholar after him.

This letter reads:

> *From Tubba al Himyari to the intercessor of the day of resurrection. O the beloved of Allah, I believe in you and the book to be sent to you. If I got blessed to see it is a blessing and if not then on the day of resurrection, please forget me not and intercede for me. I am your first Ummati; I do give my pledge to you ahead and testify that you are the messenger of Allah.*

This letter was transferred from generation to generation until it came to Abu Ayyub Al Ansari.

KHALID IBNI ZAID IBNI KULAIB (ABU AYUB)

This day when the Prophet settled in that house where now Abu Ayyub was living, and the Prophet chose to be on the ground level. Abu Ayyub had saved that letter with his servant Abu Laila. He told him to go to the prophet and to give him the letter. Abu Laila came to the Prophet and before his saying anything, the Prophet said,

"So, you are Abu Laila and you have my letter?" He said yes and gave the letter to the Prophet. The Prophet read it and said, "Peace be on Tubba, he was a pious Brother." (Muzam Ul Adyan)

MASJIDI-NABAWI

The Prophet stayed with Aby Ayyub for 7 months. Abu Ayyub, his tribe Banu Najjar, Sa'd Ibni Obadah, Sa'd Ibni Muaz and others served the Prophet wholeheartedly.

The Prophet asked about the piece of land that his she-camel sat upon twice. They told him it belonged to two orphan brothers, Sahal and Suhail, and the people of Madina used it to dry their dates. The Prophet asked these two boys if they could make a masjid therein. They said,

"Why not? This is for Allah."

The Prophet said,

"You are underage so we will pay for it."

Then the Prophet asked them and the elders about its price. They said it would cost 10 golden dinars, He ordered Abu Bakr to pay that and he did it.

Here there were some graves of *Mushrikeen*, which the Prophet ordered to be dug up and re-buried somewhere else. Then they were able to start construction. The Prophet himself pitched in to help as well. Before starting construction, Banu Najjar's chief Asad Ibni Zurarah passed away. Banu Najjar asked the Prophet to appoint them a chief. The Prophet said,

"I am your responsible person."

Banu Najjar rejoiced that the Prophet was their chief.

The masjid was made of mud bricks, with pillars made of date palms and a roof of date palm branches. It was floored with sand and small pebbles and there were 3 doors. It measured 100 x100 yards (at the time, a yard was the length of one's arm up to the elbow, which is about 18 inches of a typical man).

MADINA

The city was called Yathrib before Rasulullah. It was also known by the name of "Nakhleh" or 'Arden Nakhleh," "land of date-palm trees," as there were date gardens.

Besides its native inhabitants the tribe of Aws and Khazraj, Jews were also living there. Aws and Khazraj, it is said, were from Yemen originally and migrated there after that their water dam broke and they lost their agriculture there so they came here to this agricultural land while there were three Jewish tribes living there, but their religion took a nationalistic shape and then their tribal feuds started so they were living in different zones of Madina.

Banu Nadeer and Quraizah were allied to Aws and Banu Qanuqa to Khazraj. The Aws and Khazraj also had a history of feuds and battles between them. The Jews used to exploit Aws and Khazraj feuds for their own gains. They were illiterate farmers so these Jews who were literate skillful and businesspeople used to exploit them in different ways, including usury.

Before the migration of the Prophet, the Aws and Kharaj who had become sick and tired of their feuds, almost agreed upon Abdullah Ibni Ubai Ibni Salul to throne him as a king. But in the meantime, the Prophet came there.

When the Prophet came, the Jews recognized him, especially the learned. But they did not want to lose their status to him, so they denied him.

Allah said,

> "They know him as they know their own sons." (2:146)

> "When there came to them what they knew they disbelieved that." (2:89)

ABDULLAH IBNI SALAM

Abdullah was a great scholar of Taurat and an authentic authority for the Jews. He says,

> *I was on a date palm tree when a man called me and said that in Banu Amr Ibni Awf someone has come claiming that he is the prophet. So, I jumped down of the tree. My aunt, Khalida Bint Ul Harith, was there. She said, "If you have heard of Musa Ibni Imran, you would not have come down in such a hurry." I said, "Auntie! By God, this is the brother of Musa." So, she asked me, "Is he the someone we were talking about?" I said, "Yes, he is Ibn Salam was from Banu Qanuqa tribe. His previous name was Hussain."*

Also, Imam Bukhari narrated from Anas that Ibni Salam asked the Prophet about the first sign of "Qayamat."

The Prophet said,

> "A fire that will take people from the east towards the west will be burning them."

Then he asked about the first diet in paradise. The Prophet told him it is fish liver Then he asked him how a woman sometimes delivers a male baby and sometimes a female one. The Prophet said when the male sperm prevails, she delivers a boy and when the female sperm prevails then she delivers a girl.

Then Ibni Salam said,

"I bear witness that you are the messenger of Allah."

He said,

I was sitting with the Prophet when a group of Jews asked the Prophet for a meeting. I said to the Prophet, "I will sit in hiding and when they come, ask them about me and when they tell you about me then ask them that if he will accept Islam, then how?" The Prophet asked them, "Who is this Hussain Ibni Salam amongst you?" They said, He is our religious chief and he is the son of our chief." The Prophet said, "If he will accept me as a messenger then what?" They said, "No way, he will never, may Allah save him." Ibni Salam came out and said, "I bear witness that there is no god but Allah and I bear witness that Mohammad is the messenger of Allah". So, they lost their temper and called him evil. Ibni Salam said, "Fear Allah, why do you conceal the truth?" They said, "You are a liar."

SALMAN AL FARSI

Salman is a very big name and a very great man. Originally, he was from Faris (Iran). He was from the Esfahan area. His name was Maba Ibni Badakhshah. His family was the custodian of the Zoroastrian (fire worshippers) temple there. Once his father sent him to look after the agricultural land they had. On his way towards he passed by a Christian church. He saw people there worshipping. He liked their way of worshipping, so he stayed with them until sunset. He said,

> *When I came back, I told my father the whole story. My father told me that my religion is much better than theirs. Then my father kept me under surveillance. I let them know that if any people were going to Sham, I wanted to join them. So, when they informed me, I escaped and joined the caravan to Sham. There I got in touch with a priest, but soon I came to know that he was only accumulating money. He had filled up a few pitchers with gold and silver. After his death I informed people that he was not spending what they were giving him for the good of the religion nor on the poor, so they got enraged and thus they stoned his dead body and put it on a cross.*
>
> *After that a God-fearing man became a priest. I stayed with him and at the time of his death I asked him if he can tell me someone pious to go to. He told me about one in Mosel. I joined him. At his death he told me about someone in Amooriya, a city under control of the Romans. I went there. He was also a pious man. At his death time he gave me some money and a few goats and cows. When he was dying, I asked him for someone but he told me, "Now there is no one but now is the time, a messenger from the offspring of Ibrahim will appear, following his Millat. He will come to the land of dates (Arden Nakhleh) in between his two shoulders there will be a seal of the prophethood and he will not eat Sadaqat (charity).*
>
> *Then a caravan of Banu Kilab Arabs was passing by, I asked them if they can take me with them and I would give them all my cattle. They took me with and sold me*

to the Jews in Wadi al Qira. When my new master was taking me home, I saw the date palm trees so I knew I was in Arden Nakhleh. Then a Jew from Banu Quraizah bought me and brought me to the city of Madina. *I used to work in his gardens and the time came when the Prophet of Allah came and stayed in Banu Amr Ibni Awf. I was working in the garden, when a cousin of my master came and said to him, "May God destroy Banu Qailah (the Aws and Khazraj); they have gathered together around a man claims that he is the prophet." When I heard it, my hold of a branch loosened and very narrowly avoided falling down. I worked the whole day and, in the evening, I went to Quba to see the Prophet. I had some food and dates with me. I presented it to the Prophet and said it was charity. He didn't touch it and instead said to people around him, "Eat." I said in myself that this is one [sign]. I came back and next day I went there and presented some food as a gift. The Prophet shared it with the people around him. I said, this is another [sign]. Then one day I saw him in Baqee cemetery in connection to a burial. I came and started staring at his shoulders. He felt it and slowly he moved his cloak. I saw the seal and kissed it. Then the Prophet asked me to sit in the front. I related my whole story and I accepted Islam. He ordered me to have a Kitabat contract with my master. He agreed to that on 40 Awqiah: gold [one Awqiah is 2 ½ oz] and to arrange for him the planting of 300 date palm trees. I informed the Prophet and he ordered Sahabahs to help me with the plants. The Prophet told me, "Go and dig for the plants but not to put any plant there in until I come." Then he came and put all the trees with his Blessed hands and all these planted trees thrived.*

Then one day one Sahabi brought some gold equal to the volume of an egg. He said he found it in a mine. The

Prophet gave it to me and told me to give it to my master. I said, "But that is 40 Awqiah." He said, "Go and weigh it," so I did and it was 40 Awqiah. I gave that to my master and thus I was free.

In the Battle of Confederates the trench to protect Madina was the advice of Salman and that was the main factor in the victory of that battle. After that the Prophet said,

"Now the people will never attack you but from behind others."

That was such a victory based on Salman's advice that Ansar chanted,

"Salman is from us,"

This means the Ansar as he was living there before that the Prophet got settled there, and the *Muhajireen* said Salman is from amongst us the *Muhajireen* as he was also an immigrant there even though not from Makkah but from Persia and here the historical thing happened and the Prophet said, Salman is from us, i.e., "Ahlul Bait" What luck the Prophet counted him as his family.

In his time, there are a few sayings like 300 years and 385 years, but the most accurate one is 250 years.

THALABAH AND ASAD IBNI OBAID

Thalabah Ibni Saya and Asad Ibni Obaid were the chiefs of Banu Bahdal and Banu Quraizah. When the Prophet besieged Banu Quraizah (after the Battle of the Allies), because of their treason these two chiefs came out and accepted Islam, telling their people that this is the same prophet as elder Ibni Hailan, who migrated from Sham only to await this prophet and to believe in him and at the time of his death he told them. Then he said that a prophet from the offspring of Ibrahim will appear soon, maybe he would not meet him but they would. So when he comes, accept him, otherwise he will have all the right to shed their blood and to enslave them. So, these two accepted Islam (Ibni Ishaq). Also, he narrated that Salamah Ibni Daqish is from those who attended Badr said that in Banu Abdul-Ash'hal there was an elder.

One day he spoke about resurrection, hellfire, and paradise. The Mushriks asked him,

"Do you believe all this?"

He said,

"Of course."

They asked him,

"Why?"

He indicated towards Yemen and Makkah that a prophet would be coming from there. They asked him,

"When? Salamah says I was a little boy,"

He indicated to me, that if he grows, he will see him. Salamah says Allah blessed me with Iman and the Jews did not accept due to their jealousy.

AWS AND KHAZRAJ TRIBES

These two tribes in Madina are considered the native inhabitants of Madina and they are called Banu Qailah in the name of one of their great-grandmothers. These two tribes were cousins and they got into feuds and bloodshed. A few famous incidents and battles happened between them. The first one was known as the Battle of Sameer and the last one was Bu'aath in 616. Then the Prophet arrived in Madina and they were united on the basis of *Deen*, although some of them only pretended to accept Islam. They were hypocrites and Abdullah Ibni Ubai was one of them.

THE PROPHET AT MADINA

As we said in Madinah there were its native inhabitants i.e., the Aus and Khazraj tribes. Almost all of them accepted Islam, even though some of them were *Munafiqeen* (hypocrites) like Abdullah Ibni Ubai and his followers. Then there were the new settlers, the *Muhajireen* (immigrants) and the 3rd-largest community was that of the Jews i.e., Banu Qanuqa, Banu Nadeer, and Banu Quraizah tribes. Some Christians were also there but not in significant numbers.

Now this was a diverse community, especially among the Jews. They were influential, even though the Muslims were now growing in number as well, and majority having their own leadership, but the Prophet of Allah was a mercy of Allah and was a messenger of Allah to the whole world. He was to take all people into confidence. He was establishing a new society and a new state, system, and government to be a role model for the times to come and for sure this was to be established on the basis of honesty, truth, freedom, and justice to all to create harmony and to promote peace. For the said purpose a charter was needed to ensure that everyone's rights would be protected and also make everyone to fulfill their obligations and perform their duties.

As we know, Arab society was based and developed on tribal feuds, rancor, enmities, and bloodshed. To bring them together was a difficult job which Allah made easy for his Prophet –

Allah said:

"And remember the favors of Allah on you as you were enemies to each other, but he joined your hearts together and you became brothers to each other with his grace." (3:104)

As for the Jews living there with the upper hand financially, it was more difficult to subjugate them to a new code and leadership, but the Prophet through his wisdom made it possible as he gave them a higher status than they were expecting.

This new code was given title of Meethaqi –Madinah or Madina treaty. We can say the first ever comprehensive constitution in human history.

THE TREATY OF MADINAH

In the name of Allah, the Beneficent, the Merciful.

This is a document from Mohammad, the Messenger of Allah concerning immigrants and helpers (*ansar*) and those who followed and strove with them:

1. They are one nation to the exclusion of other people.

2. The immigrants of Quraish unite together and shall pay blood money amongst themselves.

3. The believers shall not leave anyone destitute amongst them by not paying his redemption money or blood money in kind.

4. Whoever is rebellious or whoever seeks to spread enmity and sedition, the hand of every God-fearing Muslim shall be against him, even if he is his son.

5. A believer shall not kill another believer, nor shall he support a disbeliever against a believer.

6. The protection of Allah is one and (equally) extended to the weakest of the believers.

7. Believers may support each other.

8. Whoever of the Jews follows us shall have aid and succor; they shall not be injured nor any enemy be aided against him.

9. The peace of the believers is indivisible. No separate peace treaty shall be made when believers are fighting in the path of Allah. Conditions must be fair and equitable to all.

10. It is not lawful for a believer who holds by what is in this treaty and believes in Allah and the Day of Judgment to help a criminal nor give him refuge. Those who give him refuge and render him help shall have the curse and anger of Allah on the Day of resurrection. Their indemnity is not accepted.

11. Killing a believer deliberately, with no good reason, entails killing the killer, unless the sponsor deems it otherwise.

12. Whoever you differ in a matter it may be referred to Allah and to His Messenger.

THE PACT AND THE JEWISH TRIBES

As we said, Jews were the settlers in Madinah. They had lived there for centuries. The Prophet was establishing a state, government, and community to have character and morals on one side, and peace on the other side. For that purpose, it was necessary to make them bound to certain rules, which they had to follow to achieve their goals. The Jews were of the view that they were the chosen people, the beloved of God, the most cultured and the religious people. To handle them and to make them submissive to the new rule and leadership was a difficult task, as their new leadership was a challenge to their religion, political, social, and economic status.

The Prophet wished to have a clearly defined relationship with non-Muslims to provide peace, security, and harmony to all those who have to live in this new state and new society. So, the Prophet ratified a treaty with them. The most important provisions of this treaty were:

1. The Jews of Banu Awf are one community with the believers. The Jews will profess their religion and the Muslims theirs.

2. The Jews shall be responsible for their expenditure and the Muslims for theirs.

3. If attacked by a third party, each shall come to the assistance of the other.

4. Each party shall hold counsel with the other. Mutual relation, and assistance shall be founded on righteousness, and any harm to the other party is excluded.

5. No one shall commit harm to the prejudice of the other.

6. As the Jews fight alongside the Muslims, they shall contribute to the cost of war.

7. The harmed party shall be helped and aided; however, no man is liable for a crime committed by his ally.

8. The town of Madinah shall be a sanctuary for the parties of this agreement.

9. No woman may be taken under protection without the consent of her family.

10. Whatever differences or dispute between the parties to this agreement remains unsolved shall be referred to Allah hand His Messenger.

11. No protection shall be given nor nay relation to Quraish or to their allies so they may be boycotted commercially.

12. In case of any attack on Madinah from outside all parties shall defend Madinah.

13. This treaty shall not hinder any party from seeking lawful revenge, as this treaty shall constitute no protection for the unjust and criminal.

Allah is the guarantor of piety and goodness of this treaty.

This treaty is considered a very comprehensive social contract and constitution of the state which provided social, political, financial, and religious freedom to all, provided he does not violate the laws of the land and the rights of others.

BROTHERHOOD TREATY

A having brotherhood or friendship treaty was a known aspect of Arab culture, through which people were bound to help and cooperate with each other. If one died having no heirs his property was inherited by the other one.

Here in Madinah the Prophet made a similar treaty amongst his Sahabah, the Ansar and The Muhajireen. The Muhajireen had left everything in Makkah. This agreement was made in such a way that each Ansari took a Muhajir as his brother. He provided him his basic needs and also a living place to his family.

The prophet said that the Muhajir will work with the Ansari in his farm and he will give him a portion of the output or at least some financial support. Some of these "Muwakhat" were as follows:

MUHAJIREEN	ANSAR
1. Abu Bakr	1. Kharijah Ibni Zubair
2. Umar Ibn Ul Khattab	2. Itban Ibni Malik
3. Jafar Ibni Abi Talib	3. Muaz Ibni Jabal
4. Hamzah	4. Zaid Ibni Haritha Ansari
5. Abu Ubaidah Ibn Ul Jarrah	5. Sa'd Ibni Muaz
6. Abdul Rahman Ibni Auf	6. Sa'd Ibni Rabee
7. Zubair Ibn Ul Awwam	7. Salamah Ibni Salaamah
8. Talha Ibni Ubaid Ullah	8. Kab Ibni Malik
9. Uthman Ibni Affan	9. Aws Ibni Sabit
10. Saeed Ibni Zaid	10. Ubai Ibni Kab
11. Mus'ab Ibni Umair	11. Abu Ayyub
12. Abu Huzaifah Ibni Utbah	12. Abbad Ibni Bishr
13. Ammar Ibni Yasir	13. Huzaifah Ibn Ul Yaman Ansari
14. Hatib Ibni Abe Balta'a	14. Owaim Ibni Sa'idah
15. Salman al Farsi	15. Abu Darda
16. Abuzar Ghifari	16. Munzir Ibni Amr
17. Abu Basrah Ibni Abi Rah'm	17. Salamah Ibni Daqish
18. Khabbab Ibn Ul Aratt	18. Tameem (Maula of Kharash)
19. Safwan Ibni Wahab	19. Rabi Ibni Amlan
20. Suhaib Ibni Sinan	20. Harith Ibni Shammah
21. Abdullah Ibni Makhrama	21. Farwah Ibni Amr
22. Masood Ibni Rabi'a	22. Obaid Ibni Taihan
23. Mamar Ibni Harith	23. Mo'az Ibni Afra
24. Wagid Ibni Abdullah	24. Birshr Ibni Bara
25. Zaid Ibn Ul Khattab	25. Ma'n Ibni Adi
26. Arqam Ibni Abi Arqam	26. Talha Ibni Zaid

Referring to this sacrifice of Ansar Allah said –

"And those who before them [before Muhajireen] made their abode [in Madina*] and (adopted) the faith, loved those who immigrated to them and have no desire in their hearts about that which was given to them [the Muhajireen] and they give them preference over themselves, even though they were in need of that." (59:9)*

Allah also praised them both and said:

"Verily those who believed and immigrated and strove hard and fought with their wealth and with their lives, and those who gave (them) asylum and help, they are the friends of each other." (8:72)

"And those who believed and emigrated and strove hard in the cause of Allah and those who gave them asylum and help, they are the true believers." (8:74)

One example of this sacrifice is that of Sa'd Ibnur Rabi who said to Abdur Rahman Ibni Auf,

"I am a rich man so I give you half of my wealth."

and when he gave the details then he said,

"Now the only thing remaining are my two wives, so if you want, I will divorce one of them and after Iddat you should marry her."

Abdur Rahman said,

"May Allah bless you in your wealth and family, I need none of these but show me the bazaar, and I can make my life."

He took him to the bazaar of the Jews of Banu Qanuqa. He started a small business there and soon he became a rich man.

Then in the 4th year after Hijrah when the Jews of Banu Nadeer conspired to assassinate the Prophet but the Prophet decided to let them migrate to Khaybar due to this approach of Abdullah Ibni Ubai, and the Prophet allowed each family to take a load of one camel with them and the remaining was confiscated. The Prophet said to Ansar,

> *"If you want, I will distribute amongst you and the Muhajireen. They will be living in your houses and if you will allow me to distribute this in Muhajireen and they will arrange their own houses and will leave yours."*

They said,

> *"Give all these to our brothers, the Muhajireen."*

MARRIAGE TO AAISHAH

As we have mentioned already in detail that the Prophet's first wife was Khadija and as long as she was alive the Prophet never married another, and when she died, Khaulah binti Hakeem the wife of Uthman Ibni Maz'oon (the fostering brother of the prophet), seeing the Prophet mired in grief and sorrow, advised him to marry. She also suggested Sawdah and Aaisha. After some time, the Prophet asked her if she would act as a matchmaker. She first went to Aaisha, but as she under word of her father was waiting for Jubair Ibni Mut'im. Khaulah went to Sawdah. She was a widow and later on the Prophet married her. Here, on the other hand, Abu Bakr was waiting for a word from Mut'im's family. It took time but later on the Prophet married Aaisha. Khadijah died in the 10th year of the Prophethood. Now, how old was Aaisha at the time of her marriage? Even though the wording in hadith of Bukhari is mentioned as nine, it was actually nineteen. When talking about numbers the Arabs, sometimes drop tens in an ongoing talk. So, when, for example Sabata Ashara was mentioned i.e.,17, if two people are talking casually and say, "sab'ata" they might not bother with "Ashara". So, she was 18 or 19 when the Prophet married her. Khatib Baghdadi also mentioned the same in the biography of Aaisha's sister Asma that Aaisha was younger than Asma by 10 years. Asma died in 73 after Hijrah at the age of 100 years which means at the time of Hijrah the age of Aishah was 17. So, at the time of marriage, she was 19. Aaisha died in 63 after Hijrah.

TAHWEELI QIBLAH

For about 13 years when the Prophet was in Makkah, he would face Bait Ul Maqdis in prayers, and he continued the practice when he migrated to Madinah for 16 or 17 months, as in *Riwayat* the month of Rajab and Shaban are mentioned. The Prophet went to see Bishr Ibni Bara Ibni Maroor in Banu Sal'. Ummi Bishr made some food. In the meantime, the time for Zuhr prayer came so the Prophet started leading the prayer. When he had prayed two *Rakat* and was standing up for the third, angel Jibril came and ordered him to change his direction from "Baitul Maqdis" to "Bait Ullah" in Makkah.

Allah said,

> *"Indeed, we have seen (have been seeing) your turning of face towards the heaven, so for sure we shall turn you to a "Qiblah" that shall please you, so turn your face in the direction of Masjid Ul Haram." (2:144)*

So, the Prophet turned his face towards the direction of Makkah. This required a turn of almost 180 degrees. Ten Sahabah were standing behind the Prophet and they all turned around as well. Now the case is that these 10 Sahabah behind Prophet were in the front and the Prophet as Imam was in the back, so how it worked? At that time walking and talking in prayer was allowed in certain circumstances, so the Prophet came to the front and they moved to the back. After "Salam" the Prophet neither told them why he changed the direction nor did any Sahabi ask him, as they knew that Deen is what the Prophet is doing.

Also, they were aware of that abrogation of rules is a known fact in "Shariah" even though Ikramah and Hasan Basri said,

> *"This was the first rule that was ever changed. The Prophet mentioned all these 10 Sahabah by name one by one that they are in Jannah (paradise)."*

They are:

Abu Bakr,

Umar,

Uthman,

Ali,

Saeed Ibni Zaid,

S'ad Ibni Abi Waqas,

Talha Ibni Ubaid Ullah,

Zubair,

Abdur Rahman Ibni Auf,

Abu Ubaidah Ibn Ul Jarrah.

They are known as "Al-Ashara al Mubashsharah" i.e., Ten people who received the happy news of Jannah.

Now this *Tahweel* took place during Zuhr, but whenever people received the news, they recorded the time they started facing the new direction, which is why the people of Qaba recorded the time as Fajr because they received this news at that time. Some Sahabah said "Asr" time as they received it then.

When the Prophet was in Makkah the people of Makkah used to say that he claimed to be the follower of Ibrahim, but he does not face his *Qiblah*, and the Jews and Christians were saying he opposes our *Deen* but facing our *Qiblah*. But when the direction was changed, Allah told the Prophet,

> *"Now they will object to you in a different way."*

Allah said,

> *"Soon the fools will say, 'What has turned them from their "Qiblah" which they used to face?' Say, 'To Allah belongs east and west." (2:142)*

START OF AZAN FOR PRAYER

Abdullah Ibni Umar says that the Prophet asked his *Sahabah* how to call people for prayer in *Jama'at*? Some of them suggested ringing a bell like the Christians. Others proposed blowing a horn like the Jews. The Prophet didn't like those ways and the people went home. Then Abdullah Ibni Zaid Ibni Abdi Rabbihi came and told the Prophet about his dream wherein he saw someone walking by and holding a horn in his hands. He asked him for that either as a gift or for a price. He asked me about its use and he told him,

> *"We will blow it to call people for prayer."*

He said,

"Should I not tell you something better than this?"

And then he taught him the azan. Afterwards a few Sahabah came and told the Prophet about similar dreams they had had. The Prophet asked them if they knew who the man was.

They said,

"Allah and His Messenger know the best."

He said,

"This was Jibril who came in your dreams, and then came to me and told me all this."

So, for the next prayer the Prophet asked Abdullah to stand besides Bilal giving him those words to pronounce, as he had a loud voice.

FASTING AND *ZAKAT*

Fasting is a known practice in almost every religion.

Allah said,

"O you who believed! Fasting is prescribed for you as it was prescribed for those who were before so you may become pious." (2:183)

This fasting for Muslims is prescribed in the month of Ramadan. This order also came in the second year after Hijrah.

ZAKAT

In Makkah *zakat* was not a prescribed practice but still Sahabah used to do charity. The rich used to help the poor to the best of their abilities. That's why we find the word *zakat* in Makki Surahs as well.

They used to give more than what they were obligated to give as a mandatory *zakat* later on. The Prophet called *Zakat*.

"*Qintaratul Islam*",

The treasury of Islam. *Zakat* is as important in financial rituals in Islam as prayer is in physical worship. The Prophet said,

> "*No prayer for one who does not give zakat, which means prayer will not avail such a person a reward.*"

Zakat is a purification of one's wealth and a sanctification of his nature.

Allah said,

> "*Take from their wealth the charity to purify them and to sanctify them with that.*" (9:103)

GHAZAWAT AND *SARAYA* (EXPEDITIONS)

Ghazwa technically means an expedition the Prophet himself went on, while *Sariyah* is an expedition arranged by the Prophet but he did not go. Later on, sometime the word *Ghazwa* was used for *Sariyah* and vice versa. Islamically, there are two specific words used for this purpose and these are *Jihad* and *Qital*.

Literally *jihad* means strive hard, and *jihad* means strive hard for any lawful noble cause, but to counter a wrongdoing to Muslims and Islam or Islamic state and to defend is extraordinarily noble. Therefore, mostly this word or form is used in this meaning while the word *Qital.* means fight, but if the fight is to defend Islam, Muslims and Islamic state, then *Qital.* is synonymous with to *jihad* - so if *Qital.* is for the aforesaid purpose then that is Jihad, otherwise that will be *Qital.* only and any lawful effort or striving hard for a noble cause is *jihad*, which has different types and one of that which is the more important one, is fight in the cause of Allah.

DAWAT AND JIHAD

In Islam *Dawat* is *Jihad* and *Jihad* is *Dawat*. *Dawat* means call towards Allah and His *Deen*. For this purpose, Allah sent all the Messengers. Prophet Mohammad is called *Da'e*, a caller towards Allah.

Allah says,

> *"O Prophet, we have sent you as a shahid (teacher) giver of glad tidings, one who warns and as one who invites to Allah by His leave and as a lamp spreading light." (33:45-46)*

Then the Prophet is the last and final Prophet of Allah. While people will still need someone calling them towards Allah, so his *ummah* [his followers] are bound to perform this duty.

Allah said,

> *"There may be an ummah calling towards good, enjoining good and preventing vice, and believe in Allah." (3:104)*

Now this call towards Allah is the call of Islam. So, one has to convey the message, convince a person, and convert him to Islam. This is a *jihad* as well.

Jihad is incumbent upon Muslims but it has its own prerequisites, conditions, and limits, which in brief means only when it becomes inevitable and unavoidable. Then when it is launched and a person or a group that has submitted to Islam, then there is no *jihad* against him. So eventually it took the shape of *Dawat*. And as Islam basically insists upon peace and does not encourage fighting or allow forcible conversion, if the enemy is inclined towards peace, then Muslims may incline to that as well.

Allah says,

> *"And if they inclined to peace, you also incline to it and put your trust in Allah." (8:61)*

Allah also said,

> *"And if anyone of the polytheists sought your protection then grant him the protection, so he may hear the words of Allah." (9:6)*

It means in the battlefield or otherwise if someone sought asylum, grant it to him and maybe he will hear Islam and accept it. But conversion by force is not allowed nor appreciated.

Allah said,

> *"There is no coercion [compulsion] in Deen." (2:256)*

This is another issue that if someone accepts Deen by force even, he must be treated as a Muslim.

Once in Makkah when the Makkans were torturing the Muslims, Abdur Rahman Ibni Awf said Ibni Abi Waqas Miqdar and Qadamah Ibni Maz'oon asked the Prophet if they could retaliate and fight. The Prophet said,

> *"No, be patient and stable and do not get in arguments with them as the situation is not suitable for that."*

Also, in Makkah they did not have neither a state or the upper hand, but when they came to Madinah, the Prophet established a state and a system. They were still poor there, and the people of Makkah were not leaving them alone nor sparing them. They used to instigate the surrounding areas against the Muslims to attack them and to cause them trouble. They themselves also used to invade their pastures and to take their cattle. When the Prophet heard of an uprising in the surrounding areas, he would send an expedition consisting mostly of the immigrants led by one of his own close cousins or uncles, like Sariyah of Abdullah Ibni Jah'sh and Hamzah. So, nobody may say that he is causing some unrest to Ansar who got them settled there.

So, then the Prophet decided that enough is enough and now we can and have to retaliate, and even to start a preemptive attack. These details we will talk about later on, Insha'Allah. But let's see when the basic concept of Jihad was given in Islam.

In this regard we can say that the basic concept is given in Surat Ul Hajj,

> *"Permission is given to those who have been fought (war is imposed on them) because they have been wronged and surely Allah is able to help them (give them victory). Those who have been expelled from their homes unjustly only because they said "Our Lord is Allah." (22:39-40)*

This Surah is Makki, but the basic concept of *jihad* is given there, even though, some scholars said these Ayat are Madani, as in Makkah there was no fight. But we say these Ayat are regarding this very concept to make them ready for that.

The Prophet sent a few expeditions before the historical battle of Badr. These were as follows:

SEIFUL BAH'R

Seven months after Hijrah in Ramadan, first year after Hijrah (623 after Jesus) the Prophet sent an expedition consisting of 30 horsemen under the command of his uncle Hamzah to face a caravan of Quraish coming from Sham. This caravan consisted of 300 people including Abu Jahl. When the caravan arrived in the Eis city of Juhainah, they faced this expedition and both were close to start combat, but Majdi Ibni Amr al Juhain, who was a friend and ally to both sides, intervened. In their expedition Abu Marthad Kinaz Ibni Hussain was holding a big white flag, the first ever of its type in Islam, as before that at the time of Hijrah Buraidah Ibn Ul Haseeb put his turban on a stick as a flag when the Prophet was entering Madinah.

RABIGH

In Shawwal first year (623 years after Jesus) an expedition of sixty Muslims under the command of Ubaidah Ibn Ul Harith Ibni Abdul Muttalib (the Prophet's cousin) was sent by the Prophet to come across a caravan of Quraish consisting of two hundred horsemen under the leadership of Abu Sufyan Ibni Harb. Mistah Ibni Athatha was holding a white flag of the Muslim army. The Quraish were taking rest to the left of the route to let their rides grazing in the fields. Here, both sides brought out their swords. It is said that they exchanged arrow volleys. Also, it is said that only Sad Ibni Abi Waqas shot an arrow at the Quraish. This was the first ever arrow shot at enemies in Islam. Batni Rabigh is 10 miles from Juhfah. In their caravan there were two Quraish people who were Muslims looking for a way out to get into Madina so they had joined this caravan and so they joined the Muslims and settled in Madina. These two men are known as Utbah Ibni Ghazwan Al Mazini and Miqdad Ibni Amr al Bahrani.

SARIYAH KHARRARS

In the Zul Qadah year, one after Hijrah (May 623) under the leadership of Sad Ibni Abi Waqas, this expedition of 20 people was sent to attack a trade caravan of Quraish. The aforementioned Miqdad was holding a white flag. The prophet told them not to go ahead of Kharrar. They were headed towards that place, but he instructed them to hide at night as a strategy. They arrived there on the 5th day, but the caravan had already passed.

GHAZWATUL ABAWA (GHAZWAT WADDAN)

In Safar in the second year after Hijrah the Prophet himself went out with 70 riders to catch a caravan of Quraish and Damrah. It is also said that he went after Quraish but he caught a caravan of Banu Damrah and there a treaty between Damrah and the Prophet took place. At that time Amr Ibni Makhshi was the chief of that tribe. The text of this agreement was:

> *This is a document from Mohammad the Messenger of Allah concerning Bani Damrah in which he established them safe and secure, in their wealth and lives. They can expect support from the Muslims unless they oppose the religion of Allah. They are also expected to respond positively in case the Prophet sought their help.*

This was the first time the Prophet ever went out of Madinah for 15 days. Sa'd Ibni Obadah was appointed at Madinah for these days as Amir. Hamzah was holding the army flag, which was white.

GHAZWAH BUWAT

In Rabi-Ul Awwal in the second year (623) the Prophet went with 200 people to come across a caravan of Quraish, which consisted of 1,500 camels loaded with various goods. There were 100 people of Quraish in this caravan. Umayyah Ibni Khalaf was one of them. When he arrived at Jabali Buwat from the Rudwa side, he found that the caravan had already passed. In this battle, Sa'd Ibni Abi Waqas was holding a white flag. In the Prophet's absence Sa'd Ibni Mu'ad was managing affairs at Madinah.

GHAZWAT SAFWAN

It is also called Ghazwat Badr. It took place in the first of Rabi Ul Awwal second year (September 623) under the leadership of Kuraz Ibni Jabir al Fihri. Some people attacked a pasture in Madina and stole some cattle belonging to the people of Madina. The Prophet took some 70 people to go after these thieves. He arrived in Safwan Valley but Kuraz and his people already had gone. This time Ali was holding a white flag and Zaid Ibni Haritha was Amir at Madina. This Kuraz later on accepted Islam. He was sent by the Prophet after the Arniyeen, who killed the camel guard of Baitul Mall and stole the camels. Kuraz was martyred in 8th Hijr at the conquest of Makkah time. Ibni Ishaq says this *Ghazwa* happened after Ushairah, but that is not right.

GHAZWATUL USHAIRAH

In Jumada Ath Thani or in Jumada Al Oola in the second year after Hijra (October 623), The Prophet took a group of 150 or 200 *Muhajireen* to come across a caravan of Quraish coming from Makkah. He appointed Abu Salamah Abdul Asad al Makhzoomi at Madina. He gave a white flag to Hamzah in this *Ghazwa*. When the Prophet arrived in Ushairah, the caravan had already passed. Ushairah is an area where

Banu Mudlij used to live. Then, after some time, the Prophet came out to face this caravan coming back. The Prophet entered into an agreement with Banu Mudlij and Banu Damarah.

Here in this place, Ali slept over dust and his body got dirty, so, the Prophet titled him Abu Turab. This caravan of Quraish consisted of 1000 camels fully loaded under the leadership of Abu Sufyan with 39 others from amongst them. Makhrama Ibni Naufal and Amr Ibn Ul Aas were there as well. This caravan had a value of 50,000 dinars.

SARIYAH ABDULLAH IBNI JAHSH AL ASADI

On this occasion, the Prophet ordered Abu Ubaidah Ibn Ul Jarrah to get ready but when it was the time for his departure, he broke down in tears looking at the Prophet because of how difficult it was to leave his beloved so the prophet then ordered Abdullah Ibni Jahsh Al Asadi to lead the expedition. In this expedition there were 12 *Muhajireen* with Abdullah. Each two were riding a camel by number. This was in Rajab second year (624 AD). This expedition is called "Nakhleh" also as they were going to an area of thick gardens of date palm trees.

The Prophet wrote a letter for Abdullah and told him not to open it until they had been traveling for two days, then follow the instructions, but do not force the others for this. In letter, it was written that after reading it, they were to go forth until they arrived in "Nakhleh" (a place between Makkah and Tarif), Sit there and inquire about Quraish, what they are doing and planning for. Abdullah told his fellows about the contents of this letter, and they agreed wholeheartedly. Then when they arrived there at a Mines place, Sa'd Ibni Abi Waqas and Utbah Ibni Ghazwan lost their camels so they stayed behind to look for them, while Abdullah went forth with the rest.

When they arrived in "Nakhleh", they saw a caravan of Quraish bringing skins, bears, and raisins from Taif side. In this caravan were Amr Ibn Ul Hadhrami, Uthman Ibni Mughirah, his brother Nofal, Hakam Ibni Keesan, and a few others.

The Muslims determined that it was the last day of Rajab (the sacred Month) and fighting was not allowed but tomorrow they could enter into the limits of Haram so they agreed to face them. One of them targeted Amr Ibn Ul Hadhrami with his bow and arrow.

This was the first ever person killed by Muslims. Then they attacked the caravan and captured Uthman and Hakam while Nofal ran away and escaped.

Abdullah Ibni Jahsh Reserved 1/5 of the spoils for the national exchequer and distributed 4/5 amongst his fellows, as Shariah says. These were the first-ever spoils of war in Islam and Uthman and Hakam were the first prisoners of war by Muslims. Miqdad Ibni Amr had captured Hakam. The Prophet called him to Islam and he accepted. This Hakam was the slave of Hisham, the father of Abu Jahl. This Hakam was martyred in Ghazwa "Bir Ma'oonah".

After a few days Sa'd and Utbah, who had stayed behind to look for their lost camels came to Madina. When Abdullah came back along with the camel's caravan and the two prisoners of war and related the whole story, the Prophet said,

> *"Look! I had not ordered you to fight, especially in a sacred month."*

On the other side, the Quraish exploited this incident as a propaganda against Islam and the Prophet because they had desecrated the sacred month. People used to ask the Muslims about the sacred months and the fights and killing therein only to push them to a dead end. So, Allah said,

> *[When] they ask you about the sacred month [they are asking] about fighting therein. Say, "fighting there in is a big thing [violation], but prevention from the path of ALLAH and to disbelieve in him and [prevention] from Masjidi Haram and to turn out its inhabitants therefrom is bigger than this [fighting] in the eyes of ALLAH. And fitnah is worse than killing." (2:217)*

Now, this was an immediate answer to them to counter their propaganda, that if the Muslims have done one violation, then they have done a few and these are bigger violations than those committed by the Muslims.

The Prophet then released the two captives and paid blood money to the family of Amr Ibn Ul Hadhrami.

This caused a fear to the people of Makkah about how they would carry on their trade as Madina was a major trade route. Also, they thought, these Muslims came that far, they kill, they take prisoners, and take away the caravans also. This aggravated their enmity.

Permission to fight:

In Shaban second year, Allah allowed Muslims to fight:

> *"And fight in the path of Allah those who fight you, but transgress not the limits. Indeed, Allah does not like the transgressors. And kill them wherever you find them and turn them out from where they have turned you out (or as they have turned you out) and fitnah is worse than killing. And fight them not at Masjid al Haram [inside the limits of Haram] unless they fight you there. Then, if they fought you there, then, kill them. Such is the recompense of the disbelievers. But if they ceased, then, Allah is Oft-Forgiving, Most Merciful. And fight them until there is no more fitnah and Deen (control) is for Allah.*

Then, if they ceased, then there may not be any transgression, but only against the wrongdoers." (2:190-193)

Then, the Ayat of Surah Mohammad revealed,

"So, when you meet the disbelievers, smite [their] necks and when you hurt them, then bind their bounds firmly [catch them as captives], then [after that], either [set them free] for generosity [without ransom] or for ransom, but after that the war has laid down its burden [after ceasefire]. This is [the rule]." **(47:4)**

We say that this Ayat of Surah Mohammad is the first to offer the concept of ransom. All these happenings, events, and expeditions presaged the famous "Ghazwa – I - Badr."

GHAZWA-I-BADR

We mentioned before about Ghazwat Ul Ushairah that the Prophet led 150 people to come across a caravan of Quraish, but before their arrival at Ushairah, the caravan already had passed. But when this caravan returned from Sham, the Prophet once again planned to meet it. By doing so, the Prophet was sending a message to the Quraish that now they would not keep quiet about what they (the Quraish) were doing.

"We will stop you. We will come across and we will retaliate so you should stop your plotting conspiracies against us, attacking our pastures and taking away our cattle. Also, stop instigating the surrounding tribes against us, otherwise you have to face the repercussions."

The caravan of Quraish had escaped when it was going to Sham. Coming back, it had 1000 camels fully loaded with all kinds of goods. 40 people were with this caravan. Amr Ibn Ul Aas and Makhrama Ibni Nawfal were among these forty. Abu Sufyan was the chief. The Prophet sent a group of Sahabah to catch this caravan. They had some weapons with them for defense.

CARAVAN COMING BACK

When he came to know this, Abu Sufyan sent Dam Dam Ibni Amr Ghifari to Makkah before to inform Quraish of the situation. He paid him 20 *Misqal* in gold also.

Dam Dam ripped up his shirt and slit the nose or ears of his camel to show and portray the bitterness of the situation the caravan is facing. The Quraish of Makkah took it as a challenge and started preparing for a war.

PEOPLE GOT READY:

All known people were getting ready except Abu Lahab. He gave 4,000 dirhams to Harith Ibni Hisham, the brother of Abu Jahl, to go on his behalf. Later on, he was killed in battle by Umar Ibn Ul Khattab. From Makkah, the only tribe that did not go was Banu Adi. Umayyah Ibni Khalaf was trying to stay behind as Sad Ibni Muaz had told him he would be killed. So, he was sure that the Prophet had told him so, and it would happen. Abu Jahl reproached and upbraided him with cowardice. So, he went and was killed.

First 1300 people prepared to go, but later on, 300 people of Banu Zuhrah changed their mind, so,1000 people stayed away. They had 700 camels with them and 100 horses. This cavalry and 600 infantries were coated in iron coats. The infantry was led by Sa'ib Ibni Yazid, who later on accepted Islam and was a great *Sahabi*. Imam Shafi was from his offspring.

QURAISH AND KINANAH

The Quraish also had a feud with the Kinanah, but Allah willed to bring them out, so Satan came to them in shape of Suraqah Ibni Malik Kinani, their chief, telling them,

> "*I will support you against the Muslims.*"

Allah said,

> "*And when Satan made their deeds seem fair to them and said, 'No one of mankind can overcome you this day and verily I am your neighbor [Protector], but when both the groups saw each other [came in front of one another), he turned on his heel [turned his back] and ran away and said, 'I have nothing to do with you people. Verily, I see what you see not. Verily, I fear Allah and Allah is severe in punishment." (8:48)*

QURAISH AND THEIR NUMBER

The Makkans were proud of their number and weapons as Allah said,

> "*And be not like those who come out of their homes boastfully and showing to people [their power and strength] and hindering [people] from the path of Allah,*

while Allah was encircling what they were doing."
(8:47)

Twelve chiefs had the responsibility of feeding their army. They were Abu Jahl, Utbah, Shaibah, Hakeem Ibni Hizam, Abbas Ibni Abdul Muttalib, Abul- Bukhtari, Zama'ah Ibn Ul Aswad, Obai Ibni Khalaf, Umayyah Ibni Khalaf, Nadr Ibn Ul Harith, Nabeeh Ibn Ul Hajjaj, and Munnabih Ibn Ul Hajjaj.

Allah said,

"Verily, those who disbelieved they spend their wealth to hinder people from the path of Allah [against Islam], so, they will spend it, then, it will be an anguish for them and, then, they will be overcome [defeated]." (8:36)

These people were proceeding very fast through Osfan, Qudaid, and Juhfah, when they received a message from Abu Sufyan that he had taken out the caravan safe.

The story was that Abu-Sufyan, when came close to the surrounding of **Madina**, asked Majdi Ibni Amr near Badr,

"Have you seen the people of Mohammad?"

He said,

"I have not seen any stranger and yes, I had seen two camel riders here. They rested here and made their camels sitting here."

When Abu Sufyan broke a few pieces of their dung and saw the date stone pieces in it, he knew that these were the fellows of Mohammad. So, he left the main route and took off towards the shore, and therefrom he sent Qais Ibni Imru Ul Qais to Makkah to tell them that the caravan has made its escape, so, there is no need to come, but Abu Jahl said,

"No! We will go to Badr singing there, slaughtering camels, and drinking wine. This will give a message to Mohammad and to his supporters."

Akhnas, the chief of Banu Zuhrah took his people back. Later on, it was proved that he did good. Of the Quraish, Banu Adi also did not take part in this mission.

THE MUSLIM ARMY

Now, when the Prophet learned that Abu Sufyan had taken the caravan towards the shore, while the Makkah Army is coming towards Madina through the known route, he asked Sahabah,

> "Which way should we go? To catch the caravan or to face the army?"

Now, as they were not in full pledge preparation to face the army, some of them they should go after the caravan, so, they can catch them easily as they are few in number and have no weapons so they could get a good amount of wealth as well, which they needed.

Allah said,

> "As your Lord caused you to come out of your home [city] with truth and a part of the believers were disliking it." **(8:05)**

INSPIRING RESPONSE OF SAHABAH

When the Prophet told them that they had to face the army, then, the Muhajireen made very encouraging statements. After Abu Bakr and Umar, Miqdad Ibni Amr said,

> "O Prophet of Allah! Go ahead towards what Allah has told you, we are with you. By Allah, we are not like Bani Israel who said to Musa, go you along with your Lord and fight you both, we are sitting here."

This speech by Miqdad was so inspiring that the Prophet said to people speak out. Actually, he was looking toward to Ansar, what they say, Sa'd Ibni Muaz rose up and said,

> "Maybe, O Messenger of Allah, you mean us."

The Prophet said,

> "Yes."

Then, Sa'd said,

> "We believed in you and we have seen that what you brought us is the truth. We have given you our word that we will listen and obey. Whatever you will decide, we are with you. By God, if you lead us towards the sea, we shall jump into it and not even one of us will stay behind. We will stand firmly; we are solid, stable people. We hope Allah will show you such deeds of ours as you may not be disappointed but may be proud of. If you order us to climb to the clouds, we will."

> The Prophet became happy and said, "Go ahead, as Allah has given me a happy news of victory."

In a place known as "Beir Abi Utbah", the Prophet counted his army. The number was 313. He said, this was the number of the army of Talut (Saul). Allah gave them victory over the army of Jalut (Goliath).

NUMBER OF ANSAR AND MUHAJIREEN

As we have said before, the Prophet was not sending Ansar in any expedition, but this was the first *Ghazwa*, the Prophet looked at them, and they joined the army.

This was because at the time of Bai'at Ul Aqabah, the wording was,

> "Come to Madinah and we shall help you there by hook or crook",

or because before this, the challenges were not that big, but now it was.

In this battle, the number of Ansar was 207, and the rest were the Muhajireen. They had only 70 camels and two horses. One was that of Marthad Ibni Abi Marthad Al Ghanawi and the other one that of Miqdad Ibni Amr.

The Prophet was wearing his breastplate named "Zat Ul Fudool" and his sword "Ad'b."

As the people took this attack of Mushrikeen as a challenge to their honor. That is why some young boys also came out to join, but the Prophet sent them back as they were underage. They were Osamah Ibni Zaid, Rafi Ibni Khadij, Bara Ibni Aazib, Osaid Ibni Zuhair, Zaid Ibni Arqam, Zaid Ibni Thabit, Omair Ibni Abi Waqas, Anas Ibni Malik, Abdullah Ibni Umar, and Jabir Ibni Abdullah.

Omar Ibni Abi Waqas, the brother of Sa'd Ibni Abi Waqas, was trying not to be seen to the prophet, so he was hiding. The Prophet saw him but when he told him go home, he started crying so the Prophet allowed him to stay. He was sixteen.

SAHABAH WHO WERE REGISTERED, BUT GIVEN DIFFERENT DUTIES

Though the number of Sahabah was 313, but nine out of this number were not there in the battlefield. They were given other duties; the duties are as follows:

1- Uthman Ibni Affan stayed at Madina to take care of his wife Ruqayyah, the daughter of the Prophet of Allah, who was on deathbed and nobody else was there to take her care. She died before the return of the Prophet from Badr as Zaid Ibni Haritha says,

   "The Prophet sent me to Makkah to give the happy news of victory in Badr to people in Madina, so, when I entered Madina, I saw people coming back from Jannat Ul Baqee after the burial of Ruqayyah."

2- Abu Umamah Thalabah came ready to go, but the Prophet after registering him in that army, sent him back to take care of his aged, ailing mother.

3- Abu Lubabah Abdul Munzir was left behind to take care of Madina.

4- Asim Ibni Adi was appointed as caretaker over Awali Al Madina i.e., the outskirts of Madina.

5- The Prophet sent Harith Ibni Hatib Amri to keep an eye in *Banu* Amr Ibni Awf as the Prophet received some doubtful news about them. The Prophet sent him back from "Rauhaa" (a place).

6,7- Khawwat Ibni Jubair and Harith Ibnus Shammah both were sent back from Safra as they fell sick.

8,9- Saeed Ibni Zaid and Talha Ibni Ubaid Ullah both were sent to find out the news about Quraish.

All these aforementioned people were given their due share from the spoils of war as Mujahideen.

ARRANGEMENTS

The Prophet arranged flags for different groups. The big one was that of the Muhajireen and Mus'ab Ibni Omair was holding that. The flag of Khazraj tribe was in the hand of Khabbab Ibn Ul Munzir while the flag of Aws was with Sa'd Ibni Muaz. It is said that a black flag was there in the hand of Ali, named "Oqab". This was actually Aaisha's scarf.

The Mushrikeen also had their flags, one in the hand of Abu Aziz, the brother of Mus'ab Ibni Omair, a second one in the hand of Nadr Ibn Ul Harith, and a third one in the hand of Talha Ibni Abi Talha.

BADR

This was the 17th of Ramadan when the two armies came face to face.

Allah said,

> "When you people were on the nearest side of the valley [towards **Madina**] and they were on the farther side and the caravan was lower than you [onshore side] and if you people would have to make a meeting appointment [of time and place] to face one another for sure you would have failed therein, but [you faced one another] that Allah might accomplish a matter already decreed by." (8:42)

The Prophet and Abu Bakr both were walking around when they met an old man. They asked him,

> "Do you know anything about the Quraish?"

He said,

> "When you introduce yourselves, I will tell you."

They said,

> "You should tell us, then we will introduce ourselves."

The old man said that Quraish came out on such and such day and now they will be in such and such place and Mohammad came out on such and such day. Then, he asked them,

> "And where do you come from?"

The Prophet said, from

> "Al Ma" (means water).

The old man was thinking and saying,

> "From the water of Iraq?"

The Prophet also sent Ali, Zubair and Sa'd Ibni Abi Waqas to find out about Makkans that where they are. They got two young people and brought them. The Prophet was praying. Sahabah asked them,

> "You are the companions of Abu Sufyan?"

They said,

> "We are water carriers."

Sahabah slapped them, so they said yes. The Prophet finished his prayer. He said,

> "When they told you the truth, you beat them and when they told the lie, you spared them."

The Prophet asked them.

> "Where are the Quraish?"

They said,

> "Behind the hilltop."

He asked them about their number. They said they didn't know. The Prophet said,

> "How many camels have they slaughtered every day?"

They said,

> "One day, nine; the other day, 10."

The Prophet said, then, their number is 900 to 1000. Then, he asked them about their famous people who have come. They said,

> "Utbah, Shaibah, Abul Bukhtari, Abu Jahl, Hakim Ibni Hizam, Nawfal Ibni Khuwaylid, Harith Ibni Aar, Tuaimah Ibni Adi, Nadr Ibni Harith, Zama'ah Ibni Aswad,

Umayyah Ibni Khalaf, Nabeeh Munnabih, Sahl Ibni Amr, Amr Ibni Abdi Wud."

The Prophet said to his people,

"Makkah has thrown its liver pieces to you."

QURAISH ARRIVED IN BADR BEFORE MUSLIMS

The Quraish made a basin to catch water. They got that part of the land which was solid dirt. The Muslims were tired so they fell asleep and when they woke up, they saw they could not approach the water and also, they missed the solid part of the land and got the sandy area so they cannot run as this is white sand and it is slippery, so, they were worried.

Allah said,

*"[Remember] when He [Allah] covered you with slumber as a tranquil from him and sent on you water [rain] from the sky to purify you therewith and to take away the Rij'z [whispering] of Satan and to strengthen your heart and to make your feet firm." **(8:11)***

This was such a great mercy from Allah which became the foundation of victory because the rainfall provided water to them. They filled up the pots they had. The sandy land became hard, while on the other side, it became muddy and slippery. The slumber also took away their worries and they gained courage and energy.

At night, The Prophet was praying, making *Dua* and doing *zikr* of Allah.

"Ya Hayyu Ya Qayyum",

And when the Prophet led Sahabah in Fajr prayer, then, he inspired his Sahabah in his speech for Jihad.

THE PROPHET ACCEPTED KHABBAB'S OPINION

Khabbab Ibn Ul Munzir asked the Prophet about the place he stayed, whether it was *Wahi* or his personal point of view. He asked because if it was *Wahi*, then there was no room for anybody to say something but if it was the Prophet's opinion, then he had given them the right to give their opinion. So, the Prophet said,

> *"This is my own opinion. Khabbab said if we will make arrangements in that such and such place, I know there the depth of water, we can dig well and obtain water."*

So, the Prophet accepted this advice.

SA'D'S SUGGESTION

Sa'd Ibni Muaz said that a trellis was set for the Prophet as protection. It was to be to the back of the Muslim army. In case of victory everything would be all right, but Allah forbid if any defeat happened then the Prophet would go back to Madina and be safe as all the people in Madina who stayed behind are loved him as much as they did.

A squad under the leadership of Sa'd was guarding the Prophet's trellis. This trellis was also considered a control office and headquarters as well. Once Sa'd was asked,

> "Who is the bravest person?"

He said,

> "Abu Bakr, as on that night he jumped over a few people who tried to go close to the trellis where the Prophet was staying."

That night, as Sahabah were very tired from their long march. So, they slept a sound and refreshing sleep that took away their fatigue and their worries as well. The Prophet was praying at night and making *Dua*.

That night, some Quraish also came to the Muslim side to drink water. Sahabah caught them. The Prophet said,

> "Let them go,"

And later on, those who drank there died, except Hakeem Ibni Hizam who accepted Islam later on.

Quraish sent Omair Ibni Wahab Jumahi to find out the size of the Muslim Army. He came back and told them that there were approximately 300 people with 70 camels and two horses, but swore their only shields are their swords so none of them could be killed, but after he killed one of the Quraish.

He said,

> "I saw them looking for death. So, when they will kill from you 300 people an equal to their number then how will be your living so think about that."

This man later on accepted Islam. In Uhud, he was with the Prophet of Allah.

HAKEEM ASKED OTBAH TO AVOID WAR

Hakeem Ibni Hizam came to Utbah because he was the elder and he wanted Otbah's name to be mentioned in a good way for a long time. Utbah asked him,

> *"What you mean?"*

Hakeem said,

> *"Take people back and pay the blood money of your ally, Amr Ibn Ul Hadhrami."*

After that Utbah addressed the Quraish about fighting with Mohammad, saying that they are getting nothing as from both sides they were killing your own uncles and nephews and then they would be forced to see the faces of the killers forever. So, he said,

> *"Go back and leave him with his business; if some other people killed him so you get rid of him and if not, so at least you will not be in bad shape."*

> *"Furthermore,"*

he said,

> *"If this is a cowardice, then attribute this to me, even though, I am not a coward."*

Hakeem said,

> *"Then I went to Abu Jahl and told him what Utbah said. He already had brought out his armor [iron breastplate], rubbing it with olive oil. He said it means Utbah was afraid. By God, I will not go back until he gave a*

> *decree between us and Mohammad. Utbah knew his son Abu Huzaifa is with Mohammad, so he doesn't want his son to be killed."*

When Utbah heard about the remarks given by Abu Jahl, he said,

> *"This coward blames me; now, we will see whether I am the coward or he is."*

Abu Jahl was a cunning man and knew how to plot, how to instigate, and how to set fires. He told Aamir Ibn Ul Hadhrami (the murdered ally of Quraish)'s brother that his ally Utbah wants to get rid of the battle, so he should go and ask for retribution for his brother. Aamir opened his belts, shouted, and cried,

> *"Waa Amraah!"*

Thanks to this plot of Abu Jahl, the Quraish were provoked to fight. So, Utbah said to Omair Ibni Wahab, now go and fight. He brought forth 100 cavalry and launched an attack.

The Prophet has already told his Sahabah not to start fighting without his permission. When he fell asleep, Abu Bakr told him that they have already started attack. In his slumber, Allah showed him the number of Quraish little than what they were.

> *"And [remember] when Allah was showing them to you in your dream as a few, and if he would have shown them to you a lot [then] for sure you would have been discouraged and disputed in making a decision. But Allah saved. Verily, He is All-Knower of what is in the people's hearts. And [remember] when he showed them to you when you met each other, as a few in your eyes and he made you [seem] as a few in their eyes, so, that Allah may accomplish a matter already ordained [decreed]." (8:43-44)*

The Prophet woke up and came out of his trellis. He organized the ranks and made *Dua*:

> "O Allah, these people of Makkah have come with a great pride, showing their enmity to you and belying your Messenger, so, O Allah, help me as you have promised me."

THE ARMY FACE TO FACE

At the very start, a slave of Umar named Maja came out to fight. He was shot by an arrow from Aamir Ibn Ul Hadhrami. This was the first *shaheed* of Badr. After him, the second *shaheed* was Haritha Ibni Suraqah Al-Ansari.

Aswad Ibni Abdul Asad al Makhzoomi from the Quraish side came out with a great pride, saying,

> "I promised to Allah that I would drink from the water basin of the Muslims (which means who can stop me from doing so) or I will die trying."

He came forward, Hamzah hit him with his sword on his back, and he fell on his back, but he was creeping on his back to throw himself in the basin to fulfill his oath. Hamzah caught him there and killed him. His brother Abdullah Ibni Abdul Asad was a very sincere Muslim. The Prophet once said, on the day of Judgement, Aswad would be the first one who would be given his file by the left hand while Abdullah will be the first one taking his file with by his right hand.

QURAISH VS. QURAISH

In the Arabian culture, face-to-face combat was the way that one to three people used to come out and challenge their opponents to fight. So, here also Utbah, his son Waleed, and his brother Shaibah came out and asked for a fight. Three people came out of the Muslims' side, but as they were covered in armor and helmets so they could not be known, therefore, these three people asked them about their identity. They gave their names as Abdullah Ibni Rawaha, Auf, Ansari, and Mua'awwaz Ansari. Now, as all three were from Ansar and not from Quraish, so, the Makkans said "No, not you, but our own cousins, the Quraish." They shouted, "Mohammad! Send to us our equals."

The Prophet named Ubaidah Ibn Ul Harith (the Prophet's cousin), Ali Ibni Abi Talib (his other cousin), and Hamzah (the Prophet's uncle), and they stood up and proceeded towards them. Again, they asked for their identity and when they said Ubaidah, Ali, and Hamzah, they said,

> *"This is ok."*

Utbah came towards Hamzah and Hamzah caught him with his sword and he was killed. Ali killed Waleed in an exchange of sword blows between Ubaidah and Shaibah and Ubaidah was injured severely in his leg and he fell down.

This Ubaidah was the most aged person in Muslim. Hamzah jumped towards Shaibah and killed him as well. Then, Hamzah and Ali both carried the injured Ubaidah. He asked the Prophet if he would go to Paradise if he died of his injuries. The Prophet said yes. Then he said,

> *"If Abu Talib were alive, he would be very happy with this sacrifice of mine as when the Quraish's elders came to him to hand over Mohammad to them,"*

Then, he said a verse that means,

"We will hand him over to you when we will forget about our wives and children and fight around him until we all get killed,"

In other words, over our dead bodies.

The verse was,

"Wa Nusallimuhu Hatta Nusari Hawlahu - wa Nazhalu un Abna'ina wal Hala'ili"

THE BATTLE

After this fight, The Prophet Came out of his trellis, he corrected the ranks. At that time, Siwad Ibni Aziyyah's open belly was out of the rank the Prophet touched that with his arrows unsharpened tip, and said,

"Be in line o Siwad."

He said,

"O Messenger of Allah! Allah has sent you for good, but you harmed me."

So, the Prophet opened his belly and offered him to take retribution. He hugged the Prophet and kissed his belly. The Prophet asked him that why he did? He said,

"Death is in front of us. So, I wished that my last time should be so that my body touches your body."

The Prophet made Dua for him.

The Prophet said to Sahabah if they inclined towards good, then, don't fight them. That night, the Prophet used to pray and make *Dua*. He said,

> "O Allah! If you cause this group to be killed, you will never be worshipped, never ever."

Allah says,

> "When you sought help of your Lord and he answered you, I will help you with one thousand angels coming in succession." (8:92)

And,

> "When you [O the Prophet!] said to the Believers, is it not enough for you that your Lord will help you with three thousand angels sent down. Yes, if you showed patience (stability) and avoided [cowardice], then, there will come to you right after this that your Lord will help you with five thousand angels having marks [or branding marks on those they hit]." (3:124-125)

The Prophet, after correcting the lines, went back to his trellis. He gave the Muslims a common *Shiiaar* (secret code word),

> "Ya Mansoura Ummah."

To Muhajireen, he gave the words,

> "Ya Bani Abdur Rahman."

To Aws,

> "Ya Bani Ubaid Ullah"

and to Khazraj,

> "Ya Bani Abdullah."

Using these codes, they could recognize one another as they were fully covered in armor.

Allah ordered the angels,

> *"I am with you, so, keep firm those who believed, I will cast fear in the heart of those who disbelieved." (8:12)*

THE SPIRIT OF MUSLIMS

As we said before that this battle came upon Muslims. They were not well-prepared for it, but now when it happened, they did not show any hesitation or weakness; rather, they showed their spirit of Iman to their utmost.

The Prophet said,

> *"Stand up for Jannah, whose width is the like of heaven and earth."*

Omair Ibn Ul Hammam said,

> *"Maybe I will get it."*

So, he threw the dates in his hands saying that to eat it, then, fight and get martyred is a long journey.

Awf Ibn Ul Harith asked the Prophet,

> *"Which act of a Muslim is too much liked to Allah in Jihad?"*

He replied,

> *"To put one's bare hands inside the enemies."*

He took off his armor and started fighting until he was martyred.

The Prophet picked up a hand full of pebbles and sand and threw it towards the Mushrikeen. Every one of them who got a particle of that was killed, injured, captured, or defeated.

Allah said,

> "So, you killed them not, but Allah killed them and you threw not when you did throw, but Allah threw that he might let the Believers get a good favor from him." (8:17)

The Prophet was reciting verse 45 of Surat Ul Qamar,

> "Their armies will be defeated and will turn their backs" (54:45)

ABUL BUKHTARI

The Prophet had mentioned some people of Quraish that they have been brought, as others reproached and upbraided them that you are coward afraid of death, otherwise, they were not ready to come. He mentioned Abul Bukhtari in particular and told his Sahabah not to kill him. He was the one who disagreed and led the social and economic boycott of Banu Hashim at Makkah and later on he was the one who broke it because it was wrong. At that time he said there are small children crying for food, and we were boycotting them. Majzar Ibni Ziyad saw him on a ride. "Junadah Ibni Mulaiha" was with him. Majzar told him that the Prophet said not to kill you. He asked,

> "And my colleague?"

Majzar said,

"There is no such immunity for him."

So, Abul Bukhtari said a verse which means,

"The son of a noblewoman will never leave his colleague alone until he either dies beside him or get him rescued."

He also said,

"I cannot bear the scolding of the women at Makkah."

UMAYYAH IBNI KHALAF AL JUMAHI

He was the master of Bilal at Makkah. He used to put Bilal over the hot sand, putting thorns and a big rock over his chest so he could not move. Also, his brother Ubai used to join him in this torture. This Umayyah had done some favor, to Abdur Rahman Ibni Awf some time back, and he was obliged to him. Abdur Rahman took him and his son to a hilltop to protect them, but Bilal saw them and he informed the Ansar about them. They rushed to the hilltop to get them. Abdur Rahman put his son in the front to defend his father, but he was killed. Abdur Rahman lay over Umayyah to protect him, but the people killed him beneath Abdur Rahman. Abdur Rahman's leg was very badly injured.

MU'AAZ AND MU'AWWAZ

Abdur Rahman Ibni Awf said,

> "In the rows, I saw two young boys to my right and left."

One of them asked me,

> "Uncle! Who is Abu Jahl? I said, why do you ask about him?"

He said,

> "We heard he says bad words against our Prophet and if we see him, then, by Allah, we will kill him."

The other one confirmed that as well. When I saw Abu Jahl, I indicated to them, that one is Abu Jahl. They both almost flew and attacked him and threw him down off his horse. Later on, everyone was feeling so happy that they were all boasting that they killed him themselves. The Prophet asked both,

> "Have you cleaned your swords?"

They said no. The Prophet looked at their swords and said,

> "Both of you killed him,"

But later on, Abu Jahl's belongings were given to Muaz Ibni Amr as Mua'awwaz Ibni Afra was martyred in that battle.

Muaz said,

> "When I hit him, his son Ikramah jumped at me and hit me on the shoulder. My hand got cut and was hanging by a strip of skin. As it was hindering my hits, I put my foot on it and pulled it off."

He says after my hit, Mua'awwaz jumped at him and hit him.

IBNI MASUD FOUND ABU JAHL

After that, the battle was over. The Prophet said,

> "Who will find out what happened to Abu Jahl?"

Ibni Masud said,

> "I found him. He was still alive and conscious. Ibni Masud put his foot over his neck and pulled his beard as he did the same to Ibni Masud in Makkah in Dar – an - Nadwah."

Ibni Masud said,

> "Has Allah has humiliated you today?"

He said not more than that people killed one of their own people but as he was hit by Muaz and Mua'awwaz, the two Ansar youngsters, and these Ansar were farmers, but if someone else had killed him and not these peasants. Then, he asked Ibni Masud,

> "Who earned this victory today?"

Ibni Masud said,

> "Allah and His Messenger."

Then he said to Ibni Masud,

> "O herdsman! You have climbed to a very hard [high] top peak today."

Ibni Masud chopped off his head and dragged it to the Prophet, making a hole in his nose and putting a rope through it. It is said that the Prophet said,

> "A nose for nose,"

but the head was extra as Abu Jahl had broken his nose in that incident of Darrun Nadwah and as his head was broken there as well, but it was broken only. That's why the Prophet said this.

The Prophet said three times:

> "*Allahu La ilaha illa Hoo: Allah, there is no God but only He.*"

Then, he said,

> "*Allahu Akbar: Allah is The Great, praise be to Allah, the one who made his promise true, He helped His slave and He defeated the groups alone.*"

ABBAS IBNI ABDUL MUTTALIB

Abbas was an uncle of the Prophet. He was his close friend as well. Even though he had not accepted Islam from the very beginning, he was always an alloy of the Prophet in Makkah even at Hajj time, when the Prophet would go to people in Mina and approach them for Islam. Abbas used to go with and he was the one who asked the people of Madina, at the time of the Aqabah Pledge,

> "*Will you be able to protect Him?*"

Also, he used to inform the Prophet from to time what was going on at Makkah. So, here in Badr, the Prophet said,

> "*If you people will come across Abbas in the field, then, kill him not, as he has come unwillingly.*"

Abu Huzaifah Ibni Utbah said,

> "We will be killing our own fathers and brothers sparing Abbas. By Allah, if I will see him, I shall kill him."

When the Prophet heard that, he said to Umar,

> "Would the face of the uncle of the Prophet would be hit also?"

Umar said,

> "Abu Huzaifah has become munafiq and if you will allow me, I will cut him."

When Abu Huzaifah got these feelings about the Prophet, he used to say;

> "These words of mine are killing me every time and I have a fear that I will come to a bad end."

He was martyred in Ghazwat Ul Yamamah in the time of Abu Bakr.

Umar killed his maternal uncle, Aas Ibni Hisham Ibn Ul Mughirah in this battle. Abu Bakr saw his son Abdur Rahman fighting from Makkans side, he asked him,

> "O dirty man, where is the wealth I left in Makkah?"

He said,

> "Nothing remained, only the steed, the weapons, and the sharp sword,"

and then he got out of his sight. Later on, Abu Bakr said,

> "If he had stayed there, I would have killed him for sure for the good pleasure of Allah."

Sa'd Ibni Muaz was guarding the Prophet. He said, "I wish for lot of Mushrikeen to be killed."

The sword of Okasha Ibni Mihsan was broken. The Prophet got him a stalk of tree to fight with. He shook it and it became a sword in his hand. He had that until he was martyred in battle with the apostates in the time of Abu Bakr. This sword was named as *"Al Aun."*

An Ansari captured Abu Aziz, the brother of Mus'ab Ibni Umair, so he was tying him up. He saw Mus'ab and called on him,

"Mus'ab! My brother, I hope for your help."

Mus'ab said,

"You are not my brother. This Ansari is my brother."

He said to the Ansari,

"Tie him firmly. His mother is wealthy, you can get some."

In brief, this battle was a unique example of bravery, courage, patience, and sacrifices.

THE MARTYRED

In this battle, 14 Sahabah were martyred for the noble cause. This battle and the victory therein are part of the strong foundation of Islam.

These martyred are from Muhajireen:

-Ubaidah Ibn Ul Harith

-Omair Ibni Abi Waqas

-Omair Ibni Abdi Amr (Zash, Shamalain)

-Aaqil Ibni Abi Bakr

-Maja, the slave servant of Umar

-Safwan Ibni Baida

AND FROM ANSAR:

-Sa'd Ibni Khaithamah

-Mubashir Ibni Abdul Munzir

-Haritha Ibni Suraqah

-Awf Ibni Afra

-Mua'awwaz Ibni Afra

-Omair Ibn Ul Hammam

-Rafi Ibni Mu'alla

-Yazid Ibn Ul Harith

May Allah be pleased with them.

MUSHRIKEEN KILLED

Seventy Mushrikeen were killed from Makkans. Some of them were:

Utbah Ibni Rabee'a, Shaiba Ibni Rabee'a, Waleed Ibni Utbah, Aas Ibni Saeed Ibn Ul Aas, Abu Jahl, Abul Bukhtari, Hanzalah Ibni Muttalib, Harith Ibni Aar, Hanzalah Ibni Abu Sufyan, Tuaimah Ibni Adi, Zama'ah Ibn Ul Aswad, Naufal Ibni Khuwaylid, Aas Ibni Hisham,

Umayyah Ibni Khalaf, Ali Ibni Umayyah Ibni Khalaf, Munnabih Ibni Hajjaj, Ma'bad Ibni Wahab.

THE CAPTIVES (PRISONERS OF WAR)

From Quraish, 70 people were captured. Some of them were:

Naufal Ibn Ul Harith, Abbas Ibni Abdul Muttalib, Aqeel Ibni Abi Talib, Abul Aas Ibni Rabee, Adi Ibni Khiyar, Abu Aziz Ibni Omair, Waleed Ibni Waleed Ibn Ul Mughirah, Abdullah Ibni Obai Ibni Khalaf, Abu Azzah the poet, Wahab Ibni Omair, Abu Wada'a, Sohail Ibni Amr (the known table talker).

24 dead chieftains of Quraish were thrown into a trench.

THE PROPHET STAYED IN THE FIELD FOR THREE DAYS AFTER VICTORY

Here, also he stayed for three days. On the third day the Prophet stood on that trench, named these people, and said of each one,

> *"Would you be happy if you had obeyed Allah and His Prophet? Whatever our Lord promised us, we receive, so have you found true what he promised you?"*

Omar said,

> *"O Messenger of Allah! You speak to these dead bodies? Do they hear?"*

The Prophet smiled and said,

> "I swear by the one in whose hands is my soul, you are not as good hearer to what I say to them as they are but they cannot answer."

In Ummah, it is a disputed issue whether the dead can hear. Those who believe they can present this as evidence, and those who do not believe they can say this was a special case of the Prophet for these people.

Hossain Ibni Abdullah Khuza'a was the first one who came to Makkah and told people that Utbah, Shaibah, Abu Jahl, Umayyah, Abul Hakam, and others were killed. First, they didn't believe that but later on they found out it was true.

Abu Rabi said,

> "I was sitting with Umm Ul Fazl, the wife of Abbas. Abu Lahab was there as well. Abu Sufyan Ibn Ul Harith came and said, 'By God, we were facing some strange people riding horses in the battlefield.' So, I said, 'By God these were angels.' Abu Lahab slapped me. I also tried to hit him, but as I was a weak man, he threw me to the ground. My Master Umm Ul Fazl hit him with a stone and said, 'What if his master Abbas is not here, you will slap him?'"

Abu Lahab fell sick and after 7 days he died. He remained dead for three days. His body began to smell and decompose, and then some Habshi slaves took him to a trench and buried him there.

THE HAPPY NEWS OF VICTORY

Abdullah Ibni Rawaha was sent by The Prophet to one side of Madina and Zaid Ibni Haritha to the other side to give the glad tidings to the people there. The Jews and the hypocrites had already spread the rumor that the Prophet was killed. When they saw Zaid riding Qaswa, the she-camel of the Prophet, they said,

> "Look! Mohammad is not there,"

and Zaid rode out on his she-camel. They both gave the happy news of victory. Zaid says, when we got into Madina, we saw people were coming back from "Baqee" the cemetery, they buried Ruqayyah, daughter of the Prophet and wife of Othman.

OBAIDA IBNUL HARITHA

Ubaidah, the first cousin of The Prophet who was injured when he exchanged Hits with Shaibah in the very beginning of war, was martyred at Safra. Nadr Ibn Ul Harith was also killed here. He was an archenemy of Allah who mocked the *Ayat* of Holy Quran. In Safra, The Prophet looked at this man and he said to one close to him,

> "He is going to kill me."

He said,

> "You are too cowardly".

He asked Mus'ab Ibni Omair if he could approach Mohammad,

> "As if you, O Mus'ab were in my place, I would have never liked your killing."

Mus'ab said,

> "You people were mocking the Prophet."

He was a captive in hands of Miqdad. He was expecting lot of wealth, but when he heard that The Prophet decreed his killing, he said, that is good, so Ali killed him. In another place, Irqud Dabyah another enemy of Allah, Oqbah Ibni Abi Moeet, was killed. When he was brought, he said,

> "O Quraish! Why I am to be killed in front of you people?"

They said,

> "This is because of your inhumane crimes and bullying of the weak. This dirty man once put a dirty fetus on the back of The Prophet, when He was in Sajdah."

This man was friend to Ubai Ibni Khalaf, sitting with the Prophet, as the Prophet left his food when he refused to accept The Message. He came to convince him to eat his food as this was a shame for him in that culture. Oqbah called him and asked him if he has accepted Islam. He said,

> "Not at all, but he did not take it."

He said,

> "If you want to make me believe you just go and spit on the face of Mohammad."

This dirty man tried to do that but his spit turned to a flame came back to his face and burnt his face.

Allah said,

> "And remember the day when the wrong doer will bite at his hands. He will say, oh! Would that I had taken a path with The Messenger. Ah! Woe to me, would that I had never taken so and so as an intimate friend. He indeed led me astray from the reminder after it had come to me, and Satan is to man ever a deserter in the hour of need." (25:27-29)

THE SPOILS OF WAR

We have mentioned before that Abdullah Ibni Jah'sh al Asadi in his "Sariyah" got the first ever spoils and he distributed 4/5 to his soldiers and saved 1/5 for "Baitul Maal". But that was a "Sariyah" and no proper battle happened there. While "Badr" was the first ever big *Ghazwa* and a great war happened here and the Makkans left a lot of spoils so it may be the case of that "Sariyah" was not that much propagated and also it may be that all Muslims were not aware of the rules regarding spoils, so, they asked The Prophet as Allah said,

> *"They ask you about the spoils of war (booty). Say, the spoils are for Allah and The Messenger, so, fear Allah and set right your relation to one another, and obey Allah and His Messenger if you are believers." (8:01)*

Yes, later on, Allah said in verse 41,

> *"And know that whatever of the booty you have gained, one-fifth of that is for Allah, for the Messenger, for the relatives of the Messenger, for the orphans, for the poor, and for the traveler, if you have believed in Allah and in what we had sent down to our slave on the Day of Criterion [Victory], the day when the two forces faced one another [means the help we had sent] and Allah is able to do everything." (8:41)*

SO, THE PROPHET DISTRIBUTED THE SPOILS TO THE MUJAHIDEEN THERE IN "SAFRA"

When The Prophet arrived in a place named Rauhaa. The Muslims from **Madina** had come there to welcome him and to congratulate him.

Osaid Ibni Hudair said,

> "I thought you people were going after the caravan, otherwise, I would have joined you."

The Prophet verified this.

THE CAPTIVES/PRISONERS OF WAR

The Prophet of Allah asked Abu Bakr,

> "What is to be done to them?"

He said,

> "They are our uncles and our cousins, so if we release them for ransom will be good for us."

The Prophet then asked Omar. He said,

> "I see something else: if you will allow me to kill my closest relative and to allow Hamza to kill his brother Abbas, and Ali to kill his brother Aqeel, the people may know that we will never show them any kindness."

Sa'd Ibni Muaz also suggested this.

The Prophet said to Abu Bakr,

> "You are like Prophet Isa, when people were plotting to kill him and he said, 'If you punish them, they are your slaves, and if you forgive them, you are the Almighty, the All-Wise." (5:118)

Also, he said to Omar,

> *"And you are like Prophet Nuh [Noah] when He was totally disappointed by his people and said, 'My Lord! Leave not one of the disbelievers on the earth." (71:26)*

The Prophet also did not want to kill them, but rather to ransom those who could afford a ransom and release those who could not. Also, those who did know some specific thing, like writing, reading, etcetera, they will give some to ansar service and then they will be released.

Abdullah Ibni Ruwaha advised,

> *"These people who came all the way from Makkah to fight us should be taken to some far valley and burnt [to death]."*

Omar said,

> *"The next day I came and saw The Prophet, and Abu Bakr was in tears. I asked the Prophet. He said, 'Because of what we said yesterday to go with the ransom idea, as Allah censured us."*

Allah said,

> *"It is not for a Prophet that he should have prisoners of war until he had made a big slaughter in the land. You desire the good of this world, while Allah desires the hereafter and Allah is Almighty, All-Wise. Were it not A previous ordainment from Allah, a severe torment would have touched you for what you took." (8:67,68)*

The Prophet said,

> *"If any torment was sent from the sky, no one would have escaped from it except Omar."*

Now, why did the Prophet not mention Ibni Rawaha as well? Because he had suggested that, they be burnt to death and The Prophet had said that no one else but Allah can punish them like that.

This opinion of Omar is one of those 18 or 20 places where Omar gave his opinions and then the same opinion came from the *Wahi* from Allah. The Prophet named him "Muhaddath,"

"The one who has been spoken to." (means by Allah)

Imam Shah Waliullah said it reflect things on the heart of "Muhaddath" from Allah.

Then, the basic concept of ransom was already mentioned in Quran:

"Then there (for captives) is either kindness to them (to set them free for free) or for ransom." (47:04)

So, no punishment came down, but Badr was the first *Ghazwa*, so, it was necessary to send a message to those who were to attack Muslims, so they would not plot conspiracies. But these *Ayat* frightened Sahabah to such an extent, that now they were feeling uneasy to relax with the spoils, so Allah said after these *Ayat*,

"So eat of what you have gotten of the spoils as lawful and pure." (8:69)

RELEASE FOR RANSOM AND FOR FREE

The ransom was fixed from 1,000 to 4,000 dirham. The first to pay was Muttalib, who paid for his father Harith Abu Wada'a. Later on, he accepted Islam.

Amr Ibni Suhail was a strategic orator and mediator. He used to talk bad against The Prophet and against Islam. He was amongst the captives. Omar said,

> "O Prophet of Allah! If you allow me, I will break his teeth, so he may not say what he used to say."

The Prophet said,

> "If I do this, Allah will break my teeth."

This Suhail also accepted Islam later on.

ABBAS, THE UNCLE OF THE PROPHET

Abbas, the uncle of the Prophet, was amongst the captives. The Prophet said.

> "Uncle! You will pay the ransom."

Abbas said,

> "You know about my Islam."

The Prophet said,

> "I know if you are truthful, but now you have to pay the ransom of your nephews, Aqeel Ibni Abi Talib and Naufal Ibn Ul Harith and so of your ally Amr Ibni Jahdam."

Abbas said,

> "But I don't have that much wealth."

The Prophet said,

> "You have planned the wealth you have given your wife, Umm Ul Fazl, if I am killed, give it to my sons Abdullah Ubaid Ullah and Fazl."

Abbas said,

> 'This is not known but to me and my wife only. I swear that you are The Messenger of Allah."

Abbas also had 20 Awqiah gold with him, The Prophet said,

> "As that we got in the battlefield, it is booty."

Allah says,

> "O Prophet! Say to the captives who are in your hands! If Allah knows any good in your hearts. He will give you something better than what has been taken from you, and He will forgive you, and Allah is All-Knower, All-Wise." (8:70)

When Abbas heard this, he said.

> "I wish, you had taken more from us."

ABUL AAS

Abul Aas was the nephew of Sayyidah Khadijah from her sister Halah. Zainab, the daughter of the Prophet, was his wife. He was captured around Badr. For his ransom, Zainab sent a necklace that she had received as a gift from her mother, Khadijah. The Prophet when he saw it, said to Sahabah,

> "Please send it back to Zainab and release Abul Aas."

They agreed to that. The Prophet said to Abul Aas,

"You will let Zainab to come to Madina."

He agreed to it. One month later, The Prophet sent Zaid Ibni Haritha and he brought her to Madina. Later on, Abul Aas also accepted Islam and came to Madina. The Prophet sent her back to Abul Aas, but according to some scholars, a new *Nikah* took place, while others said it was simply based on the previous contract. In any case, The Prophet was the lawgiver, so, when he did something, it became law for that issue, either as a general law or as a special case.

Zainab had one daughter from Abul Aas named Omaimah. Fatima, at the time of her death, said to Ali that he should marry Omaimah and later on he did so.

WAHAB IBNI OMAIR

Among these captives was Wahab Ibni Omair. Once, his father was sitting with Safwan Ibni Umayyah in "Hijr" (Hateem) in Bait Ul-lah. They were talking about their dead in Badr, thrown in the trench there. Safwan said,

"Since then, life has become very bitter."

Omair said,

"If my life had not straitened enough to take care of my family and pay my debts, then for sure I would have gone to get rid of Mohammad."

Safwan said,

"If you are serious, then that is on me."

When Omair got word of this, he took his sword and left for Madina. He made his camel sit outside the Masjid. Omar saw him. He told Sahabah,

> "Keep an eye on this man, he is capable of anything."

He came to the Prophet and informed him also. The Prophet said,

> "Bring him straight to me."

Omar got hold of the string of his sword and brought him. The Prophet said,

> "Leave him."

Omar asked him,

> "Why have you come here?"

He said,

> "To ask you to do a favor for my son."

The Prophet said,

> "And what else?"

He said,

> "That is all."

The Prophet said,

> "Then what is this sword for?"

Omair replied,

> "Perished be these swords. Have these saved us from you?"

Then, the Prophet told him about his talk in Hateem with Safwan. He was looking at The Prophet when he was telling him what they talked about. He said,

> "There was nobody but me and him."

Omair said,

> "I used to belie your Wahi. By Allah, this is true and you do receive the truth from Allah."

He accepted Islam. The Prophet said to His Sahabah,

> "Teach him the prayer and some parts of The Quran, then, hand over his son to him."

From all these captives, the Muslims received 20,000-dirham total.

Nadr Ibn Ul Harith used to mock the *Wahi* by reading storybooks and saying there was not such a big difference between him and Mohammad and The Prophet ordered his killing in a place known as Afra and Ali killed him. His sister, Qateelah, when she found out, recited some poetry verses, in which, she spoke about her brother:

> "Alas! The swords of his cousins killed him."

Also, she said,

> "If you had released him and forgiven him, you would have been known for that as a man of firm will, courage, and bravery, as he was your relative as well."

The Prophet, when heard it, broke down in tears and said, if "I had received word from her before, I would have released him for sure."

THE REASONS FOR VICTORY

As we mentioned before, the Muslims were not very ready for a battle, as they had few people or weapons, but still, they were victorious.

HOW? AND WHAT BROUGHT THEM THIS VICTORY?

The first and utmost important in Islam is a full and perfect sincerity when a Muslim does something, especially when he does it for the sake of Allah. So, as we have mentioned, the Muslims were few in number and even fewer in weapons but they headed to war with full sincerity and no fear of death; rather, they were looking for martyrdom in the path of Allah and such a zeal and spirit could not be defeated very easily.

We also mentioned before that the angels came down in a big number, which encouraged them further,

a) that now this is an acceptance by Allah because he sent the angels.

b) if we are going to face anything, otherwise, so, these angels are very alert there.

Ali says a very strong wind blew 3 times, and that was the coming down of the angels.

Abu Yaseer was very slim, but he caught Abbas, who was a very strong man. He was asked,

"How did you do that?"

He said,

"A stranger helped me."

The Prophet said,

> *"That was the angel."*

A man from Banu Ghifar said,

> *"My cousin and I were on a hilltop. At that time, we were not Muslims. Suddenly, a cloud passed by very swiftly and we heard the neighing of horse in it. My cousin was frightened, fell down, and died at the spot and I narrowly escaped."*

The Prophet said,

> *"I saw Jibril, dirt was seen on his robes."*

Abu Dawud Zamani and Sahl both said,

> *"We were trying to hit someone and before our swords touched, his head was already cut off."*

Huwaitib Ibni Abdul Uzza said,

> *"I was in the Makkans Army and I saw the angels hitting our people."*

The Prophet came out of his canopy and was reciting,

> *"Soon, this group will be defeated and turn around [run away]" (54:45).*

The Prophet said,

> *"I swear by the one in whose hands my soul is, whosoever will fight today wholeheartedly will go to Jannah [paradise]."*

Omair Ibn Ul Hammam had some dates in his hands and was eating them. He threw them and said,

> *"Oh, so, this is the barrier between me and paradise."*

Ahmad narrated from Ummi Salmah that The Prophet said,

> "Whosoever was at Badr or Hudaibiyah will not go to Hell."

Also, The Prophet said from Allah,

> "O people of Badr! Do as you wish; I have forgiven you."

Even, the weapons used in Badr earned respect. Zubair hit the eye of Ubaidah Ibni Saeed Ibn Ul Aas with his spear. The Prophet took it from him. Later on, this was with all the four Khulafa and then with Abdullah Ibni Zubair.

THE DEATH OF RUQAYYAH, THE DAUGHTER OF THE PROPHET

Ruqayyah was the elder daughter of The Prophet.

She and her sister Ummi Kulthum were engaged to two sons of Abu Lahab before Islam, but Abu Lahab, the uncle of The Prophet (who was the first one to throw sand and pebbles towards The Prophet when he gave a call towards *Tawheed* for the first time and said bad *Dua* to The Prophet), asked his sons to break their engagements and instigated them both to go to The Prophet and insult him. They both broke their engagements and Otaibah was the one who ripped up the Prophet's tunic and spit on him. The Prophet said,

> "O Allah! Set One of your dogs on him."

Later on, when he was going on a business trip to Sham in a caravan and they were taking rest somewhere in a rest area *Azzarqa* ("the place"), a lion rushed to him like lightning, lifted him up, and threw him very roughly. His head was crushed. The lion did not touch anybody else. His brother, Utbah, later on, accepted Islam.

Anyhow, Ruqayyah married Uthman, and as we said before that Uthman's name was registered in Mujahideen and he came well-prepared, but The Prophet sent him back to take care of his wife, who was fighting for her life. She passed away in the absence of The Prophet. The Prophet sent Zaid Ibni Haritha riding the Prophet's she-camel to give the victory news to those who were in Madina. He said,

> *"When I entered Madina, they were coming back from the burial of Ruqayyah."*

Uthman had a son with her, who died at the age of six.

THE MARRIAGE OF FATIMA, THE DAUGHTER OF THE PROPHET

Four and a half months after the marriage of The Prophet to Aaisha, The Prophet arranged for Fatima to be engaged to Ali and after seven months, they married.

Before Ali, Abu Bakr and Umar also asked for Fatima, but The Prophet did not agree. Then, Umar told Ali,

> *"You should ask for her."*

He said,

> *"But I do not have anything."*

A slave girl of Ali's used to insist on Ali to go and ask. So, once he came to The Prophet and sat with him quietly. After some time, The Prophet himself said,

> "Have you come to ask me for Fatima?"

Umar said,

> "Yes!"

The Prophet asked him,

> "Do you have something [for a bride-price]?"

He said,

> "I don't have anything."

The Prophet said,

> "What about the coat of mail I gave you?"

He said,

> "But that is "Hutaimah", (made by the Hutami tribe), and not worth more than 400 dirham."

The Prophet said,

> "Sell it, and I will agree to your Nikah with Fatima."

He said to Ali at the time of marriage,

> "Tonight, meet me, then talk to your wife."

Then, The Prophet did *wudu* and splashed that water on Ali. He rinsed his mouth and splashed the water on Fatima's head and chest. For everyone, he made *Dua* separately and collectively:

> "O Allah, bless them both and their offspring [and keep them] from Satan."

He made the same splash between the shoulders of both of them. This marriage took place in second year after "Hijrah".

Fasting and *zakat* both became *Fard* in Ramadan, this second year of Hijrah, while Eid Ul Fitr was celebrated and Sadaqat Ul Fitr became *Wajib* as well. In other words, all these gifts are given to Muslims in appreciation to their sacrifices or as a way of thanks to Allah for their great victory.

Allah said,

> "And remember when you were few in number, and you were reckoned weak in that land and you were afraid that the people might abduct you, but He provided a safe place for you, He strengthened you with His help and provided you with pure things so you may pay thanks to Allah. (8:26)

EXPEDITIONS BETWEEN BADR AND UHUD

The Battle of Badr was a foundation of Islam and the Islamic State, which gave courage to Muslims and strengthened them in their faith and belief. Also, it frightened not only the people of Makkah, but also the Jews and the hypocrites at Madina who wanted to eliminate Islam and the Islamic State. The tribes around Madina had little use for gods and faith, but they used to rob here and there. Now, all of them were thinking about how to weaken this nearly established state even as it grew stronger day by day. All of them started conspiring in one way or the other.

The Prophet and the Muslims also became further alert as they thought,

"All these wicked people will not accept our victory. They will try to their best to turn over the situation."

That's why so many expeditions happened in this regard, as whenever The Prophet heard of any uprising or conspiracy in the surrounding areas, he took a pre-emptive step to stop it or at least to warn them that they were well aware of any plots or machinations and could face any situation.

GHAZWAH BANI SULAIM

Seven Days after Badr, The Prophet was informed that Banu Sulaim and Ghitfan were plotting to attack Madina. So, The Prophet appointed Siba Ibni Urfuta Al-Ansari as caretaker at Madina and along with 200 horsemen went to "Kud'r" in Najd area, located between Makkah and Sham. He ordered Amr Ibni Qais (Ibni Ummi Maktoum) to lead the prayers. This Amr was the son of the Khadijah's maternal aunt. His mother's name was Attika, daughter of Abdullah. Thirteen times on different occasions he led the prayer at **Madina** in The Prophet's absence with his appointment. It is said that in the time of Umar, he was holding the flag and was martyred. It is also narrated that he was injured and then died at Madina.

In this expedition, Ali was holding a white flag. When Banu Sulaim came to know that The Prophet was proceeding towards them, they ran away and left 500 camels, which the Muslims got. After one-fifth of Baitul Mal, every soldier got two camels. The Prophet stayed there for three days. He got one captive also. His name was Yasar. The Prophet set him free. This Expedition took place in Shawwal second year after Hijra.

GHAZWAH BANU QAINUQA

As we mentioned before, The Prophet came to Madinah and established a state and government there. For this purpose, he wrote a treaty for how this state would be run. In this treaty, the first ever written constitution in human history, he gave full rights to all citizens and made them bound to loyalty. But the Jews (Banu Qanuqa, Banu Nadeer, Bani Quraizah) used to plot and conspire against this state, The Prophet, and the Muslims from day one. One example of this was an old Jew, Shas Ibni Qais. When he saw Aus and Khazraj, the two hostile tribes became too close to one another on the basis of Islam, so he sent a young man to sit with them and give a talk about the Battle of Bu'aath, in which so many people from both sides were killed, and mention these killed in such a way to inspire both side and to instigate them against one another, so they would start fighting again. The Prophet was informed so he rushed to them along with some of Sahabah and he said, "Again towards ignorance and bloodshed, after that Allah has blessed you with Islam, honored you and brought you out of disbelief and ignorance and made you as one body."

Allah said,

> *"O you who believed! If you will obey a group of those who had been given The Book, they would render you disbelievers after your Iman [make you denounce Islam]. And how would you disbelieve while the Ayat of Allah are recited to you and among you there is His Messenger. And whoever holds firmly to Allah, then, he is indeed, guided to the right path. O you who believed! Fear Allah as he should be feared, and die not, but as Muslims. And hold firmly to the rope of Allah and be not divided among yourselves. And remember the favor of Allah on you as you were enemies [to each other] so, he joined your hearts together and you became brothers [to*

one another] with His grace. And you were on the brink of a pit of fire, so, He saved you from that. The same way Allah explains, in detail to you his verses, so you may be guided." (3:100-103)

The Jewish people in Madina were either tradesmen like carpenters, masons, blacksmiths, goldsmiths, etc. or they were in business, while Aus and Khazraj, the Madinites were farmers. The Jews used to give them loans for their farming and earn interest from the loans. The usury was so high that these poor people used to give the majority of their profits to them.

Also, these Jewish people were literate people and the Madinites were illiterate. So, these Jews had their upper hand on them both economically and mentally. Now, when The Prophet came there, both their positions were at stake as The Prophet was educating people and also, he was against exploitation.

The Banu Qanuqa were professional people. Ibni Masud relates from Abu Awn that an Arab lady came to the bazaar of Banu Qanuqa to sell some of her silver ornaments to a goldsmith. As she was covering her face, they asked her to show her face. She refused. A wicked man tied the lower part of her gown to her back. When she stood up, it revealed her back, so, they laughed at her and said bad words to her that she refused to not show her face but now her whole back was visible. She cried and shouted that they were shameless. A Muslim, when he saw all that, he couldn't control himself, and jumped upon that man and killed him. The Jews there jumped on that Muslim and killed him in retaliation and the situation quickly spun out of control. The Jews used to do conspiracies on a going on level, but The Prophet had been very nice to them giving them warnings and giving them time to stop their plots, but they persisted. This incident upset the Muslims. They came out to fight the Jews. Ibni Abbas said The Prophet called them towards Islam, but they said,

"You think we are like Quraish that you are frightening us. If you wage war on us, you will see the result."

The Prophet Mohammad besieged them for 15 days. Their crime was high treason as they threatened the state and the head of the state, which has always been a capital offense. The Prophet was also thinking of capital punishment, but they approached their old ally, the chief of hypocrites, Abdullah Ibni Ubai to approach The Prophet to give them a pardon. On two occasions, The Prophet didn't answer, but when he asked a third time, he put his hand in the mail coat of The Prophet, indicating that he would not leave until the Prophet did what he wanted. The Prophet got angry until his face turned red and said to Ibni Ubai,

"Leave me,"

But Abdullah said,

"By God, I will not until you pardon my allies."

The Prophet, once again said,

"Woe to you, leave me."

Abdullah said,

"No, are you going to kill these many hundreds of people? This will further aggravate the situation."

The Prophet said,

"I am going to leave them alone, but they must leave Madina."

He also said that they were not allowed to take anything with them. The Prophet ordered Mohammad Ibni Maslamah to go there, check on them, and confiscate their belongings. He ordered Obadah Ibni Samit to take care of this whole process. They had gathered lot of weapons, which Obadah confiscated. Obadah took them to a mountain named Dubab, so they would go to "Azru'aat."

When The Prophet was in their area for 15 days, he has appointed Abu Lubabah at Madina. The Prophet distributed 80% of their belongings to the Mujahideen and 20% to Baitul Mal. In this *Ghazwa*, The Prophet got three coats of mail, three long lances, and three swords. He gave one coat to Sa'd Ibni Muaz and another one to Mohammad Ibni Maslamah. The Prophet also got three bows named Katoom, Rauha, and Baida. Katoom was a silent bow: no sound was made when it shot arrows.

One mail coat's name was "Fidah" and the other one was "Saghdia". It's said that this was the coat that Dawoud (David) was wearing in his battle with Jalut (Goliath). Hamza was holding a white flag in this battle.

GHAZWAH-I-SAWEEQ

The Battle of Badr had caused the Makkans a big rage and anger. Abu Sufyan took an oath that he would not bathe until he had his revenge. So, in Dhul Hijjah second year of Hijrah, he came out with 200 horsemen towards Najdiyah and stayed near Raneeb Mountain, 12 miles out of Madina on a channel of water. At night, secretly, he came to the chief of Banu Nadeer, Huyai Ibni Akhtab in Madina. He knocked out his door, but he, himself, was feeling fear, so, he didn't open it. So, Abu Sufyan came to another chief, Sallam Ibni Mishkam. He welcomed him and offered him wine, and also gave him some news and advice. He went back to his people and in the last part of night, he sent a few people to attack the area. They came and lit some fire in some date groves and killed Ma'bad Ibni Amr Al-Ansari and his colleague in their sleep. The Prophet Mohammad found out, so, he took 200 people and went after them, but they had already fled. The Prophet arrived in an area called Qar Qarat Ul - Kadr and got a big bunch of roasted, sweetened flour of barley called *Saweeq*, which the Makkans had left there. Sahabah asked The Prophet,

"Is this Ghazwa, even if no fight took place there?"

He said,

"Yes, this is. The Prophet has appointed Abu Lubabah Ibni Abdul Munzir at Madina as a caretaker."

GHAZWAH-I-ZEE AMAR

In Muharram, 3rd year after Hijra, The Prophet got the news that a group of Muharib and "Banu Thalabah" had gotten together in Zee Amar under their leader Da'thur Ibni Harith Al-Moharibi to attack Madina. The Prophet took 450 Sahabah with him to face them and appointed Uthman Ibni Affan at Madina. The Muslims got hold of one, Jabbar Tha'aalibi, and brought him to The Prophet. The Prophet called him towards Islam and he accepted it. Then, he guided the Muslims towards his group, but when they heard of this Muslim Army, they fled to the mountains. The Prophet told Bilal to teach Jabbar about Islam. Later on, Da'thur, the leader also, when saw a miracle of The Prophet, accepted Islam. He convinced many others and they accepted Islam as well. The Prophet stayed in the area in the month of Muharram and Safar to send a message to the people in the area.

THE MARRIAGE OF UMMI KULTHUM

As we have mentioned before that The Prophet was in Badr when his daughter Ruqayyah, the wife of Uthman, passed away. Then, Uthman asked Umar for his daughter Hafsah, who was a widow of Khunais Ibni Huzafa. He said,

> "Let me ask the advice of The Prophet as Sahabah used to do regarding their affairs."

The Prophet said to him,

> "Should I not tell you the best one for your daughter and for Uthman, a better one than your daughter?"

Then, he told him,

> "I will marry my other daughter, Ummi Kulthum, to Uthman and you will marry your daughter to me."

By this, not only Umar became happy, but when he told the same to Uthman, he became happy as well. Ummi Kulthum's *Nikah* took place in Rabee Ul Awwal, the 3rd year after Hijra (migration to Madina) and the marriage took place in Jumad Al Oola the same year. She also died in the fourth year after Hijrah. The Prophet said to Uthman,

> "If I had another daughter, I would have married her to you as well."

It is worth mentioning that Ruqayyah and Ummi Kulthum were engaged to Utbah and Otaibah when "Surat Ul Lahab" revealed to The Prophet. Abu Lahab and his wife, Ummi Jamil, the sister of Abu Sufyan and an archenemy of The Prophet, asked their sons to divorce their wives and to insult Mohammad. They both divorced them and Otaibah insulted The Prophet and torn in his shirt and spit on Him. The Prophet made a *Dua* on him saying,

> "O Allah! Set one of your dogs on him."

Later on, Otaibah was going on a business trip to Syria with his colleagues. They were in "Az Zarqa", a lion approached the group. Otaibah recalled the words of The Prophet and said,

"Woe to my brother. He took me there and Mohammad made Dua on me."

Utbah said,

"This lion will eat up his brother for sure."

The lion rushed and jumped on Otaibah like lightening, picked him up, and crushed his head.

THE MARRIAGE OF HAFSAH

Hafsah was the widow of Khunais Ibni Huzafah. The Prophet married her in Shaban, year 3 after "Hijrah" and thus, The Prophet became the son-in-law of Abu Bakr and Umar, the first and second Khalifa and the father-in-law of Uthman and Ali, the third and fourth Khalifa. Hafsah passed away in the time of Muaa'wiyah.

KA'B IBNI ASHRAF (A VILLAIN)

Ka'b was from Banu Nabhan Arabs. His father Ashraf killed someone and fled to Madina. He asked Banu Nadeer, the Jews for asylum, and they gave him the same. Later on, he married the daughter of Abul Huqaiq, a Jewish chief, named, Aqilah. She delivered Ka'b, and as in Judaism, the lineage goes to the mother. Kab was a handsome man having a lot of wealth. He was a scholar of "Taurat", he was a poet also and saying bad against The Prophet, Islam, and Muslims, mocking them. He was also instigating the Quraish against The Prophet in his poetry. He was the one who went to Makkah and instigated them and the Battle of Badr happened. The Prophet's victory at Badr almost broke him, as when Zaid Ibnu Haritha and Abdullah Ibni Rawaha brought the news of victory to Madina, he asked people,

> "Do you believe this is true, and if this is, it is better to get gutted in the ground."

Then, when it became true, he went to Muttalib Ibni Abi Wada'a in Makkah, provoking the Quraish to take revenge of their elders who were killed at Badr. To determine to what extent he is serious, Abu Sufyan asked him,

> "What do you think our religion or the religion of Mohammad is the best?"

He said yours. Abu Sufyan said then,

> "Why do you not make a sajdah to our Gods Jibt and Taghut?"

And he did the same.

Allah said,

> "Have you not seen those, who have been given a portion of [knowledge of] The Book, believing in Jibt and Taghut and say regarding those who disbelieved, that they are better guided than those who believed." (4:51)

In his poetry he was speaking foul and dirty language against chaste Muslim women. The Prophet said,

> "Who is for us regarding this degenerate?"

Mohammad Ibni Maslamah from Banu Abdul-Ash'hal was accompanied by Abbad Ibni Bishr and Abu Naila Salkan Ibni Salamah. Abu Naila was the foster brother of Ka'b. Also, it is said that Ka'b was related to Mohammad Ibni Maslamah from his mother's side. They were joined by Abu Abas Ibni Hurr and Harith Ibni Aus as well. Mohammad was the "Amir" of the group. He asked The Prophet,

> "Is a strategy allowed?"

The Prophet said,

> "Yes."

The Prophet found out that after taking this job and responsibility Mohammad was eating very little. The Prophet asked him,

> "Why?"

He said,

> "I am not sure I will do it or not, that's why I lost my appetite."

The Prophet said,

> "Take it easy."

Then, he went to Ka'b and said to him,

> "We have nothing to eat and this Prophet asked us for donations, so can you lend me one or two Wasaq (a measurement) of grain?"

Ka'b said,

> "But how I can trust you that you will pay it back? Give me something as collateral."

Mohammad said,

> "What do you want?"

He said,

> "Your women."

Mohammad said,

> "How can we do that? You are a handsome man."

He said,

> "Your children, then."

Mohammad said,

> "The people will mock us for putting our sons up as collateral for grain. But we can put our weapons with you even though we need it."

He agreed. Abu Na'ilah later on, also made a deal with him for himself and for his other colleagues. These five people later on departed for their mission. The Prophet accompanied them to Baqee and made *Dua* for their success. There was a full moon that night. Abu Na'ilah then called him from outside. His new bride said,

> "Don't go out. I felt this call, as if the blood is dripping of it."

He said,

> "But this is my brother Abu Na'ilah."

So, he came out. He welcomed them, thinking that the weapons they have brought were the collateral. Abu Na'ilah had already told his colleagues that he uses perfume, so, he decided he would ask him to bring down his head so he could smell it and he would hold his head then, jump on him at once. First, they sat with him then, they said,

> "Let's take a little walk."

When they took him on a distance from his house, Abu Na'ilah put his plot into motion and said,

"What is that fragrance?"

He said, actually,

"I have the best Arabian scented wife."

Abu Na'ilah said,

"Can I smell it?"

He said,

"Of course,"

And he lowered his head. Abu Na'ilah put his finger in his hair combing it through. He also asked his colleagues to smell it and they also did the same, then, they carried on walking. After a while, Abu Na'ilah asked him for the same once again and this time he grabbed him from his hair very firm and his colleagues hit him with their swords. He cried out loudly and the lights in the fortress were lit. Harith was injured by one of his colleagues' swords, which is why he came out little bit late. They chanted,

"Allahu Akbar (God is great)" altogether

When they got together in *"Hamrat Ul Areed."* The Prophet heard it and he said *"Takbeer"* as well. They got his head cut and brought it to The Prophet. The Prophet said,

"These faces (or chiefs) succeeded."

They said,

"And your bright face as well, O Prophet!"

Then, he put his saliva over the injury of Harith's wound and he recovered.

This incident put fear in the hearts of Jewish tribes and for some time they started showing loyalty and obedience to the state. This happened in Rabi Ul Awwal year 3. The Prophet, after this, turned his attention to the conspiracies outside Madina.

IBNI SUNAINAH

Ibni Sunainah was another such villain. When Muhayyisah Ibni Masud heard of the murder of Ka'b, he went and killed Ibni Sunainah. His brother Huwayyisa said to him,

> *"Your fat belly comes from his food and yet you killed him. He said if you do the same, I will kill you as well."*

This wording touched Huwayyisa's heart and he accepted Islam.

THE ASSASSINATION OF A FEW VILLAINS

Abu Rafi Sallam Ibn Abil Huqaiq was killed in Jumada al Akhira year 3 after "Hijrah". He used to torture the prophet mentally. He was living in a fortress in Hijaz.

The prophet arranged a group of *ansar* having Abdullah Ibn Ateeq as their leader. When they arrived there, the sun was setting. Abdullah said to his colleagues,

> *"You should wait here."*

He proceeded further, covering himself with his cloak and sitting in such a way that it appeared he was relieving himself. The gatekeeper thought he was one of the fortress people. So, he called him with a louder voice to hurry up as he is going to close the gate. He said,

"*I entered with them and sat somewhere in hiding.*"

The gatekeeper closed the doors and left the keys hanging with a standing wood.

Abu Rafi was talking to the people in his loft until late. When the people left him, Abdullah said,

> *I went to the keys, opening the doors one by one and entered his room. I called Abu Rafi and he responded so I jumped over the place. I heard the response from and tried to hit him, but I was not able to. He shouted with his loud voice, so I rushed out of the room. When he slept again, I entered the room once again and said, "Abu Raf, what was this shout?" He said, "May you be perished, somebody tried to hit me." So again, I jumped to the voice and stabbed my sword in his belly so forcefully that it went straight to his backbone. I came out, coming down the stairs in the dark. I thought, the next step would be the ground, but it was not and I broke my leg. I tied it with my turban, came out and sat on the gate to confirm his death in the morning and when his death was announced then I came to my colleagues and informed them. Then we came back to the prophet. The prophet touched my leg and it healed like it was never broken at all. (Bukhari)*

ABU AFAK AND ASMA

Abu Afak was from the tribe of Banu Amr Ibni Auf. He was a bad mouth poet, saying bad things against the prophet and Muslims. One Muslim, Saleem Ibni Omair, took an oath that he would get rid of this villainous man, so he went and killed him when he was sleeping.

Asma, daughter of Marwan, was the same like woman from the Banu Umayyah Ibni Zaid tribe. Omair Ibni Awf was from a not-very strong tribe but he went. He found her baby sleeping with her, so he put the baby to one side and then he killed her. After her burial, her tribe came to Omair and asked whether he killed her. He said,

> *"Yes. What can you expect of me if someone using this type of abusive and humiliating language against someone and she was doing the same against our prophet? And let me make it clear, if anyone repeats that, he will suffer the same fate."*

This bravery from such a weak person convinced that tribe and they accepted Islam.

THE BATTLE OF NAJRAN

In Rabi Uth Thani year three, the prophet took 300 people with him to Najran in Hejaz. He stayed there in Jumada al Oola also. Later on, he came back to Madina.

SARIYAH OF ZAID IBN HARITHA

The Quraish were in shock and fear after Badr and thinking of taking revenge. They learned that the prophet was entering into treaties with people living on shore. That was on their trade routes and they know whether he would continue to allow them to use that route in the future.

> *"We depend on trade with Sham in winter and with Habshah in summer,"*

This is what Safwan their trade's caretaker for that year said.

> *"Aswad Ibni Abdul Muttalib said then this year we should take the Iraqi route and as this a long route and we are not that much aware of it, we will take Furat Ibni Hayyan of Banu Bakr Ibn Wa'il with us as a guide."*

Saleet Ibni Noman was sitting with Nuaim Ibn Masud al Ash'jaee drinking wine. At that time Saleet had accepted Islam and Nuaim had not, so Saleet came to the prophet and informed him about the Makkans' plan. In this trip Huwaitib Ibn Abdul Uzza was accompanying Safwan. Among their goods they had a big bunch of finger rings with precious stones in them. The prophet arranged an expedition of a hundred horsemen under the leadership of Zaid Ibn Haritha – Al - Kalbe. The caravan of the Makkans was staying at a water fountain, Qirad, in the Najd area. When Zaid arrived, Safwan and others fled away when they saw that Zaid was approaching, but first the guide was caught. It is said that two other people were also captured. Zaid brought a lot of booty to the prophet. The prophet took one-fifth for the "Baitul Mal" and distributed the rest to the Mujahedeen. Furat accepted Islam there. It is said that this booty was almost 100,00 dirhams. After this for Makkans there was only to surrender or to attack Madina. And as they were thinking of the Badr revenge for the last one year, they started getting ready to attack Madina.

GHAZWA-I-UHUD (THE BATTLE OF UHUD)

This battle took place on the 5th of *Shawwal* year 3 after Hijrah. It was a Saturday.

Abdullah Ibni Rabee'a, Ikramah Ibni Abu Jahl, Safwan Ibni Umayyah and a few others came to Abu Sufyan and they talked to Abu

Sufyan about the fact that the Caravan, which was the primary cause for the battle of Badr and its wealth is not distributed to owners, so they wanted to know if he would help them with that to get revenge on their tribesmen who were killed in Badr. Abu Sufyan said,

> "We and the Bani Abdi Manaf tribe are agreed."

The original value of all the goods of the caravan, was almost 1000 camels and 50,000 dinars, and the profit was 50,000 as well. Abu Sufyan said,

> "The capital will be to its owners and the profit is for that expedition."

So, the Quraish and their allies Banu Kinanah and Tiyamah purchased weapons and armor for the battle with that money. Allah said regarding such spending, *(8-30-37)*

> "Verily those who disbelieved spending their wealth to hinder [people] from the path of Allah, so they will be spending it [so], but it will be an anguish for them [in the end], and then [still] they would be overcome. And those who disbelieved will be gathered into the hell in order that Allah may distinguish the wicked from the good, and may put the wicked over one another, heap them together and cast them into hell. They are those who are the losers."

ABU AZZA

Abu Azzah was a poet badmouthing the prophet, Islam, Muslims, and also women. He was captured as a prisoner in Badr, but he cried to the prophet that,

> "I have daughters and they have no one to take care of them, I am very sorry for what I have done in the past. I apologize. In the future I will never say any bad against you and Islam."

The prophet released him for free. In Makkah Safwan Ibni Umayyah said to him,

> "Inspire and instigate the people against Islam, Muslims, and the prophet."

He said,

> "But I was released so I could take care of my daughters."

Safwan said,

> "Look! If you will come back alive, I shall make you a rich man enjoying life and if you are killed, I shall take care of your daughters like they were mine."

He again refused that I have given Mohammad my word. But Safwan was forcing him to break his promise so he got ready.

SAFWAN AND JUBAIR

Tuaimah Ibn Adi, the uncle of Jubair Ibn Mut'im, was killed in Badr by Hamzah; so, he said to Wahshi Ibni Harb an Abyssinian slave,

> "If you will kill Hamzah then you will be free."

It is said also that the daughter of Tuaimah told Wahshi to kill Hamzah or Ali or Mohammad and she would free him and offer a lot of money. He was a skilled archer and sniper. Safwan also took another poet with him. His name was Musafi Ibn Abdi Manaf Jumahi.

THE QURAISH ARMY

The Makkans arranged an army of 3000 fighters as they had with them their allies, the *Ahbash* Banu Mustalaq, Banu Haun Ibni Khuzaimah and others as well. Hind Bint-Utbah, the wife of Abu Sufyan's father, Utbah, brother Waleed, and cousin Shaibah, were killed in Badr, joined the army to instigate and inspire them with her singing. She had other women beside her as well. The wife of Ikrimah Ibni Abi Jahl, Ummi Hakim Bint Tariq, and the wife of Amr Ibn al Aas, Reeta Shamiyah were amongst them. They were singing,

> "We are the daughters of Tariq, walking over soft cushions. If you people will go ahead [in fight] and face the enemies, we will embrace you but if you show your back to the enemies, we will leave you and never join you again."

QURAISH'S DEPARTURE

On Shawwal 5th, the 3rd year after Hijrah, they departed from Makkah to Madina. The uncle of the prophet Abbas had not accepted Islam and he was also one of their financiers. This time he refused to join them or even to fund them, because he had seen the result at Badr, and as long as the Muslims followed the instructions of the prophet then it was almost impossible to defeat them. He was a close friend of the prophet also. In Makkah, he used to keep him company and that is why some historians are of the view that he had accepted Islam but he had not disclosed it to the prophet. He wrote a letter to the prophet and informed him about the situation. His messenger travelled so fast that he arrived in Madina in only three days and nights.

The prophet was in Quba when he received this letter. He gave it to Ubai Ibni Kab to read. The prophet told him to keep it secret. Then the prophet went to Sa'd Ibni Rabee and told him about this and also told him not to disclose it to anyone. When the prophet left. Sa'd's wife asked her husband what the prophet had told you? He said,

"None of your business."

She said,

"But I heard everything."

And she told it to Sa'd. Sa'd got hold of her firmly and brought her to the prophet that she heard it herself, I have not told her,

"I brought her to save my Iman and ultimate end."

The prophet said.

"There is no problem."

EMERGENCY DECLARED

The prophet after that announced an emergency at Madina so all the entrances to Madina were guarded, keeping an eye on every comer. The Muslims used to have their weapons with them even in prayers. The chiefs of Ansars like Sad Ibni Ubadah. Sad Ibni Muaz and Osaid Ibni Hudair used to guard the prophet's house.

QURAISH ARRIVAL

When the Quraish army approached Madina, they came via the Aqeeq valley. At night they came to a place named Ainain near the Uhud mountain. This mountain is north of Madina. The prophet once said that Abu Qubais at Makkah and Uhad at Madina are the mountains of paradise. When the prophet came back from Tabuk and he saw Uhud, he said,

> "Uhud loves us and we love it."

On Shawwal 6th, they arrived on their way to Madina when they were in Abawa where the grave of the prophet's mother was located. Hind wanted to demolish it in anger but the people stopped her, reminding her that doing so would have its repercussions and also would establish a very bad precedent for generations to come.

THE PROPHET AND HIS COMPANIONS

In Islam, consultation and seeking advice is important. Allah said regarding good noble Muslims in their qualities,

> "And in their system is a mutual consultation amongst them." (42:38)

And the prophet was very eager in this regard.

Abu Hurairah says,

> "I have not seen anybody else doing more consultation as the prophet used to." (Tirmizi)

So, the prophet consulted his companions. He told them,

> *"I dreamt of a cow being slaughtered. I saw a breakage in my sword. Also, in the dream I put my hand in a very strong armor jacket, and I was dragging a big ram."*

Then he himself interpreted it and said that the cow slaughter meant that some of the Sahabah would be martyred. The breakage in his sword meant that someone from his own family would be martyred as well. Putting his hand in the jacket is Madina: it will be safe and someone big of them would be killed by someone very close to me. Later on, the same things happened. Seventy Sahabah were martyred. Hamzah was amongst them. And the ram was the Makkans. Their carrier Talha Ibni Uthman Alabdari, the ram of their Army, was killed by Ali.

Then the prophet was of the opinion that they should stay inside Madina and let the Makkans enter. They did not know the streets so they would get stuck and the Muslims could hit them with stones and arrows from the rooftops. The elders, both from Ansar and Muhajireen, had the same opinion. The prophet sent someone to Abdullah Ibni Ubai to ask his point of view also. He said the same thing. He didn't know the opinion of the prophet and other people.

But those who couldn't join the Badr Battle were eager for a day like that. "So," they said,

> *"This is not looking good for us to allow them, to enter our city. So, we should go out and face them."*

This was Hamzah's opinion as well. Ibni Ubai said,

> *"Our history is like this: whenever someone entered Madina he is defeated, and whenever we have gone out, we are defeated."*

Noman Ibni Malik and Sad Ibni Ubadah also said,

> *"We should face them outside Madina."*

Hamzah said, By Allah,

> "I will not eat until I go out and use my sword on them."

He said,

> "O messenger of Allah! Please do not deprive us of paradise, I want to go to paradise today."

Ibni Ubai said,

> "Look, if they will come inside, our women can join us, pelting stones on them from the rooftops."

As there was no *Wahi* in this regard, the prophet listened to them and decided to go out.

THE PROPHET PREPARED

This was Friday so the prophet gave his *khutbah* and led the *Jumma* prayer. Later on, he prayed *Asr* also in its time. Then he entered his house and put on two armor breastplates. Abu Bakr and Omar tied his turban. He hung his sword from his shoulder. The people from Awali the out skirts of Madina also came.

Here in Masjid Sad Ibni Muraaz and Osaid Ibni Hundair said to people that they insisted the prophet go out, so when the prophet came out, these people reproached themselves and said,

> "O prophet of Allah! Whatever your opinion is, we will go by that."

But the prophet said,

> "This is not for a prophet when he decrees and puts on his armor to change his mind but rather let the decision take its course."

The prophet put Abdullah Ibni Ummi Maktoum as "Amir" on Madina.

THE PROPHET MADE THREE FLAGS

One flag for Muhajireen, which he gave to Ali or Musab Ibni Omar (both names are there in narrations so maybe they took turns carrying it). The second flag was for Aws, Osaid Ibni Hudair was carrying that, while a third one was for Khazraj and Khabbab Ibni Munzir was holding it. Sa'd Ibni Obadah and Sad Ibni Muaz were both wearing armor. They were marching in front of the prophet. Altogether there were 100 people in armor.

The prophet saw a group marching at some distance. He asked about them, and the Sahabah told him,

> "These are the Jewish allies of Khazraj tribe. Ibni has Obai brought them?"

The prophet said,

> "Tell them to go back, for we do not seek their help."

Allah said (3:121)

> "And remember when you left your household in the morning posting the believers in encampments for war and Allah is the All hearer, the all Knower."

The prophet did not allow underage boys to fight When this army arrived in a place known as Shaikan, the prophet sent back Thabit, Abu

Saeed al Khudri Numan Ibni Bashir Sammurah Ibni Jundub, Rafi Ibni Khadij, Bara Ibni Aazib, Amir Ibni Hazm, Zaid Ibni Arqam, Arabah Ibni Aws, Sad Ibni Ageeb, Sad Ibni Juhainah and Zaheer Ansari. Rafi Ibni Khadeej cried. Sahabah interceded for him, telling the Prophet that he is an expert archer. They saw Sammurah Ibni Jundub in the same situation. They interceded for him; also, Sammurah himself said,

"I can defeat in wrestling."

The prophet said,

"Let's see."

So Sammurah, it is said, asked Rafi,

"Please do me a favor and let me defeat you as the prophet will not send you back now, as he has given his word to you already."

Rafi did him the favor and thus they both joined.

The prophet stayed at night there. He offered Fajr prayer at *Shawt*.

Mohammad Ibni Maslamah guarded the Muslims the whole night while Zakwan Ibni Abdi Qais was guarding the prophet.

IBNI UBAI RETURNED

The chief hypocrite who was a cheap man known for his heinous acts took three hundred people back to Madina on the grounds, that the prophet preferred youth's opinion and disregarded his. So he did not feel he could join him. Now only seven hundred Muslims remained.

This hypocrisy of Ibni Ubai harmed the feelings of Muslims; for a while some Muslims were so angry that they said those hypocrites should be killed first. Even two tribes, Banu Salamah, and Banu Haritha, intended to go back. It was not possible for seven hundred people to fight three thousand, but Allah protected them and provided them with courage.

Allah said (3:122)

> *"When two parties [tribes] from among you were about to lose heart, but Allah was their protector. And in Allah should the believers put their trust."*

WAR SKETCH AND PLAN

The Muslims had only two horses with them. The prophet took with him Abu Khaithamah al-Ansari: He passed by Banu Haritha arrived at the garden of Rabe Ibni Qaiz a hypocrite. He was blind but he heard their footsteps. He said,

> *"Who is there? If you are Mohammad, then you are not allowed to enter to my garden."*

A few Sahabah rushed to him but the prophet stopped them and said,

> *"His heart is as blind as his eyes."*

But before that the prophet could finish, Sa'd Ibni Zaid already had jumped over him and hit him on the head.

The prophet arranged, organized, and disciplined the army. He arranged their ranks in such a way that the mountain was to their back and Qanat valley and Ainain mountain were to their left and thus the Makkans army was in between them and Madina. From the Ainain side there was a fear of attack through a crack there. So, the prophet put fifty archers under the command of Abdullah Ibni Jubair on the hilltop which was later known as "Jubal Ur Rumat," the archers' hill. The prophet told them,

> *"If you saw that even the birds are snatching us, you should not leave this place and if you saw that we defeated them, or they overtook us, you should not leave this place."*

He put Munzir bin Amr on "Maimanah" (right forwards) and Zubair Ibn Ul Awwamon "Maisarah" (the left forward). Also, he put Miqdad Ibn Ul Aswad with Zubair. He said to Zubair to face the Khalid platoon. The prophet put the combatant fighters in the front. This plan and sketch were the best ever plan in that field.

The Makkans put on their right forward Khalid Ibn Ul Walid, on their left forward Ikramah Ibni Abu Tahla. They put Safwan Ibni Umayyah or Amr Ibni Hesham on their infantry and Abdullah Ibni Rabee'a as leader of their archers. Tulaiha Ibni Abi Talha was holding their flag, which is why the prophet switched the Muhajireen flag from Ali to Mus'ab Ibni Omar, who was from the tribe of Tulaiha from Banu Abdud Dar.

THE PROPHET'S SWORD

The prophet brought out a sword and said,

> *"I want to give it to someone who can do with it what it deserves."*

A few Sahabah come forward, like Abu Bakr Omar Ali and Zubair, but when Abu Dujanah Simak Ibni Kharshah stood up and asked for, the prophet gave it to him. Abu Dujanah said, I take it for what it deserves but what does it deserve? The prophet said, to use it on enemies so much it gets crooked.

Abu Dujanah whenever was going forward for a combat, wrapped his head and tied it with a red scarf. He walked forward showing his muscles. When he was walking, the prophet said,

> "This is a walk Allah only wants to see in battle."

Abu Sufyan, the leading general of the Makkans, said,

> "Banu Abdul Dar! You know we had given our flag to your tribesman Nadar Ibn Ul Harith in Badr but you know what happened there [he was captured). So, if you cannot qualify then give it back to us as nations get rise and fall with their flag."

They said,

> "You will see tomorrow, what we can do."

It is worth mentioning that when Qusai Ibni Kilab had given different statuses and responsibilities to different tribes of Quraish in Makkah, at that time the flag carrying was given to Banu Abdud Dar.

THE STRATEGY OF QURAISH

Abu Sufyan sent a message to Ansar:

> "Leave us alone with our own cousins, the Quraish."

By this he tried to separate them from the prophet, but they said,

> "We have given the prophet a word in our pledge of Aqabah that we will defend you as we defend our honor, which means at the cost of our lives."

Then from the ranks of Makkans came Abd Amr Ibni Saifi Aby Aamir - Ar - Rahib. This man was originally from Madina but became a puppet of Caesar of Rome and was living in Makkah. He had told the Quraish,

> "When I will go out and my people will see me, they will leave Mohammad alone and will go back."

He called on his tribe, the Aus, saying,

> "I am Abd Amr Abu Amir!"

They said,

> "Oh, the villain! may you perish."

He said,

> "Oh! my people have gone astray."

He had a group of people with him. They started throwing rocks on Muslims. The Muslims retaliated in the same way, so they ran back.

Then Talha Ibni Abi Talha al- Abdari came out. He was called "Kabsh Ul Kateebah," the ram of the force. He challenged the Muslims. Ali came out and hit his legs, he fell down and his trousers got open and he became exposed. Ali turned around not to look at him, but there from Zubair came out and killed him.

The prophet said, "Allah u Akbar!" and the Muslims did the same.

After him his brother Uthman Ibni Abu Talha came out. He raised the flag. The women were singing behind him saying,

> "The flag careers must either color the spear with blood or break it."

Hamzah hit him and that was his end. Then his third brother, Abu Saeed Ibni Abi Tallah, came out. Sad Ibni Abi Waqas targeted him with his arrow. It entered his throat and thus he was killed. Then after that Musafi the son of Talha Ibni Abi Talha came out and got the flag.

Aasim Ibni Thabit Ibni Abi Aflah hit him with an arrow, and he was killed. Then his brother Harith raised the flag. Aasim killed him with an arrow as well. Then their third brother raised the flag. Zubair killed him, then the fourth son of Talha came out. His name was Jallas. Talha Ibni Abdullah killed him. After that Artat Ibni Sharabeel got the flag. He was killed by Ali. In the same series Abu Zaid Ibni Amr was killed by Qazman. Then Shuraih Ibni Qariz kept the flag. Qazman killed him as well. Then the son of Sharjeel got it. He was also killed by Qazman. This Qazman was a hypocrite but ego brought him. Then the slave of Sharjeel Sawwab raised the flag and he was killed him as well.

The first six people were from one family and altogether, 10 people were killed one after the other and all of them were from Banu Abdud Dar. Actually, Abu Sufyan had reproached them, so they tried to wash out the blame.

This slave Sawwab showed his bravery when both his hands were cut so he was holding his hands between his chin and chest. But after him there was none to hold it and it was lying on the ground.

ABU DUJANAH AND THE PROPHET'S SWORD

As we have mentioned before that the prophet offered his sword to one who can do with it what it deserves, and Abu Dujanah got it. Hind Bint Utbah was along with some other Quraish ladies inspiring their army with their songs. Once she came under the sword of Abu Dujanah, but he refrained from hitting her, not because she was a woman, but he said,

> *"I thought it unsuitable to kill a woman with the sword of the Prophet."*

Zubair, who had asked the prophet for this sword but couldn't get it, says that Abu Dujanah did what the sword deserved. He says that whenever any Mushrik hit a Muslim, I wished if he came across Abu Dujanah and in a few cases it happened.

THE BRAVERY OF MUSLIMS

The Muslims showed their bravery in a proper way and they defeated this big army of Makkans and put them on the run out of the field. In this combat, the code words of the Muslims was "ummah ummah" while that of the Makkans was *"Ya lal uzza ya lal Hubal,"* calling their respective gods.

HAMZA WAS KILLED

Along with this bravery, some losses also happened to the Muslims. The big loss was the killing of Hamza the uncle of the prophet. As we mentioned before, Islam became strong with the Iman of Hamza and Umar at Makkah, as the people of Makkah were very much afraid of them both, their bravery, and the way they used to face and fight. In the battle of Badr, Hamza had killed Utbah, the father of Hind, his son Waleed and also, he killed Tuaim Ibni Adi, the uncle of Jubair Ibni Mut'im. Jubair offered his slave Wahshi Ibni Harb his freedom if he killed Hamza. Also, Hind offered him a big amount for killing him. He was a good archer from far with his spear, but facing Hamza was very difficult. So, it was necessary to hit him from afar.

WAHSHI IBNI HARB RELATES HIS STORY:

The following story was related by Wahshi himself. He says that I was looking for such opportunities when Siba from Makkah side came out and asked the Muslims to come out and to fight him.

Therefrom Hamza came out and said,

> "Oh the son of Ummi Anmar the one who used to circumcise the women! You have come to fight Allah and the prophet of Allah."

So, he hit him and killed him.

> "But when he was going back, passing by, I threw my spear on him and it hit his vital part below the belly button, and he fell down and died."

Wahshi said,

> "I took no part in this battle before nor any after this. I came back to my tent as I got what I came for."

In his story he says that at the time of the conquest of Makkah when the prophet declared him a war criminal along with a few others, he ran away towards Ta'if. But when the people of Taif were also defeated by the prophet and their representatives were going to Madina for the release of their prisoners, he accompanied them. When the prophet saw me, he asked me,

> "Are you Wahshi? I said yes."

He said,

> "You killed Hamza."

I said,

> "It happened like this."

Then I said,

> "Oh Messenger of Allah! You have said and we have heard it, that one who has committed an illegal sex act or killed someone or committed theft will face the torment, so is there any room for my forgiveness?"

He said,

"Wait!"

Then he said,

> "But one who repented and believed and practiced righteous deed then these people, Allah will change their evil deeds into good deeds. And Allah is the most forgiving, Merciful." (25:70)

So, I said, maybe I will not be able to practice righteous deeds. He said wait, then he said,

> "Verily Allah does not forgive when associates are attributed to him, while he forgives anything except that to whom he wills." (4:48)

So, I said, maybe he will not will the same for me as I did the worst. He said, "Then wait!" Then he said,

> "Say, to my slaves who have transgressed against their own selves, despair not of the Mercy of Allah verily, Allah forgives all sins verily he is the most forgiving, Merciful." (39~53)

Then I said,

"Now the matter is clear."

So, I accepted Islam.

Wahshi says,

> *"I made a strong will if I can do such a good thing for Islam, which can take off the burden, my conscience was carrying, because of the killing of Hamza to have it as an expiation for it. Then the time came when the Muslims were going to fight Musailamah Al Kazzab and his people in the time of Abu Bakr. I joined them with the intention that I will kill Musailamah. In the field I rushed towards him, He was among his security. I hit him with my spear in the middle of his chest. An Ansari hit him on his head with a sword and he fell down. From*

the rooftop a woman shouted, oh! a black man killed Amirul Momineen."

He said,

"Coming back towards my people I was chanting, 'Thank God!' I had killed the best of Muslims, and today I killed the worst of the infidels and maybe it is an expiation for that act of mine."

HANZALAH IBNI AAMIR

This young man got married the day before he joined the Muslim Army for the good pleasure of Allah. He jumped to Abu Sufyan and almost killed him. But Shaddad Ibn Al Aswad cut off his hit and killed him. When the prophet ordered his companions to gather together the bodies of Martyred in the path of Allah, they found the body of Hanzalah with water dripping down his beard and head. Jibril informed the prophet that the angels had bathed his body. The prophet said to Sahabah to ask his wife, she said, he was in state of Janabat after meeting her, but he couldn't bathe and rushed to the field when was informed. The Muhaditheen called him *"Ghaseel Al Malaika," "the one washed by the angels."*

The rules of Shariah state that the body of a martyred should not be washed unless the person was martyred while in a state of *Janabat* (impurity after sex).

Now the Makkans ran out of the field towards Makkah and the Muslims spread here and there.

THE ATTACK OF MAKKANS

When the Makkans fled and the Sahabah started collecting the booty, they left. Then at that time those archers who were on the hilltop under the leadership of Abdullah Ibni Jubair, they said, to Abdullah that our brothers fought and got tired and now they are collecting the spoils also. So, we should go and help them to give them time to take rest. But they were also thinking that they didn't take part in the war, so if they do not join them in collecting these spoils then maybe they would not be given any share in that. Even though they had pushed the Makkans back from this side, Abdullah said to them,

> "As long as we do not receive a new order from the prophet we should not go down."

But they were of the view that this was to keep an eye on Makkans so they may not attack here from, and when they tried, the Muslims pushed them back but now that they have left the field then there is no need to keep standing here. So, forty of them came down.

At that time Khalid Ibni Waleed came back along with his platoon and attacked the remaining 10 archers and martyred them, and as Muslims were not alert, he attacked them, which caused the Muslims to run out. They were so disturbed and confused that they didn't know which way to run. Even they forget their code word, "ummah ummah", and that's why some of the Muslims were attacked by their own people, and in this way Yaman, the father of Huzaifah, was mistakenly killed by the Muslims. Huzaifah shouted,

> "My father, oh the servants of Allah! And May Allah forgive you!"

The Prophet offered him blood money later on, but he refused it, saying,

> "That is for the Muslims."

Abdullah Ibni Qamee'al Laithi killed Mus'ab Ibni Omair when he was wearing armor. At that time, he resembled the prophet. Ibni Qamee'ah thought he was the prophet. And that is why, when Mus'ab Ibni Omair fell down, the rumor spread that the prophet was martyred and this was another reason that people ran off the battlefield. In such a situation the prophet did not change his place. He was standing there still.

In the disturbance and turmoil some Muslims climbed the mountains and some of them they arrived in Madina. Some weak people even thought that now that the prophet is martyred and the Makkans have the upper hand, they should ask Abdullah Ibni Obai to ask the Makkans to give them a peace (protection).

ANAS IBNI NADR

He was the uncle of Anas. He couldn't go to Badr, so he said more than one time to the prophet,

> *"I wish I had an opportunity like that and O prophet! Then you will see what I will do."*

He was passing by a group of Muslims sitting their half-dead. Umar and Talha were amongst them. He asked this group,

> *"What is going on?"*

They said that the prophet was martyred. He said then,

> *"What are you waiting for? Stand up and be martyred for the same cause the prophet was martyred for."*

He said,

> *"O Allah! I disconnect myself from those who did wrong."*

He was proceeding towards Mountain Uhud, Sa'd Ibni Muaz asked him, where? He said,

> *"I feel the paradise fragrance from Uhud's side."*

He went ahead and fought the enemy wholeheartedly until he was martyred. He was so cut up that his sister recognized him through his fingers only. He took more than eighty hits and grave wounds on the front of his body. Sa'd later said to the prophet,

"What Anas Ibni Nadr did today, I could never do."

But in fact, he lived up to his promise to the prophet.

THABIT IBNI DAHDAH

Thabit also addressed Ansar, saying,

"If Mohammad is martyred, then what? Allah is alive and eternal. Stand up and fight for the cause of Allah. He is your helper. He will give you success."

Some Ansar joined him and they came towards the platoon of Khalid Ibni Waleed and fought until Thabit was killed by Khalid.

THE PROPHET WAS INJURED

When the Sahabah got attacked in such a way, they tried to escape. Nine people remained with the prophet, among them there were seven Ansar and two Muhajireen. When the prophet saw this, he called on them saying,

"Come to me...I am the messenger of Allah."

The polytheists recognized him so they attacked him. These nine people fought whole heartedly but the Mushriks were big in number. The ansar was martyred one by one and now only Sa'd Ibni Abi - Waqas and Talha Ibni Obeidallah, the two muhajir remained. Utbah Ibni Abi Waqas, the brother of Sa'd Ibni Abi - Waqas threw a stone on the prophet, which broke his teeth and tore his lower lip. Abdullah Ibni Shahab injured his forehead while Abdullah ibn Qamee'ah al Laithi hit the shoulder of the prophet, but that day prophet was wearing two layers of armor so no injury happened there. But due to that strong hit, the prophet had severe pain in his shoulder for almost a month afterwards. Then that dirty man hit his face and two rings of the helmet hir the face of the prophet. Ibn Qamee'ah when hit the prophet said.

"Take this, this is from Qamee'ah."

The prophet said,

"May Allah crush you."

Ibn Hajar says that later on once this man was grazing his sheep and goats. A ram butted him and he rolled down the hill and got smashed.

The prophet fell into a trench, a few of which Abu Aamir Al Fasiq had dug in that area and covered with some grass. These disbelievers shouted,

"Mohammad is killed."

Kab Ibni Malik Al-Ansari was the first one who saw him injured. He recognized him by his eyes. He shouted with a louder voice,

"O Muslims! Congratulations! Here is the prophet of Allah, he is alive."

Then, a group of Muslims including Abu Bakr, Umar, Ali, Zubair Talha and Harith Ibn Simmah came over. Ali got hold of the hand of the prophet and Talha helped him onto his feet. Abu Obadiah ibn Ul Jarrah cut off the ring of the helmet in his face with his teeth so the prophet would not be further harmed and he lost a tooth.

The father of Abu Saeed al Khudri named Malik Ibni Sinan sucked the blood of the prophet and swallowed it. The prophet told him to spit it out. He said,

> *"By God! I will never."*

Then the prophet said,

> *"Whoever wants to see a man of paradise on earth should look at this man."*

Later on, he was martyred also.

The prophet said,

> *"How will those who dyed the face of their prophet with his blood succeed?"*

As implicitly this could have meant a bad *Dua* on them also, so Allah said.

> *"Not for you is the decision, (but for Allah) whether to return on them or to punish them verily they are the wrong doers." (3:128)*

Later on, the prophet made a *Dua*.

> *"O Allah, guide my people as they do not understand."*

Sa'd Ibni Abi - Waqas said, I made up my mind that I will go ahead either to be martyred or to approach the prophet to defend him. Going ahead, I saw someone whose face was bleeding but couldn't recognize him as there was Miqdad between me and him. I was to ask Miqdad, to tell me who is the man but before this Miqdad himself said.

> *"Sad! This is the prophet.' The prophet got some sand and pebbles in his hand and threw that towards the disbelievers a few times so they started running away towards the mountain. Miqdad said to me that the prophet is calling you. So, I went to him. He made me sitting front of himself and made a Dua in my favor. O Allah, make his target perfect and accept his Dua."*

I started shooting the arrows when mine were finished, then the prophet was giving me his arrows saying.

"Shoot it my parents be sacrificed of you."

This day Sa'd shot hundreds of arrows and the prophet was saying this to him.

Ali said,

"I never heard the prophet saying the same to anyone except for Sa'd. We say it means in Uhud otherwise he said the same to Zubair in Ahzab."

THOSE WHO STAYED FIRM

In this hustle and bustle, fourteen Sahabah stayed firm and these are.

Abu Bakr,

Umar,

Abdul Rahman,

Sa'd Ibni Abi Waqas,

Talha Ibni Ubaid Ullah,

Abu Ubaidah Ibn Ul Jarrah, and Zubair Ibn Ul Awwam, while from

Abu Dujanah,

Kabbab Ibn Munzir,

Aasim Ibni Thabit,

Harith ibn Simmah,

Sahl ibn Hunaif,

Sad Ibni Mu'aaz, Osaid Ibni Hudair.

The prophet himself shot so many arrows that his bow was broken.

TALHAH IBN OBAIDULLAH

Imam Nasai narrated from Jaber Ibn Abdullah that the Ansar were sacrificing their lives, then Talha ibn Obaidullah came forward. He fought with the strength of eleven people. His hand got cut off, means fingers so he said.

"Huss."

The prophet said,

"If you had said 'Bismillah' then the angels would have lifted you up and the people would have been looking at you."

Imam Hakim relates that.

"Talha had injured 35 or 39 people with his hand. He pushed the polytheists back."

Qais ibn Hazim says,

"I had seen that hand of Talha (Bukhari)."

Imam Tirmizi narrated that the prophet said that anyone who wished to see a martyred one walking on earth should look at Talha.

Abu Dawud relates that Abu Bakr whenever he was talking about Uhud, he used to say,

> "That whole day was the day of Talha."

Imam Bukhari narrated from Sa'd Ibni Abi - Waqas that he saw that day that two people wearing white were fighting around the prophet i.e., Jibril and Mika'eel.

A FEW OTHERS WHO WERE DEFENDING THE PROPHET

Abu Talha from ansar, shot so many arrows that he broke three bows. He was shielding the prophet. If the prophet raised his head, Abu Talha used to say,

> "My parents were sacrificed for you, raise not your head, my chest is a shield for your chest."

Shammas Ibni Uthman al-Makhzoomi was also defending the prophet until he was injured. He was brought to Ummi Salamah and after one day and night he died.

The prophet said on that day you cannot compare shammas but with a shield only.

Sahl Ibni Hunaif was also busy to defend the prophet, and the prophet was saying give arrow to Sahl.

Qatada ibn Numan Ansari was protecting the prophet's face with his own. An arrow came and it hit his eye and his eyeball came out and was hanging on his cheek. The prophet fixed it with his holy hand. Tabari relates that it was then looking much more beautiful than the other one and its sight was also better. Ibn Ishaq also narrated the same.

OTBAH IBN ABI WAQQAS WAS KILLED

Utbah ibn Abi Waqas hit the prophet with a rock on his mouth, broke his teeth, and tore his lip. Hatib ibn Abi Balta'a followed him and hit him with his sword in such a way that his head was separated from his body. Hatib got both his horse and sword. Sa'd Ibni Abi - Waqas said,

> "I was eager to kill my brother but Hatib got the opportunity."

Abdur Rahman Ibni Awf was hit hard in the mouth. On that day he got twenty injuries, one of which was on his leg. Later on, he used to walk lame.

UMMI AMMARAH

Her name was Naseebah Binti Ka'b Al Mazaniyah. She said,

> "I was giving water to the injured people. The fight was in the Muslims' hands, but later on when the position was changed, I rushed to the prophet and started fighting. I was using my sword and shooting arrows as well. I was injured by Ibni Qamee'ah when he was approaching the prophet and was saying, 'Where is

Mohammad? I may not be safe if he is safe' so Mus'ab Ibni Omair and I both started fighting him. He hit me and I was injured. I also hit him but he was wearing two layers of armor." On this day her husband Zaid Ibni Asim and her two sons Abdullah and Habib were in the field as well. When the prophet saw them, he said, *"O the family! May Allah bless you."* Naseebah said O prophet of Allah! Please make a Dua that Allah will give us your company in Paradise. The prophet made that Dua then Naseebah said, *"Now I don't care whatever hardship I may face in this world."*

The prophet said,

"On that day, whichever direction I was looking at, there was Ummi Ammarah fighting to defend me. On that day she got twelve injuries."

She had joined Bai'at-I-Aqabah, Ghazwa-I-Uhud, Bai'at – Ur - Rizwan and Battle of Yamamah in the time of Abu Bakr.

MUS'AB IBNI OMAIR

Mus'ab had accepted Islam in a very young age and his family turned him out of their house and when the people of Madina asked the prophet for a teacher at the time of Bai'at-I-Aqabah, he sent Mus'ab Ibni Omair with them. He is the one who did land-leveling work at Madina as a center of Islam and the Islamic state.

In Uhud, he was holding the flag of the Muhajireen. Mohammad Ibni Sharabeel Alabdari says, that he was defending the hit by Ibni Qamee'ah so his right hand got cut off. He held the flag with his left hand and used to say,

"And Mohammad is but a messenger of Allah."

While these words were yet not come to the prophet. His left hand was cut so he held the flag to his chest with his upper arms and then he gave it to Ali. In this attack, the prophet came to Muslim army. Ka'b Ibni Malik recognized him. In the meantime, Uthman ibn Abdullah Ibn Ul Mughirah, a polytheist horse rider, came to attack the prophet and the prophet also got ready to counter him, but Uthman's horse fell into a trench. So Harith Ibnus Simma hit his leg and took his weapon and came to the prophet. Another polytheist rider, Abdullah ibn Jabir, hit the shoulder of Harith Ibnus Simma and he was injured so Abu Dujanah jumped at him and cut off his head with his sword.

THE MUSLIMS AND DROWSINESS

Drowsiness is a beneficial for tranquility and healing. The Muslims suffered a lot so Allah made them drowsy to get tranquil Allah says.

> *"Then after the distress he sent down for you a tranquility, i.e., a drowsiness overtaking a group of you."* (3:154)

Abu Talha said,

> *"I was in this group and my sword fell out of my hand a few times."*

THE PROPHET AND THE MUSLIMS TOWARDS THE MOUNTAIN

Under the cover of this fight, the Muslims and the prophet tried to go towards the mountain valley. Ali brought some water in his shield to the prophet, but the prophet didn't drink it because it did not smell good.

Ali washed the prophet's wounds with it. It is also narrated that Ali poured the water and Fatima washed the wounds and as the bleeding was not stopping, so they burned a piece of mat and put its ashes on the wounds. Mohammad ibn Maslamah brought some water. The prophet drank it and made *Dua* for him. As he had lost a lot of blood and he was wearing two armor coats, he couldn't climb. Then Talha sat down and took the prophet on his back.

The prophet prayed his *Zuhr* prayer in sitting and the Sahabah prayed behind him sitting as well and that's why some jurists are of the view then when imam due to reason prays in sitting then those behind him must pray in sitting without reason. But we say this was because most of them were injured or as the polytheists were still there in the surrounding area and if they were to see someone, they shoot arrow on him, that's why they prayed sitting down so as not to be seen. Also, later on in his last days of life, the prophet led them and he was sitting while they were standing behind him. When the prophet was going towards that valley, Obai ibn Khalaf came across and said,

"*I may perish if you got escape.*"

Sahabah asked the prophet,

"*Should we kill him before he approaches you?*"

He said,

"*Let him come.*"

The prophet got a spear from Harith ibn Simma and scratched Obai's neck with its tip and he shouted,

"*Mohammad killed me.*"

The Quraish said,

> "How? This is only a scratch without even any blood."

He told them that once in Makkah, he threatened Mohammad for that he fed his horse every day such and such amount of grain to ride it and to kill you. The prophet responded,

> "But I will kill you." And this is what happened to me. Even if he had just spit on me, he would have killed me and this is a spear hit."

They accused him of cowardice. Imam Hakim related he was sounding like a bull saying,

> "The pain I feel if distributed to all people gather in Zul Majaz. [an annual market of Arabs] they would have died of it."

Then, the polytheists again made an attack here under the command of Khalid but a group of Muhajireen and ansar pushed them back.

MUTILATION OF THE MARTYRS

After this attack, these people came back and getting ready to go back to Makkah while their ladies started mutilating the martyred. Hind Gar landed herself the organs of Hamzah. They cut off Hamzah's chest, brought out his liver and tried to chew it and then she spit it out. Actually, she was fulfilling a pledge to do that. When the prophet saw this, he took an oath that this is a war crime and by God he would do the same to seventy of them. Jibril came and recited the following verses to the prophet:

> *"And if you punish [as a revenge) then punish the like of what you have been punished with and if you endure patiently, for sure that is good for the patient people. And you may endure patiently and your patience is not but only from Allah and grieve not over them nor be distressed because of what they plot." (16:126, 127)*

Then the prophet said,

"Then I shall be patient,"

And thus, he fasted 3 days as an expiation for the breaking of his oath.

THE BRAVERY OF MUSLIM WOMEN

We have already described how Ummi Ammarah fought around the prophet. Anas says that he saw his mother, Ummi Sulaim, and Sayyidah Aaisha bringing skin bags full of water on their backs for Muslims. Ummi Saleet Ausaria was doing the same.

When Ummi Aiman saw the Muslims fleeing, she threw some dust to their faces reproaching them and demanding that give her their arms. She ran to the battlefield and started giving water to the Muslims.

> *It is narrated that Hiban Ibni Araqah hit her with an arrow, she fell down and some of her body was exposed. On this Hiban laughed so the prophet gave Sa'd Ibni Abi Waqas an arrow to hit him with. He did it and Hiban fell down and his hips were also exposed so the prophet also laughed. (As Seerah – Al - Halbia)*

ABU SUFYAN REJOICED

Abu Sufyan went to an elevated spot and called on Muslims, is Mohammad there? The Muslims looked at the prophet to see if he would allow them to answer but he didn't. Then he asked,

"Is the son of Abu Quhafah (Abu Bakr) there?"

They didn't answer. Then he asked about Umar, but they didn't answer. He asked about these three personalities as he was of the view that Islam is because of these three. At this, Umar couldn't hold himself and said,

"O enemy of Allah. All three are alive to cause you grief."

Then Abu Sufyan said,

"I have not ordered the mutilation of your dead but I feel no shame for that."

And then he said

"Habal! Go high."

The prophet said to the Sahabah,

"You don't want to answer him?"

They said,

"What should we say?"

The prophet said,

"Allah is the exalted and magnificent one."

Then Abu Sufyan said,

> "We have Uzza and you people do not."

The prophet said, you people don't answer? They said,

> "But what?"

The prophet said,

> "Allah is our helper and you don't have a helper."

Abu Sufyan said.

> "Ok! This day is a revenge of Badr and war has terms."

Umar said,

> "Not like this, as our martyred are in paradise and your dead are in hell."

Then Abu Sufyan said to Umar,

> "Come tome."

The prophet said,

> "Go what he says!"

Umar went to him. He asked him,

> "Have we killed Mohammad?"

Umar said,

> "No, He is listening to you now."

Abu Sufyan said,

> "You are more trusted to me than Ibni Qamee'ah."

He said, I have killed Mohammad. Ibni Ishaq narrates that Abu Sufyan announced,

> "We will see you again next year in Badr."

The prophet said to Umar,

> "Tell him that is done."

Ibni Hisham writes that the prophet said to Ali,

> "Go and see whether they have mounted their camels and their horses are going empty. If they have mounted their camels, then they are going to Makkah and if they are riding their horses, then they want to go towards Madina and then we have to give them a lesson."

Ali came back and told the prophet that they had mounted their camels.

Hafiz ibn Hajar says that the prophet sent Sa'd ibn Abi Waqas for this purpose so it may be that he sent them both one after the other.

Now it appeared that the polytheists had won the battle but actually they had not, as they were afraid and trying to get out of the area as soon as possible.

THE MARTYRED AND THE WOUNDED

When the Muslims were sure that the Makkans had left for Makkah, they started looking for the injured and the martyrs. Among the injured ones, they found Amir ibn Thabit Al Asram. The Muslims didn't know that he had come because whenever someone was asking him to accept Islam, he was refusing it so they asked him,

"Why are you here?"

He replied,

"I have accepted Islam."

Then he died. Sahabah told about him to the prophet. He said,

"He is in paradise."

Abu Hurairah said,

"He is a man who never prayed a single prayer, nor has he fasted one day but he still went to paradise; what a lucky man he is."

Qazman was another one among the injured. He had killed seven or eight people. They brought him to Bani Zafar zone. The Muslims congratulated him for Islam and martyrdom. He said,

"I didn't fight for Islam but to defend my people."

And then because of pain he killed himself. The prophet said,

"He is in hell."

Mukhaireeq, a Jewish man from Banu Thalab said to his people,

"Look! you are bound by the treaty of Madina to help Mohammad."

They said,

But this is "Sabat" [Saturday, the Jewish Sabbath], when we cannot do anything. He said may you not have any "Sabat" so he went on his own to the field and made

a will, if I am killed, my belongings are for Mohammad. Ibni Hisham says,

The prophet later on said.

"Mukhaireeq was a best Jew."

SA'D IBN RABEE

Mohammad ibn Maslamah says,

"The prophet sent me to acquire about Sa'd ibn Rabee, whom he had not seen. I found him injured. I told him, 'The prophet is asking about you and sent me to inquire and he said if you found him, say my Salam to him.' Sa'd replied, 'And peace be upon the prophet of Allah.' He also said to me, 'Tell the prophet that I feel the fragrance of paradise and tell my people if you are alive and something happened, to the prophet, then no excuse of yours is acceptable.' The prophet said, 'That may Allah have mercy on Sa'd in life and death both, he was sincere to Allah and his messenger.'"

THE MARTYRS

Some people had taken their martyred to Madina already but the prophet ordered them to bring them back and bury them in their own clothes along with their blood.

Abdullah bin Amr Ibn Hiram and Amr Ibn Ul Jamuh both were buried in one grave. Hanzalah ibn Aamir was bathed by the angels as he came to the field on the very first night of his marriage and was martyred. His wife came and told the prophet that when he was coming, he needed a Fard shower. Now the prophet was to arrange for his *ghusl* as in shariah a martyr one is in no need of shower unless he was in *Junabat*. The Angel Jibril came and told the prophet that the angels will bathe him. So, a piece of cloud came down, lifted him up and then brought his body back. Water was dripping off his beard and head. Hamzah's body was mutilated. His sister Safiya came to see her brother. The prophet told her son Zubair to take his mother back because she might not be able to bear the sight of her mutilated brother, but Safiya said,

> *"I know that and that is for Allah, so I will say only that indeed we belong to Allah and indeed we go back to him and I shall show patience."*

He was buried with his nephew who was his foster brother also named Abdullah ibn Jah'sh in one grave.

Imam Ahmad narrates from Khabbab that a cloak was brought to shroud Hamazah therein, but it did not quite cover his whole body so the prophet said,

> *"Cover his head with it and cover his feet with grass."*

The same thing happened to Mus'ab ibn Omair as well (Bukhari).

Wahab and his nephew Harith Ibni Utbah had brought their sheep and goats for grazing. They heard that the prophet had left for Uhud regarding a Battle. They left their herd and rushed to Uhud. When Khalid and Ikramah both attacked, then the Wahab fought very bravely. A group of the polytheists came forward, the Wahab pushed them back with arrows. A second group came and he returned them with his sword. Fighting a third group he was martyred along with his nephew. The polytheists mutilated his body as well. The Prophet was standing beside their bodies, indicated to the Wahab, and said,

> "May Allah be pleased with you; I am pleased with you."

As his cloak was also short, the prophet himself covered his feet with grass. When Umar and Sa'd ibn Abi Waqas saw this, they said,

> "We wish to go towards Allah in form of this Muzani."

When the "Janazah" of Abdullah Ibni Amr Ibn Ul Hiram was lifted up, the prophet heard the cry of a woman. The prophet said,

> "Tell her not to cry as the angels were shadowing him with their wings."

Jabir ibn Abdullah says the prophet saw me very grieved, so he asked me. I said, my father was martyred and left behind a big family and a lot of debts. He said,

> "Should I not give you happy news, about how Allah met your father? Allah spoke to him. He said to your father, ask what you want to ask for. He said, if you give me another life to get martyred in your path once again. Allah said, but that is not going to happen again."

Allah said,

> "And think not of those who are killed in the path of Allah as dead. No! They are alive with their Lord and they have been given provisions. They rejoice in what Allah has bestowed upon them of his bounty and rejoice for the sake of those who have not yet joined them but are left behind that on them no fear shall come nor shall they grieve." (3:169)

Amr Ibn Ul Jamuh was lame so his family and friends told him not to go as you are excused. He said, but I want to be lame like this in paradise, so he was martyred. His son Khallad was also martyred. Amr's wife was the sister of Jabir's father, Abdullah. He was martyred as well. She was coming toward Uhud when she was informed about the Martyrdom of her brother, husband, and son, one after the other. With everyone she said,

> "Indeed, we are for Allah and indeed we are going back to him."

She used to ask constantly,

> "How is the messenger of Allah?"

And when she saw the prophet she said,

> "Every calamity is nothing to me now."

When the prophet arrived in Bani Abdul Ash'hal, he saw a few women crying for their dead. The prophet wept and said,

> "Hamzah, there is no one to cry for."

So Sa'd ibn Abi Waqas came towards these women and said,

> "Go to the prophet and mourn the death of his uncle."

They came and did the same.

Note: Ar that time, mourning was not yet forbidden. Then the very next day, the prophet forbade it.

The prophet met his cousin Hamanah Bint-I-Jahsh on his way back. He consoled her over the death of her brother Abdullah Ibn Jah'sh. She said,

> "We belong to Allah and indeed we shall return to him."

On his condolence for her uncle Hamzah, she said the same but when the prophet consoled her for the death of her husband, Mus'ab ibn Omair, she cried. The prophet said,

"For a woman the husband is much more than anyone else."

On his way he saw the mother of Sa'd ibn Muaz coming on a ride. Sa'd said,

"O messenger of Allah! My mother is here."

The prophet consoled her for the death of her son Amr. She said,

"When you are unharmed then there is no worry."

The prophet of Allah made *Dua* for all people. Ummi Sa'd said,

"And make Dua for all those who stayed behind,"

and the prophet did it. The prophet came to Madina on Saturday Shawwal – U l- Mukarram. He gave his sword to Fatima to wash. Ali also gave her his sword to wash. He said,

"May this sword made me true today."

The prophet said,

"And with you Abu Dujanah and Sahl Ibni Hunaif too."

Ibn Ishaq says that 22 Makkans were killed. But after thorough study, it seems that 37 people of them were killed. From the Muslim side four Muhajireen were martyred, while from Aws there were 24 and from Khazraj their number was 41.

THE PROPHET (SAW) VISITED THE SHUHADA

Later on, when the Prophet (SAW) was in Madina he used to visit the *Shuhada* of Uhud on Saturday.

Once he came and said,

> *"I am the fore-sent treasury for you and by Allah. Indeed, I see my pond now and indeed I have been given the keys of the earth and indeed by Allah I don't fear of you doing shirk after me, but I have a fear that you will compete each other in accumulating wealth."*

EMERGENCY DECLARED MADINA

We mentioned that in the very beginning the Muslims got victory, but later on the scene got changed, so here in Madina an emergency was declared and the Sahabah started guarding Madina from all around not to be attacked by the Makkans. Allah said (3:121-129):

> *"And [remember] when you left your household in the morning, placing the believers at their posts for the battle. And Allah is the all-hearing, All-Knower." (3:121)*

> *"When two parties from among you were about to lose heart, but Allah was their protector and in Allah may the believers put their trust." (3:122)*

> *"And indeed, Allah had assisted you at Badr when you were weak [few in number without enough weapons]. So, fear Allah that you may pay thanks to him." (3:123)*

> *"When you were saying to the believers is it not enough for you that your Lord should keep you three thousand angels sent down." (3:124)*

> *"Yes, if you remain patient [stable] and pious [stick to your job?] and the enemy comes rushing at you, your Lord will help you with five thousand angels having marks [or have been making marks on the hit one]." (3:125)*

> *"And Allah has not made it but a happiness for you and that your hearts may get satisfaction with It, while there is no help but from Allah the all-mighty, the all-wise." (3:126)*

> *"So that he may cut off a part of those who disbelieved to humiliate them so they may retire frustrated [disappointed]." (3:127)*

> *"Not from you is any part of the affair (O Mohammad)! whether He [Allah] forgave them or punished them. For surely, they are the wrongdoers." (3:128)*

> *"And to Allah belongs all that is in the heavens and all that is on the earth. He forgives whom he wills, and he punishes whom he wills. And Allah is the oft-forgiving, most-merciful." (3:129)*

Allah relates the story of Uhud but in between he reminded them his help to them in Badr to tell them that lost is not for you always as you got victory in Badr, even though you were few in number and weapons, and here also He protected Banu Salamah and Banu Haritha from cowardice even though they had lost heart and were to go back but Allah saved them. And then He made it clear to them not to be weak or worried as He said:

Holy Quran 3:139 - 160

> *"And be not from infirm nor grieve and you will have the upper hand (will be superior and victorious) if you are believers (truly)." (3:139)*

"If a wound has afflicted you [in Uhud] then a wound like this had afflicted that nation also [at Badr], and these are the days [incidents] we give to people by turns, and to know [distinct] those who believed and to take martyrs [or expert as failure teaches a lot] from among you. And Allah likes not the wrongdoers." (3:140)

And that Allah may purge those who believe and to efface the disbelievers." (3:141)

"Did you think that you will enter the garden [paradise] and Allah will not have yet known [distinct] those who strove hard among you and will not have yet known the stable [patient]." (3:142)

"And indeed you had been wishing for death before you met it so indeed you have seen it and you were looking at it." (3:143)

"And Mohammed (SAW) is but a messenger. Indeed, messengers have passed away before him. So, if he dies or is killed then will you turn back on your heels? And whoever turns back on his heels he cannot harm Allah a little bit. And Allah will give reward to the grateful [obedient]." (3:144)

"And this is not for a person to die but with the leave [order] of Allah as an appointed term and whoever desires the reward of this world, we shall give him that and whoever desires reward from the hereafter we shall give him that. And we shall reward the grateful [obedient]." (3:145)

"And how many Prophets fought in his company, a lot of the people of Lord. They never lost heart for that which did befall them in the path of Allah nor did they

weaken, nor they abuse themselves. And Allah loves the patient [stable]." (3:146)

"And their saying was no other than that they said, our Lord, forgive our sins and our transgression in our affairs and make firm our feet [make us stable] and give us victory over the disbelievers." (3:147)

"So, Allah gave them the reward of this world and the best reward of the hereafter. And Allah loves those who do good." (3:148)

"O you who believe, if you obey those who disbelieve they will turn you back on your heels and you will become losers." (3:149)

"Nay, Allah is your patron [protector] and He is the best of helpers." (3:150)

"Soon we will cast terror into the hearts of those who disbelieved because they set up with Allah that for which he has not sent down any authority. And their abode is fire, and how bad is the abode of the wrong doers." (3:151)

"And indeed Allah made his promise true to you when you were cutting them ([slaying them] with his permission [or his decree] until when you became weakhearted [lost your courage] and disputed regarding the order [of the Prophet for the archers over the mountain whether it was until the new order or until victory which we got] and you disobeyed after that and he showed you people what you loved [means the victory and the booty]. Among you there are some who wish this world, and among you there are some who wish the hereafter. Then He [Allah] turned you away from them in order to

test you. And for sure He has pardoned you. And Allah is gracious to the believers." (3:152)

"[remember] when you were running away [dreadful] without turning to anyone [without looking at anyone] and the Messenger was calling you from your back (not to run away and come back) so He [Allah] gave you one distress over the other [more than one distress to be used to] so you may not grieve at what had escaped you not at what befell you and Allah is well aware of what you do." (3:153)

"Then after the distress He sent down on you peace, i.e., a slumber overtaking a group of you, while another party whom their own selves rewarded anxious, thinking about Allah unjust i.e., thinking of ignorance [foolishness]. They were saying, 'Do we have any part in the affair [or we do not have any part in the affair)?' Say [O Mohammed] affair, as a whole belongs to Allah. They were concealing in themselves [their hearts] what they were not revealing to you. They were saying, 'Had we any hand in the affair we would not have been slain here.' Say [O Mohammed] had you remained in your houses, those for whom the death was decreed would certainly have gone forth to the places of their lying down [death places] and that Allah May test what is in your breasts and may purge what was in your hearts. And Allah is the all-knower of what is in the heart." (3:154)

"Verily those who turned back on the day when the two armies met [in Uhud], it was Satan who caused them to backslide [run away] on account of some of what they had done and for sure Allah has pardoned them. For sure, Allah is forgiving, forbearing." (3:155)

> "Do you who believe, be not like those who disbelieved and who said regarding their brethren when they travelled on the earth or they were in fight, if they would have been with us, they would not have died, nor killed so that Allah may make it an intense regret in their hearts. And Allah gives life and causes death. And Allah is all-seer of what you do." (3:156)

> "And if you were killed or died, for sure the forgiveness from Allah and mercy is for better than what they amass [accumulate]." (3:157)

> "And if you were killed or died, unto Allah you shall be gathered for sure." (3:158)

> "And by the Mercy of Allah you deal with them gently and had you been rough and harsh hearted they would have certainly broken away, [dispersed] from around you, so pardon them, and ask forgiveness for and take council with them in the affairs. Then when you have taken a decision then put your trust in Allah. Verily Allah loves those who trust." (3:159)

> "If Allah helps you, then no-one can overcome you, and if he forsakes you then who is there to help you after Him. And in Allah let the believers put their trust." (3:160)

Then as some of them said where from this misfortune befell us? They were saying things so to correct them Allah said,

Holy Quran 3:165-167

> "[what's the matter?] When a misfortune befell you even though you have afflicted in double of that, you say where from this happened? Say [O Mohammed] this is

from your own selves. Verily Allah has power over everything." (3:165)

"And what befell you on the day when the two armies met [at Uhud] was by the leave of Allah in order that he might know [test and distinct] the true believers." (3:166)

"And that He might know [test] the hypocrites and it was said to them, come fight in the path of Allah [in the front] or defend in the rear] or defend [in the rear or defend yourselves] they said, 'Had we know fight, we would have followed you for sure, [but we do not know how to fight or had we known that you are going for fight we would have followed you]. They were that day nearer to disbelief than themselves to faith. They say with their mouths what is not in their hearts. And Allah is the best knower of what they conceal." (3:167)

"Those who said regarding their brethren [the martyred one] if they would have followed us [and would not have gone to Uhud] they would not have been killed. Say [O Mohammad] then, avert death from yourselves if you are truthful [in what you say]." (3:168)

"And think not of those who were killed in the path of Allah as dead. Nay, but they are alive with their Lord, been provided [with permission]." (3:169)

"Rejoicing what Allah has given them, of His bounty. And they are getting glad tidings about those who have not yet joined them but are left behind that on them there is no fear nor shall they grieve." (3:170)

"They rejoice in the grace and bounty from Allah and that Allah does not waste the reward of the believers." (3:171)

> *"Those who answered [responded positively the call of] Allah and the messenger after that an injury had touched them. For those who did good [responded sincerely] from among them and feared [Allah or feared and avoided cowardice] there is a big reward."* (3:172)

> *"Those onto whom the people said that people [the Quraish] have gathered against you so fear them [and don't go to face them] so this increased [enriched] them in faith and they said, Allah is sufficient for us as he is the best disposer [of the affairs]."* (3:173)

> *"So, they came back [from that journey] with grace and bounty from Allah [and] no harm touched them, and [as] they followed [looked for] the good pleasure of Allah. And Allah is the owner of the great bounty."* (3:174)

> *"Verily this one is Satan frightening you of his friends [the disbelievers] so fear not them, fear me only if you are believers."* (3:175)

Allah made it clear that in worldly life some time one side will prevail and sometime the other. This is also a test that who remains firm in both situations. Also, it is narrated that after Badr some Muslims used to say,

> *"If we will meet our enemy once again?"*

But now when it happened like this then they said as if this was death? So, Allah said,

> *"You people were asking for this death. The lesson was not to wish a fight and if you get defeated then don't lose your heart."*

Also, when the views of the martyrdom of the Prophet Mohammad was spread and they lost their heart, then Allah said that he was a messenger and he has given the message and was mortal. But you people may carry on his mission after him.

Some hypocrites said to the Muslims,

> *"Let's go and ask protection for us from Abu Sufyan."*

So, Allah said,

> *"If you people listen to them, you will be ruined."*

Also, some Muslims said,

> *"Allah had promised us help and victory, but where is it?"*

So, Allah said he had made his promise true and they had received victory and bounty as well but they came down of the hill so they lost their victory, but still that is good for them as they became accustomed to grief, they learned a lesson, and also people became distinct from each other in situations where they were tested. Also, you came to know that neither going to the battlefield is death nor staying at home is security. Every day is not the same; be ready in life for situations.

And when a cloak was lost of the booty and some hypocrites said maybe the Prophet had taken it. then Allah said,

> *"What nonsense is this? This messenger is the grace of Allah; why are you causing the anger of Allah to yourselves by saying such things?"*

Then he told them that the Martyred got a new life and provisions as well.

Regarding Badr it is proven that angels came there but regarding Uhud, there are only sayings in this regard.

GHAZWAH, HAMRA-UL ASAD

The Prophet Mohammad (SAW) came back to Madina on Saturday. Ansars were guarding his house at night. The Prophet Mohammad himself was thinking that maybe they will attack back.

Waqidi related that in the morning Abdullah Ibni Amr came to the Prophet Mohammad and said,

> "At night, I came to Malal [a place] with a few friends. The Quraish were staying there and saying that they should have followed them to Madina to get rid of them. Then some of them said they should go now, and attack Madina but Safwan ibn Umayyah said to them, 'Be not foolish, do you think they will spare you if you attack their city? Lot of Khazraj people were taken back by Abdullah Ibn Obai yesterday. But now if you enter the city, they will join them and you will get stuck.'"

When the Prophet (SAW) was informed of this talk, he said,

> "Even though Safwan is not a reasonable man, this talk of him is a reasonable one. I swear by Allah, he had prepared branded stones for them if they would have come."

On Sunday, the Prophet ordered Bilal to announce that they would follow the Makkans, but only those who were there in Uhud yesterday would be permitted to join them. Abdullah Ibn Ubai said,

> "I want to go also,"

But the Prophet (SAW) refused him.

Jabir said,

> "O The prophet of Allah! I wanted to join you but yesterday my father was going and he ordered me to stay behind to take care of my seven sisters,"

So, the prophet allowed him to join. The Prophet (SAW) sent three Muslims to enquire about the Makkans. Two of them met Makkans at Hamra-Ul-Asad. So, they killed them both. When the third, named Thabit Ibni Oahhak, arrived, he found their bodies so he buried them. The Prophet (SAW) said to Umar,

> "The Quraish will never be defeated as long as we do not do Istilam of Rukni Yamani."

He told Talha,

> "Until we conquer Makkah, they are not defeated properly."

The Prophet (SAW) appointed Abdullah Ibni Ummi Maktoum as Amir at Madina. He gave the flag to Ali when he arrived Hamra-Ul-Asada, outside Madina by eight miles. Ma'bad Ibni Abi Ma'bad al Khuza'a came and accepted Islam. He said,

> "We are very sorry for what happened yesterday. We wished you to be in good form."

The Prophet (SAW) said to him to go and to frighten Abu Sufyan. He went and found them in a place named "Rauha" some 36 miles from Madina. When he came there, they asked him what was there behind him. He said,

> "Mohammad, with a big army."

Abu Sufyan said,

> "But we want to go back to Madina to uproot them."

Ma-bad said,

> "Listen, be not foolish and flee towards Makkah. This was a muscle fight."

A caravan of Abdul Qais was going towards Madina. Abu Sufyan said to them,

> "Tell Mohammad we are coming back to Madina. If you do this, I will honor you with a big quantity of Raisin when you come to Okaz."

In some narrations the name of Nuaim Ibn Masud is mentioned that Abu Sufyan told him to do this, but according to our study it seems that this case of *Nuaim* was regarding Badr – as - Sughra, while Abdul Qais did it here on this occasion.

Some Mufassireen like Mujahid (applied these verses 173-175 which we have quoted to Badr-as-Sughra. But we say these verses are regarding Hamra-Ul- Asad as Allah has said it right after the battle of Uhud is narrated and after Uhud this Hamra-Ul-Asad happened. Mujahid said that the wording (3:174)

> "So they returned with grace and bounty from Allah, no harm had touched them."

And that was in Badr-as-Sughra, where they sold their goods and made a profit. But we say that to frighten the enemy to flee without a fight is also a great grace and bounty. After Uhud, some people thought that the Muslims would never stand and rise up, but they did and this was a great grace and bounty that a message was spread that those who think like this about Muslims, they are living in a fool's paradise. So, Allah said, in verses 172-175 as we have mentioned before.

A BELIEVER IS NOT TO GET BITTEN TWICE FROM THE SAME HOLE

Abu Azzah was a poet from Makkah. He was captured in Badr and he was supposed to be killed, as he used to scoff at Muslims in his poetry, even the women and at the Prophet, but he cried to the Prophet that he had only daughters and there was no one to take care of them. He promised that he would not badmouth the Muslims again and the Prophet released him, but later on he started the same practice again. Now he got captured here. Again, he started crying to the Prophet in the name of his daughters, but this time the Prophet said,

> "A believer is not to get bitten twice from the same hole."

So, he ordered Zubair or Zaid or Asim Ibni Thabit to cut him, and it was done.

MU'AAWIAH IBNI MUGHEERA IBNI ABIL AAS

The paternal grandfather of Abdul Malik Ibni Marwan came to his cousin Uthman Ibni Affan in Madina and Uthman asked the Prophet to give him permission to stay in Madina for three days.

Now when the Prophet left for Hamra – Ul - Asad, he broke the promise and stayed long spying for Quraish so the Prophet sent Zaid Ibni Haritha to go and kill him and he died.

The Prophet stayed in Hamra-Ul-Asad for three or five days. This could be called an addendum to Uhud or a separate mission.

Uhud gave a few lessons or benefits to the Muslims:

1. Hypocrisy will always out.

2. When the Prophet orders a thing to be done, then don't do your own deductions as long as he has not fixed a time for his order.

3. When you gain victory, then never be careless unless the fear is totally gone.

4. In this world things will happen alternate.

5. Tests will happen but never be coward or disheartened.

6. Martyrdom is a high rank.

7. You learn a lesson when you discover a shortcoming.

8. Difficulties and hardships strengthen one.

9. Who stands firm in either situation is the most stable.

10. With the Mission of Hamra-Ul-Assad you made it clear that we are not going to lose courage.

MISSIONS AFTER UHUD

SARIYAH ABU SALAMAH

News came to Madina that Talha and Salamah the sons of Khuwaylid along with their people had gone to Banu Asad asking them for help against the Prophet.

The Prophet sent Abu Salamah Ibni Abdul Asad with 150 people including Abu Ubaidah Ibni Jarrah, Sa'd Ibni-Abi Waqas, and Osaid Ibni Hudair and other great Sahabah from Muhajireen and Ansar. The Prophet told them to travel at night to surprise them. When they arrived in their area, Banu Asad fled away and the Muslims got their cattle. This was in Muharram Ul Haram year 4th (Zad Ul - Maad].

SARIYYAH ABDULLAH IBNI ONAIS

In the same Moharram news came that Khalid ibn Sufyan al Huzali plans to attack Madina. The Prophet sent an expedition under the command of Abdullah Ibn Onais. Khalid was killed. Abdullah brought his head. The Prophet gave him his staff to be a sign on the day of judgment. Abdullah made a will to put it with him in his grave (Zad Ul Maad)

SARIYATUR RAJEE

This is also called Sariyah of Asim Ibni Thabit in the month of Safar year 4th after *Hijra*. Banu Lahyan tribe said to Adl and Qarah tribes,

> "*If you ask the Prophet to send us some people to call towards "Deen", then we will give you some wealth.*"

They sent seven people pretending that they are Muslims. The Prophet sent six people with them: Asim Ibni Thabit, Marthad Ibni Abi Marthad-al-Ghanawi, Abdullah Ibni Tariq, Khalid Ibni Bukair, and Khubaib Ibni Adi. Imam Bukhari mentioned the number as ten people.

When these Sahabah arrived at "Rajee" a well of the Huzail tribe, which according to Wa Qidi and Ibni Ishaq is between Makkah and Ta'if near Mirat, these seven people of Adl and Qarah called on Huzail. They came with their swords and attacked the Sahabah. Asim Ibni Thabit and his colleagues brought out their swords. These people of

Huzail were swearing to them that they were not going to kill them, but Asim, Khalid and Marthad told their colleagues that these people were not trustworthy. So, they fought and were martyred. Zaid Ibni Dathinah, Abdullah Ibni Tariq and Khubaib came down from the hill. They tied their hands. Abdullah said,

> "This is the first cheating"

So, he opened his hands and attacked them and was martyred when they hit him with a big rock. They brought Zaid and Khubaib to Makkah and sold them to the Makkans. Safwan Ibni Umayyah bought Zaid to kill him for his father who was killed in Badr. He handed him over to his slave Nastas to kill him. Abu Sufyan asked Zaid,

> "Do you wish Mohammad to be in your place and you with your own people?"

He said,

> "I wish the Prophet to be safe wherever he is and I don't want to be with my people,"

So Nastas killed him.

Abu Sufiyan said,

> "I have never seen people having that much love for their leader."

Khubaib

Hajeer Ibni Abi Ihab – At - Taimi bought Khubaib. He was the ally of Oqbah Ibni Harith of Banu Nawfal. Oqbah wanted to kill someone for the killing of his father.

When Khubaib was in their custody, they started insulting him. He said,

> "I have never seen such a characterless people that they do such like thing to their prisoners,"

So, they were ashamed.

The lady in whose custody he was named as Maria said,

> "At night when Khubaib was reciting Quran in his prayer, we ladies used to cry."

Maria asked him,

> "Can I do anything for you?"

He said,

> "Give me soft drinking water and bring me no meat that is not slaughtered in the name of Allah."

He also asked to be notified that he was to be killed the day before.

She said,

> "When I told him that today they were going to kill him, he asked me for a razor. My baby son had gone into his room. I was afraid that since he had the razor maybe he would kill my son. I rushed to his room, and I saw he had my son sitting on his knee. When he saw me, he said, 'Did you think I would harm him? We don't do that.'"

She said,

> "I saw him eating grapes when there were no grapes to be in Makkah in those days.

When he was brought to be killed, they asked him,

> "Do you want Mohammad to be in your place?"

He said,

> "I don't even want a thorn to prick his foot."

They asked him his last wish. He said,

> "To pray two Rakat."

He prayed and then said,

> "If I wasn't worried that you will think of me that I want to delay my killing I would have asked you to allow me to pray another two Rakat but I don't."

Abu Sirwa'a brought him to the crucifixion place.

He said some verses that mean.

> "I don't care when I am getting killed as a Muslim, whichever side they want to lay me down, as this is for the sake of Allah and if he wills, He will put his blessing in each cut of my joins."

Then they crucified him. His body was upon the cross and they put guard on it. Amr Ibni Umayyah Ad - Damari and another Ansari went to Makkah if they can kill Abu Sufyan. They got the body of Khubaib as the guard was sleeping. They departed towards Madina with the body on their horse. Sometime later when the guard woke up, he couldn't see the body so he along with others ran towards Madina. They said,

> "When they came close to us, we brought down the body and put it on the ground and we saw the earth swallowed it."

Muhaditheen titled Khubaib a "Balee - Ul - Ard" "swallowed by the earth."

AASIM IBNI THABIT

In Uhud, this Asim had killed the son of Salafah Bint –i- Sa'd. She had made a pledge that she would drink wine in Asim's skull. The Huzail people tried to cut his head and to bring it to that woman to get a bounty. But when they were approaching his body, a lot of wasps came and protected it. They waited for nightfall, but at night from somewhere a flood came and took away the body. He is called,

> *"Hami –Ud- Dabar" and "Hameel –Us- Sail," "the protected by wasps and taken away by flood."*

He was the father-in-law of Umar. Umar said, How Allah made this pious man true in his wish as he had asked Allah that his body may not be touched by a *Mushrik* alive or dead.

SARIYYAH-I-BEER-I-MA'OONAH

This is an expedition like other expeditions but also a big tragedy and cheating by Banu-Aamir. This expedition is also called expedition of "Qurra" the reciters. They were forty or seventy in number. Also, this is called *Sariyah* of Munzir Ibni Amr al-Khazraji. This happened in Safar 4th after *Hijra*.

Abu Bara Aamir Ibn Malik Ibn Jafar Al Aamiri, who was known as a player of spears (Mula Ibn Ul Asinnah) because of his expertise in spear fighting and targeted throws, came to the prophet. The prophet presented Islam to him, but he did not accept it and said,

> *"This is a good call and concept, so if you will, send with me a few companions of yours to convey it to my people. Maybe they will accept it."*

The prophet said,

"But one can expect any evil from the people of Najd."

He said,

"But they are in my shelter and refuge,"

So, the prophet sent forty or seventy Qurra with him under the leadership of Munzir ibn Amr.

When these people arrived there at the Ma'oonah well located between Banu Salim and Banu Aamir, they gave a letter to Haram Ibn Malham, the brother of Ummi Sulaim and the maternal uncle of Anas ibn Malik in the name of Aamir ibn Tufail ibn Malik-Ibni Jafar al Kilabi. He was the nephew of Abu Bara. When he arrived there and gave the letter to him, he killed him without even looking into the letter and said to his people,

"Let us kill all these people."

They said,

"But they are in refuge of Abu Bara."

They refused to do it. So, he approached three tribes of Banu Sulaim: Ra'l, Asiyyah, and Zakwan. They agreed to it and made him their Amir and leader. Here the Muslims became concerned about Hiram when he didn't come back so they went after him. These people who were big in number surrounded them and killed all of them, except one Ka'b ibn Zaid an Najjar who was so badly injured and the enemies thought him dead as well, but he survived. Then Amr ibn Umayyah Ad Damari and Munzir Ibni Oqbah came after these Muslims. Munzir, when came to know what happened to his fellows, challenged these disbelievers, and fought them and was martyred and Amr Ibn Umayyah was captured. Amr ibn Tufail, when he learned that this captured man is from Mudar tribe, he brought him, cut a few hairs of his forelock, and freed him on behalf of his mother, who had vowed to do so.

Amr ibn Umayyah, when he was coming back, was taking rest under a tree in a place named Qar Qarah. Two men from Banu Kilab also came there and slept in the shade. Amr ibn Umayyah killed them as a revenge when he came back and related his whole story to the prophet, the prophet told him,

> "But those two people were in a treaty and you killed them."

He said,

> "By Allah, I never knew of it."

The prophet then started reciting Qunut – I - Nazilah in Fajr prayer to curse these cruel tribes who killed the missionaries (non-combatants) for no reason. Anas said,

> "The prophet did it for one month then Allah ordered him not to do so, so he stopped."

Then the prophet paid blood money to the families of the two men who were killed as they were in a treaty with the prophet, but Amr was not aware of that treaty.

Among those martyred was the liberated slave of Abu Bakr, Aamir Ibn Fuhairah, who used to bring his goats to the cave of Thaur to give fresh milk to the prophet when he was staying there for three nights at the time of migration to Madina. He was killed as well. He was riding with the prophet at the time of Hijrah. He was the one who wrote a document of protection for Suraqah, the one who came after the prophet at the time of "Hijrah" to catch him or to kill him and his horse was caught three times by the earth and then he asked for forgiveness and got a protection letter from the prophet. Jabbar ibn Aamir Sullami killed Ibni Fuhairah and tried to chop his body up but the body flew and disappeared. Jabbar then asked Amr Ibni Umayyah about him. He told him this was Aamir Ibn Fuhairah and then Jabbar accepted Islam. Abu

Bara fell in such a grief because of the treacherous act of his nephew that he died in a few days.

THE GHAZWAH OF BANU NADEER

As we mentioned before that at the time of Hijrah there were big tribes of Jews in Madina:

1) Banu Qanuqa, which the prophet turned out of Madina when they started teasing Muslims especially the women and plotting in the Capital,

2) Banu Nadeer

3) Banu Quraizah.

All these people were given their due rights as citizens and they were bound to be law abiding loyal and faithful to the state. But they started their conspiracies and treason from day one. The prophet warned them a few times but they never stopped. Then what happened at Uhud Rajee and in Beer –i- Ma'oonah to the Muslims gave them confidence. They started contacts with Mushrikeen at Makkah and hypocrites in Madina to get rid of Islam and Muslims. As we mentioned before, Amr ibn Umayyah ad-Damari killed two people from Banu Aamir and that was a mistake as they were in a treaty with the prophet.

The prophet said,

"Now we have to pay them blood money."

This was also written in the treaty of Madina that all these who are in the state, including the Jewish tribes, will be bound to defend the state and to pay whatever is binding on them. So here in this case also the Jews were bound to pay their share to the blood money. The prophet came to their village near Quba to talk to them in this regard.

CONSPIRACY

When the Prophet told them and asked them for their share, they said,

> *"Why not? For sure we will fulfill our obligation, but amongst themselves they said this is a prime opportunity to get rid of Mohammad once for all, as this procedure will be going on and maybe we will never get such an opportunity again. So, look! Mohammad is leaning to a wall so someone should go to the wall top from the back and throw down a heavy rock onto him."*

Amr Ibn Jahsh said, I will do this. Sallam ibn Mishkam said,

> *"No, this is treason, as we are bound by treaty and I am sure you cannot do this as Allah will inform him, and then you people will be of nowhere."*

But they did not listen to him and Amr went up to the wall from its back, but Allah informed his Prophet so he stood up in a hurry and departed pretending, that he would come back. Here the Jews involved his companions in talk, but when the companions felt that the Prophet is gone or something had happened then they also departed towards Madina. On their way back someone told them that the prophet had already arrived in the masjid. They also rushed to the masjid. The prophet told them the whole story, what they had plotted and this was a case of high treason so prepare as soon as possible.

THE PROPHET'S WARNING

The prophet first sent to them Mohammad ibn Maslamah al Ansari to tell them that they must get out of Madina in 10 days otherwise they would be attacked. Now they did not have any choice but to leave. They started gathering their things to leave but the chief of hypocrites, Abdullah Ibni Obai, came to them and told them not to leave, because this was their place.

> *"We are with you and Banu Quraizah and Banu Ghifar will support you as well."*

They had even arranged camels in a place named Zul - Jadr, but this supportive talk encouraged them and they refused to leave. This whole story is mentioned in "Surat Ul Hashr."

Because of this verbal support of hypocrites, their chief, Huyai Ibni Akhtan, sent a message to the prophet that they were not going anywhere.

Now they had plotted against the state and tried to assassinate the prophet who was head of the state which is high treason and the punishment for this crime is execution. The prophet showed mercy to them, but they ignored his order. The prophet appointed Abdullah ibn Ummi Maktoum as Imam at Madina. He gave the flags to Ali and ordered the Sahabah, "Let's go!" They chanted the slogan "Allahu Akbar". The prophet came close to their township. He led Asr prayer there. When Banu Nadir saw them marching towards them, they closed the gates of fortresses and went to the rooftops and started shooting arrows and throwing stones at the Muslims.

They hypocrites, true to their nature, did not come to help them nor did the Banu Quraizah Jews show up.

THE SIEGE

The prophet besieged them. They were inside their fortresses and their thick gardens of palm trees were also a shelter and shield for them and an obstacle and hindrance to the Muslims. So, Allah ordered the prophet to cut their trees that were making their job difficult so the prophet cut some of their trees and burned them. They shouted,

> *"You always used to stop people from such like acts but now you did it."*

Anyhow their siege was for some 15 days. So, they were very afraid. They sent a message that they were ready to surrender and to go out of Madina as ordered, but they requested some kindness, to take their possessions with them. The prophet said,

> *"Every family (married couple) can take one loaded camel with them."*

They started breaking their buildings to pluck out certain precious things from. The Muslims also helped them in this regard. Altogether they took with them 600 loaded camels.

THE "FAY"

When the Muslims get *Ghanimah*, spoils of war, 80 percent was distributed to the Mujahideen and 20 percent went to the Treasury to be distributed to the prophet, his family, the orphans, the poor and the travelers.

Here in this case, it was "Fay" where no war happened properly but their wealth came to the Muslims as a treaty, and the Fay as a whole went to Baitul Mal. Imam Abu Hanifa said The Prophet distributed this whole to the aforementioned five categories while Imam Shafi said,

> *"The prophet distributed that to the 'Muhajireen' so the Ansar may be free of their responsibility for them."*

Yes, the prophet gave Abu Dujanah and Sahal ibn Hunaif from Ansar as they both were poor. The prophet bought with that money the horses and weapons. A famous sword of Sallam ibn Abul Huqaiq, he gave that to Sad ibn Muaz.

This expedition took place in Rabee-Ul-Awwal 4th year after Hijrah. Kinanah Ibni Rabee, Sallam, and Huyai Ibni Akhtab from among Jewish leaders went to Khyber while others went to Jarash, a place in Sham. Ma'ad ibn Wahab and Yameen Ibni Omair Ibni Ka'b accepted Islam and they kept their whole property safe.

In this battle, Ali killed Azuk while Abu Dujanah and Sahl Ibni Hunaif also killed a few of them. The story is narrated by Abdur Razaq and Abu Dawud is like this that after Badr, the Mushrikeen of Makkah wrote to Bani Nadeer, telling him to either fight Mohammad and turn him out of Madina or be ready for the consequences. So, they consulted for a treason. They sent a message to the prophet to bring thirty people with him out of Madina and they would bring the same number of people. They will talk and if they could be convinced, they would accept Islam. Their plot was to kill these thirty known people along with Mohammad and then to handle the others would be very easy. But later on, they changed their mind and decided that they would not be able to fight these thirty as every one of them was ready to fight to the death and you were doing it for life. They said to the prophet that in sixty people it will be difficult to decide so there may be only three people from either side. A lady from Banu Nadeer talked about this conspiracy to her nephew. He came and informed the prophet so the prophet attacked them the next day and asked them for a new pledge of Allegiance but they refused. Then the prophet came to Bani Quraizah and asked them for the pledge and they did it. So, there is no conflict in both the stories. These both are the reason, meaning their clear-cut high treason.

Note: Until this tragedy and high treason, the prophet had a Jewish inscriber but he totally lost his trust in them. It didn't matter how lenient and sincere you are to them; they were not trustworthy so the Prophet now ordered Zaid Ibn Thabit to learn Sami and Hebrew languages to replace the former writer.

Allah said,

> "Whatever is in the heavens and whatever on earth glorifies Allah, and He is the all mighty all wise." (59:1)
>
> "He [Allah] is the one who turned out the disbelievers among the people of the book [Jews of Banu Nadeer] from their homes at the first gathering [of their force]. You never thought that they would go out and they thought that their fortresses would [defend] protect them even from Allah. But Allah came upon them from such a direction which they never thought of, and he cast terror [fear] in their hearts, so they [started] destroying their houses with their hands and by the hands of the believers. So, take a lesson [admonition], O you who have eyes [power of thinking and reflection]!" (59:2)
>
> "And he had not written [decreed] on them the exile then for sure he would have punished them in this world and for them in the hereafter there is fiery torment." (59:3)
>
> "This is because whoever opposes Allah receives His severe punishment." (59:4)
>
> "What you [the Muslims] cut down means the palm trees or you let it standing on its stems, so that was by the leave of Allah and [that was] to disgrace the outlaws [rebellions]." (59:4)
>
> "And whatever Allah has given as 'Fay' [bounty without war] to his messenger from them, so you have

spared neither horses nor camels against them, But Allah gives control to his messenger over whomever he wills. And Allah is able to do all things." (59:5)

"To what Allah has given as 'Fay' to his messenger from the people of the townships that is for Allah, for his messenger, for the kindred [of the messenger] the orphans, for the poor, for the wayfarer so it may not become the fortune [wealth] of only the rich among you. And whatever the Prophet gives you, take it and whatever he forbids, you then abstain from and fear Allah. Verily Allah is severe in punishment." (59:6)

"For the poor immigrants who have been expelled from their homes and their properties, seeking bounties from Allah and [his] good pleasure and helping Allah and his messenger [by helping his Deen] they are the truthful people." (59:7)

"And those who got abode [therein)], and adopted Iman [true faith] before them [meaning before the immigrants came to them] and they loved one who immigrated to them and they entertain no desire in their [breasts] hearts for what has been given to them [to the immigrants] and they give them preference over themselves even though if hunger [poverty] had afflicted them And whoever is saved from his self-covetousness, they are the successful people." (59:8)

"And those who came after them, they say "Our Lord! Forgive us and our brothers who have proceeded us in faith and put not in our hearts any hatred against those who have believed, our Lord!" You are indeed full of kindness most merciful." (59:9)

"Have you not looked at those who did hypocrisy, they were saying to their brothers [friend] who disbelieved

among the people of the book, if you got expelled then for sure we will go out with you [leaving Madina as a protest] and we will not obey anyone in you [in your case], and if you are attacked, we will help you for sure. But Allah knows that verily they are liars." (59:10)

"If they got expelled, they [the hypocrites] will not go out with them [even to see them off or to say goodbye to them] and if they [the Jews] were attacked they [the hypocrites] will not help them and suppose if they help them even, they will turn their backs and then they will not be helped [pardoned]." (59:11)

"Indeed, you are more fearful in their hearts than Allah. That is because they are people who comprehend not." (59:12)

"They will not fight you together but in fortified townships or from behind walls. Their enmity among themselves is severe. You think they are together, but their hearts are divided. That is because they are people who do not sense." (59:13)

"Like those before them shortly, they tasted the evil result of their conduct and for them there is painful torment." (59:14)

"Like Satan, when he says to man, disbelieve, but when he disbelieves, he says I am free of you. I fear Allah the Lord of the worlds." (59:15)

"So then the end of both is that they will be in the fire abiding therein and that is the recompense of the wrong doers." (59:16)

GHAZWA-I-ZATUR RUQA

Ruqa means "patches." But how did this *Ghazwa* got this name? There are a few reasons mentioned in this regard:

1) This *Ghazwa* happened close to a known tree, named "Ruqa"

2) The flags in the battle were made of patches (pieces of cloth)

3) The Muslims walked that much that their feet got blisters and torn. So, they tied fabrics on their feet.

4) This is the name of a mountain that has black and red stones patched up on one another, But in the verse of "Da'thur" the poet he mentioned Zatur - Ruqa as a place. The *Ghazwa* is also called Ghazwa-Bani Thalabah, Ghazwa-Muharib, Ghazwa Bani Anmar, and also Ghazwa Salat Ul Khawf, as prayer in a different way was prayed therein.

Ibni Ishaq narrated that after Ghazwa Bani Nadeer, The Prophet was in Madina for the month of Rabi-Ul'Awwal, Rabi'ath Thani and a few days in Jamaad al Awwal and then he departed towards Najd to face Banu Muharib and Banu Ghitfan in Zatur-Ruqa. He came across Banu Ghitfan, but no battle happened. Here the prophet prayed salat Ul Khawf as Imam Bukhari related. The salat Ul Khawf is mentioned there in Surat - Un - Nisa 4:101-104 as follows:

> *"And when you (O Mohammad!) Travel in the land, there is no sin on you if you shorten the prayer if you fear that the disbelievers may put you in fitnah [disruption or attack you]. Verily the disbelievers are open enemies unto you." (4:101)*

> *"And when you are there among them and lead them in prayer, Then let one group of them stand up with you [for prayer] taking their arms [with them], they do prostrate [pray half of the prayer] then they may be in the rear [to take position for defense] and let the others group come who have not prayed, So they may pray with you [the remaining half of the prayer] and may take all*

> *the precautions, and their arms and Those who disbelieved wish if you ignore your arms and your stuff [other defense tools]. So, they may attack you at once. And there is no sin on you if you lay down your arms (the heavy one) because of difficulty caused by rain or illness. But take precautions [with light arms] verily Allah has prepared for the disbelievers a humiliating torment." (4:102)*

> *"Then when you finish the prayer, remember Allah in standing, sitting, and [lying down] on your sides. Then when you feel satisfaction [no fear and the situation is normal], then perform the prayer [in its normal way] verily the prayer is enjoined on the believers in its appointed time." (4:103)*

> *"And do not be weak in pursuit of the enemy (nation). If you suffer, for sure they will suffer as you do and you expect from Allah what they do not expect [i.e., a reward] And Allah is all-knowing and all-wise." (4:104)*

This rule came at the time of *salat Ul* Asr as the disbelievers saw the Muslims praying at *Zuhr* time together so they said,

> *"We should have attacked them at that time."*

So, some others said,

> *"Asr time is coming and that prayer is much more important to them. So, we will attack them at that time."*

And they were in Safar so they had to do qasr?

So now there are two rules, one is *qasr* when traveling and the other one is *salat Ul Khawf*, to pray the prayer in a different way mentioned in the "Ayat". Now the condition

> *"And when you travel in land."*

Is regarding *qasr*, while the condition

"If you fear that the disbelievers will attack you."

Is regarding *salat Ul Khawf* so when travelling, there is *qasr* even if there is no fear and *salat Ul Khawf* is when there is fear of attack by enemies, otherwise the prayer is to be prayed in its normal way and when fear is there but they are not travelling than they will pray complete prayer i.e., without *qasr*, but in this different way.

Then this way of *salat Ul Khawf* was because the Sahabah were eager not to miss prayer behind the prophet, otherwise the Muslims now can pray in different groups normally. But if they want to pray it this way, then this is the rule,

Regarding this *Ghazwa* the Prophet got the news that the disbelievers were getting together to attack Muslims. The Prophet informed the Sahabah, so four hundred Sahabah got ready to go. The Prophet appointed Abu Zar or Uthman Ibn Affan as Amir in Madina. He took the army and arrived in Shaqrah. He sent a few groups forth to find out if any uprising is going on. They came back and told the Prophet that they could not see anything. The Prophet marched ahead to a place called Nakh, a village of Ghitfan in Najd, but no battle happened.

There is a "Riwayat" that this expedition happened after Ghazwa Khyber as the names of Abu Musa and Abu Hurairah are mentioned therein and they had accepted Islam at Khyber.

GHAZWA-I- BADR AS-SAGHRA

It means the *Ghazwa* of Badr the small one: We have mentioned before that Abu Sufyan, when going back from Uhud, called upon the Muslims challenging them for another combat next year in Badr. As that year remained dry, he wanted to delay it for another year. But the

Prophet of Allah took fifteen hundred Sahabah with him and departed for Badr in the month of Shaban year four after Hijrah. They also had ten horses with them. The Prophet appointed Abdullah Ibni Rawaha as the Amir of Madina. Ali was carrying the flag in this expedition.

Abu Sufyan also came with two thousand people having fifty horses with them up to Murruz Zahran. But he said to his people,

"This is a dry year. Battles should take place in fertile years so I am going back."

The people taunted him,

> "So you came here to drink Sattu (the roasted barley flour they used to put in drinking water in hot weather)?"

That is called *Saweeq* in Arabic and that's why this mission got the name Saweeq.

Abu Sufyan had come out only to honor his word. He was not ready for a fight and that is why he had sent Nuaim Ibni Masud al Ash'jaee towards Madina to frighten Muslims so they would not come out and they will have a good excuse to go back without being blamed for cowardice. But the Prophet said to the Sahabah,

> "Even if nobody goes, I will go alone."

The Sahabah got ready. The Prophet stayed in Badr for eight days with these fifteen hundred Sahabahs. Some of the Mufassireen and Muhaditheen applied the following verses of Surat Aali Imran to this event and we have related these verses in the story of Ghazwa Hamra-Ul Asad the very next day after Uhud in verses 172 and what is mentioned therein support that these verses came at that time. But anyhow due to similarity of both the situations these verses 173-175 are applicable to both so maybe it came there in that situation, but may be the Prophet related that in this one situation also, and the Holy Quran is not confined to place and time or even a specific event, rather it is applicable to any place or time to a similar situation, especially in rules and laws.

> *"Those who answered [responded positively to) the call of Allah and of the messenger after that big injury had touched them. For those who did good [responded sincerely] from among them and feared [Allah or feared and avoided cowardice] there is a big reward." (3:172)*

> *"Those unto whom the people said that people [the Quraish] have gathered against you so fear them [and don't go to face them] so this increased [enriched] them in faith and they said, Allah is sufficient for us and he is the best disposer [of the affairs]." (3:173)*

> *"So, they came back [from that journey] with grace and bounty from Allah, [and] no harm touched them, and [as] they followed [looked for] the good pleasure of Allah. And Allah is the owner of the great bounty." (3:174)*

> *"Verily this one is Satan frightening you with his friends [the disbelievers] so fear not them, fear me only if you are believers." (3:175)*

This Ghazwa is also called "Badr al Mau-id," Badr the promised, Al - Badr Ath - Tania," Badr the second. In this year a son of Uthman from Ruqayyah named Abdullah passed away in the age of six. Hussain Ibni Ali was born this year. Also the Prophet married Ummi Salamah in this year.

GHAZWAH DOOMATUL JUNDAL

In Rabi Ul Awwal, the fifth year the Prophet received the news that people near Dooma't Ul Jundal were robbing people there and they were so great in number that they were thinking of attacking Madina even.

The Prophet appointed Sibah Ibni Urfuta al Ansari as Amir in Madina and along with one thousand Sahabah he left for the area on 25th of Rabi Ul Awwal. The Prophet also got a guide from Banu-Azirah. His name was Mazkur. They used to travel at night and to disperse and hide at daytime here and there. So, they may attack them suddenly. This was a journey of 15 nights. But when they arrived there, these people had already gone away, so maybe they had heard the news. Ibn Ul Athir says that the Muslims got some camels that they left there. In this expedition the prophet made a treaty with Oyainah Ibni Hisn.

MARRIAGE WITH ZAINAB BINT JAHSH

In the time of *Jahiliyat* (ignorance) Arabs had so many bad customs, that had become as their *Deen* and faith. One of these customs was that an adopted son is just like a real son, even in terms in prohibition of *Nikah* [betrothal] based on blood relation, and in inheritance, etc. This was an imagination of Arabs and imagination can never be a fact. In other words, imagination cannot change facts or realities. This is playing game with nature, and no civilized people will ever alter it or accept it. But *Jahiliyat* is *Jahiliyat*. The Prophet addressed the issue a few times but it was so curved in their mind they had reservations about it. So, Allah willed to abolish and nullify this custom through the practice of his prophet as actions speak louder than words. So, first Allah said:

> *"And he has not made your adopted sons like your real sons. That is only your saying with your mouths. And*

> *Allah speaks the truth and he guides to the right path. Call them [attribute them] to their fathers, that is more just, with Allah and if you do not know their fathers then they are your brethren in faith and your friends [so call them a brother or friend!]." (33:3,4)*

So, the prophet was ordained to get his first cousin Zainab binti Jahsh married to his adopted son Zaid Ibni Haritha. Also, it was told that eventually he would divorce her and would get her married and by doing so this bad custom will get abolished forever. When the prophet told Zainab about her marriage with Zaid, she said,

> *"Is this a suggestion or an order?"*

The prophet said,

> *"It is an order."*

She said,

> *"Then it is all right."*

But as we said, it didn't work as it was not meant by Allah to work. So once Zaid came to the prophet asking him if he can divorce Zainab. The prophet said,

> *"Don't do that."*

But later on, when Allah told the prophet that this is the time then he told Zaid,

> *"You should divorce Zainab."*

He did it and as it is in the text of Quran that Allah did her *Nikah* with the prophet; no *Iddat* was required as no consummation had taken place, Allah said,

> *"It is not for a believing man or a believing woman, when Allah and his messenger have decreed a matter*

that they will have an option in their [Allah's and the prophet's] decrees [or in their own personal affairs even] and whoever disobeys Allah and his messenger Then he indeed has strayed in a plain error." (33:36)

"And [remember] when you said to him [Zaid] on whom Allah has bestowed grace [with Iman] and you bestowed on him a favor [by emancipating him], keep your wife to yourself and fear Allah, and you were hiding in yourself what Allah was to make it manifest, and you was afraid of people [meaning their propaganda that 'Oh! He married his daughter in law'] while Allah is more deserving to be afraid of him. So, when Zaid had no desire for her, then we gave her in marriage to you, so that there may not be and difficulty [discomfort] for the believers in terms of [marrying] the wives of their adopted sons when they do not have any desire for them. And the order of Allah is to be done." (33:37)

"There is no blame on the prophet in that which Allah had made lawful for him. That had been the way of Allah with those who have passed away before [the prophets] and the command of Allah is a decree determined." (33:38)

"Those who convey the messages of Allah and fear him and do not fear anybody but Allah alone. And Allah is enough to be a reckoner." (33:39)

"Mohammad is not the father of any of you men, but a messenger of Allah and the seal (last and final) of the prophets and Allah is ever all-knower of everything." (33:40)

She was a very generous person. Once Umar sent her twelve thousand dirhams. She distributed it to the poor and then she made a *Dua*:

"O Allah, may you not bring this time again on me to take the Hadiyah of treasury."

She died after that. Umar led her Janazah; Mohammad Ibni Abdullah Ibni Jahsh and Usamah Ibni Zaid laid her to rest. The Prophet, in his last moments when all his wives were too sad and they asked him which one of us will join you the first, he said,

"The one who has the longer hand."

Then they looked at their hands to determine their length, but the prophet had meant their generosity. And she was the first one of them who died.

GHAZWA-I-AHZAB

Ahzab is the plural of *Hizb*, which means "the groups," and as these groups got together and made an alliance against the prophet of Allah to attack Madina, we can translate this name as the Battle of Allies or Battle of Confederates and on this occasion the prophet ordered for a trench to be dug on the side of the city to make it safe. That's why it is sometimes also called the Battle of the Trench. And when did it happen? Some historians say it happened after *Ghazara – I - Muraisee*, which is also known by the name *Ghazwa-I-Bani Mustalaq*. They say Ghazwa-I-Bani Mustalaq happened in year 5 after Hijrah, while Ghazwat Ul Ahzab also happened the same year but after Muraisee in the month of Zul-Qadah. But Muhmmad Ibni Ishaq says that Ghazwa-I-Ahzab happened in Shawwal year 5, while Muraisee happened in Shaban year 6 after Hijrah – it is to be noted that the marriage of Zainab binti Jahsh took place in Zul Qadah year 5 and that was after Ghazwat Ul Ahzab. Both stories are mentioned in *Surat Ul-Ahzab*. Even though the Quran is not a book of history that presents events in sequence, it did mention these two stories in sequence.

A RESERVATION AND ITS ANSWER

In some narrations it is mentioned that when the hypocrites created a mess in this expedition of Ghazwa-I-Bani Mustalaq, some heated words were exchanged between Sa'd Ibni Muaz and Sa'd Ibni Ubadah, while Sa'd Ibni Muaz died of the injury he received in Ahzab by a stray arrow. So, it means that Muraisee (Bani Mustalaq) took place before Ahzab. But we say that in authentic narrations, the name of Osaid Ibni Hudair is mentioned instead of Sa'd Ibni Muaz. Aaisha herself mentioned the chief of Aus only and he was Sa'd Ibni Muaz. and after his death Osaid Ibni Hudair Ibni Ishaq also mentioned that Osaid Ibni Hudair talked to the prophet. Ibni Qayyim and Ibni Hazm both also said that Ahzab was before Ghazwa – I - Muraisee.

THE BACKGROUND OF GHAZWA-I-AHZAB

We mentioned before that the Banu Nadeer were driven out because of the treason they plotted against the state and its leader. Their chiefs Huyai Ibni Akhtab, Sallam Ibni Mishkam, Kinanah Ibni Abil Huqaiq, Haudah Ibni Qais Wa'ily and Abu Aamir al Fasiq came to Quraish in Makkah to instigate them against the prophet. The Quraish said,

"How can we trust you to support us as you believe in a divine religion and Mohammad claims the same."

They asked them,

"How will you believe us?"

They replied,

> "If you express our Deen and make Sajdah to "Jibt" and "Taghut" [their two known idols] is better than the Deen of Mohammad,"

So, they said it and did it.

Allah said:

> "Have you not seen those who were given a portion (of the knowledge) of the book that they believed in "Jibt" and "Taghut" and said in favor of those who disbelieved they are better guided in path as regard to those who believed." (4:51)

Then these Jews also convinced the Ghitfan tribe to join in war against the prophet.

THE INVADERS MARCH

Under the leadership of Abu Sufyan, the Quraish came from south. Ghitfan's sub-tribe Banu Fazarah under their leader Oyainah Ibni Hisn, another subtribe Banu Murrah under the leadership of Harith Ibni Auf and a third tribe Banu Ashja under their leader Mis'ar Ibni Rakheelah came from the other side, joined by Banu Sulaim and Banu Asad tribes as well. There were more than 10,000 people.

THE SHURA

When the prophet was informed of this, he summoned the *Shura* council to ask their opinion on how to defend and protect Madina. Madina was bordered by thick date palm tree gardens on three sides, but on one side, where Mount Sila was located, was not covered Salman al Farsi said,

> *"In Persia we dig a deep, wide trench so the enemy forces may not cross over towards a city or a strategic place."*

The prophet liked this idea and ordered for a trench near Sila in the open area. The prophet, along with the Sahabah, started digging the trench. Imam Bukhari narrated from Sahl Ibni Sa'd that the prophet when working was saying:

> *"O Allah there is no pleasant life but only the life in the hereafter so forgive the Ansars and the Muhajirs."*

Then we were answering with this:

> *"We are those who gave their pledge to Mohammad on jihad as long as we live."*

And Bara Ibni Aazib narrates that the prophet was reciting the verses of Abdullah Ibni Rawaha,

> *"O Allah! If you had not been there, we would never have given charity or prayed, so you sent down Sakinah (mental peace and satisfaction) on us and strengthened our feet when we face the enemy. Verily, these people invaded us and if they have intended to force us to fitnah (sedition), we reject that."*

When they were digging the trench, they encountered a hard white rock. The Sahabah tried to break it but they couldn't. Salman Farsi told the prophet about the rock. The prophet came and hit it with a sledgehammer in the name of Allah and its one part was smashed.

The prophet said,

> *"I have been given the keys of Sham."*

He dealt it another blow and said,

> *"I have been given the keys of Persia,"*

and with a third blow, the whole rock was gone. He said,

> *"I have been given the keys of Yemen."*

These were the prophesies he gave about these areas that would soon come under Islamic State.

Then three thousand Muslims came with the prophet and were stationed on different fronts on some distance from the trench to Madina side. The prophet gave his Sahabah a code word, *"Hamim La Yunsaroon,"* so they would not harm their own people at night.

THE INCIDENTS

10,000 enemies came, but couldn't cross over the trench, so they were stationed on the other side. The Muslims shot arrows towards them at intervals so they could not come close to the trench to fill up some of it with dirt in order to cross over. But from somewhere Omar Ibni Abdi Wadd, Ikramah Ibni Abi Jahl and Darrar Ibn Ul Khattab got out, and Amr challenged Muslims, so one may come and fight him face to face. Ali Ibni Abi Talib came out and killed him and the other two ran away. Ikramah left his lance behind. It has also been narrated that two other people were also with Amr: one was Munnabih Ibni Uthman; he was hit by a Muslim arrow and was injured and died at Makkah. The other one was Naufal Ibni Abdullah. He slid down into the trench and the Muslims started stoning him. He said,

> *"If you can kill me at once it will be better."*

So, Ali went down to the trench and killed him. Sa'd Ibni Muaz was wounded by a stray arrow and a few days later he succumbed to his injury and was martyred. Imam Bukhari narrated that at that time he made a *Dua*:

> *"O Allah, if the Quraish still want to fight after this, then keep me alive because they have betrayed your prophet, and if they are not going to fight again then give me shahadat." Ibni Hisham also narrated that he also made a Dua: "O Allah! Give me comfort regarding Banu Quraizah."*

BANU QURAIZAH

As we mentioned before, the Jews in Madina plotted against the state from day one, even though they were citizens and thus obligated to be loyal. For treason, two tribes, the Banu Qanuqa, and the Banu Nadeer, were turned out from Madina, but the Banu Quraizah remained. The chief of Banu Nadeer Huyai Ibni Akhtab came out to Ka'b Ibni Asad Al Qurazi and knocked his door. Ka'b didn't open the door at first, but when he insisted then he opened the door and Huyai said to him,

> *"Look! I have brought Quraish Ghitfan and all these allies but now this is up to you people to attack the Muslims from the rear so we may get rid of them and this is the opportunity."*

First, he said,

> *"I am under oath,"*

But Huyai insisted, so he got ready to break his treaty and to attack Muslims from the rear. It is noteworthy that when the prophet and the Muslims were going out of Madina they sent their families to the area of Banu Quraidah for safety, which means the Muslims trusted the Banu Quraidah. Once the aunt of the prophet and the mother of Zubair Safiya saw a Jew walking around the fortress. She said to Hassan Ibni Thabit,

> "Go and kill him as I am sure that he is up to no good."

Hassan said,

> "You know I am not the man for the job!"

So, Safiya picked up a long stick, came down of the fortress, and killed the Jew with that stick. She said to Hassan,

> "Now you should go and take whatever is with him as I cannot touch a strange man,"

But he replied,

> "I don't need it."

The Prophet was informed of the treason of the Banu Quraizah. So, he sent Sa'd Ibni Muaz, Sa'd Ibni Obadah, Khawwat Ibni Jubair and Abdullah Ibni Rawaha to find out the facts. The prophet told them,

> "If this news is wrong, then come and tell me openly; and if this is true then give me some indication only so the Muslim may not worry."

When these Sahabah went, the Banu Quraizah said,

> "We are not bound by any treaty with Mohammad."

When they came back, they said,

> "Adlun wa Qarah,"

The tribes who cheated before and killed the missionaries.

THE QADA PRAYERS

The Prophet and the Muslims were so engaged that it caused them to miss a few prayers. Imam Bukhari related that the prophet prayed Asr after sunset and then he prayed maghrib. Imam Shafi and Imam Ahmad said that they missed more than one prayer so the prophet led them at night in one time for Zuhr, Asr, Maghrib and Isha. In this battle six Muslims were martyred and ten disbelievers were killed.

A STRATEGY TO CREATE A DISUNITY

War is fought with weapons but based on tactics and strategies. The prophet said once that war is a strategy. This news about Banu Quraizah was very shocking so the prophet said to Sa'd Ibni Muaz and Sa'd Ibni Obadah,

> *"If we will enter into a treaty with the chiefs of Ghitfan Oyainah Ibni Hisn and Harith Ibni Auf to take Ghitfan back, we will give them one-third of the dates of Madina."*

They both replied,

> *"If this is an order by the prophet then from the bottom of our hearts but if you want our protection and defense*

then no way. When we were idolaters, we never surrendered, nor did we pay anything to them. Now when we are Muslims and we are here for Islam, so how can we do that. With us there is nothing for them except swords."

The prophet said,

"I was trying that for your protection, as all Arabs and non-Arabs have jumped at you."

Nuaim Ibni Masud Ibni Aamir of the Ghitfan tribe came to the prophet and said,

"My people do not know anything about my Islam, so will you allow me to use a tactic?" The Prophet said, "Go ahead, as war is tactics."

He came to Banu Quraizah and told them,

"You know my people have a friendship with you so let me tell you one thing that your case with Mohammad is totally different than that of Quraish. They will go back but you will stay here under his rule and then you will pay the price of what you are doing."

They listened to him, and said,

"Yes, you are right, but tell us what we should do?"

He said,

"Take some people from Quraish as a surety in your hands that if they will leave you alone then you should kill them."

They thought this was good advice. Then he came to Quraish and told them that Banu Quraizah blamed themselves for breaking their treaty with Mohammad. He added that they were going to ask for some people to be in their hands as surety. But they would hand them over to Mohammad.

The very next day Quraish and Ghitfan asked Banu Quraidah to attack Mohammad from the back. They said,

> *"Today is Saturday and we do not do anything on Saturday, so later on we can do it but you have to hand over some people to us to keep them as a surety."*

When the Quraish and the Ghitfan received this message, they said.

"Oh! Nuaim was right!"

THE PROPHET PRAYED AND INVOKED ALLAH

The Prophet was invoking Allah against these allied forces, so Allah sent on them a very cold and terrible wind that uprooted their tents. Their camels and their horses broke their ropes and ran over them. The angels started shouting on them terrorizing them. They thought that it was the Muslims attacking.

The prophet sent Huzaifah Ibn Ul Yaman to see what was going on. He came and told the prophet that they were terrified. Huzaifa said,

> *"When I was among them in dark, they were so afraid that Abu Sufyan addressed them."*

Huzaifah said,

> *"I asked a man, 'Who are you?' in order to make him unable to ask me."*

Abu Sufyan left afterward and when the leading general departed all the others followed him. These people stayed there for twenty days or so. Now when the prophet was informed that they are gone, he told his Sahabah,

> *"From now on Quraish will never think of fighting unless you want to fight them."*

This story is mentioned there in Surat Ul Ahzab which is named after this war.

> *"O you who believed, Remember the favor of Allah to you, when there came against you hosts [troops] and we sent on them a wind and forces [angels] which you saw not. And Allah is the all-Seer of what you do." (33:9)*

> *"When they came at you from above you and from below you and when the eyes grew wild and the hearts reached to the throats and you were harboring various assumptions about Allah." (33:10)*

> *"There the believers were tested and afflicted with severe shaking [convulsions]." (33:11)*

> *"And when the hypocrites and those in whose hearts there was a disease were saying that Allah and his messenger promised us but a delusion." (33:12)*

> *"And when a party of them said, "O people of Yathrib [the name of Madina before the Prophet came therein] there is no stand for you, so go back," and a group of them was asking for permission of the prophet saying, "Indeed our homes are empty [unprotected] while they were not empty. They intend not but to flee only." (33:13)*

"And if the troops had entered on them from all sides of it [Madina] and they would have been asked for fitnah [to seduce] they would have done it for sure and they would not have delayed it but for a little while." (33:14)

"And indeed, they had made a covenant with Allah before this that they will not turn their backs and a covenant with Allah must be questioned." (33:15)

"Say [O Mohammad!] Flight will not avail you [of anything] if you flee from death or killing, and they would be given but a little enjoyment." (33:16)

"Say [O Mohammad!] who is the one who can protect you from Allah if he intends to harm you or intends a mercy on you? They will not find themselves any protector or any helper." (33:17)

"Indeed, Allah knows among you the hinderers and those who say to their brethren, "Come here towards us while they themselves do not come to the battle but a little." (33:18)

"Being miserly towards you. Then when fear comes you see them looking to you and their eyes are revolving like one overcome by death. Then when the fear departs, they smite you with sharp tongues indisposed towards good. They have not believed so Allah has rendered their deeds worthless and that is ever easy for Allah." (33:19)

"They think that the allied forces are not gone, and if they will come [again] they will be wishing if they were with the Bedouins [i.e., far away in the desert] inquiring for your news and if they happen to be among you, they will not have fought but a little." (33:20)

"Indeed, in the Messenger of Allah there is a good model for you, for one who hopes for Allah and the last day [i.e., fear of them both] and remembered Allah a lot." (33:21)

"And when the believers saw the allied forces, they said, this is what Allah and his messenger promised us and Allah and his messenger has spoken the truth. And it did not increase them but in faith and submission." (33:22)

"Among the believers there are those who have made what they promised with Allah true and of them there is one who has fulfilled his obligation and of them there is one who is still waiting, but they have not changed it at all." (33:23)

"So that Allah may reward the truthful people for their truth and perish the hypocrites if he willed or accept their repentance. Verily Allah is Oft-Forgiving, Most Merciful." (33:24)

"And Allah drove back those who disbelieved in their rage; they got no advantage. And Allah sufficed for the believers from fighting. And Allah is All-Strong, All-Mighty." (33:25)

"And he brought down those who backed them from the People of the Book from their forts and he cast terror in their hearts so a group of them you killed and another group you made captives." (33:26)

"And he gave you their land [for free], their homes and their wealth and [also] a land upon which you had not trodden. And Allah is able to do everything." (33:27)

GHAZWA-I-BANU QURAIZAH

As we mentioned, the Banu Quraizah was a tribe of Jews living in Madina. Before them, two tribes of Jews committed treason against the state and they were supposed to be executed as traitors, but the prophet turned them out of Madina instead. This third tribe was to attack the prophet and the Muslims from their back (from the Madina side), even though the prophet trusted them to such an extent that he had sent the women and children to their town for safety. Though as a strategy by Nuaim it did not happen as it was the plot but their treason was proven. When the prophet came back from the trench side and put off his weapon and armor coat, the angel Jibril (Gabriel) came and said,

> *"O Messenger of Allah! You put off your weapon and we angels have not yet, because the case of Banu Quraizah is not resolved yet."*

The Prophet came out and ordered the Mu'azzin to make an announcement, that whoever hears it must obey and not pray Asr prayer, but in Banu Quraizah.

Ibn Hisham wrote that he appointed Abdullah Ibn Ummi Maktoum at Madina as Amir. He gave the flag to Ali along with a group of Sahabah. When these people arrived in Banu Quraizah, they made some derogatory remarks about the prophet of Allah. They were coming back to inform the prophet, so they came across the prophet coming towards Banu Quraizah.

Ali said,

> *"O Messenger of Allah, if you will not go that is better."*

Maybe he was thinking that they would harm the prophet or say the same things in his presence. The prophet said,

> *"Maybe you heard them saying things, but when I am there, they will not say then."*

The Prophet went there and addressed them,

> "O the brethren of monkeys! Has Allah not disgraced you? Has He not sent His torment on you?"

They said,

> "O Abul Qasim! You are not unaware of this."

When he was passing by Sadrain, a place towards Banu Quraidah, he asked the people there.

> "Have you seen anyone passing by?"

They said,

> "Yes, we saw Dihyah al-Kalbi on a white mule."

The Prophet said to his companions this was Jibril, came to put terror in their hearts.

The Prophet besieged Banu Quraizah for twenty-one or twenty-five days, depending on the source, the first by Waqidi and the second by Ibn Ishaq. In all these days, the Muslims only ate dates provided by S'ad Ibni Obadah.

THE ADVICE OF KA'B IBNI ASAD

When Banu Quraizah came to know that the prophet was not going back, then Ka'b Ibni Asad al-Qurazi told them,

> "Now this calamity has come on us, so I give you three pieces of advice."

> "All of you know that he is a messenger so let believe in him and you will save yourselves in this world and in the coming one as well."

But they said,

> "We will never leave our Deen."

Ka'b said,

> "Then let us kill our women and our children with our own hands and then we will attack them all at once, so if we will remain alive, we can get other women and start a new life, and if we are killed then at least we will not grieve that at the time of our death they will take our women and children."

They said,

> "We do what we do to protect our families, so if we kill them ourselves, then is the point of any of this?"

Ka'b then said,

> "Today is Saturday and Mohammad is not alert from our side, as he knows that we do not do anything this day, so let's attack them now."

They said,

> "Our forefathers did what they did on Saturday and they got results."

Ka'b became angry at them and said,

> "Since the day your mothers delivered you people have you ever used your common sense?"

ABU LUBABAH

Rifa'a Ibni Abdul Munzir, known as Abu Lubabah, was from their ally tribe Aws. They said to the Prophet,

> "Send him to us,"

Meaning that they wanted to ask his opinion. The prophet sent him. Their women and children started crying to him asking him,

> "What should we do, what is your opinion?"

He pointed to his own throat, which means that they would be slaughtered. He said,

> "Right after this I recalled what I said and why I said it, so I said to my own self that it was a betrayal to Allah and his messenger."

So, he came straight to the masjid and tied himself to a pillar and said,

> "I will stand so here until I die or Allah accepts my repentance, and then I will never step into the city of Bani Quraizah."

His wife used to untie him for prayer. As he didn't come to the prophet, the prophet said,

"Where is Abu Lubabah?"

Sahabah told him his story. The prophet said,

> "If he had come to me and I would have asked Allah for him, he would have forgiven him. But now when he has adopted this way so I cannot do anything."

Then when his repentance was accepted and Jibril told the prophet, Ummi Salamah came and gave him this glad tiding and then the prophet himself untied him.

SA'D IBNI MU'AAZ AND ARBITRATION

It was freezing cold and the Muslims were tired, as they had been at the trench for twenty days or more. Now here Ali said,

> "By Allah either like Hamzah I will be martyred or I will force the Banu Quraizah to open their fortress."

The Banu Quraizah had a big stockpile of supplies so they did not have any shortage of food, but because of this constant siege they were fed up with the situation and thinking of coming out.

Here the Aws tribe of Ansar said to the prophet,

> "You have done favors to the Banu Nadeer before this and they were the allies of Khazraj tribe and they asked for that favor, so can you please do them a favor as well, as they were our allies?"

The Prophet said,

> "Then why should not one of you decide this matter?"

They agreed. So, the prophet said,

> "Here is Sa'd Ibni Muaz in the tent of Rufaidah Al-Aslamiyah's as she treats him."

She was a doctor at that time. Sa'd was injured with an arrow as we said before and the wound was bleeding. He was too weak. So, he was riding a camel or a donkey. The Prophet said,

> "Stand for your chief."

This was a respect for Sa'd and a message to Banu Quraizah that we will honor what he will decide. The Prophet said to him go and decide the matter. The Aws tribe used to ask him,

> "Please do some favors for them."

Sa'd said,

> "Now this is time for Sa'd that no one will blame him regarding the Deen of Allah."

Now the Aws came to know the decision. Sa'd asked the prophet whether his decision was effective on the Banu Quraizah. The Prophet assured him it was. He asked,

> "And on Muslims?"

The Prophet said,

> "And on Muslims also."

Then he said,

> "And on me?"

The Prophet said,

> "Yes, and on you as well."

Then he said then men might be killed, and the women and children might be made captives and their wealth distributed. The Prophet said,

> "You decreed in accordance with the command of Allah."

It is noteworthy that when Sa'd was injured in Ahzab, he was making *Duas*, one of these *Duas* was,

> "O Allah! Give me the comfort of my eyes regarding Banu Quraizah."

And thus, he got it.

PLOTS OF THE BANU QURAIZAH

The Banu Quraizah had committed treason. They had been plotting to eradicate Muslims as they gathered fifteen hundred swords, two thousand lances, three hundred armored coats and five hundred helmets. The Prophet had ordered to gather their women and children in the house of Bint - Ul - Harith and their men in the house of Osamah Ibni Zaid. Then their men were brought in groups and were killed. Their number was between six and seven hundred. When Huyay Ibni Akhtab was preparing Ka'b Ibni Asad for this treason, he told him,

> "Whatever will be the result I will be with you people."

So, he was killed along with them. Whenever a group was being taken, they used to ask Ka'b Ibni Asad, what is going on what they are doing with us? He said,

> "See you not that the caller is calling and taking groups and no one is coming back."

Huyay Ibni Akhtab had made holes in his robe, which was a king's or chief's robe. He said,

> "I want to make it useless so it can neither be counted in spoils nor be used by someone else."

When he was brought in, his hands were tied behind his back. He said to the Prophet,

> "I have not shortened in your enmity but Allah gives victory to whom he wills."

These people were killed by Ali and Zubair. Only one of their women was killed but she was killed in retribution. Aishah said,

> "She was sitting with me when she was called; I asked her, what is the matter?"

She said,

"I would be killed."

Her name was Bananah. It turned out that she had killed a Muslim, Khallad Ibni Suwaid, with a millstone. In fact, her husband had asked her to kill someone with this stone. The whole thing was actually a plot by her husband so she would be executed as retribution and could not remarry. Khallad was a great Muslim who attended Badr, Uhud, and before that he was in Bai'at – I - Aqabah.

EXEMPTIONS

The prophet ordered the adults to be killed. Atiyeh Qurazi could not grow a beard yet so he was left alive. Later on, he accepted Islam. Harith Ibni Qais Ibni Shammas asked for Zabeer Ibni Bata, or it is said that the prophet himself gave Zabeer to Thabit to reciprocate him as he had sheltered him in a battle in the time of ignorance. The Prophet said,

> "This is up to you whatever you want to do with him."

Thabit willed to spare him, but he said to Thabit,

> "For God's sake, please send me to my brothers,"

meaning, *"Kill me,"* so he killed him.

His son Abdur Rahman Ibni Zabeer remained with Thabit and later on he became Muslim. Umm Ul Munzir Salma Bint – I - Qais An'najjaria asked for Rifa'a Ibni Samwal and later on he accepted Islam as well.

A few people from the Banu Quraizah had come out before this treason so they were not touched or harmed. One Jew named Amr had not joined this treason; he came out and Mohammad Ibni Maslamah saw him but ignored him, and later on nobody knew where he was gone.

DISTRIBUTION OF SPOILS OF WAR (BOOTY)

The Prophet after taking out one-fifth from the booty, distributed the rest to Mujahideen. He made three thousand and seventy-two shares as there were also thirty-six horses for mujahideen. So, he gave every horse two shares. This is the *madhab* of Jumhur, while Abu Hanifa says a horse also merits one share, and there are Ahadith in this regard.

The Prophet also sent some captives with Sa'd Ibni Zaid from Banu Abdul Ash'hal to Najd to exchange them for some weapons and horses. One lady, Raihana binti Amr, asked the prophet to keep her with him and later on she became Muslim. (Ibn Ishaq)

Sa'd Ibni Muaz died after this whole process. Sa'd died when the Sahabah were carrying his body. They said,

"He was such a healthy man and his body is so light."

The Prophet told them that the angels were holding him.

Also, in this besiege time Abu Sinan, the brother of Okasha, died.

EXPEDITIONS AFTER AHZAB

KILLING OF SALLAM IBNI ABUL HUQAIQ

The Jews in Madina showed their actual intentions. Also, it was disclosed that their friends from outside instigated them against the state and some of them did it very openly and they had been doing this for quite a long time. Ka'b Ibn Ul Ashraf was killed because of such treasons by the tribe of Aus. Now the Khazraj tribe asked the Prophet if they could kill another big conspirator, Sallam Ibni Abil Huqaiq, to gain the same virtue as of their cousin tribe. The Prophet gave them permission under the leadership of Abdullah Ibni Attik. A group of five departed the job. The other four were Abdullah Ibni Onais, Abu Qatada, Aswad Ibn Ul Khuza'a and Sa'ud Ibni Sinan. Abdullah said,

> "I am going to make a strategy as it is not easy to approach him."

So, before sunset when all the fortress people started going inside, Abdullah was covering himself with his cloak in the open area as if he was answering the call of nature. The gate keeper started giving the call to enter the fort as he is going to close the gate. So, he also stood up and rushed to the gate and entered with the other people.

He said,

> I was looking at the gatekeeper. He closed the gate and all the doors and then then he hung the keys on a hook. At night Sallam was talking to his people until late, as usual. When all the people left, I went to the upper story. I did not know where he is so I called on him by his nickname, Abu Rafi. "He said, "Who is this?" I

rushed toward the voice and tried to strike him, but in vain. He shouted. I came out and hid when all the people who had come to him with his shout went back and it was quiet. I went there again and asked him, "What happened?" He said, "Somebody tried to hit me." So again, I went toward the voice and hit him on his belly with my sword in such a way that it went through his backbone and I was sure that he was dead. Then as I took the keys as I noticed where they were, so I started opening all the doors one by one. I fell down on the stairs and broke my leg. I tied it with my turban, waiting for daybreak, then it was announced from the fort top that Abu Rafi had died. Then I came to my colleagues and we came back to Madinah. I related the whole story to the prophet. The prophet put his hand on my leg and it healed as if it had never been broken.

It is also narrated that another colleague of Abdullah Ibni Onais also had gone with him as in some narration it is said that he killed Abu Rafi. This is also related that in the beginning the wife of Abu Rafi asked him who are you? So, Abdullah Ibni Attik talked to her in "Ibram" (Hebrew) language, and Abdullah Ibni Onais said to her,

"Don't make noise."

But maybe she realized that they were Jews because he spoke to her in Hebrew. This event happened in Zul 'Qadah or Zul Hijjah year five after Hijrah.

SARIYAH-I-QARTA

This happened in Muharram year six after Hijrah. It was led by Mohammad Ibni Maslamah Ansari so it was named after him. In this expedition there were thirty people. The Prophet ordered them to travel at night and to hide at daytime to surprise them. So, when they attacked the sub-tribe of Bakr Ibni Kilab, the tribespeople ran away, but the Sahabah took their livestock. These were one hundred and fifty camels and three thousand goats. The prophet traded ten goats for one camel. This expedition took nineteen days. They also captured the chief of Banu Hanifa Thumamah Ibni Athal as he was coming towards Madina to assassinate the Prophet, dispatched by Musailamah. He was tied to a pillar in a masjid.

The Prophet came out and asked him,

> *"What good do you have?"*

He said,

> *"I have good. If you kill, then you kill a person having blood [meaning a sacred blood] and if you do good then you do that to one who is thankful, and if you need wealth, then tell me, how much?"*

The Prophet passed by and left him. The next day he asked the same question and received the same answer, and also the third day as well. Then the Prophet said,

> *"Release him."*

He went to a nearby date palm garden, bathed, and came back and accepted Islam. He said to the Prophet,

> *"By God, before this your face was the utmost disliked face to me on earth and now that is the utmost beloved face in my eyes, and same is the case of your Deen in my eyes now."*

He continued,

> *"But I also had the intention of umrah when your army caught me."*

The prophet said,

"*Now you should go for umrah.*"

When he came for *umrah* and the Quraish saw him doing *umrah* in an Islamic way, they said,

"*So you have turned to Sabi [a term they used to use for one who accepted a new Deen different from the Deen of Quraish]?*"

He said,

"*No, but I have become a Muslim.*"

He said to them,

"*Now you will not see a single grain from Yamamah unless the prophet wills it.*"

When he went back, he stopped the grain for the Quraish until they begged the prophet to order Thumamah to end this siege and the prophet did it. Later on, when the *fitnah* of Musailamah became apparent, he stayed strict to Islam and used to tell people,

"*This is a mess and misleading. So don't listen to him.*"

GHAZWA BANU LAHYAN

These people had betrayed ten Sahabah of the prophet and killed them. Now the prophet was to teach them a lesson. The Prophet arrived in Makheez and then to Batra. After that he turned to the right towards the mountains of Yamen, then he went straight to Qahjah and later on to Gharran and then to Saya. In this Ghazwa there were 200 people and twenty horses. He had appointed Ibni Ummi Maktoum as Amir at

Madina. Those people got frightened and fled to mountains. As a strategy he gave Abu Bakr ten riders to pass by Kuragh Ul Ghameem. So, the Quraish may know that we are on alert. In this mission the prophet was out of Madina for fourteen days.

RAID OF OYAINAH IBNI HISN

The Prophet had barely arrived in Madina when Oyainah Ibni Hisn raided the camels of the Prophet. He had his riders along with Zarr Ibni, Abi Zarr was guarding these twenty camels. His wife Laila was also with him. They killed the guard and took away the camels along with the woman. One night when these people were sleeping, Laila mounted the prophet's she-camel named Adba and came to Madina. They gave chase after her, but in vain. She said,

> "I made a pledge that if I arrived in Madina safe, then I will sacrifice this she-camel."

The Prophet said,

> "She saved your life and you want to sacrifice her?"

The Prophet said,

> "There is no Nazr for a sin and no Nazr in what one does not own."

SARIYYAH-I-GHAMR

Ghamr was a well belonging to the Banu Asad on the way towards Makkah at a distance of two days' travel form Fahd Fortress: Okasha Ibni Mihsan led an army of forty people. Banu Asad fled away. One man informed these Sahabah about two hundred camels of Banu Asad so they got it. This Sariyah is also called Sariyah -I- Okasha.

SARRIYAH MOHAMMAD IBNI MASLAMAH

In this expedition Mohammad Ibni Maslamah al-Ansari took ten people with him towards Banu Thalabah in Rabi Ath' Thani in year six after Hijrah. In the beginning Banu Thalabah did not show any reaction, but at night they started shooting arrows at them when they were sleeping. So, they also retaliated and countered them. Mohammad Ibni Maslamah and Maslamah Ibni Maslamah got injured and one man from the enemies got killed as well. The place where it took place is called "Zul - Qissah."

SARRIYAH ABU OBAIDAH IBNUL JARRAH

In Rabi Ath' Thani, in year number six, the Prophet gave Abu Ubaidah forty men toward the aforesaid Zul-Qissah. The people there, they fled to the mountains but the Sahabah took their camels and goats along with a captive who later on accepted Islam. The expedition of Mohammad was sent because the prophet heard a report that the people of Banu Thalabah and Anmar planned to attack Haifa, a pasture of the people of Madina. Also, Maslamah Ibni Maslamah was martyred because of the injuries he received in the Sariyah of Mohammad Ibni Maslamah. So, the Prophet sent this Sariyah of Abu Ubaidah.

SARRIYAH ZAID IBNI HARITHA

Zaid Ibni Haritha came to Marruz - Zahran to Jamoom, a water place of the Bani Sulaim. A lady named Halima from the Muzainah tribe guided him towards Banu Sulaim. He caught their camels, goats, and a few people as well. Also, he forgave that lady and her husband.

SARRIYAH EIS

The Prophet got the news that a caravan of the enemy was coming from Sham. He sent one hundred and seventy men under the command of Zaid Ibni Haritha to catch that caravan. He caught them. Among the caravan was Abul Aas, the husband of Zainab, the daughter of the Prophet. Also, the sister of Khadijah, Ummi Halah, was among these people. Zainab, the daughter of the Prophet, asked the Prophet, if he would give the assets of Abul Aas to him back, and he did it. When Abul Aas went to Makkah, he started giving back the *Amanat* (the wealth of people he was entrusted with) to the people to go to Madina and accept Islam. He came back to Madina and accepted Islam. The Prophet sent Zainab back to him. Now Jumhur said that after a few years she was sent back based on the previous *Nikah*. But Abu Hanifa said she was sent back with by a new *Nikah*. He was of the view if one half of the couple accepts Islam, then some time is to be given to the other one to decide whether she/he will accept Islam, then they can live together on their previous *Nikah*. But it should not be a long period of time.

From Zainab, this Abul Aas had a daughter named Umamah. The Prophet once put her on his shoulders and then prayed with her still up there.

SARRIYYAH ZAID IBNI HARITHA

In Jumada – Al - Ukhra, a mission of fifteen people under the leadership of Zaid Ibni Haritha was sent towards Banu Thalabah. They fled but the Muslims got twenty of their camels.

SARRIYYAH ZAID IBNI HARITHAH

In Rajab of year six after Hijrah, twelve people including Zaid went to Wadil Qura area to see what they were plotting. They attacked them. None of them were martyred there, and Zaid came back with two hostages.

SARRIYATUL-KHABT

The historians mentioned that this happened in Rajab in year number eight after Hijrah. But its narrative does not go along with what happened as the Muslims were not stopping the caravans after Hudaibiyah so it could have happened before, such as when the Quraish broke the treaty or after that. Jabir said,

> *The Prophet sent us three hundred people under the leadership of Abul-Ubaidah Ibn Ul Jarrah to stop a caravan of Quraish. We began to starve, so one man slaughtered three camels one day, and more the second and third day as well. Then Abu Ubaidah stopped him. Then one day the ocean threw out to us a fish called Anbar. We used to eat of it for one month or so and used*

its fat on our hands and faces to keep them moisturized. Abu Ubaidah erected one of its ribs and a tall man or even a camel could pass beneath. Also, we brought some of its meat with us and related the story to the prophet. The Prophet said, "This was a provision by Allah." He asked if we have some of it. So, we sent him some.

SARRIYAH ABDUR RAHMAN IBNI AWF

This is also called Doom Atul - Jundal. Before this in Rabi Ul Awwal year number five, Abdur Rahman had an expedition to Doom Atul Jundal, we have mentioned that before. This time the Prophet made him sit in front of him, and he had a black turban on his head. The Prophet took it from Abdur Rahman's head and tied it again with his own hands. This was a blessing and a mark of the Prophet's trust in him. Then the prophet said to Bilal,

"Give me the flag."

The Prophet after Hamd and Salah said,

"Abdur Rahman! Take this flag and fight those who refuse, but do not exceed the limits, not break the promise or cheat. Do not dismember bodies or kill children. You have been given this duty from Allah and this is the Seerah of your prophet."

Abdur Rahman took the flag and departed towards Banu Kalab. The Prophet said,

"If they accept Islam, then marry the daughter of their king."

Abdur Rahman took seven hundred people under his leadership and went into Doomah. He called them to Islam. For three days they were reluctant, but eventually they accepted Islam. Their king, Isbagh Ibni Amr, a Christian, also accepted Islam. Abdur Rahman married his daughter Tamadur. She was a *Sahabiyah*. Her nickname was Ummi Bint Abi Salmah. Later on, Abdur Rahman divorced her and he died while she was in Iddah. So, she was entitled to her due share and Uthman decreed the same accordingly. The heirs of Abdur Rahman gave her as *Takharuj* 83,000, dinars. She was one of his four wives at that time and this was 1/32 share of his estate, or even less.

SARRIYAH ALI IBNI ABI TALIB

In Shaban, year six, Ali took one hundred *mujahideen* towards Banu Sa'd Ibni Bakr. The Prophet got the news that these people were trying to gather people for the Jews of Khyber. So, he sent this expedition towards them. When the Muslims attacked them, their herdsmen fled. Ali brought five hundred camels and two hundred goats of them.

Now as we said, Ibni Ishaq said that Battle of Confederates happened in Shawwal year number five and the Bani Mustalaq happened in Shaban year six. So, this Sariyah of Ali was either before Bani Mustalaq or after that, but it was in the same month.

GHAZWAH - BANI-MUSTALAQ

Bani Mustalaq was a sub-tribe of Khuza'a, and Muraisee was the name of the well there. As we mentioned before, according to Ibni Ishaq, the battle of confederates happened in Shawwal or Muharram in the fifth year before this *Ghazwa*, or Shaban year six. This is supported by the details of the story of slandering against Sayyidah Aaisha as she said, and we will talk about it in detail later *inshallah*, That Safwan Ibni Muittal - As - Sullami was seeing me before "hijab." And it is obvious that rules about hijab are either in Surat Ul Ahzab or in Surat An Nur. Now this slandering story is mentioned in Sura-I-Nur. So, it means that these rules had already come to the prophet. Then Surat Ul Ahzab definitely came before Surat An Nur and this story of a false charge is there in this surah. The only reservation is that after this story it is said that when the prophet complained against Abdullah Ibni Obai, Sa'd Ibni Muaz, the chief of Aws said,

> *"If he had been of our tribe, we would have taken care of him but he is from our brethren's tribe, the Khazraj, so you can order and we can get rid of him."*

The chief of Khazraj Sa'd Ibni Obadah said,

> *"You cannot do anything, but you say so, because he is from Khazraj. If he was of your tribe, you would not have been so excited or angry."*

To make a long story short, we say that if Ahzab happened before Muraisee, Sa'd Ibni Muaz's hand was injured there in Ahzab and later he died from his wounds. So, in some *Riwayat*, the name of his cousin Osaid Ibni Hudair is mentioned in the context of hot words exchanged between him and Sa'd Ibni Obadah. But in some *Riwayat*, instead of naming the chief only chief of Aws, is mentioned and Sa'd Ibni Muaz was the chief; while after his death Osaid became chief, so it is believed that this was Sa'd Ibni Muaz. No but it was Osaid Ibni Hudair

Also, it is noteworthy that the prophet married Zainab binti Jahsh in the month of Zul' Qadah after the battle of Ahzab. The story is mentioned in Surat Ul Ahzab. And Hamanah binti Jahsh, Zainab's sister, is also mentioned in the slandering story and this may be because of a natural rivalry of her sister and Aaisha, as both of them were deeply in love with the prophet, both as a prophet and as a husband. But we keep quiet here as Humamah is a Sahabiyah. Because of all these, Hafiz Ibni

Hazm and Hafiz Ibni Qayyim have both given priority to what Ibni Ishaq said. Also, it is said that after this slander by Abdullah Ibni Ubai, Osaid Ibni Hudair talked to the Prophet in this regard.

THE BACKGROUND

The Prophet was informed that Harith Ibni Darrar al-Khuza'a was plotting to attack Madina and had raised an army, so the prophet planned to counter him before he could execute his plot. A group of hypocrites also joined him. The Muslims had thirty horses with them. The prophet appointed Abu Zar Ghifari or Zaid Ibni Haritha as Amir at Madina. The Prophet was accompanied by both Aaisha and Ummi Salamah. The Muslims also killed a spy of Harith al-Khuza'a in this expedition. His name was Numailah Ibni Abdullah al-Laithi. After this, Harith and his people fell in fear. From Qudaid's side the Prophet arrived at Muraisee. He disciplined the army for fighting. He gave Abu Bakr the flag of Muhajireen and the Ansar's flag to Sa'd Ibni Obadah. In the beginning some arrows were exchanged on both sides, but then the Prophet attacked them, killed ten people at once, and caught seven hundred as captives.

Ibni Qayyim said that no proper battle took place, although some incidents did happen, and these people were captured. In one incident, Hisham Ibni Dubabah was accidentally killed by an Ansari from the group of Obadah Ibni Samit, as he thought he was an enemy. Among these prisoners was the daughter of Harith. When the prophet was giving these prisoners to the Sahabah as slaves, she came in part of Thabit Ibni Qais. She did "Mukatabat" with him: if she or someone on her behalf would pay him that amount, she would be freed. The Prophet paid that amount and then he married her. She was the wife of Musafi Ibni Safwan who was killed in this "Ghazwa." Her name was Barrah, but the Prophet changed it to Jawairiyah. After this marriage the Muslims set many captives free because now, they were the in-laws of the

Prophet, so they did not want to keep them as slaves. Also, after this marriage the whole tribe and their king, Harith, became Muslims.

When the prophet migrated to Madina, the hypocrites used to defame him, along with the other Muslims and Islam in general. They spared no opportunity to slander them. As we said they, practiced their dirty practices in both peace and war. We have mentioned what they did at the time of "Uhud" and what they were saying at the time of "Ahzab." And what nonsense they propagated at the time of Zainab's marriage.

THE CONSPIRACY OF ABDULLAH IBN UBAI

Before that we mention the false accusation story, we would like to mention another story that happened at Muraisee. Muraisee, as we said is a water well or fountain, and the Banu Mustalaq tribe was living around it. A servant of Umar Ibn Ul Khattab name Jahja al-Ghifari and an Ansari named Sinan Ibni Dabar al-Juhani exchanged some hot words with one another at Muraisee. Jahja slapped him. He called on Ansar and said,

"Ya Lal Ansar!" (O Ansar, help!).

Jahja also called,

"Ya Lal-Muhajireen."

Both of these people came out of their tents and from under their canopies to help their men. The Prophet also came in between them both and said,

> "Do you dare make these calls of 'Jahiliyat' while I am among you?"

So, both groups went back to their resting places. Ibni Ubai exploited this also and passed over his remarks that these people (*Muhajireen*) were biting the hand that fed them. He also said,

> "If [or when] we go back to Madina, then for sure the more honorable [he meant himself] will expel therefrom the meaner [he meant the messenger of Allah]."

He also told his people,

> "You sheltered them, you people shared your property with them, now if you will wait longer, you will be turned out of Madina."

A boy named Zaid Ibni Arqam was sitting there. He heard all this nonsense and relayed it to his uncle. Then he told the Prophet. Umar was sitting with the Prophet. He said to the Prophet,

> "Tell Abbad Ibni Bishr to kill this hypocrite [Ibni Ubai]."

The Prophet said,

> "Then people will say, 'Mohammad has started killing his own companions.'"

The Prophet ordered to depart and that was a time when he never ordered to depart at that time. Osaid Ibni Hudair said,

> "O the Prophet of Allah! Today you ordered us to depart at a time you never have before, so why this unusual departure?"

The Prophet said,

> "Have you not heard what your colleague has said?"

He asked what and who said it. The Prophet said,

> "Ibni Ubai said that the most honorable one will expel the meaner one."

Osaid said,

> "O the Messenger of Allah! By Allah he is the utmost of the meaner and you are the utmost of the honorable."

He further said,

> "O Messenger of Allah! Leave him as we were to crown him as king of Madina. Then you came and that plan was ruined. He thinks he lost it because of you."

The Prophet was travelling the whole day and the whole night and a part of the next day as well, and then he stopped and the people slept. Ibni Ubai was informed of it so he rushed to the Prophet and said,

> "O the Prophet of Allah! By Allah, I have not said what you heard. That boy may have misheard or gotten confused."

Zaid Ibni Arqam said,

> "The grief I felt that day was unlike any I had ever felt before, but I felt better when Allah sent the verses of Surat Ul Munafiqun."

SURAT UL MUNAFIQUN

> "When the hypocrites come to you, they say, we testify that you are indeed the messenger of Allah. Allah knows

that you are his messenger. And Allah (also) testify that these hypocrites are liars for sure." (63:1)

"They have made their oaths as a shield; thus, they hinder from the path of Allah. Verily, bad is what they used to do." (63:2)

"That is because they believed and then disbelieved so their hearts got sealed so they do not understand." (63:3)

"And when you see them, their bodies [i.e., how they look] it please you, and when they speak, you listen to their words. They are like blocks of wood propped up. They think every shout is against them. They are the enemies so beware of them. May Allah destroy them [or curse them] for how they were pushed to lie." (63:4)

"And when it is said to them, "Come, so the messenger of Allah may ask forgiveness for you from Allah," they shake their heads and you see them turning away their faces in pride." (63:5)

"It is equal to them whether you ask forgiveness for them or you do not ask forgiveness for them, Allah will never forgive them. Verily, Allah guides not the rebellious people." (63:6)

"They are those who say, spend not on those who are with the messenger of Allah so they may desert him. And to Allah belongs the treasures of the heavens and the earth. But the hypocrites comprehend not." (63:7)

"They say, if [or when] we will return to Madina, indeed the more honorable will expel therefrom the meaner. And to Allah belongs the might [and the honor]

and to his messenger, but the hypocrites know not."
(63:8)

THE STORY OF "IFK" OR FALSE ACCUSATION

On this trip, Sayyidah Aaisha was with the prophet. After that the mission was done the Prophet was bivouacking with his army. Sayyidah Aaisha went for some humanitarian needs. When she came back, she realized that she had lost a necklace she had borrowed from her sister. She went back to look for it, but when she returned to the campsite, the army had already departed. She sat there, hoping that they would soon realize that she was not in the litter. She figured that they had not noticed the difference in weight when they lifted up the litter because the women were not eating much in those days, so they were very light. She slept while she waited.

She said,

> *"I woke up when Safwan Ibni Mu'attal as-Sullami saw me and said 'Inna Lillahi wa Inna Ilaihi Rajioon.'"*

He had also remained back for some reason. He recognized her because he had seen her before the rules of "Hijab" were in place. Aaisha said,

> *"He ordered his camel to sit and I mounted it. He didn't say a single word to me. At midday when the army was taking rest, we rejoined it. The hypocrites started spreading filthy propaganda, accusing us of sexual relations."*

Abdullah Ibni Ubai was the ringleader of this plot. He was angry not only because he lost his kingship as the Prophet arrived in Madina. He plotted at Uhud time and brought three hundred people back to Madina, and when he stood up after Friday prayer saying,

> "Allah has blessed us as he brought his prophet to Madina,"

Some people shouted at him calling him a hypocrite and grabbed him from his shirt to make him sit and he then crossed over people's necks and went out saying,

> "I was supporting him but people shouted at me."

An Ansari told him,

> "Go back and ask the Prophet for forgiveness."

He said,

> "Absolutely not,"

Which is mentioned in verse number five in Surat Ul Munafiqun. So, all this had caused him so much anger, and that is why he was looking for an occasion to take revenge.

THE SON OF ABDULLAH IBNI UBAI

This hypocrite had a son. His name was also Abdullah. He was a sincere Muslim. When he heard all that, his father did, he also heard that Umar asked the Prophet if he could kill him or order Abbad Ibni Bishr or Muaz Ibni Jabal or Mohammad Ibni Maslamah to kill this dirty man. But the Prophet said,

"No, people will say that Mohammad is killing his colleagues."

So, his son Abdullah pulled out a sword and stood at the entrance of his house to wait for his father, saying,

"I will show him who is the more honored one and who is the meanest one."

He also said,

"My father cannot enter the house unless the messenger of Allah says so."

When the Prophet came to know all this, he called Abdullah and said to him,

"Let him come to his house."

He said,

"O the Prophet of Allah! Whenever you want him to be killed, so tell me and nobody else. I will do it."

THE PROPHET ASKED ABOUT

Here when the prophet of Allah arrived in Madina. He was very upset. He asked Osamah Ibni Zaid,

"What do you think?"

He said,

"Aaisha is a noble lady."

The Prophet asked Ali. He said,

"If there is anything like this, then there are so many women in the world."

[It can mean that why then Allah had ordered you to marry Aaisha while some people said like as Ali was indicating toward divorcing her. But this is not right].

Ali also said,

"You can ask Bareera, her slave girl."

She said,

"I have never seen anything amiss except that sometimes she falls asleep and leaves the bread dough unattended and the goat eats it."

The Prophet asked Umar also. He said,

"Has she come to your house on her own?"

[meaning, she has come there with the leave of Allah so if there is anything he will tell you). The Prophet also asked Zainab binti Jahsh. She said,

"I have never seen anything but good in Aaisha."

Then the Prophet came to the pulpit and said,

"Who is for me from this hypocrite?"

Osaid Ibni Hudair said,

"I can do it."

At that time the chief of Khazraj, Sa'd Ibni Obadah said,

"You can't do anything to him,"

And noise erupted there. The Prophet made them quiet and left the scene.

AAISHA GOT THE NEWS

Aaisha was not aware of all this. She had not been feeling well for almost one month. The only thing she felt that the prophet due to the situation was not giving her that much attention. In those day the women used to go out to relieve themselves at night after *Isha*. She was going with Ummi Mistah, and she tumbled on a stone and said,

> *"May Mistah get punished."*

Aaisha said,

> *"Mother! Why would you say that?"*

She said,

> *"Do you not know what he has said?"*

And she told her the whole story.

Aaisha said,

> *The next day I asked the Prophet if I could go to my parents' house and he allowed me. I was weeping for two days and nights. One day the prophet came and told me that if I was innocent, then for sure Allah would reveal my purity. I asked my father to answer on my behalf. He said what can I say. Then I asked my mother. She said the same thing. I said, "If I say so, you people will not believe me." She said, "I was so stressed that I forgot the name of the prophet Yaqoob, referring to him what he said" so I said, "I will say only what the*

father of Yusuf said, 'A good patience (is good for me) and only Allah is to be asked for help against what you people describe (12:18).'" Then I lay down on my bed. I was very sure that Allah would reveal my purity, but I was not expecting that it would be in the Quran, but rather in a dream of the Prophet or as inspiration. Then I saw that the Prophet covered himself in his cloak, which I did know through my observation that he does that when he receives Quran. Then when it was done and he uncovered himself and he was smiling and said, "Aaisha, give thanks to Allah! He revealed your innocence." and thus he recited these verses.

"Verily, those who brought forth the slander (fabricated lie and false) are a group among you consider it not a bad thing for you (from all angles), but that is good for you (from some angles). For every man among them is what he has sinned. And the one who has taken on himself the big portion of it [made it] for him is the biggest torment." (24:11)

"Why not then when you heard it, the believing men and believing women thought good of themselves [meaning their own people], [and why not] they said that this is an obvious lie." (24:12)

"Why did they not brought forth four witnesses and when they have not produced witnesses on it then they are the liars with Allah." (24:13)

"And had there not been the bounty of Allah and his mercy on you in this world and in the hereafter then for sure a big torment would have touched you for that which you had fallen in." (24:14)

"Because you were propagating it with your tongues and you were uttering with your mouths what you had

no knowledge of and you counted it a little thing while with Allah that is a big thing." (24:15)

"And why not when you heard it said, it is not okay for us to speak of this, Glory be to you [O Allah!] [or amazing] This is a big lie." (24:16)

"Allah advises [forbids] you to go back to the like of it (to repeat it) if you are believers." (24:17)

"And Allah makes the rules clear for you. And Allah is all-knower, all-wise." (24:18)

"Verily, those who like evil to spread among those who believe, for them there is a painful torment in this world and in the hereafter. And Allah knows while you know not." (24:19)

"And had not the bounty of Allah been on you and his mercy [as well you would been punished] And [know that] Allah is ever Compassionate, ever Merciful." (24:20)

"O You who believed! Follow not the footsteps of Satan (devil). And whosoever follow the footsteps of Satan, he [Satan] commands the evil practice and forbidden things. And had it not been the grace of Allah on you and his mercy [as well], none of you would have been escaped among you. But Allah saves [protects] whom he wills. And Allah is all hearing, all knowing." (24:21)

"And let not those among you who are dignified and wealthy, swear not to give (any help) to their kins, the poor, the emigrants in the path of Allah, and they may pardon and turn their face [meaning do not be vengeful] Do you not love that Allah should forgive you? And Allah is oft-forgiving and most-merciful." (24:22)

> "Verily those who accuse chaste women who have nothing to do with unchastity and are believing, they are cursed in this world and in the hereafter and for them there is a big torment." (24:23)
>
> "On the day when their tongues, their hands and their legs [feet] will testify against them regarding what they used to do." (24:24)
>
> "On that day Allah will pay them their actual recompense and they will know that Allah is the manifest truth [reality]." (24:25)
>
> "Bad habits [bad talk/ bad actions] are for [or of] bad people and bad people are for bad actions [words or habits] and good habits [talk or actions] are for good people and good people are for good words [habits or deeds]. They are innocent of what these [bad] people say. For them there is forgiveness and a respectful [or generous] provision." (25:26)

My father Abu Bakr and my mother both said,

"Give thanks to the Prophet."

I said,

> "I will give thanks to Allah. Mistah was the cousin of Abu Bakr. Their mothers were sisters. As he was a poor man, so Abu Bakr used to help him a lot. He swore upon Allah that I would never help him anymore."

But verse 22 said,

> "And let not the people of virtue and wealth, swear not to give to their relatives, to the poor, and to those who

migrated in the path of Allah. Let them pardon and forgive. Do you not love that Allah should forgive you? And Allah is oft-forgiving, most merciful."

Abu Bakr said,

"Yes, I love it."

So he took some things to Mistah's house. The verse indicated too that he said it. That is not good, but he is your relative, he is poor, and also, he is a muhajir. And furthermore, for sure you are in love of pardon and forgiveness.

SARAYA AND MISSIONS AFTER BANI-MUSTALAQ

SARIYYAH ZAID IBNI HARITHA

In Ramadan year six, Zaid Ibni Haritha was taking a caravan to Sham. When this caravan was in Wadi-Qira, they came across some people of the Fazarah, a sub-tribe of Banu-Badr. They beat them and stole their goods. Zaid informed the prophet about it so the prophet gave him an army to teach them a lesson. They captured a Fazarah man and killed him. They also caught their Queen, who was named Ummi Qarafah, the daughter of Rabee'a Ibni Badr. She was captured by Qais Ibni Mohsin or Ibni Sahl or Ibni Mohsin; three names are mentioned there. She was also known as Sariyah Abu Bakr. Perhaps the prophet sent this support to Zaid under the leadership of Abu Bakr, as Salamah Ibn Ul Akwa said,

I was in this army. We attacked them after the Fajr prayer. We caught them on their water so Abu Bakr killed some of them. I saw a group of them with women and children so I shot arrows between them and a mountain in front of them so they may not flee to it. And thus, I caught them and brought them to Abu Bakr. Ummi Qarafah was among them with her very pretty daughter. Abu Bakr gave me that girl, but I did not touch her until I brought her to the Prophet. The Prophet gave her to the people of Makkah in exchange for releasing a few Muslims. Ummi Qarafah had arranged thirty horsemen, all of whom were her relatives, to assassinate the Prophet. They were all killed. When they came back, Zaid came straight to the Prophet. He knocked at the door and the Prophet came out in hurry. He hugged Zaid, kissed him, and asked about the details.

THE MISSION OF IBNI RAWAHAH

We have already mentioned that a wicked man, Ibni Abil Huqaiq, was killed by Muslims as the prophet ordered. Then the Jews appointed Aseer Ibni Razam as their leader. He was the one who suggested taking Ghitfan with them and attacking Madina and killing the Prophet. When the Prophet found out, he sent Abdullah Ibni Rawaha along with three other people to inquire about this news. Abdullah went to Khyber and came back and told the prophet that it was true. Here Kharijah Ibni Haseel told the Prophet,

"*I have seen Aseer arranging an expedition and coming to you.*"

The Prophet told his Sahabah about this and thirty of them got ready to counter them. The Prophet appointed Ibni Rawaha as their

Amir. They went to Khyber and met Aseer Ibni Razam and told him that the Prophet had sent them to take them there. He also arranged a group of thirty people. Now the arrangement was like this that on every camel a Jew will ride and a Muslim behind him on the same camel. On his way Aseer tried to take Abdullah Ibni Rawaha's sword from him, but Ibni Rawaha killed him and thus every Muslim killed the Jew who was sitting behind him. When they came, the prophet said,

> "Allah saved you from these dirty people."

UKAL AND ORAINAH TRIBES, AND KURAZ'S MISSION

Eight people of the Ukal and Oriana tribes came and pretended that they had accepted Islam. In Madina they fell sick. They became pale and their bellies swelled up. They said to the prophet,

> "We are not used to the weather here."

The Prophet told them to go to Harrah where there are the camels of state and drink their milk and urine. In a few days they felt better. So, they killed Yasar the herdsman. They drove thorns through his eyes and disemboweled him and took away the camels. They buried him in Quba. When the Prophet was informed, he sent Kuraz Ibni Jabir al-Fihri a Quraish man who had accepted Islam after Hijrah and gave him twenty fighters to catch them. When they brought them, the Prophet said,

> "Cut out their organs, drive thorns into their eyes and throw them on sand in scorching heat to die in pain in Harrah."

Allah says,

> *"Verily, the recompense of those who wage war against Allah and his messenger and do mischief and spread mischief [disorder] in the land is not but they shall be killed or crucified, or their hands and their feet be cut off from the opposite side or be expelled from the land [they are in]. That is their disgrace in this world and for them there is great torment in the hereafter."* (5:33)

Regarding this punishment for robbery, the interpretations are different. Imam Malik says,

> *"If they have killed someone [in the course of the robbery], they should be killed or crucified."*

He says they may choose between these two types of punishment, while for disemboweling or exile there is no option. Imam Shafi and Ahmad said,

> *If they have taken away the property and killed someone also, then they may be killed and crucified both." If they have taken away only [the wealth], then their hands and feet are to be cut off. And if they have only terrorized the people, then they may be expelled from the area.*

Imam Abu Hanifa says,

> *"If they have taken the wealth and have killed someone also, then their hands and feet could be cut off and they could be killed; this also means both punishments are allowed at once."*

Another issue is that of drinking of the urine of edible animals. Imam Malik and Imam Ahmad said that their urine is pure, while Hanafites and Shafiites say that it is un-clean. If less than one-fourth of (to Abu Hanifa and Abu Yusuf) of a shirt is soiled with this type of urine and someone wears it to pray, then his prayer is done, because its uncleanliness is minor, while the urine of other animals is severely unclean. And this hadith is about treatment. So, if no other medicine is available, then treatment like this is allowed.

PACT OF HUDAIBIYAH

The Prophet saw in a dream that he had entered Bait Ullah along with his Sahabah and that he had the key of Bait Ullah and performed *Tawaf* and *Umrah* as well, and that some of his Sahabah had shaved and some others had trimmed their hair. He told the Sahabah about his dream. They all thought that this would happen this year. The Prophet also planned *Umrah* and asked his Sahabah to get ready.

The Prophet mounted his she-camel named Qaswa and appointed Abdullah Ibni Ummi Maktoum as Amir in Madina. In one *Riwayah* it is said that he appointed Ibrahim or Numailah al-Laithi as Amir. Maybe one of them was Amir and another one was Imam for prayers.

The Prophet departed Zul Qadah year number six after Hijrah. It was a Monday. Ummi Salamah, the wife of the Prophet, was with him. In this trip some fourteen or fifteen hundred Sahabah accompanied the Prophet. They did not have weapons with them, as they were doing *Umrah*. At that time, swords were not considered weapons in normal circumstances, and at that time the Arabs wore them hanging at their sides. But this time they had packed them in their luggage.

THE PROPHET PUT ON HIS IHRAM

When the Prophet arrived at Zul - Hulaifah he put on *ihram* and prayed two *Rakat*. Ibni Ishaq relates that the prophet had seventy camels with him and seven hundred Sahabah. Maybe this was the number at Zul - Hulaifah and later on others were joining him and ultimately, they were fourteen or fifteen hundred as we said before.

The Prophet sent a Khuza'a man ahead to inquire about the conditions. When the prophet arrived in Osfan, a place there, Bishr Ibni Sufyan al-Kalbi came and told him that the Quraish had come out along with their milking she-camels to face them. He said metaphorically that they have worn cheetahs' skins and have erected their tents in Zee Tuwa valley. Also, Khalid Ibni Waleed arrived at Kura – Ul - Ghameem valley along with his horsemen.

The Prophet's informer also came and told him that Ka'b Ibni Lu'ai has gathered for you the Ahbash. Ahbash were the tribes known as the Banu-Harith Ibni Abdi Manat, Banu Mustalaq, and Haya Ibni Sa'd, who had entered into a treaty with Quraish on a mountain named Habshi in Noman Ul-Arak.

The Prophet said to his Sahabah,

"The Quraish are war psychics."

He asked his companions,

"Should we handle the Ahbash or go straight to Haram?"

Abu Bakr said,

"As we came here for Umrah, so we should go straight to Haram and if someone gets in our way then we will do what we need to do."

But when they arrived in Kura-Ul-Ghameem, they saw Khalid and his horsemen. They prayed *salat Ul-Zuhr*. Khalid thought at Asr prayer time that he could attack them but he could not find an opportunity, as the Prophet prayed it as *Salat Ul-Khawf*.

To avoid trouble, the Prophet changed the route and turned to the right. He left the usual route of Tan'eem. The Prophet took with him a guide named Hamzah Ibni Amr from the Aslamah tribe.

In Tahiyyat – Ul - Mura, Qaswa the she-camel tumbled. A Sahabi said,

> *"She is tired."*

The Prophet agreed,

> *"This not her habit but the one who stopped the companions of elephants, stopped it."*

Then he made it stand and she started walking. The Prophet came near a pod in Hudaibiyah and stopped there. When the water in the puddle was gone, and the Sahabah told the prophet about it, he gave them an arrow to place in it. It is said that Najdiyah Ibni Jundub or Bara Ibni Aazib or Obadah Ibni Khalid erected it. Imam Bukhari narrated from Bara Ibni Aazib that it was a well that was almost dry. So, the Prophet put some water in his mouth and then spit it into the well and asked them to wait a little bit, and the water rose up. So maybe Bara called that puddle a well and maybe the prophet has ordered them to plant the arrow and he threw the water in as well. Also, Bukhari and Muslim narrated from Jabir that the prophet put his fingers in a cup of water that had a little water inside and the water flew off his fingertips. They made *wudu* and drank and filled up their pots as well. So maybe all these happened there but Ibni Hiban related it as two different events.

THE DELEGATIONS TO THE PROPHET

As we mentioned before, in none of the battles or expeditions did the Muslims show any weakness. The Prophet defeated them at Badr and Ahzab, while in Uhud also he defeated them in the beginning. Even the Makkans never thought of it that we have won and that's why they didn't come back, even though Abu Sufyan had said it. And after Ahzab the Prophet said,

> *"From now on, they will never attack you but if you attack them or they will plot some conspiracies."*

Now after all this, it was clear to other people that now the Makkans had no place. So now when the prophet was entering Makkah even for worship, they thought it would be way too much for them, that he would enter along with his Sahabah. They thought to get some people in between to convince him not to come but to go back and thus people will say that they did not allow them to come, even though this was totally against the very known policy and practice, to stop people to come to their holy place even though if they are enemies.

They used different tactics. Budail Ibni Warqa-al-Khuza'a came and reported to the Prophet that the Makkans were very much ready to fight. The Prophet said,

> *"But we have not come to fight, but for umrah; as you see, we are in Ihram."*

He went back to the Quraish and told them that he had met him and seen them in *ihram*.

Then they asked Mukhriz Ibni Hafs of the Banu Aamir. When the Prophet saw him, he said he was a traitor but still he told him what he had told Budail before. He also came back and told them the same way.

Then they sent Halees Ibni Al-Qama of Kinanah to go to the prophet. He was the chief of the Ahbash. The Prophet said,

> "He is from such a tribe who honor the haram sharif, the visitors of haram and the sacrificial animals as well."

So, the Sahabah welcomed him with *Talbiyah*. He then went back and told the Quraish,

> "I saw them in ihram and also their sacrificial animals. They do not have any intention of war or fighting."

This man had not talked to the prophet in this regard at all when he saw the scene. The Quraish became angry with him and insulted him saying,

> "Shut up, you farmer!"

He also became angry with them and said,

> "You have to let him enter and perform umrah otherwise I will withdraw from the treaty as that is an alliance against those who want to fight you or us."

The Quraish came to their sense and apologized to him. Urwah Ibni Masud also told them,

> "He is giving you a reasonable solution so listen to him."

They asked him to go and talk to the prophet. He said,

> "But I saw how you dealt those who went before me."

They said,

> "We will never blame you for anything."

Urwah came to the Prophet. The Prophet told him the same thing he had told Budail and Mukhriz. Urwah was requesting that the Prophet should go back to avoid any unpleasant situation, otherwise he was worried that his own colleagues would desert them. Abu Bakr, who was known for his softness, became angry and said to Urwah,

> "Kiss the hidden part of 'Lat'—we will desert?"

Urwah asked the prophet,

> "Who is this?"

He said,

> "This is Ibni Abi Quhafah."

Urwah said,

> "I wish you had not done a favor for me! (Meaning, "I would have answered you")*.*

That favor was that in the time of ignorance, Abu Bakr had paid blood-money on his behalf.

When Urwah was talking to the Prophet he kept taking his hand towards the beard of the Prophet, perhaps in supplication. Mughirah Ibni Shobah was standing beside him, stopping his hand with the tip of his sword not to touch his beard as he thought that a *Mushrik* should not touch this holy beard. Urwah said,

> "Who is this stopping me every time?"

They said,

> "This is Mughirah Ibni Shobah."

Urwah said,

> "O the traitor! Would that I had not helped you in your treason."

Mughirah was his nephew. In the time of ignorance, he had killed thirteen men of the Thaqeef and stolen their belongings and wealth. But after that he accepted Islam. The Prophet said,

> *"He has accepted Islam, so what he has done in the time of ignorance I have nothing to do with."*

Urwah was watching the Sahabah. When he came back to the Quraish he told them,

> *I have seen Qaisar and other Kings, but I have not seen such a king whose people give him that much respect. By Allah! They do not allow his saliva even to fall on ground. They take it with their hands and rub it on their bodies. They even fight one another for the water of his wudu. When he speaks, they listen to him very attentively and when he orders they rush to obey it. So, my suggestion is let him do umrah and go back as he said it to me. This is the reasonable solution.*

But Quraish didn't accept his suggestion. So Urwah went back to Taif along with his people. Later on, after Thaqeef's mission, Urwah accepted Islam.

Ibni Ishaq says that the prophet gave his camel named Thalab to Kharash Ibni Umayyah and sent him to the Quraish. Instead of listening to him the Quraish cut off the camel's ears and wanted to kill Kharash but Habush told them not to do this.

The Quraish tried to instigate Muslims so they would start a fight. So, some seventy or eighty people from the Tan'eem mountain's side came at night to infiltrate the Muslims' camp but Mohammad Ibni Maslamah caught them, tied them up, and brought them to the prophet. The prophet then released them, as he was not there for any mischief.

UTHMAN ON MISSION

The Prophet said to Umar,

> "If you will go talk to Quraish and make it clear to them that we are only here for umrah and nothing else."

He said,

> If you order it, I will do it, but none of my tribe, the Banu Adi Ibni Kab, have remained there in Makkah, so the Quraish will listen to me because of him, but I suggest someone who is much more respected in the eyes of Quraish than I am; and also his tribesmen are there so they will listen to him and will not harm him because of his tribesmen there and that is Uthman Ibni Affan.

The Prophet accepted this reasonable suggestion. He sent Uthman. When he entered Makkah, he met his first cousin Aban Ibni Saeed Ibn Ul Aas. Then he went to Abu Sufyan. He talked to them. They said,

> "If you want, since you are in ihram, you can perform umrah."

He said,

> "As long as the Prophet has not done it, I will not."

The Quraish stopped him for some time so they could think about what Uthman has told them and then in Hudaibiyah a news spread that Uthman is killed. The Prophet said,

> "If this news is true, then there is no other way but revenge."

BAI'AT-I-AQABAH

This is also called "Bai'atur Rizwan." The Prophet took a Bai'at on this from his Sahabah. The first one he gave his Bai'at was Abu Sinan - Al- Asadi, the brother of Okasha Ibni Mihsan. Salamah Ibn Ul Akwa gave his Bai'at three times on death. The prophet gave his holy hand as borrow to Uthman so that if he is alive so he may not be deprived from this blessing.

He said,

> "This hand of mine is for Uthman regarding this Bai'at."

This shows how much the Prophet loved and trusted Uthman, as this was a pledge for death. When the Bai'at was completed, Uthman came back alive. No one stayed behind except Jadd Ibni Qais, a hypocrite. Allah says,

> "Verily, those who gave "Bai'at" [pledge] to you they are giving their pledge to Allah. The hand of Allah is over their hands." (48:10)

Also, he said regarding these people.

> "Indeed, Allah is pleased with the believers when they were giving their Bai'at (pledge) to you under the tree. He knew what was in their hearts. He sent down tranquility upon them and he rewarded them with a near victory." (48:18)

THE PACT OF HUDAIBIA

After thinking about the message of the Prophet given by Uthman, the Quraish sent Suhail Ibni Amr a good table talker, orator, and a statesman from Banu Aamir Ibni Lu'ai to the Prophet. When the Prophet saw him, he said,

"It seems that this man has come for a reconciliation."

He made a lengthy prologue before his talk. After that, there remained no possibility of war and was instead an atmosphere for a peace treaty.

Umar came to Abu Bakr and said, Is Mohmmad not a Prophet of Allah? He said,

"Why not?"

Then Umar said,

"Are we not Muslims?"

Abu Bakr said, why not. He said,

"Are the Quraish not Mushrik?"

He said,

"Why not?"

Umar said,

"Then why are we showing this weakness?"

Abu Bakr said,

"We must listen to the Prophet and obey and follow him."

Umar said,

"I bear witness that he is the prophet of Allah."

He went to the prophet and said the same things to him. The Prophet said,

> "I am the prophet of Allah and his messenger as well and I will never disobey him in any commandment."

Umar realized that this is the order of Allah. Umar said,

> "After talking to the prophet, I was feeling sorry for myself so I started praying, fasting and freeing slaves in order to feel better."

In some Riwayat it is narrated that first he spoke to the prophet and then to Abu Bakr, but to us the former narration seems more accurate.

THE PACT

The Prophet ordered Ali to write the text of the pact, and he wrote,

> *This is what Mohammad the messenger of Allah and Suhail Ibni Amr made a peace on. Suhail said if I was to know and believe that you are the messenger of Allah, then there would have been no dispute, nor we would have stopped you from the house of Allah. So, write your name and your father's name.*

Now Ali was not to erase the words,

> "The Messenger of Allah"

consent fully so the prophet himself erased it and said,

> "Write Mohammad the son of Abdullah."

Note- Ali had started the treaty with "in the name of Allah, the Beneficent, the Merciful." And now Suhail objected to the word "Rahman." So, Ali erased it, but he showed resistance to erase the word "the messenger of Allah." Why? The answer is that even a single word "Allah" or "Allahumma" was sufficient there, as it has all the required attributes and have it. But the prophethood was not that much clear just from mention of the name Mohammad only.

THE ARTICLES OF THE PACT:

1) Mohammad will go back this year without performing *umrah* and he and his followers can come next year and can stay at Makkah for three days with their swords inside their luggage and the Quraish will go out of the city for these three days, so they may not face one another.

2) This treaty is good for ten years: neither party will fight the other.

3) Whoever wants can join Mohammad in this treaty, or he can join the Quraish, and he will be considered a part of the treaty.

4) Whoever will go to Mohammad from Quraish's side without the permission of his or her elder will be returned to the Quraish and whoever comes to Quraish from Mohammad's side they are not bound to return give him back to Mohammad.

The Khuza'a tribe joined the Prophet at the time of the treaty. They were the allies of Abdul Muttalib in the time of ignorance as well, while the Banu Bakr joined the Quraish. It is said that what Umar said to Abu Bakr and then to the prophet was before signing this treaty. So, until it was signed, these were only suggestions and the prophet had given them the right to speak if they did not agree. But when something is formally decided then it is to be obeyed.

Suhail said,

"I will keep this document."

So, Mohammad Ibni Maslamah wrote out another copy for the Muslims. In the beginning no one except Abu Bakr was ready for some contents of the treaty, especially the third part. In this treaty it was written,

"The secrets of the past are to be kept secret."

This means that what happened in the past, who did wrong and what was the result, should not be disclosed. Another sentence was,

"There will be no cheating or stealing."

THE WISDOM IN TREATY

As we mentioned before, the contents of the treaty were not acceptable. But the wisdom therein was known to the prophet and that is why he accepted it. As for as the case of Abu Bakr was concerned, he accepted it from the very beginning because of his utmost obedience and because his heart was getting reflection from the prophet. The Quraish stipulated the conditions and they were surprised that the prophet accepted it, as they themselves were not aware of the wisdom therein.

THE WISDOM THEREIN WAS

(i) Before this they did not consider the prophet as a legitimate power in the area. Now for the first time they agreed that Muslims were an equal political power and that Madina is a legitimate state as they considered them equal to them, and thus Allah said: *"Indeed we have given you a clear victory." (48:1)*

So, this treaty itself was considered a victory. This was the prophet's victory on the external side, while on internal side this was the manifest victory that the contents were not acceptable to Sahabah. But they accepted it whole-heartedly and that is the manifest victory for a leader, that his followers showed full obedience without resistance.

(ii) For the first time, the Quraish admitted that the Muslims had the right to come to Bait Ullah. Yes, they succeeded in stopping them for only one year.

(iii) After this treaty the Muslims were free to move anywhere in peninsula, which was good for the spread of Islam and for their trade and financial activities. They went to Makkah to visit their relatives and the Makkans came to Madina as well and they were learning about Islam, Muslims, their values, and ethics. As they began to understand the perfection of the prophet's personality, they became interested in Islam and many of them converted.

(iv) When the Muslims did not have to worry about this side due to the peace treaty, the prophet now started writing letters of *dawah* towards Islam to different kings and rulers. Also, he started sending missions to different areas to call people towards Allah, so we see that at the time of Hudaibiyah there were fourteen hundred Muslims and only two years later, this number increased that when the prophet was going to Makkah in Ramadan year 8: he had 10,000 Sahabah with him. The only thing the Quraish apparently won in this treaty was that the prophet had to return their men if any came to him, while they did not have to give back their men. But this was also in favor of Muslims: if someone became apostate, he must stay away as he is unclean and will create a *fitnah* if he remains in Muslim society.

The Prophet said,

> "Whoever from our side will go to them, so Allah has taken him away. And the one who will come out of them and accept Islam if he cannot take shelter at Madina, then the land of Allah is spacious. Habshah was spacious for Muslims before."

(v) This is what the prophet indicated to it when he said,

> "And whoever of them will come to us, then Allah will give him a way out and a relief [Muslim]."

It is said that the Prophet got a few people to witness the treaty and they were Abu Bakr, Umar, Uthman, Abdur Rahman Ibni Awf, Sa'd Ibni Abi Waqas, Abu Ubaidah, and of course Ali, as he wrote it, while from Quraish's side he got Huwaitib and Mukhriz.

ABU JUNDAL

When Suhail Ibn Amr was sitting with the Prophet and Ali was writing the document, Suhail's own son Abu Jundal came with chains around his hands and feet, as he had accepted Islam and they had chained him. When Suhail saw him, he said the to the Prophet,

> "This is the first I ask for his return to us."

The Prophet replied,

> "But the treaty has not been signed yet."

Then he said,

> "So I am not going to do anything."

The Prophet said,

"Give him to me."

He said,

"Not at all."

Suhail slapped Abu Jundal in the face and then grabbed him. Abu Jundal was shouting,

"O the Muslims, will I be given back to them to be tortured?"

The Prophet said,

"Abu Jundal! Be patient, Allah will give you and all other oppressed a way out and a relief. We have agreed on something so we don't want to cheat."

Umar jumped up and walked with Abu Jundal, telling him,

"Be patient! They are polytheists. Their blood is like dog's blood."

He was talking close to him, one hand on the hilt of his sword so he could hit his father with it, but Abu Jundal didn't do that.

THE PROPHET CAME OUT OF IHRAM

After the treaty was signed the prophet told his Sahabah to slaughter their animals and to come out of *ihram*, but nobody stood up even though they used to sacrifice their lives whenever he asked. The Prophet came to Ummi Salamah and said,

"What happened to them?"

She advised him not to tell them to slaughter, rather you go and slaughter your animal, then you will see what they do. The prophet did the same and when Sahabah saw him, they stood up and slaughtered their animals and took off their ihram. The Prophet slaughtered the camel of Abu Jahl that he had obtained in Badr. He distributed the meat to the locals there. Kharash Ibni Umayyah Ibni Fazl al-Khuza'a shaved the prophet's head. In an another *Riwayah* it is mentioned that Muaa'wiyah Ibni Abi Sufyan shaved his head as he had accepted Islam secretly and disclosed it after the conquest of Makkah.

Ibni Abbas said that some Sahabah shaved their heads while others merely trimmed. The prophet said,

> *"O Allah! Have mercy on those who shaved."*

The Sahabah said,

> *"And those who trimmed."*

So, the prophet made *Dua* three times for those who shaved and one time for those who trimmed. So that is why the scholars say shaving after *ihram* is *sunnah* and trimming is allowed.

Note – For one who shaves his head or trims his hair while in *ihram* due to some necessity, a *Fidyah* is due on him after in shape of sacrifice or *Sadaqah* or fasting. This rule was made when Ka'b Ibni Ojrah had shaved his head and Allah said,

> *"And whosoever of you is sick or having an ailment in his scull he must pay a Fidyah of either fasting [three days] or give Sadaqah [feeding the sick and/or the poor] or sacrifice [a goat or lamb]." (2:196)*

Musa Ibni Oqbah Zuhari and Bayhaqi narrated from Urwah Ibni Zubair that on that day a Muslim said,

> "Is it a victory that we couldn't perform umrah and we also returned a Muslim to them?"

When the prophet heard about this, he said,

> *He has said wrong. Of course, this is a victory that they agreed that we will go back without a war, while they agreed that we will do umrah next year and they inclined to this peace treaty when they heard about your pledge on death. Have you forgotten Uhud when I was calling on you and you were running away, or you have forgotten Ahzab when the hearts had reached the throats?*

The Sahabah said,

> *"Of course, you have said right."*

Umar later cut down the thorny tree under which the prophet took the pledge so the people would not start worshipping it.

SURAT UL FATH

Translation

> *"Indeed we have given you a manifest victory." (48:1)*

> *"That Allah may forgive you your sins of the past and future and complete his favor on you and guide you on the straight path." (48:2)*

> *"And that Allah may help you with a mighty help." (48:3)*

> *"He is the one who sent down [put] tranquility into the hearts of the believers so they may grow in faith more*

along with their faith [i.e., enrich their faith]. And to Allah belong the hosts of the heavens and the earth. And Allah is ever all-knowing, all-wise." (48:4)

INTERPRETATION

(48:1) Regarding the plain victory Jalal – Al - Muhalli, Qazi Beidawi and some other scholars said, *"This is a happy news about the conquest of Makkah. You people accepted this treaty where a few conditions were not acceptable apparently, so Allah will give you the victory of Makkah as a reward."* And some others said, *"It means this victory was a glad tiding about the victory of Khyber which happened after this event."*

But we say it means this treaty itself where:

(i)   They accepted Muslims as an equal party.

(ii) They could not impose a war on Muslims in their own area.

(iii) They admitted that Muslims have the right to enter Makkah next year and to perform *umrah* and thereafter whenever they wanted to

(iv) Muslims won the right to move freely and go to the peninsula, even to Makkah, without fear.

(v)   Muslims became free of any concern from this side so they can focus on mission work.

(vi) Muslims showed some resistance to some of its articles but when the prophet said, *"This is an order,"* then all of them accepted that whole-heartedly. This shows their faith in Allah and in his messenger and obedience to the leadership even they thought that certain conditions are not acceptable, and

(vii) A message went out that this messenger is an angel of peace even though before that these people introduced them as an axis and pivot of evil and mischief.

"That Allah may forgive your sins." (48:2)

What it means is that The Prophet never committed any sin as he was sent as a role model. And a role model has to be perfect. So, it means either the sins of his followers or it means some small mistakes in the process, and this concept could be approved by the following sentences,

"And to complete his favor on you and to guide you to the straight path and to help you with a perfect help [i.e., more correction and development]."

(And he did, as Islam spread to other parts of the peninsula. Also, some Makkans accepted Islam as they came to know the reality when they mingled with Muslims and this was a gateway to the conquest of Makkah.)

"He sent down tranquility [satisfaction] into the hearts of the believers." (48:4)

Means that in the beginning, they were disturbed at being prevented from doing *umrah* and some other conditions that were unacceptable. But later on, when the prophet told them, *"This is an order,"* then they were satisfied.

"Verily those who were giving you the Bai'at, indeed they were giving their Bai'at to Allah, the hand of Allah was over their hands, then whoever breaks it he breaks it only to his own self [i.e., harming his own self] And whoever fulfilled what he has covenanted with Allah, Allah will bestow on him a great reward." (48:10)

Then he said regarding these people:

> "Indeed Allah is pleased with the believers when they were giving you a pledge under the tree. He knew what was in their hearts so he sent down the tranquil upon them and he rewarded them with a near [or easy] victory." (48:18)

> "And abundant spoils that they will capture. And Allah is ever all-mighty, all-wise." (48:19)

Regarding not allowing a war to happen, Allah said:

> "And he is the one who has withheld their hands from you and your hands from them in the midst of Makkah after that he had made you victors over them. And Allah is ever the all-seer of what you do." (48:24)

This verse either means that at the time they were in Hudaibiyah and they tried to attack you from the Tan'eem side but they were captured or it means that they were safe under that treaty in Makkah when they will come for *umrah* next year and victory is that not only they won the right to entry and *umrah* but also, they turned them out of Makkah for three days, even though it is their city.

And some Muslims said,

> "Where is the dream that we will enter Makkah shaving our heads and trimming?"

Allah said:

> "Indeed Allah has made to his prophet the dream come true, that you shall enter to Masjid al-Haram if Allah wills, secure shaving your heads and trimming having no fear, so he knew what you knew not so he granted you a near [or easy] victory." (48:27)

This near or easy victory also either means this treaty where you [Muslims] got a lot or it means to some *Mufassireen* the victory at Khyber.

Regarding the objection of Suhail to the word *"the messenger of Allah"* which saddened the prophet as well,

Allah said:

> *He is the one who has sent his messenger with guidance and with a Deen of truth to make it prevail over all religions and sufficient is Allah as a witness. (48:28)*

> *That Mohammad is the Messenger of Allah and those who are with him are utmost harder for the disbelievers and kind among themselves to one another, you see them bowing and prostrating [in prayer] seeking a bounty from Allah and satisfaction. There are marks on their faces from repeated prostration. That is their description in 'Taurat,' and marks in Injeel like a crop [seed] that has sent forth its shoots, then made it strong and became thick so it stands straight on its stem, delighting the farmer that he may enrage the disbelievers with them. Allah had promised forgiveness and a great reward among those who believed and practiced righteous good deeds. (48:29)*

ABU BASEER ARRIVED IN MADINA

When the Prophet arrived in Madina, there came Abu Baseer Utbah Ibni Osaid Ibni Haritha Ath Thaqafi from Makkah. The Quraish sent two people to Madina to take Abu Baseer back. The Prophet gave him back to them per the terms of the treaty.

When they were eating there in Zul-Hulaifah, Abu Baseer said to one of them,

> "Oh! Your sword! he said take it and see."

He took it and killed a man named Khunais with it. Another man who was with him fled to Madina. After a while Abu Baseer also came back to Madina.

He said,

> "O the Prophet of Allah! You have fulfilled your promise."

The Prophet said,

> "The action of your will lit a fire."

He understood that if the Quraish asked him for the second time, the prophet would give him back to them. So, he left Madina and went to Saiful-Bahr in Sham. When Abu Jundal got the news of Abu Baseer's arrival there, he came there also and later on whoever was accepting Islam in Makkah he came there and thus their number became three hundred. This was on the trade route of the people of Makkah, so whenever a caravan was passing by, they stopped it and looted everything from them and thus the Quraish were unable to take anything to Makkah. So, they requested the prophet to bring them to Madina.

The Prophet wrote to Abu Baseer to come to Madinah (along with Abu Jundal, and to let other Muslims to go to their respective areas) and let the Quraish continue their business in peace. When Abu Baseer received the letter, he was in his last moments. He died while reading it. Abu Jundal buried him there and made a *masjid* close by, and he himself came to Madina along with a few other Muslims.

Abu Bakr said,

"There was no greater a victory then the pact of Hudaibiyah, as Islam spread after this even in Makkah."

THE WOMEN AND THE RETURN

As we mentioned, there was the condition to return whoever came from Makkah and thus the prophet returned a few men as Muslims, but this condition was not applicable to the women. Allah says,

> "O those who believed! When there come to you believing women as emigrants, take a test of them [regarding Iman] Allah knows well their belief. Then if you found them believing then do not give them back to the disbelievers. Neither they are lawful for them nor they can be lawful for them [these women] and give them [their husbands] that [amount] which they have spent [given to them as their bridal money]. And there is no blame on you to marry them if you have given them their mahr [dowry]. And do not hold to the ties [marriage contract] of disbelieving women and ask for what you have spent [as dowry] and let them [the disbelievers] ask for what they have spent [given to their wives]. This is the command of Allah; he judges between you [with]. And Allah is all-knowing, all-wise." (60:10)

> "And if any of your wives deserts you to the disbelievers and you followed it up [to have your mahr returned but you could not get it] Then give those whose wives are gone the equivalent of what they have spent and fear Allah the one whom you believe." (60:11)

Umar divorced two of his wives that day. Later on, Muaa'wiyah married one of them and Safwan Ibni Umayyah married the other.

Ummi Kulthum, daughter of Oqbah Ibni Abi Mo'eet, had accepted Islam before Hijrah. Now she came to Madina on foot with a man from Khuza'a. Her two brothers, Ammarah, and Waleed came there asking for her return, but the prophet said the wording of the treaty did not apply to women, so they left.

GHAZWAT UL GHABAH

This is also called Ghazwa Zi-Qirad. Oyainah Ibni Hisn attacked the pasture of the prophet and he killed his herdsmen as well. Salamah Ibni Amr Ibn Ul Akwa al-Aslami said,

> *The prophet sent me with Rabah, the prophet's slave. We were both riding the horse of Abu Talha. When we were there in that place, I told Rabah take the horse to Abu Talha. I went to an elevated place and called for help. Then I followed these people and started shooting arrows at them. Until I got them into a narrow canyon in between the mountains and continued shooting arrows at them. They started leaving the camels of the Prophet behind them one by one. They also threw behind, thirty shawls [cloaks] and thirty spears. I was putting a sign on everything so the prophet may recognize it. There I sat in a place until I saw the horse-riders of the prophet. Ahzam came then Abu Qatada and then Miqdad. Abu Qatada killed Abdur Rahman – al - Fazari. These people fled to Zi-Qirad well to drink therefrom but I did not spare them to drink water. Then the Prophet arrived there. I asked the prophet to cut them off but he said, "Now leave them." The Prophet said, "This day Abu Qatada is our best horsemen and Salamah is the best among those on foot." He gave me*

two shares that day and made me ride behind him on Adba the she-camel.

In this Ghazwa, the flag-bearer was Miqdad, while Ibni Ummi Maktoum was Amir at Madina. The prophet prayed salat Ul-Khawf in "Zi-Qirad."

LETTERS TO THE KINGS AND LEADERS

As we mentioned before, when the pact of Hudaibiyah was made, the prophet had no more concern from Quraish's side so now he wanted to give *Dawat* to the kings and leaders of different areas. Among them there were Qaisar and Kisra.

The Persian empire had overtaken Sham, Misr and some parts of Asia and was now threatening the Romans in Constantinople, the religious center of Christianity.

When the Prophet came back from Hudaibiyah, he decided to send a message to the rulers and who to use as messengers. So, he selected those who used to go to the respectable areas in connection to their trade and business, as they were aware of the local customs. He was told that the rulers did not receive an unsealed, unstamped letters. So, he ordered Abu Bakr to make him a seal and he had a silver ring made by a goldsmith, upon which the words "Mohammadur Rasulullah" were engraved.

Later on, this ring was with Abu Bakr the Umar and then Uthman, but once Uthman was sitting on Bismic of Arees Well, so it was in his hands but fell down therein. Sahabah looked for that for three days in the well, but they couldn't find it and that was the year when Uthman was martyred. These letters are,

LETTER TO CAESAR THE KING OF ROME

Imam Bukhari narrated the letter the Prophet wrote to the king of Byzantines, HiraQal" (Hercules):

> *In the name of Allah, the Beneficent, The Merciful. From Mohammad the slave of Allah and his messenger, to Hercules the great [King] of the Byzantines. 'Peace be on one who followed the guidance. I invite you to Islam, submit to be safe. Allah will give you your reward twice, but if you turn your face then the sin of the downtrodden will be on you." [Then he wrote the verse 3:64]*

> *Say, O people of the Book! Come to the word which is equal [equally revealed] to us and you, not to worship any but Allah, and not to associate with him anything, and not to take one another as lords besides Allah. Then, if they turn away, then say, "Bear witness that we are Muslims".*

The Prophet gave this letter to his envoy Dihyah Ibni Khalifa al Kalbi. He was told to give it to the King of Busra, he will send it to Caesar. When Hercules received the letter, he was surprised. He ordered the Arabs in his area to come to his palace. At that time a few Arabs were there in the area on business. Among them there was Abu Sufyan. Hercules asked them,

> "Who amongst you is closest to Mohammad?"

Abu Sufyan looked at the Arabs and saw that none of them was as close to the prophet as he was. So, he said,

"Me."

Hercules asked him,

"How close are you?"

He said,

"He is Mohammad, son of Abdullah, son of Abdul Muttalib, son of Hashim, son of Abdi Manaf; and I am Abu Sufiyan, son of Harb, son Umayyah, son of Abd Shams, son of Abdi Manaf."

Hercules asked him,

"What is his family's *status?*"

He said,

"They are the noblest of the noble."

He asked him,

"What was Mohammad like before?"

He replied that he was known as honest and trustworthy. Then he asked him,

"What did he call people towards?"

He answered,

"Towards the oneness of Allah."

Then he posed another question about who accepted his call and who refused it. Abu Sufiyan said,

"Only the downtrodden people accepted his message."

Then he asked,

"Has anyone denounced it since?"

He said,

"We put them through so much, but no one has ever denounced it."

Abu Sufyan confessed later that that once or twice he intended to lie, but then I thought,

"If someone from these Arabs exposes me then we will lose our dignity as Arabs."

So, the King said,

"If what he said is true then for sure his message will spread to this area of ours also."

It is also narrated that one morning Hercules was in Baitul Maqdis, he woke up incredibly stressed and when he was asked why, he said,

"I had a dream that a circumcised one has appeared and is a threat to my kingdom."

Then he said,

If I had been there, I would have washed his feet. Then we heard a noise and he turned us out. I told my colleagues now Abu Kabsha's son Mission has gone forth [Abu Kabsha was the name of an infamous grandfather from the prophet's mother's side and the Arabs, when they wanted to put someone down, they used to mention him by the name of an infamous grandfather. And this was the only opportunity for Abu Sufyan to put the prophet down). I told them also that it means that the king of Rome is also afraid of him. I was now very sure that Mohammad's mission will prevail and then Allah blessed me with it as well.

Imam Bukhari narrates then that Hercules called Roman elites to his Hims city palace. He closed the doors and told them,

> *"If you people are looking for honor, then follow this man."*

The elites became angry that he was suggesting that they abandon their own religion and they rushed towards the gates, but they could not get out. Hercules called them back and to calm them down, he said,

> *"I was testing you to see how strong you are in your faith,"*

And thus, they prostrated to him.

JUZAM ROBBED DIHYAH

Then Hercules gave some gifts to Dihyah. The Juzam tribe looted that from him and Dihyah told the prophet what happened. The prophet gave a group of soldiers to Zaid ibn Haritha to give a lesson to Juzam. He attacked them. Some of the people were killed while some others Zaid captured. They were almost one hundred along with one hundred camels and two thousand goats. Then Zaid Ibni Rifa'a - Al - Juzami came. He had accepted Islam before, along with a few others. He had tried at the time of robbery also to defend Dihyah, so the prophet gave him everything back and released the captives.

LETTER TO "KISRA" (KHOSROW) THE PERSIAN EMPEROR

In the name of Allah, the Beneficent, the Merciful. From Mohammad the messenger of Allah to "Kisra" (Khosrow) the King of Persia! Peace be upon he who followed the guidance, believed in Allah and his messenger, and testified that there is no god but Allah alone having no partner with him and that Mohammad is the slave of Allah and his messenger and I invite you with the invitation of Allah, verily I am the messenger of Allah to all mankind to warn one who is alive and that the charge will prove against the disbelievers so submit to be safe otherwise you will have the sin of the Magians.

Abdullah Ibni Huzafah took this letter to the king of Bahrain and through him he took it to Khosrow. He was a proud man, so when he read the letter, he said,

"A wicked person wrote his name before my name,"

So, he tore it and threw it to the ground. Now when the prophet was informed of this, he said,

"May Allah smash his Kingdom,"

And then it happened later on. Khosrow wrote to his governor in Yemen, a man named Bazan, to send two powerful people to bring this man to him. Bazan sent his treasury secretary, Babwaih, and a Persian man, Khar Khosrow, to the prophet, giving them a letter ordering the prophet to go with these two people to Khosrow. Bazan told them both to go and talk to him and inform him what he says. They came to Taif and asked some Quraish people about the prophet. The Quraish told them that he is in Madina. They went there and Babwaih talked to the prophet.

There were two people with shaved beards and long moustaches. The prophet asked them, why and how are you like this?

They said,

> "Our lord [Khosrow / Chusroes] has ordered us."

The prophet told them,

> "Now go take rest, both of you, and come to me tomorrow."

Allah informed his prophet that Khosrow had been killed by his son Sharawaih.

Waqidi says that this was in 10th Jumada – al - Oola year 7 and it was a Tuesday night. In the morning when these two men came to the prophet, he told them about Khosrow. They said,

> "What you say?"

They meant if this was a lie then the prophet would pay a heavy price. The prophet said,

> "Just go and tell your Governor the same, and also tell him, My Deen will approach the kingdom of Khosrow, and wherever else humans and animals can go. Also tell him, if he accepts my Deen, I will keep him as Governor."

They went and told their lord all this. After a little while a letter from Sharawaih came to Bazan to suspend the case of Mohammad. This caused Bazan and the people of Yemen to accept Islam. Babwaih also told Bazan that he had never seen a person so venerated. He asked him whether he had any guards around him; they said no. Then the prophet kept him as the Governor there until Hajjah –Ul- Wida.

LETTER TO NEGUS THE ABYSSINIAN KING

"Najjashi" (Negus) was the title of the King of *Abyssinia* (Ethiopia). His name was *As 'Hamah Ibni Abjar*. The Prophet wrote to him at the end of the 6th or in the beginning of the 7th year in the month of *Muharram*. *Amr Ibni Umayyah Ad Damari* took this letter to him. So, this letter was of course after *Hudaibiyah*, while *Imam Tabari* mentioned a letter which seems to be a letter that the prophet wrote when he was at *Makkah* and some *Sahabah* were migrating to *Abyssinia*. Because in the end of that letter it is written

> *"And I have sent to you my cousin Jafar along with a few Muslims."*

The text of this letter was:

> *In the name of Allah, the Beneficent, the Merciful. From Mohammad the messenger of Allah to Negus the king of Abyssinia: Peace be upon one who accepted the guidance.*
>
> *And after that I praise you Allah the King, the holy, the source of peace, the provider of peace [the guardian of faith] the preserver of safety, I bear witness that Jesus son of Mary is the spirit of Allah, his word which he cast into Mary the virgin, the good, the pure, so she conceived Jesus from his spirit and breath, as he created Adam with his hand; and I call you to Allah, the one having no partner and to his friendship [based] on his obedience and to follow me to believe in what has come to me, for I am the messenger of Allah. I invite*

> you and your hosts to Allah the almighty and I communicate and advise this sincerely. Peace be upon one who accepted the guidance. And I have sent my cousin Jafar, along with a few Muslims."

Some scholars have related this letter as the prophet's letter after Hudaibiyah and they did not mention the last sentence regarding Jafar, but to the best of our study we say that the letter after Hudaibiyah is the one narrated by Ibni Ishaq and Bayhaqi and that is,

> In the name of Allah, the Beneficent, the Merciful. From Mohammad the messenger of Allah to Negus As'hamah, the great of Abyssinia! Peace be upon him who accepts the guidance and believes in Allah and in his messenger and bore witness that there is no God but only Allah who has no partner, neither a wife nor a son and that Mohammad is his slave and messenger; and I call you with the call of Islam for I am his messenger, so submit to be safe, "Say [O Mohammad] O people of the book, come to the word which is equal [equally revealed] to us and you, not to worship but Allah alone and not to associate with him anything and not to take one another as lords besides Allah, then if they turn away, then bear witness that we are Muslims. So, if you refuse then, thereupon you will bear the sin of Christians from your people.

Now some Ulama say that this letter the prophet wrote to a different Negus, namely, the successor of the first one, but we say but the name As'hamah is mentioned there so this letter was to the same Negus and he wrote his answer to the prophet.

> In the name of Allah, the Beneficent, the Merciful. To Mohammad the messenger of Allah from Negus As'hamah Ibni Abjar. Peace be upon you O the prophet of Allah, his mercy, and his blessings as well that Allah where there is no god but only, he the one who guided

me to Islam. Thereafter there came to me your letter, O messenger of Allah! what you have mentioned regarding Isa so, I swear by the lord of the heaven and earth, Isa is not more than what you have mentioned, and we knew what you have been sent to us with and we have treated son of your uncle and his colleagues. So I testify that you are the messenger of Allah in truth and we trust it and I give Bai'at to you and I give Bai'at to your uncle's son and submitted on his hands to Allah the lord of the worlds and I have sent to you my son Arha Ibni As'hamah as I don't own but myself and if you want me to come then I will O the messenger of Allah!

Now here he has mentioned his hospitality to Jafar, even though he had done that before, but Jafar and others were still there so he referred to. It again Ibni Ishaq said that Negus sent his son along with sixty-two people in a boat, but the boat sank. Also, the prophet asked him to send Jafar and others, so he sent them in two boats and they came and joined the prophet in Khyber. This Negus died in Rajab, the 9th year after Tabuk. The prophet announced his death in masjid, and it is narrated there that the prophet performed his *Janazah* there, which is a special case of the prophet or a special case for Negus according to Abu Hanifa as to them there is no *Janazah* in the absence of a body. To others that is allowed in cases. The prophet also wrote a letter to his successor, but it is not mentioned whether he accepted Islam or not.

THE MARRIAGE OF UMMI HABIBA

This is mentioned worthy here in this chapter that Abu Sufyan's daughter Ummi Habiba had accepted Islam in Makkah and she had migrated to Abyssinia along with her husband Obaidullah Ibni Jah'sh, but he denounced Islam there so Ummi Habiba left him. Mohammad Ibni Umar says,

> *"The prophet sent me to Negus to do his nikah with Ummi Habiba."*

Negus sent his slave girl Abraha to Ummi Habiba to tell her that the prophet had proposed to her. She became very happy, and she gave some of her jewelry to that girl. Negus appointed Khalid Ibni Saeed Ibn Ul Aas as a representative from the prophet's side and solemnized the *nikah*. Negus fixed her *mahr* (bride price) at 400 dinars and gave it to Khalid. The slave girl took that money to Ummi Habiba. She gave 50 *Misqal* to that girl, but she said,

> *"The king has ordered to give you that jewelry back." The girl told Ummi Habiba that she had also accepted Islam and asked Ummi Habiba to give her Salam to the prophet. She said, "When we came to Madina the prophet had gone to Khyber. When he came back, I gave him the Salam of that slave girl. He said, 'And peace be upon her.' When Abu Sufyan was informed of this nikah, he said 'What a girl, you cannot stop her from making her own choices.'"*

The prophet did this *nikah* by the leave of Allah, to console her as she suffered because of apostasy of her husband and also by this, her father will think of Islam as well. In one narration it is said that she had appointed Uthman as her representative for this Nikah. She had a daughter by the name of Habiba and that is how she got the nickname Ummi Habiba. Her real name was Ramlah.

LETTER TO MUQAUQAS THE KING OF MISR (EGYPT)

Muqawqas was the title of the Egyptian viceroy. His name was Binyamin or Juraij Ibni Mutta (possibly both, as some people have more than one name). The prophet wrote,

> *In the name of Allah, the Beneficent, the Merciful. From Mohammad the slave of Allah and his messenger to Muqawqas, viceroy of Egypt. Peace be upon one who followed the guidance. After that, I invite you to Islam. Submit to be safe; submit, Allah will give you your reward double, but if you turned your face then upon you is the sin of the Copts. "Say [O Mohammad] O people of the scripture come to the word equal [equally revealed] to us and you, not to worship but Allah alone and not to make anything partner with him and not to make one another as lords, but if you turn away then bear witness that we are Muslims."*

Then it is said that the prophet chose for this mission Hatib Ibni Abi Balta'a. When Hatib arrived in Misr, he found out that the King is in Alexandria, so he went there. When he gave the letter to him, Hatib said,

> *"Before you in this area there was a king [Pharaoh] who claimed to be the god, so Allah made him a lesson for generations to come. So, you may take a lesson from him and make not yourself a lesson for others."*

Muqawqas said,

> *"We have our own religion so we cannot desert that, but if we found a better one."*

Hatib said,

> *"But we invite you to Islam the Deen of Allah."*

This messenger of our invited people to it so the Jews refused it bluntly, while the Christians showed a little softness towards it.

Through "God" Moses gave glad tidings regarding Jesus and Jesus gave the same regarding Mohammad and the holy book. We invite towards it like you invite the people of *Taurat* towards Injeel. And we are not taking you away of religion, but we invite you towards the complete and perfect one. Muqawqas said,

> *"We came to know that this messenger is neither a magician nor a soothsayer, and not a liar even."*

Then he put the letter in a box made of *Aaj* (ivory) and sealed it. He gave it to a female servant and ask for his inscriber and ordered him to write a letter. This letter is,

> *In the name of Allah, the Beneficent, the Merciful. To Mohammad, son of Abdullah, from Muqawqas, the King of Copts: Peace be upon you.*
>
> *Thereafter, I read your letter and I understand what you have mentioned therein and call towards, and I knew that a prophet was to come but I thought he would be in Sham. I indeed honored your envoy and sent you two girls of high status among the Copts, and some clothing and a mule for you to ride and peace be upon you.*

The prophet used to ride this mule, which he named "Duldul." It is said later on it was with Ali. This was the first mule in the area. It was a shining white. Even though Muqawqas did not accept Islam, he respected the prophet's letter and envoy as well. The presents he sent were accepted by the prophet. The girls mentioned were of the status, which is why it is said that they were the nieces of the King. They were Mariya Qibtiyya, who married the prophet and gave birth to his son Ibrahim, who died when he was nine months old. The other girl, named Serin, was given to Hassan Ibni Thabit al Ansari, the prophet's poet. Serin gave birth to Abdur Rahman Ibni Hassan. Nassif beg has given a test of these gift as under;

1: Maria Binti Shimon

Her mother was a Roman lady.

2: Sirin,

    Was another young lady. At that time, it was the custom to offer the marital relation as a symbol of love and friendship or to accept that for services and specially in Egypt as the Heksus King had given his niece Hagar to the wife of Ibrahim Sara and she asked Ibrahim to marry her to have children, and she delivered Ismael.

3: A third girl who was a slave, named Qaisr.

4: Another Abyssinian slave girl named Bareera.

5: A slave man named Habu.

6: A shining white mule named Duldul.

7: A saddled horse named Maimun.

8: A white donkey named Yafur.

9: A small box having a comb, oil bottle, scissor, *Siwak*, and Kuhl (Black eyeliner).

10: One thousand gold *Misqal*.

11: *Ud*, perfume and musk.

12: Some silky Egyptian dresses.

13: A cup made of glass

14: Honey from Nabha a place. The prophet liked it and made *Dua* for it.

    It is also said that he also sent a doctor, but the prophet told him,

"You can go back because we don't eat unless we feel hungry and when we do, we do not gorge ourselves, so we are rarely ill."

On his way back Hatib used to talk to Maria and Siren about Islam, and they accepted it.

MARIA QIBTIA (COPTS)

There are two points of view about whether Maria was a slave girl, and the prophet had a son with her or whether she was a free woman and the prophet did *nikah* with her. To us, this second point of view is preferable. The prophet had a son, Ibrahim, with her as we mentioned before. The prophet built her a house in the Bani Nadeer area. She used to stay there, and the prophet used to go to her. That area is called "Al-Awali" [the outskirts]. Ummi Bardah used to suckle Ibrahim. Maria passed away in the 6th year of Umar's Khalafat and he led her *Janazah* prayer.

LETTER TO HARITH IBNI ABI SHAMIRR' AL GASSANI

Harith was the ruler of Damascus under Caesar of the Roman empire. The prophet wrote to him,

"In the name of Allah, the Beneficent, the Merciful. Peace be upon one who followed the guidance believed in Allah and believed it true. I invite you to believe in

Allah alone who has no associate then your kingdom will remain for you."

This letter was taken to him by Shuja Ibni Wahab. He says,

When I arrived in Damascus, he was getting ready to go to Caesar in Baitul Maqdis. I was sitting at his gate for three days. I was telling the gate keeper whose name was Mari that I was the envoy of prophet Mohammad and I want to meet Harith the ruler. He said, "One can meet him when he himself comes out and the day is known." I used to talk to this gate keeper about the prophet and he used to cry telling me, "I was thinking that this prophet will appear in Sham, but he appeared in that part of Arabia." He said, "I believe in him.'

One day Harith came out with his crown on his head. I was taken to him. He threw the letter on the ground and said, "Who can take away my kingship? I will come to this man on my own even if he is in Yemen." He ordered an army to get ready and told me, "Just go and tell him this".

He also informed Caesar about me and the letter. At that time Dihyah Kalbi was still there with Caesar so Caesar told Harith not to do what he intended and come to me. He came back to senses and gave Wahab some dresses and money also.

LETTER TO HAUDAH IBNI ALI, THE RULER OF YAMAMAH

Haudah was the chief of Banu Hanifah a Christian tribe. The prophet wrote a letter to him and gave it to Sulait Ibni Amr-Al-Aamiri. It reads,

> *In the name of Allah, the Beneficent, the Merciful. From Mohammad the messenger of Allah to Haudah Ibni Ali. Peace be upon one who followed the guidance and know that my Deen shall prevail to the end of shoe and hoof. So, submit to be safe and save whatever is under you, in your hands.*

Haudah respected Sulait a great deal and wrote to the prophet that what he was inviting is very excellent thing but make for him some share therein as he held a high status in Arabs. He gave Sulait some dresses of Hajar. When the prophet read his letter he said,

> *"By Allah I will never give him a small piece of land." Furthermore, he said, "He and his kingdom will both be destroyed." After the conquest of Makkah, Jibril informed the prophet that Haudah died. He said, "In Yamamah a falsifier will emerge who will claim falsely that he is a prophet and after me he will be killed." Someone asked the prophet, "Who will kill him?" He said, "You and your followers."*

Later on, there emerged Musailamah-al-Kazzab, and he was killed in the time of Abu Bakr in battle of Yamamah, which is also called the Battle of Banu Hanifah, the name of the tribe.

LETTER TO MUNZIR IBNI SAWA GOVERNOR OF BAHRAIN

> *In the name of Allah, the Beneficent, the Merciful. From Mohammad the messenger of Allah to Munzir Ibni Sawa peace be upon you. I do praise to you Allah, the one where there is no other god, but He and I witness that Mohammad is the slave of Allah and his messenger. Thereafter, I remind you Allah the Almighty whoever accept the sincere advice then he does the same for his own good and whoever will obey my envoys and follow their order then he has obeyed Me and whoever will think of their good then he has thought of my good and verily My envoys praised you so I accepted your intercession regarding your people so leave for Muslims what they have submitted to and I have pardoned the offences of the offenders so you may accept it from them [pardon them]. And you as long as you do good, we will not depose you and whoever wants to live with his Judaism or Magian faith, should be made to pay Jizyah (tax).*

The prophet sent this letter by the hand of Ala-al-Hadhrami (Zad Ul Ma'ad). From this letter it seems that the prophets had sent his envoys to him before this and that he had accepted Islam with the first letter and also some others had also done the same. The prophet wrote to him *"peace be upon you,"* which he only used when writing to a fellow Muslim, and he wrote a letter to the prophet calling him the messenger of Allah. His letter reads,

> *To the messenger of Allah from Munzir Ibni Sawa. Thereafter O the messenger of Allah! I read your letter to the people of Bahrain. Some of them liked Islam and they accepted it while some others disliked it, while in my land there are Magians and Jews, so tell me how to treat them.*

When this Munzir passed away, Amr Ibn Ul Aas was with him. This is also mentioned in writings about his liberated slave Nafi Abu

Suleiman that he also had visited the prophet (Usd Ul - Ghabah, Ibni Qani, Tabari).

LETTER TO THE KING OF OMAN JAIFER AND HIS BROTHER ABD S/O JALANDI

These were two bothers to whom the prophet sent a letter by the hands of Amr Ibn Ul Aas which is read as.

> *In the name of Allah, the Beneficent, the Merciful. From Mohammad Ibni Abdullah to Jaifer and Abd sons of Jalandi. Peace be upon one who followed the guidance. Thereafter I invite you with the invitation of Islam. You should both submit to be in peace. I am the messenger of Allah to all mankind to warn one who is alive, and the word become true upon the disbelievers. If you will both admit Islam [into your realm] I will appoint you as rulers but if you refuse to accept Islam, then your kingship is gone and my horses shall enter your yard and my prophethood shall prevail over your kingship.*

Obai Ibni Kab wrote this letter. Jaifer was the older brother, but Abd was very reasonable person. Amr Ibn Ul Aas said,

> *I went to Abd and told him, "I am the envoy of the prophet of Allah to see you both." He said, "You should see my brother, as he is my elder and he is the king, but what is the subject of the letter you are going to read it*

to my brother?" I said, "The prophet calls you to believe in Allah alone with no partner, to desert other deities and to believe that Mohammad is the slave of Allah and his messenger." Abd said, "You are from a noble family but what did your father do in this regard?" I said, "He died before believing in Mohammad's mission. I wished he had accepted it, but Allah guided me." Abd asked, "When did you accept Islam?" I answered, "When I was in the court of Negus and Negus accepted it." Abd pressed, "But what did his people do?" I told him, "They did the same." He asked me about Negus' bishop and monks. I said they also accepted it. He said, "Beware, no one is as bad as he is." I said, "I never tell lies, for my own Deen does not allow it." Then he asked me, "Did Hercules know about Negus's Islam?" I said yes. He asked me, "But how do you know that?" I said, "Because Negus stopped paying the tax he used to pay. Hercules's people told him to take an action against Negus, but he said, 'Nay, I would have accepted the same if I didn't have the fear of my kingship.'" He asked, "What did your prophet tell you to do?" I said that he tells us to worship Allah alone, to be pious, to be kind to our kith and kin. He also forbids us to commit adultery, idolatry or to drink wine or worship the cross.

Abd said, "What fair and pure beliefs and actions. I wish my brother will listen to it and follow me to believe in it and to accept Mohammad's religion, but I think he will not sacrifice his kingship to be a follower." I said, "If he accepts Islam, the prophet will give him the authority on his people to take zakat from their rich and to distribute it to the poor." He said, "That is good but what is zakat? I said, "A rule of Allah to take a portion of rich people's wealth and to give it to the poor." Abd said, "I doubt it will work with our people." Then Amr

Ibn Ul Aas stayed for a few days and then he was taken to Jaifer. His courtiers were holding me by my arm. He said, "Leave him," and I was going to sit but they said no. He asked me to say what I want to. So, I gave him the letter. He opened it and read it. Then he gave it to his brother. He read it as well. Then he asked me, "But what did the Quraish do?" I told him that they followed him some of them willingly and some other when got defeated and now they prefer Islam over any other religion and now no one remains but him. "And if you will not accept then his horses will crush you so submit to be safe and to maintain your kingship."

He said leave me today and come to me tomorrow. The next day I went to him but they did not allow me so I came to his brother, so he took me there. This day his tone was different, more threatening. So, I told him I was leaving tomorrow. Then he talked to his brother privately and then called me to tell me they both accepted Islam. Now it seems that this letter was sent after the conquest of Makkah as Amr said people accepted Islam, but some of them after that this mission prevailed and this was after the conquest of Makkah. These missions made it clear to the world that now the Deen will spread and now no power can stop it. Also, this embodies the bravery of the prophet and his strong belief in Allah as he challenged these rulers all at once. Also, by their reaction the prophet came to know that who is who and how to deal with.

THE BATTLE OF KHYBER

This *Ghazwa* happened in Moharram in the 7th year after Hijrah. Khyber is 60 to 70 miles from Madina, a sandy but fertile area. Mostly here the Jews were living, and they used to create *Fitnahs* (intrigues) as they were the one who plotted the battle of allies. The prophet had ordered the killing of their gang lords Ibni Abil Huqaiq and Aseer Ibni Razam. Now when the prophet was less worried about the Quraish, he wanted to get rid of this *fitnah* center, so he decided to launch a mission in Khyber. It was very important to be free of *Fitnahs* and to propagate Islam to other areas, and the Jews used not only to stop the spread of Islam but even attempt to assassinate the prophet.

THE FORTS IN KHYBER

The Jews had been living in walled fortresses for generations. The details of these forts are as follows:

1: Natat, which had four forts inside it:

(a) Na'im

(b) Sa'b Ibni Muaz

(c) Al Kateebah

(d) Baqlah

2: Shaq, which had two forts inside,

(a) Obai

(b) Barri

3: Kateebah, which had three fortresses inside,

(a) Wateeh

(b) Qamoos

(c) Salalim

SOME SCHOLARS HAVE MENTIONED IT AS FOLLOWS

(1) Na'im, (2) Sa'b and (3) Azzabir were in the Natat zone; (1) Obai and (2) Nazar were in Shaq; while in the Kateebah zone there were (1) Qamoos the fortress of two sons of Abul Huqaiq, (2) Wateeh and Salalim. There were some other fortresses also. The forts in the Natat and Mushq zones are where the battle happened while the Kateebah zone surrendered without a struggle.

THE PROPHET AND HIS ARMY

On this occasion the prophet had 1600 people with him. Two hundred of them were horsemen. Ummi Salmah accompanied the prophet on this trip as she did in Hudaibiyah. The prophet appointed Siba Ibni Urfuta al Ansari as Amir at Madina. Ibni Ishaq says that he appointed Nameelah Ibni Abdullah Al Laithi but the first narration is the preferred one.

The *Mufassireen* said that Allah had promised the prophet spoils in plenty at the time of Hudaibiyah and these spoils of Khyber were from among these promised spoils as Allah says.

> "*Allah has promised you spoils in abundance so he has hastened for you this [victory of Hudaibiyah] and he has*

restrained the hands of the people [Quraish] from you so that it may be a sign for the believers and that he may guide you to the straight path. And other [spoils] which you have not overtaken yet but Allah has encompassed them and Allah has the power over everything." (48:20-21)

In the same way it is also said that only those who were in Hudaibiyah, they joined the prophet, and they were 1400 so maybe these two hundred horsemen were from amongst these 1400, but some historians counted them as extra. They didn't think that they would overtake other areas and become victorious getting spoils but they did, as Allah had decreed that, so the spoils of Khyber are from the promised spoils.

And as the Prophet said,

"Only those who were in Hudaibiyah can join us, so those who did not join him in that mission they said we want to go with you so Allah said 48;15: "Those who lagged behind, will say, when you will go forth to have the spoils [you have been promised with] leave us follow you. They want to change the words [decision] of Allah, [that only those will go who were in Hudaibiyah] say, you cannot follow us. Thus, Allah has said beforehand. Then they will say, but you envy us [so we may not get any share in spoils]. Nay, but they do not understand in depth but only a little [as these spoils are just a reward for those who were in Hudaibiyah]."

At this time Abu Hurairah came to Madina and accepted Islam. The Amir at Madina Siba Ibni Urfuta gave him some dates and urged him to go and to join the prophet at Khyber. Abdullah Ibni Ubai, the chief of the hypocrites, informed the Jews in Khyber that Mohammad was coming towards them, but fear him not. The people of Khyber sent Kinanah Ibni Abil-Huqaiq and Howdah Ibni Qais to the Ghitfan tribe asking them for help against the prophet. They agreed and asked for half of the crops of Khyber.

THE PROPHET ON HIS WAY TO KHAYBER

The prophet passed by "Jabali-Asr" then by "Sahba" until he arrived in "Rajee' valley. There between him and the tribe of Ghitfan was a travel distance of one day and night. When Ghitfan got the news, they departed to Khyber, but they heard some noise from there back and they thought like as the Muslims have attacked their families, so they returned to their houses.

The prophet had two guides to guide the army to Khyber so he asked one of them named Haseel to guide them through an effective way from the north side, so the Jews may not flee to Sham. They brought him to an intersection and told him the names of all the routes going there. These names were Heizn, Shash, Hatib and Marhab. The prophet chose Marhab as a good omen because it means "welcome." He had prayed Salati Asr in Sahba. He asked for the roasted Barley flour called *Saweeq* and ate it, and then prayed Salati Maghrib. It means he did not renew *wudu* when he ate something roasted with fire. Imam Bukhari narrated from Salamah Ibn Ul Akwa,

> *We were going with the prophet to Khyber. We used to Marah at night. One man said to my brother, Aamir, will you not recite to us some of your poetry? So, he started "O Allah! If you had not guided us, we would not have done any charity nor we would have prayed. So, forgive for what we missed we will sacrifice ourselves, and strengthen our feet if we encounter the enemy. And bestow upon us tranquility as whenever we have been shouted at [by others] we refused.*

The prophet said,

"Who is this?"

They said,

"Aamir Ibn Ul Akwa."

The prophet said,

"May Allah give His mercy to him."

They said,

"If you had allowed us to get the benefit of him."

It means that they knew whenever the prophet makes a *Dua* of mercy for someone, he is martyred, and then it happened, and he was martyred. When the prophet arrived close to Khyber, he stopped and made a *Dua*:

> *O the lord of the seven heavens and what it has shadowed, the Lord of the seven earths and what it has carried, the Lord of Satan and whatever they have taken astray, we ask you for the good of this village, the good of its people and the good therein, and we seek protection of the evil of this village, the evil of its people and the evil therein.*

THE MUSLIM ARMY AT THE BORDERS OF KHYBER

The Muslims arrived at night in Khyber in four days. They spent the night there. The prophet prayed *Fajr* in dark and they saw the Jews were going to their jobs and farming with their tools. When they saw Muslims, they shouted,

> "Mohammad, by God, Mohammad and the army!"

So, they ran back to their city. The messenger of Allah said,

> "Allahu Akbar! Khyber is destroyed."

He said it twice and then he said,

> "When we entered the center of a city, bad is the morning of the warned people."

The prophet fixed a place close to Natat fort. Habab Ibn Ul Munzir asked whether this is *Wahi*, or opinion? He said it was opinion. So Habab said,

> *This is very close to Natat fort, and all their fighters are in this fort. They know all about our situation and we do not. Also, they can shoot their arrows very easily as they are atop of us while our arrows will not approach them. And here are the date-palm trees also, so if we will set in another place.*

The prophet accepted this.

Now this new place was in between the Jews and the Ghitfan so there was no way for the Ghitfan to come and to join them. The prophet gave his flag Oqab to Habab Ibn Ul Munzir and another flag to Sa'd Ibni Obadah. The prophet made a place for prayer also and ordered to cut the nearby date-palm trees, so they cut almost 400.

THE BATTLE

The prophet was wearing two coats of chainmail. Also, he had a helmet on head. He was riding a horse named Zarb, holding a shield and a spear. A Jew threw a grinding stone at Mahmud Ibni Maslamah, the brother of Mohammad Ibni Maslamah and thus he was martyred. The prophet fought the Jews of Natat fort for seven days. He took Mohammad Ibni Maslamah with him every day and left Uthman there in the station place. The Jews were not coming out to the open field. If they were suffering losses, they would retreat into the fort and close the gates.

On sixth night of this fight a Jew came to the Prophet and told him that tonight they were going from Natat fort to Shaq fort. He also told him that in there was an underground room full of weapons the Sa'b zone of Natat and offered to lead them.

ALI ON MISSION

The prophet was suffering from a migraine, so he was sending Sahaba, but the fort was not surrendering. He told Mohammad Ibni Maslamah that tomorrow he would give the flag to a person who loves Allah and his messenger and Allah, and his messenger love him and Allah will give him success. The next day he called Ali, who was suffering from ophthalmia. The prophet gave him white flag and put his saliva in his eyes. Ali says that after that he never got any problem in his eyes afterwards. The Prophet made a *Dua*.

> "*O Allah, protect Ali from cold and heat*".

Ali says,

> "*After this, I was never uncomfortable, even if I wore a thick woolen robe in scorching heat or thin fabric in freezing cold.*"

Ali took the flag and said,

> "I will fight them till they are like us,"

Meaning submission. The prophet told him,

> "Call them to Islam first. If they refuse then fight them in the name of Allah, but even if one person is guided through you, that is better for you then a herd of red camels."

He left and erected the flag close to the Na'im fort, the fort of Marhab, which held nearly one thousand people. The first one who came out of the fort was Marhab's brother Harith. He was a good fighter, but Ali caught him under his sword and killed him. Then Marhab came out with two swords, two turbans with a helmet over them, and a spear. He was also saying some verses;

> "Indeed, Khyber knows me as Marhab the user of weapon brave and expert. When the battle is shooting flames."

Salamah Ibn Ul Akwa says,

> "My uncle Aamir came forward. They exchanged sword blows, but my uncle was martyred."

The prophet said,

> "Indeed, he has two rewards."

And he tapped his two fingers together and said,

> "Very rarely has an Arab gone this way."

Then again Marhab repeated what he said before. This time Ali came forward. Salamah says, Ali said answering him,

> "I am the one whose mother named him Haidar like a lion of the forest with a frightening shape."

Then he hit the head of Marhab and then he died.

Then when Ali came close to their forts, a Jew came to the tarres of the fort and asked him,

> "What is your name?"

He said,

> "Ali" (which means "excellent").

He said,

> "So, you became excellent, I swear by what had been sent to Musa,"

Which means by *Taurat*.

Yasir, brother of Marhab: After that there came out the brother of Marhab named Yasir. Zubair Ibn Ul Anwam came out to confront him. Safia Zubair's mother was there, and she said,

> "O the messenger of Allah, this man will kill my son."

The prophet said,

> "Not at all; your son will kill him."

THE MUSLIMS TOOK OVER A FEW FORTS

In this battle, the Jews could not fight the Muslims. So, they went from Na'im fort to Sa'b and the Muslims entered Na'im under the leadership of Habab Ibn Ul Munzir. The Muslims attacked this fort. For three days they could not overtake it, so Banu Sahm asked the prophet to make *Dua*. He said,

"*O Allah, I cannot do it, please give us this fort.*"

So, before sunset they overtook it. This fort was full of grain, cooking oil and other supplies. Ibin Ishaq related that after this victory the Muslims were cooking donkey meat. The prophet came and said,

"*No more Mut'ah nikah and donkey meat.*"

So, the Muslims poured the contents of their cooking pots onto the ground.

After this the Jews went to the Zabeer fort, which was over a hilltop. One Jew came to the Prophet and told him that even if they besieged it for one full month, nothing would happen as they have a lot of necessary supplies inside the fort and there is water flowing into it from outside. So, they should block the water flow, which the Prophet did. So, the Jews came out and a fierce battle broke out. Ten Jews were killed and a few Muslims as well. But the fort was overtaken by the Muslims.

Then the Jews went to Obai fort. Two Jews came forth, challenging the Muslims to a face-to-face fight. They were killed by Abu Dujanah Simak Ibni Kharshah. After killing them, Abu Dujanah rushed to enter to the fort and he entered along with a group of Muslims and a very severe battle was fought there inside the fort. So, the Jews abandoned this fort.

THE CATAPULT AND THE CONQUEST OF NAZAR FORT

After Obai fort, the Jews entered the last fort of this part Nazar fort. This was the strongest fort of this portion and the Jews were of the view that Muslims will not be able to enter this fort and that's why they had put their women and children therein. The Muslims besieged this fort but they could not find any access points. The Jews did not emerge but were throwing rocks and shooting arrows. The Prophet ordered a catapult installed in order to hit the walls with big rocks to break it. It worked, and the Muslims entered the fort and fought inside. The Jews left their women and children and ran out of the fort. So, all the fort of Natat zone were overtaken and the Prophet ordered his army to march to the Kateebah zone.

THE KATEEBA ZONE

After taking over the Natat forts the Prophet came to the Kateebah zone. In this zone there was Qamoos fort belonging to two sons of Sallam Ibni Abil Huqaiq and also two other forts, Salalim and Wateeh. Ibni Ishaq says,

> "Qamoos was taken by force while the other two by a treaty,"

But Waqidi says, all three were taken by treaty as the Jews surrendered and agreed to peace. This siege lasted fourteen days.

THE SURRENDER AND THE PEACE TREATY

The son of Sallam Ibni Abil Huqaiq, when he realized there was no way out, asked for peace and shelter. He said that they would leave everything for Mohammad and leave Khyber. The Prophet agreed to this and made it clear to them that if they hid, stole, or took anything, then they would be charged for treason and cheating, and they agreed to this.

The Muslims received therefrom one hundred mail coats, four hundred swords, one thousand lances, five hundred Arabian bows and a few volumes of *Taurat*. They asked for the *Taurat* later on and the Prophet gave it to them. They also left their cattle and some gold and silver, and of course their land was there. The two sons of Sallam Ibni Abil Huqaiq were hiding some wealth, including the wealth and jewelry of Huyai Ibni Akhtab, as the daughter of Huyai Safia was the wife of one of them. Kinanah Ibni Rabee Ibni Abil Huqaiq was brought to the Prophet. He asked him about the wealth. He said he did not know. Another Jew told the Prophet,

> *"I used to see this man roaming around in the desert every morning."*

The Prophet said to Kinanah,

> *"If we find it, then you deserve to be killed?"*

He said,

> *"Yes"*

Then the Prophet ordered digging of the area the other Jew mentioned. Some of the valuables were found. He was asked once again about the remaining but once again he denied it. So, Mohammad Ibni Maslamah killed him.

THE *NIKAH* OF SAFIA

Huyai Ibni Akhtab used to live in Madina but later on they were turned out of there when they tried to assassinate the Prophet. So, they went to Khyber. Huyai's daughter Safia was married to one son of Sallam Ibni Abil Huqaiq. Now she was among the captives, so she was given to Dihyah Al Kalbi, but it is said that he or someone else told the Prophet that she was the daughter of the king, and others also endorsed this warding if the Prophet would marry her. As we have mentioned more than once, the marriages of the Prophet were with by the leave of Allah for certain reasons and wisdoms therein. So, the Prophet asked her if she would accept Islam and she did. Then when they were in "Saddus Sahba" coming back to Madina, Ummi Sulaim betrothed her and sent her to the Prophet. She was a beautiful girl, 17 years of age.

The Prophet saw some signs of abuse on her face and asked her about that. She said before your coming to Khyber, I saw in my dream that the moon fell down of its place into my lapse. She mentioned it to her husband, so he slapped her that you want to be the wife of that king of Madina, which means Mohammad.

Her name was Zainab but the Prophet selected that from the booty for himself and this type of selection by the Prophet was called Safia (the chosen one or the chosen thing).

DISTRIBUTION OF SPOILS OF WAR (BOOTY) AND MUKHABARAH

The Jews asked the Prophet if he would allow them to do *Muzara'-at* in this agricultural land.

> *"You people will take some of the output and we will take as well."*

In other words, the pay would be a portion of the crop, and the Prophet agreed to that.

The Prophet made it 3600 shares. 1800 shares were kept for the needs of *ummah* while rest were distributed to the Muslims. Since there were 1400 people with 200 horses, the Prophet gave everyone 1 share and to every horse, he gave 2 shares. Now Jumhur said that riders had to take three shares as we mentioned, while Abu Hanifa says the riders were to be given two shares. They were 1600, and as we will mention later on people like Jafar, Abu Musa and their colleagues also got their share. So, these people were other than the people of Hudaibiyah who joined the Prophet at Khyber. This was limited to only those who accompanied the Muslims in Hudaibiyah and those who were in Madina at that time and did not join the Prophet in Hudaibiyah were not to take. While these extra people were from outside.

So, the Jews worked as farmers and they took half of the crop.

Imam Bukhari narrates from Ibni Umar that after this wealth *Muhajireen* were no longer in need to the money of Ansar.

THE POISONOUS LAMB

The wife of Sallam Ibni Mishkam named Zainab sent a roast lamb to the prophet. When he put a piece of it in mouth, he spit it out and said,

> *"This meat told me, 'I am poisoned.'"*

Bishr Ibni Bara Ibni Maroor was with the Prophet. He had swallowed a morsel of meat and died from it. The Prophet asked the lady,

> *"Why did you do this?"*

She said,

> *"To get rid of you if you are only a king, and to know the validity if you are a Prophet."*

Thus convinced, she accepted Islam.

In these battles in Khyber 15 to 18 Muslims were martyred people, while 93 Jews were killed.

JAFAR AND ABU MUSA JOINED THE PROPHET

Abu Musa Al Ashari says,

> *We heard that the Prophet had gone to Khyber, so some fifty plus people from Yaman took a boat to go to him but the wind took us to Abyssinia and there we met Jafar and his fellows. Then all of us came to the Prophet. He kissed the forehead of Jafar and said, "I don't know what to be happier about: the conquest of Khaybar or for the coming of Jafar." The Prophet gave us some of the booty as well."*

It is said that Jafar came back when the Prophet sent Amr Ibni Umayyah Ad Damari to Negus to send them back. There were sixteen people.

THE FADAK

When the Prophet arrived in Khyber, he sent Muhayyisah Ibni Masud to the Jews of the Fadak area to call them to Islam but they delayed him there and when Khyber was conquered then they also asked the Prophet to keep them in Fadak like the Jews in Khyber and they would send him half of the output of Fadak. And as the Prophet received this without a fight, it was for him only. He used this income for the good of state and Muslims, and after the death of the Prophet it went to Baitul Mal as per the rules of Islam. On his way back to Madina the Prophet ordered some rest at night. He said to Bilal,

"You should be awake to give Azan for Fajr."

First, he started praying to keep himself awake. But then he began to lean to his camel and fell asleep. Then all of them woke up with the warmth of sun. The Prophet asked Bilal,

"What happened? He said, "The same as what happened to all,"

Meaning sleep. The Prophet ordered Fajr and led them in *Qadah* prayer.

GHAZWAT WADIL QIRA

This is a valley between Taima and Khyber with a few villages. Some Jews were living there when the Prophet was coming back to Madina these people started shooting arrows at them. A slave of the Prophet named Mud'im was killed with arrows.

The people said,

> *"Congratulations to him; he has gone to paradise."*

But the prophet said, referring to something he had taken from the Booty before distribution,

> *"That thing will hit a fire on him,"*

So here someone brought one or two strings to the Prophet. The Prophet said,

> *"A string or two of fire."*

The Prophet told Sahabah to be ready to fight them. He gave four flags to four people: Sad Ibni Obadah, Hubab Ibn Ul Munzir, Sahl Ibni Hunaif, and Abbad Ibni Bishr, and then asked the Jews to convert but they refused. One man came out and gave a challenge to the Muslims. Zubair Ibni Awwam came forward and killed him. Then another one came out; Zubair killed him as well. A third one came and Ali killed him. Almost eleven men were killed, one after another, and then they surrendered and handed over their belongings to the Prophet and it was distributed according to the rules. The Prophet used to pray the prayer of the time and to start the fight. After killing every challenger, he was calling them to Islam or to surrender but they refused.

The Prophet appointed Amr Ibni Saeed Ibn Ul Aas as governor of Wadial Qira. When the people of Taima heard all this news, they asked Amr Ibni Saeed if they could get the same protection. He gave this message to the Prophet that and he wrote a document for them. He appointed Yazid Ibni Sufyan as governor of Taima, as Yazid had accepted Islam the same day. This document was written by Khalid Ibni Saeed.

The Prophet came back to Madina at the end of the month of Safar or in the beginning of Rabi Ul Awwal. The Muslims at Madina welcomed him with "Takbeer!" and "Tahleel!" in their loudest voices. The prophet said,

> *"Relax, you are not invoking an absent one or a deaf one but the nearest one and the all-hearer."*

SARIYAH OF ABAN IBNI SAEED

When the prophet was leaving Khyber, he knew that some Arab tribes were looking for an opportunity to invade Madina when it was empty, and that's why the Prophet dispatched a mission towards Najd under the command of Aban Ibni Saeed to warn those people that they were aware of the plot. There from Aban left Khyber. On his arrival he found that Khyber had been overtaken by the Prophet.

A note on "Ghazwa Zatur Ruqa": Regarding this *Ghazwa* the historians have two points of view. One is that it happened after Khyber so they have mentioned it after that and another point of view is that it happened in the year after Hijrah, where the prophet offered Salat Ul Khawf for the first time and we have mentioned it there after *Ghazwa* Bani Nadeer.

MISSIONS AFTER KHYBER

After Ghazwa Khyber, the prophet dispatched a few missions:

1: The prophet sent Umar with 30 people towards Hawazin tribe in Turbat so they ran away.

2: The prophet sent Abu Bakr with a group of Sahabah to Banu Kilab in Najd area. He killed some of them and captured a few.

3: Under Bushair Ibni Sa'd of Ansar the prophet sent thirty people towards Banu Murrah. They captured their camels and goats, but on their way towards Madina, Bani Murrah attacked them. They fought the whole night but they ran out of arrows so they escaped to Madina with difficulty. All these three missions took place in Shaban, the 7th year after Hijrah.

4: Before these missions the prophet under the leadership of Ghalib Ibni Abdullah Allaithi had sent in Safar or Rabee Ul Awwal a group of Sahabah to Ban Ul Muluh who had killed the colleagues of Bashir Ibni Suwaid. The Muslims killed a few of them and took their cattle. When they were on their way to Madina a big army came after them but suddenly a heavy rain fell and a big flood developed between Muslims and that army. So, they arrived safely in Madina.

5: In Ramadan the prophet gave a group of one hundred and thirty people to Ghalib Ibni Abdullah Al Allaithi and sent them toward Najd to the people of Manee'ah some ninety miles or more from Madina. They killed a few of them and took their cattle.

In this mission Osamah killed Nuhaik Ibni Mirdas who said the "Kalimah" but Osamah Ibni Zaid killed him and when the prophet asked him why after "Kalimah"?

He said,

"He had said it to save his life,"

Meaning not from his heart. So, the prophet said to him in harsh tone,

"Then why you did not cleave his heart?"

Meaning to look into his heart whether he has said it wholeheartedly or not. So, Osamah apologized a lot for that.

6: SARIYAH BUSHAIR IBNI SA'D AL ANSANI

In the month of Shawwal, the prophet sent Bushair Ibni Sa'd with three hundred Sahabah to Yemen and Jabar to the area of Ghitfan tribe where Oyainah Ibni Hisn had gathered people to attack Madina, but when they heard about this they fled. Bushair brought lot of their cattle he got in the area.

7: SARIYAH ABU HADRAD AL ASLAMI

A man from Jashm Ibni Muaa'wiyah had gathered lot of people in Ghabah trying to convince people of Qais also to wage war on Muslims. The prophet sent two people to Abu Hadrad to inquire. He went and sat on one side of those people hiding and his two colleagues were on the other side. The herdsman of the enemy was delayed so their chief came in his stead. Abu Hadrad shot him with and rendered him unable to speak. Abu Hadrad said "Allahu Akbar" loudly from one side and his two colleagues said it from the other side so the army ran away and these three Muslims took a big number of their cattle.

Note: Waqidi mentioned that in this year in the month of Muharram the prophet sent his daughter Zainab to her husband Abul Aas as he had accepted Islam. There are two opinions on this: one that she went to him based on the previous *nikah* contract and another that she went with a new *nikah*.

Waqidi also narrates that Hatib Ibni Abi Balta'a brought the gifts of Muqawqas this year and also the prophet started to be on the pulpit for *khutbah* from this year. Before the pulpit he used to lean on a standing date palm trunk when he was giving *khutbah*. But Tabari say that this was started in the 8th year.

UMRAT UL QADA

In Zul-Qadah year 7th after "Hijrah" the Prophet said,

"Those who were in Hudaibiyah should get ready for umrah."

So, all those who were still alive got ready. Also, some others prepared to go. This Umrah is called *Umraht Ul Qadah*. But the interpretation is different according to different jurists. Imam Abu Hanifa and Imam Ahmed call it 'Qadah' and stated that it was the making of the *umrah* they missed last year and could not go because of the Quraish blockade. But according to Imam Malik there is no *Qadah* of *umrah* as they were prevented from and they came out of Ihram by slaughtering the sacrificed animal. It was called Qadah as it was promised in the travel of Hudaibiyah. This is also called *Umraht Ul Qisas* as it was a retribution.

The Prophet appointed Owaif Ibni Adbat or Abu Rahm al Ghifari as Amir at Madina. Some two thousand people joined the prophet, half on horseback. They had sixty camels with them for sacrifice. Najia Ibni Jundub al Aslami was taking care of these camels. The prophet put on his *ihram* from Zul-Hulaifah and the Muslims as well and all of them recited "Talbia". They were taking weapons with them to be ready if the Quraish cheated.

They put the weapons in a place called Yajaj and left Aws Ibni Khawli Al Ansari there along with two hundred people. The prophet entered Makkah riding his she-camel Qawsa. The Muslims had hung their swords at their sides and they were looking at the prophet and reciting "Talbia."

The Quraish left Makkah to the Muslims per the terms of the treaty and they went to the top of mountain Qaiqa'aan to the north side of Makkah to look at the Muslims there from that viewpoint as they were saying that the fever of Madina has weakened them. The prophet said,

> *"Keep your right shoulder open and do Ram'l in the first three rounds of Tawaf."*

When the Quraish saw them, they said,

> *"Oh! They are strong."*

Abdullah Ibni Rawaha was reciting his verses:

> *O the sons of the disbelievers!*

> *Be on side from his path.*

> *Be on side as the whole good is in his (Allah's) messenger.*

> *Verily the Beneficent one has sent down in his revelation and in scriptures recited to his messenger.*

> *O my Lord! I believe in his word. Indeed I have seen truth in his acceptance.*

> *That the best killing is of one in his path.*

> *Today we will hit you with his revelation.*

Such a hit will take the skull from its place and will take away a friend from his friend.

Anas said that Umar said to Ibni Rawaha,

> "How can he do this when it is "haram?"

The prophet said,

> "Umar! Let him recite, as it goes through their bodies better than arrows."

Then the prophet did *"Sai."* He made the sacrificial animals near *Marwah*,

He said,

> "This is the place of sacrifice and all the streets of Makkah are its place."

Then he sacrificed there.

Later he ordered two hundred Sahabah to go to *Yajaj*, which was eight miles from *Makkah*. He ordered them to guard the weapons there and those who are there will come to perform their *umrah*. On the fourth day *Suhail Ibni Amr* and *Huwaitib Ibni Abdul Uzza* came to the Prophet and said,

> "We are here to remind you that the pact says three days."

Sa'd Ibni Obadah started to say something but the prophet stopped him.

When the prophet was departing *Makkah*, a daughter of *Hamzah* was coming, calling the prophet *"O Uncle! O uncle!"* because *Hamzah* was also the foster brother of the prophet. Ali wanted to be her guardian, but *Jafar* and *Zaid* were also eager to take care of her but the Prophet gave her to Jafar as her maternal aunt was his wife and as *Imam Abu Hanifa* said, after one's mother, one's aunt has the right to be the guardian of a nephew or niece.

THE MARRIAGE OF MAIMUNAH BINT UL HARITH

Maimunah was the sister of Umm Ul Fazl, the wife of Abbas. They were from Banu Aamir. Before entering to Makkah, the Prophet sent Jafar Ibni Abi Talib to Maimunah, so she appointed her brother-in-law Abbas as her representative to decide upon the bridal money. He fixed 400 dinars and he himself paid it as well. The Prophet appointed Abu Rafi to bring her.

Abu Rafi said,

> *"When we were coming out of Makkan a few wicked youths passed some remarks about insulting the Prophet. I warned them that our horses and weapon are still in Yajaj so they ran away."*

At the time of marriage her age was 51 years. This was the last wife of the Prophet. And she was the last one who died as well.

KHALID AND AMR

Khalid Ibni Waleed was Maimunah's nephew, the son of her sister and Amr Ibn Ul Aas was the close friend of Khalid. They were fighting generals. They both accepted Islam so this relation may have been one of the factors in their conversion. But as we mentioned before, Amr had accepted Islam near Negus when the Quraish had sent him there but maybe he disclosed it at that time. Usman Ibni Talha Al Abdari also accepted Islam with them.

The story of Amr is that after the Battle of Allies he told the Quarish,

> Now there is none to stop Mohammad, and he himself wants to go to Negus. If Mohammad overtakes then we will be under Negus and that is better than being under Mohammad; and if our people win then we will come back." Then I said, "We also have to take some gifts to Negus." Tanned leather was a famous product in our area so we took some of that. Jafar and his colleagues were there since they had migrated from Makkah. We were sitting with Negus when Amr Ibni Umayyah Ad Damari arrived. I said to my colleagues that if Negus would hand him over to me, I would kill him and then the Quraish will give us a lot of respect for having killed the envoy of Mohammad. Then after that we met Negus we prostrated to him, as this was the protocol. He asked for gifts as this was the custom as well, so we presented him with the leather. He became very happy when he saw that. Then I said, "O King, I wish if you had given that man to me who came from Mohammad a little while ago because he has killed lot of our people so if I will kill one of his men." Negus lost his temper and hit me on my nose so hard that I though my nose was gone. So, I apologized to him and said, "By God, I did not know my words would cause you such an anger, otherwise I would not have said." He said, "You are talking about such a personality to whom Jibril comes who used to come to Moses." I said, "Is that so?" He said "Woe unto you. Go and believe in him as he will overtake his enemies like Musa [Moses] did to Pharaoh."

This means that the people of the Book did know that he is the messenger and his message is like that of the message of Moses, and he will prevail like Moses. Amr said,

I said to him, "Now you can take my pledge for Islam and thus he did and I became Muslim." Then I came to my colleagues but never disclosed my faith to them. Then I was going to Madina so I saw Khalid going in the same direction. I asked him "Where are you going?" He said, "By God, he is the messenger, I am going to Madina to accept Islam." This was before the conquest of Makkah. He asked me and I said the same thing. So, we went to Madina and we accepted Islam.

When I was offering my pledge, I said, "My sins are to be forgiven." The Prophet said, "Islam, Hijrat and Hajj demolish whatever sins are before that."

Now Negus was a Tabi'ee as he never met the Prophet while Amr Ibn Ul Aas is a Sahabi but he had accepted Islam by giving his pledge to a Tabi'ee.

Zubair Ibni Bakkar says, someone asked Amr why the truth was disclosed so late to such a clever and smart person? He said, "Actually we had such smart people that their intellect was like tall mountains: when they died then the realities and facts were revealed to us where they had once been hidden."

THE ISLAM OF KHALID

Khalid Ibn Ul Waleed a well-known general was responsible for the weaponry and cavalry of Quraish. He says,

At the time of Umraht Ul Qadah I went to hiding. My brother Waleed Ibn Ul Waleed who had accepted Islam, had come for Umrah with the Prophet. He tried to meet me but couldn't find me so he wrote a letter to me:

"In the name of Allah, the Beneficent, the Merciful. It is perplexing to me that still you are refusing Islam though you are exemplary in wisdom. Islam cannot remain unacceptable for a wise man. The Prophet asked me about you, I said, 'Allah will bring him.' He said, 'Such a person cannot remain unaware of this true Deen more if he will use his skill for Deen will be good for him, and we would have given him priority.' O my brother! You are so deprived of these opportunities of jihad, so this is the time to get it."

Khalid says,

What the Prophet said about me affected me a lot, so I had a dream that I entered from a dry desert into a green land. Then when I was departing for Madina, *I saw Safwan Ibni Umayyah. I said Abu Wahab, "Do you not see that Mohammad's mission is spreading, so let's go and accept Islam." But he was reluctant because his father and brother had been killed in Badr. Then I went to Ikramah Ibni Abu Jahl and said the same thing to him. His answer was no different than that of Safwan. They both said they would never accept Islam, not even if all the Makkans did. I asked them not to disclose my secret. Then I came to Uthman Ibni Talha – Al - Hajabi. His father Talha, his uncle Uthman and his four brothers Safi, Hallas, Harith and Kilab all six were killed in Uhud, but he was my close friend so when I told him, he accepted it. Then we agreed that whoever will depart first, he should wait for the other one in such and such place. Then we met there in the appointed place in Haddah and we met Amr Ibn Ul Aas also. We told each other what the mission was.*

When we arrived in Madina, *I met my brother Waleed and I changed my clothes. My brother told me the*

Prophet was very happy for me. So, I came and accepted Islam. The Prophet said, praise be to Allah, who guided you. I was sure that a wiseman like you will come towards this good. I requested the Prophet to make a Dua so Allah may forgive my sins. He said, Islam demolishes whatever someone has done before." Then after me Amr Ibn Ul Aas and Uthman Ibni Talha also accepted Islam.

At Hudaibiyah people had locks of the Prophet's hair. I got one and sewed it in my cap and whenever I entered into a fight with that cap on my head, I won. He may have gotten it when the Prophet did umrah from Ji'irranah later on.

Khalid passed away in Hims (Sham) in year 21 after Hijrah in the time of Umar. He was over 40 at the time of his death.

THE BATTLE OF MUTA

A big part of the nearby area world was under the control of Roman Empire. The Prophet now wanted the *Dawat* of Islam to be extended out of "Jazeeratul Arab" (peninsula) to the north. So, he wrote a letter to Harith Ibni Ibi Shemar al- Ghassani the ruler of Busra. The envoy of the Prophet Harith Ibni Omar al Azdi the bearer of the letter was staying there in "Muta". So, the ruler of Sham Sharabeel Ibni-Abi Amr al Ghassani killed him. It was unheard of to kill an envoy. Also, the companions of the Prophet who were giving *Dawat* to Islam were killed in "Zat Ul-Tallah". The killing of religious mission was also a crime of such a nature. Also, four out of five missionaries to Banu Sulaim were killed, as we mentioned before. These were some of the reasons the Prophet arranged an army of three thousand people towards Muta.

THE PROPHECIES ABOUT MARTYRDOM

The Prophet appointed Zaid Ibni Haritha as Amir of the army and said,

> "If he is martyred then Jafar Ibni Abi Talib should lead, and if he is also martyred then Abdullah Ibni Rawahat should be the Amir, and if he receives the same fate then you people should select an Amir on your own."

By saying so the Sahabah came to know that may be all these three will get martyred. Also, it is known from this appointment by the Prophet that in circumstances like this there was a ready-made contingency leadership of three ranks. The Prophet gave them a white flag.

A Jewish person by the name of Naghman was sitting there. He said,

> "O Mohammad! Before you, any Prophet who appointed more than one Amir for a mission one after the other was martyred, so no one of these three will come back."

He said to Zaid,

> "If Mohammad is a Prophet, then make a will."

Zaid said,

> "By God, he is a true messenger."

The Prophet said to Zaid,

> "Approach the place where Harith Ibni Omar was martyred. Call the people there to Islam. If they accept, then that is good, otherwise go ahead in the name of Allah and fight them."

This army got together in Jawf. The Prophet addressed them:

> *Go! Fight in the path of Allah in the name of Allah with those who have refused Allah. Betray not and do not attack at night when they are not informed. Kill not the old, the women, or the children, nor a monk sitting in a monastery. Cut not the trees and date palms nor demolish any buildings.*

When the army was departing, Ibni Rawaha broke in tears. They asked him, why? He said, "Allah says,

> *'There is no one but he will enter it [hell]. This is on your Lord a decree incumbent. [he has decreed so on himself].' So, I cry as entering is proven but how will be the coming out means to pass over it?"* (19: 71)

The Muslims, said "May Allah bring you people back safe." So Ibni Rawaha said a few verses.

But I ask from the Beneficent one forgiveness and a *Wast* [strong] hit taking away the head or a thrust in Zee-Harran with a spear piercing through entrails and liver so that when they pass by my grave, say,

> *"May Allah guide he who did jihad' and indeed he is a guided one."*

THE ARMY DEPARTED

The Prophet came with them up to Tahiyyat Ul Wada and said goodbye to them. These people marched towards north until they arrived in Ma'aan. They got the news that Hercules or his brother had gathered together 100,000 troops of Balqan in Ma'aab and another hundred thousand more of Lakhm, Jizam, Balqan and Bala tribes would join them as well.

The Muslims stayed in Balqan for two days consulting. They thought to inform the Prophet about the situation, so he may either send them support or advise them to try something else. But Ibni Rawaha objected to this and said,

> "Why do you have concerns about what you have come for [meaning martyrdom]? We cannot compete the enemy in power and number but we can fight them based on Deen, with which Allah has empowered us. Go forth as there is one of the two benefits for us, victory, or martyrdom."

So, it was decided unanimously. Then the army marched forth until it arrived in Masharif where there were the platoons of the enemy so the Muslims avoided to face them and thus, they arrived in "Muta" and got ready for fight. The Muslims appointed Qutbah Ibni Qatada on *Maimanah* (the right wing of the army) and Obadah Ibni Malik on the left side.

Under the command of Zaid, they started the battle and he was martyred. Then Jafar took the command after him. He was fighting on horseback, but when he was stuck in face-to-face fighting, he fell to the ground and slaughtered his horse so the enemy would not take it if he was martyred. In battle his right hand was cut so he held the flag in his left hand. Then his left hand also got cut so he held the flag with his cut hands to his chest and was leading the Mujahideen until he was martyred. Imam Bukhari narrates from Ibni Umar that he had taken almost fifty hits and injuries all on his front, which means that he had not turned his back at any point.

The Prophet said,

> *"Allah gave Jafar two wings in paradise for his hands so he is flying."*

That's why he is called Zul - Janahain and At - Tayyar, it means *"the one with two wings"* and *"the flying one."*

Then Ibni Rawaha took over the leading. In the beginning he was debating whether to fight on foot or on horse. But then he made up his mind and started fighting on foot until he was martyred as well.

Ibni Rawah was from the Khazraj tribe and he was there in Bai'at-I-Aqabah. His name was Abdullah Ibni Thalabah.

THE NEW LEADERSHIP

When all three generals appointed by the Prophet were martyred at the time of martyrdom of Ibni Rawaha, Thabit Ibni Arqam from Banu Ajlan picked up the flag and shouted out,

> *"O Muslims! Decide on a leader."*

They said,

> *"You are our leader now."*

He said,

> *"No, but if possible, then get behind Khalid Ibni Waleed,"*

And they did so.

Khalid Ibni Waleed changed the formation of the army. He ordered those in the back to come to the front and he made the same change to Maimanah and Maisarah.

This was a strategy and psychology as the enemies thought some new force and support had come to the Muslims. Ibni Ishaq says,

> "He fought for 7 days and tried to push the enemy back."

Khalid says,

> "During this time some nine swords broke in my hand."

The Prophet of Allah in Madinah was giving a commentary regarding war field. He told people about the martyrdom of Zaid, Jafar and Ibni Rawaha and then told them that now the Muslims got together behind Khalid and now the leadership flag had been taken by Khalid, a sword from the swords of Allah, and thus it became Khalid's title. As he was telling them all this he was in tears. In this battle twelve Muslims were martyred but it is not known how many enemies were killed.

The victory of this battle by so few Muslims against so many enemies frightened people, so the Aslam, Ghitfar, Zubyan, Fazarah and Ashja tribes all accepted Islam.

Yala Ibni Umayyah was the first one who came back. The Prophet said,

> "Do you want to tell me what happened or should I tell you?"

and when the Prophet told him all the details he said,

> "By God you have not missed a single thing that happened there."

This was a war and battle itself but we can say this was a prologue for the conquest of Rome.

The ruler at Ma'aan named Farwah accepted Islam and sent a white mule to the Prophet as a gift and sent a letter to the Prophet expressed his Islam therein. When the emperor of Rome got this news, he invited him and hanged him at a well named Afrain in Philistine. Ibni Ishaq says he recited a verse in front of the Romans,

> *"Inform the leader of Muslims that my bones and joints are presented to my Lord [meaning I sacrifice it]."*

It is narrated that he hanged him in the 9th year after the conquest of Makkah.

SARIYYAH ZATUS SALASIL

When the Prophet learned that some Arab tribes were forming an alliance against Muslims, while Quza'a and others were thinking to attack Muslims on their own, and this type of uprisings were either because they were thinking that coming back of Muslims from Muta is their defeat, but that was not a defeat, but a strategy. They came out safe as they were too few, or these enemies were of the view that they came back victorious so now they will attack again so the other tribes decided to get together and stop them. The Prophet was also planning to stop these alliances so he gave three hundred people to Amr Ibn Ul Aas with twenty horses. The mother of Amr was from Balha and this army was sent towards Balha and Azirah.

Salasil means chains, as the enemy tied themselves to one another with chains so nobody may run away. Another explanation for the name is that this battle happened near a well named Salsil, and that's why this battle called Zatus Salasil. The Prophet gave one white flag and one black one to Amr Ibn Ul Aas. These people used to march at night and to go into hiding during the day. When these people arrived there, they discovered that the enemy was large in number, so they sent Rafi Ibn Ul Makeeth to the Prophet for further support. The Prophet sent two hundred more people under the command of Abu Ubaidah Ibn Ul Jarrah and gave him a flag as well. In this group there were Muhajireen and Ansar like the first group, including Abu Bakr and Umar. When this group joined the first group, Abu Ubaidah thought he would be the imam but Amr told him, "You people came as support," so Amr led the prayer and Abu Ubaidah subjugated himself.

For one hour they fought the enemy and defeated them so they fled and the Muslims came back victorious.

SARIYYAH ABU OBAIDAH IBNUL JARRAH

This *Sariyah* is also called *Sariyyat Ul - Khabt*, while Imam Bukhari named it Saiful Bahr as it happened on the coast. In the month of Rajab, in the 8th year after "Hijrah". The Prophet of Allah sent three hundred people under the command of Abu Ubaidah Ibn Ul Jarrah towards Juhainah to get hold of a caravan of Quraish. Umar was also part of this mission. In this mission their food supplies were exhausted so the sea wave threw out to them a big fish called Anbar. They ate it for many days, otherwise they would have had to start eating leaves as they had nothing else. Then in Shaban the Prophet sent fifteen people under the command of Abu Qatada towards Ghitfan as they were gathering in Khudrah in Najd. So, they killed a few of them and captured a few along with their cattle. Abu Qatada stayed out of Madina for fifteen days.

In Ramadan of the 8th year the Prophet sent Abu Qatada in 8 people towards Izam, 36 miles outside of Madina, so the Quraish would know that Muslims were alert, as they had broken the treaty of Hudaibiyah.

When Abu Qatada was on his mission, somewhere in the middle he met Aamir Ibni Adbat al Ash'jaee. He said "Salam" to them, but Mihlam Ibni Ju'thamah, whose actual name was Yazid Ibni Qais, killed him and grabbed his camel and belongings. When they came back, they informed the Prophet about this incident. So, Allah said,

> *"O you who believe! When you go in the path of Allah then verify the truth (make things clear and inquire) and say not to one who said 'Salam' (or expressed his Islam) to you, that you are not a believer. You seek the goods of the life of this world, so there are lot of treasures with Allah. You were the same before this, then Allah conferred on you his favor, therefore inquire [about things], for verily Allah is ever well-aware of what you do." (4: 96)*

This passage means everyone is considered a believer with the expression of Islam and what is in one's heart is known to Allah alone.

As Abu Qatadal could not find any group of disbelievers and got the news that the Prophet had already left for Makkah so they also left to join him. They joined him in Suqya. Yazid Ibni Qais asked the Prophet if he can ask forgiveness for him but the Prophet said,

> *"May Allah not forgive you."*

He started crying and on 7th day he died. He was put in a grave a few times but the earth threw him out. Then he was thrown in a creek between two mountains and covered with rocks. The Prophet said,

> *"The earth accepts much more evil people but this is a lesson for you people."*

It means, when one thinks of him- or herself is Muslim, his expression and admission of Islam is enough and s/he is to be treated as Muslim.

THE CONQUEST OF MAKKAH

We mentioned there in the story of Hudaibiyah that Allah said,

> "Indeed, we have given you a manifest conquest." (48: 1)

To Hafiz Ibn Ul Qayyim and Jalal Uddin - Al Muhalli this was a promise by Allah that we have decreed for you the victory of Makkah. Ibni Masud and Bara said that you people think that is the conquest of Makkah while we consider the pact of Hudaibiyah the victory (Bukhari).

Imam Ahmad relates from Majma Ibn Ul Haritha that when the Prophet recited this verse one man said,

> "Is this a victory?"

The Prophet said,

> "Of course, I swear by the one in whose hand is the soul of Mohammad."

And that's why the spoils of Khyber were distributed among those who were there in Hudaibiyah.

KHUZA'A AND BANU BAKR

In the pact of Hudaibiyah it was mentioned that anyone from different tribes who wanted to join either party could do that. So, the Khuza'a tribe joined the Prophet and the Banu Bakr joined the Quraish.

The Khuza'a were also the allies of Abdul Muttalib in the time of ignorance when there was a dispute between Abdul Muttalib and his uncle Nawfal for the custody of Bait Ullah.

Khuza'a and Banu Bakr had been fighting since the time of ignorance but when Islam prevailed then these disputes calmed down. But after the pact of Hudaibiyah, a man from Banu Bakr recited some verses defaming the Prophet. Someone from Khuza'a jumped on him and broke his head and thus a battle broke out as Banu Bakr attacked Khuza'a under the leadership of Nawfal Ibni Muawiya Addili near a watering hole when Khuza'a people were taking a rest there. The Banu Nufathah, a subtribe of Banu Bakr, asked the Quraish to help them with weapons and they did it. Some people from Quraish even joined them secretly. They killed 20 people or more from the Khuza'a. Ikramah Ibni Abu Jahl, Safwan, Shaibah Ibni Uthman, Huwaitib Ibni, Abdul Uzza, and Suhail Ibni Amr were among those who took part in this battle. Fortunately, all these people accepted Islam later on. Banu Bakr were fighting with Khuza'a until they pushed them to the house of Budail Ibni Warqa al- Khuza'a and the house of Rafi, an ally of Khuza'a.

There Banu Bakr said to Nawfal,

> *"Your God is your God, which means his rules do not apply to us."*

Nawfal said,

> *"This is a very big word. Just carry on and take your revenge o Banu Bakr as you were committing theft in Haram, so will you not take your revenge therein?"*

QURAISH WERE AFRAID

When the Quraish helped Banu Bakr against Khuza'a and ended the battle, they came to sense that they have broken the pact and were not sure what to do now. Therefore, Harith Ibni Hisham came to Abu Sufyan. Abu Sufyan said,

> *"I was not there nor I was unaware of it, but this is something happened and now I am sure that Mohammad will fight us. He will not keep quiet. Also, my wife Hind has seen in her dream that a flood of blood has come from Hajun and stopped at Khandamah which means something is going to happen."*

AMR IBNI SALIM FROM KHUZA'E

After this incident Amr Ibni Salim al Khuza'a came to Madina. The Prophet was sitting in masjid with his Sahabah. He recited some verses,

> *- O my Lord! I remind Mohammad the pact of his father and our father.*
>
> *- O Mohammad! You were young and we were older, then we accepted Islam and we never drew our hand back.*
>
> *- So help, may Allah help you a strong help and call other slaves of Allah to come for help.*
>
> *- The Quraish have broken your treaty.*
>
> *- They have broken your strong pact and made us worry with their watching us.*
>
> *- They thought we will not ask anyone for help, while they are very mean and little in number.*

> *- They attacked us in water when we were praying Tahajjud, bowing down and prostrating.*

When the Prophet heard him, he broke down in tears. He stood up pulling his cloak and said,

> *"If I will not help you the way I help myself, then it means I haven't done anything."*

Aaisha said,

> *"At that time he seemed very angry."*

Budail Ibni Warqa also came there along with a few others and gave details to the Prophet about how they broke the treaty and how the Quraish helped them.

The Prophet told them,

> *"Go to mountains and hide there."*

On the other hand, the Quraish were in a condition of fear. The Prophet said to Sahabah,

> *"Soon you people will see Abu Sufyan coming here."*

On his way to Madina, Abu Sufyan came across Budail Ibni Warqa and asked him,

> *"Where are you coming from?"*

He replied,

> *"From some people of Khuza'a in that valley."*

Abu Sufyan said to his colleagues,

> *"Let's see where these people were resting, to see the dung pieces of their camel, if in that there are the date-*

stone pieces then for sure they are coming from Madina,"

And when they checked that they found that they were there and now they were sure that they are coming from the Prophet.

ABU SUFYAN IN MADINA

Abu Sufyan came to Madina straight to the house of his daughter Ummi Habiba the wife of the Prophet. When he entered the house, he saw a bed and tried to go to it and to sit. But Ummi Habiba hurried to it to fold up the coverings. Abu Sufyan said,

> *"I don't know whether you have given priority to the bed on me or to me on bed?"*

She said,

> *"As you are polytheist and this is the sitting place of the Prophet of Allah so a Mushrik cannot sit on it."*

Abu Sufyan said,

> *"It means you have lost your manners."*

She said,

> *"This is not the case but Allah has blessed me with guidance so I worship him and you still worship the stones, while you are the head of the Quraish and from you this type of faith and action is bewildering."*

He said,

> *"Then should I desert the religion of my forefathers and accept Mohammad's religion?"*

After that, he came to the Prophet and requested him to renew the treaty. The Prophet did not give him any answer, so he came to Abu Bakr to speak to the Prophet but he refused. Then he came to Umar and asked him for the same thing. He not only refused but said,

> *"If I had but a corn straw in my hand, I would fight you with that."*

Then he came to Ali and requested him for the same appeal. He said,

> *"Woe unto you! There is no room for such an appeal."*

Fatima was sitting there with Hasan, a small boy. He said to Fatima,

> *"Can you request the same thing for us through this boy?"*

Fatima said,

> *"He is too small to say such a thing and there is no one to go ahead of the Prophet in this regard. He is the only one who can do this."*

Now, he came to know that there is no way. He asked Ali if he can give him any suggestion he can do. He said,

> *"I do not know any suggestion. You are the chief of Banu Kinanah, so go and announce in public that I am here for peace."*

Thus, he left Madina getting nothing.

It is also narrated that the Prophet sent Damurah to tell the Quraish to do one of these three things:

- Give the blood money of all the people killed from Khuza'a.

- Withdraw from the alliance with Banu Nufathah
- Declare that the pact of Hudaibiyah is not intact anymore.

Abu Sufyan came back to Makkah and said that he couldn't get anything from Mohammad.

THE PROPHET WAS GETTING READY

The prophet was preparing for Makkah but as a strategy he was keeping it secret. Aaisha was preparing the Prophet's travel kit. Abu Bakr came and asked Aaisha,

> "These are not the days to go towards Banu Asfar, so what is the program?"

She said,

> "I don't know."

The *Sariyah* of Abu Qatadal of 8 people as we mentioned was a part of this strategy so the people would not think about the Prophet's mission towards Makkah.

THE STORY OF HATIB'S LETTER

A slave lady who used to serve Banu Hashim in Makkah came to Madina seeking help from the Prophet. The Prophet asked Banu Hashim to help her and they did. When she was going back, Hatib Ibni

Abi Balta'a asked her to take a letter to some people in Makkah and also gave her some money as a compensation. Hatib Ibni Abi Balta'a had sensed that the Prophet is going towards Makkah.

The Prophet was informed by Allah about that letter. The Prophet sent Ali, Zubair, Miqdad and Abu Marthad after that woman and told them that you will get her in Raudat Ul - Khakh, a rest area, so get that letter from her anyway. They went and found her there and asked her for the letter but she denied she had any type of letter. Ali threatened her with a strip search if she did not produce the letter. She got scared and brought out the letter from her Tresses. They brought it to the Prophet. He opened it. It was from Hatib. The Prophet called Hatib and asked him,

> *"What is this?"*

He said,

> *"O messenger of Allah! Don't hasten in my case. I swear by Allah I am a believer, I have not denounced Islam, nor I am a munafiq [hypocrite], But I was living among the Quraish even though I am not one of them. My family is still there and don't have any relative to take care of them. That's why I wrote this letter so they will protect my family as a reciprocation to it."*

The Prophet said to his Sahaba,

> *"He spoke the truth."*

Umar became angry and said to the Prophet,

> *"Just allow me to cut the head of this hypocrite."*

The Prophet said,

"He is from those who were in Badr and Umar! You know what Allah said regarding people of Badr? He said, whatever you do after this, I have forgiven you,"

So, Umar began to weep and said,

"Yes, Allah and His messenger know the best."

In this regard Allah said,

> 59: 1: "O you who believe! Take not (make not) my enemies and your enemies as Auliya [friends or protectors] offering to them affection, while they have disbelieved in what has come to you means the truth. They have driven the messenger and you as well, because you believed in Allah, your Lord, if you have come forth for jihad [fight] in my path [cause] and seeking my good pleasure, you offer them lovely friendship secretly, and I know what you concealed and what you revealed. And whosoever of you does this, then for sure he has lost the right path.
>
> 2: If they will get an upper hand over you, they will be your enemies and will stretch forth their hands and tongues badly against you and they wish you to disbelieve.
>
> 3: Neither your relatives nor your children can give you any benefit on the day of resurrection. He will judge you and Allah is all seer of what you do.
>
> 4: Indeed there is a good model for you in Ibrahim and in those who were with him, when they said to their people, 'Verily we are free from you and whatever you worship besides Allah, we have rejected you and there has started between us and you the enmity and hatred forever.' But if you believe in Allah alone, yes except the

saying of Ibrahim to his father, 'Verily I shall ask forgiveness for you but I don't have the power of doing anything for you against Allah.' O our Lord! In you we have put our trust and to you we turned and to you is our final return."

The text of the letter of Hatib was,

"The Prophet has declared and announced to people the jihad. I think he is coming towards you so I thought to show some kindness to you people."

In other narration the text is,

"O Quraish! The Prophet is coming with a big army to attack you like a flood. By Allah if he will come alone, Allah will give him the victory and fulfill his promise with him, so think about yourselves."

Now the text does not indicate any conspiracy; rather, it embodies the suggestion to surrender, to be safe. He wrote it in the name of Suhail Ibni Amr, Ikram al Ibni Abi Jahal, and Safwan Ibni Umayyah.

THE ARMY MARCHED TOWARDS MAKKAH

The Prophet told Abu Bakr (and in some narratives, Umar) about his mission. He mustered an army of ten thousand people. This was the 10th of Ramadan in the 8th year when he departed. He also sent in front of him his intelligence on every path and road to keep an eye on every strange or unknown person, so nobody may inform the people in Makkah before time. He appointed Abu Rahm Kulthum Ibn Ul Hussain Ibni Khalaf al – Ghifari Amir at Madina. He had accepted Islam when the

Prophet had come to Madina. He was hit with an arrow in his throat at Uhud. Allah saved him but his throat was badly injured, and that's why he was called "Manhur" (the slaughtered or the sacrificed one).

Dumyati narrated that Abdullah Ibni Ummi Maktoum was appointed as Amir but it may be that one of them was the imam for prayers and the other one was for administrative affairs.

The Prophet and Sahabah were fasting. He broke his fast in Kudaid in between *Osfan* and *Omj* after Asr. He also announced that who cannot fast they should not. When he arrived in Juhfah, Abbas and his family joined him there. They had come from Makkah. In Abawa the son of Prophet's uncle Abu Sufyan Ibn Ul Harith Ibni Abdul Muttalib and the son of his paternal aunt Abdullah Ibni Abi Umayyah al – Maohzami came to him as well, but the Prophet turned his face from them, as they used to say bad words against Islam and the Prophet. Ummi Salmah said,

> "O the messenger of Allah! May your cousins not be unlucky,"

Which means she was asking him to forget about the past and forgive them.

Ali said to Abu Sufyan,

> "Go to the Prophet and say what the brothers of Yusuf had said to Yusuf when they observed his nobility and character and recognized him and they were ashamed of what they had done to him."

And that was,

> "They said, By Allah! Indeed Allah has preferred you above us and indeed we were for sure the sinners." (12: 91)

Abu Sufyan did and said the same so the Prophet said what Yusuf said to his brothers after that:

> *"He said, no reproach on you this day. May Allah forgive you and He is the most merciful of those who show mercy." (12: 92)*

Abu Sufyan Ibn Ul Harith was a very good poet so he said a few verses *ex tempore*:

> *"I swear by your life when I was carrying a flag so that the horses of Lat [the statute] may overtake the horses of Mohammad.*
>
> *So, I was confused in darkness like one whose night is darkened, now this is my time when I got the guidance.*
>
> *That guide guided and introduced me to Allah whom I had rejected badly.*
>
> *To the best of my efforts, I used to stop and go away from Mohammad and I was called to Islam but no connection was coming up.*
>
> *They [the disbelievers] are what they are, when one does speak according to their wish, even if he is a man of opinion he is blamed and called fool.*
>
> *I used to please them and not turning my face from those people and tell Thaqeef tribe, this is my caravan and I do not want to fight them.*
>
> *And I was not in that army which disgraced Aamir and no harm happened from my tongue or from my hand.*
>
> *There were tribes came from very far areas and were fighters equipped with arrows and armor coats."*

The Prophet hit him on his chest and said,

> "You had rejected me totally."

Hafiz Ibni Qayyim said due to his shame from his past after his Islam even he never looked at the Prophet straight. He used to look at him from the side or when the Prophet was not looking at him, and at the time of his death when his family was crying, he said to them,

> "Cry not. By Allah! After Iman I have never committed sin nor spoken a word of sin [Zad Ul – Ma'ad]."

This Abu Sufyan was the fostering brother of the Prophet because Halima suckled him. When Hamza accepted Islam, he was eager for Abu Sufyan to accept Islam as well. He had too much resemblance with the Prophet like Hasan, Jafar, and Qutham Ibni Abbas.

Abdullah Ibni Umayyah was the son of Atikah Bint Abdul Muttalib and he was the stepbrother of Ummi Salmah. Ummi Salma's mother's name was also Atikah, but she was the daughter of Aamir Ibni Qais. Abu Sufyan, as we mentioned, used to say bad verses regarding the Prophet and the Prophet said to Ummi Salmah,

> "This cousin of mine has attacked my honor and dignity."

Hassan Ibni Thabit used to answer him with verses as he said,

> "Beware! Take it to Abu Sufyan from my side that this affair [prophethood] has become clear [open or overtaking]. You said bad regarding Mohammad so I answered that and with Allah there is a reward for that."

The Prophet also said that this other cousin of his, Abdullah Ibni Umayyah, didn't know what he said in Makkah. Allah said,

17: 90 – And they said, we shall not believe in you until you cause a spring for us to gush forth from the earth.

91 – Or you have a garden of date palms and grapes and you cause river therein to gush forth [and flow].

92 – Or you cause the heaven to fall on us in pieces as you pretend or you bring Allah and angels to us face to face.

93 – Or you have a house of adornments [gold and silver] or you ascend up into the sky, and we will never believe in your ascension until you bring down for us a book that we can read [means therein materials of our choice]. Say [O Mohammad!] Glory be to Allah [amazing as these words they used to say in amazing] I am not but a human and a messenger.

THE MUSLIM ARMY AT MARUZ – ZAHRAN

As we mentioned before, this army was 10,000 people altogether. But some Arab tribes joined them on their way to Makkah and to some historians mentioned the number as 12,000, and the number which is mentioned in *Seerat Ul Halbia* is 6,900, so that 10,000 is those who gathered together in the very beginning in Madina and the others who joined them later on. This book has given the details of the first gathering as well and that is, there were 7,000 Muhajireen with three hundred horses, 4,000 with 500 horses Ansar, 1,000 from the Muzainah with one hundred horses, 40 from the Aslam tribe and its colleagues with thirty horses, and Juhainah, along with its colleagues, sent 800 with fifty horses. The total number of horses was thus 980.

This big army arrived in Marruz – Zahran at Isha time. So, the Prophet told the army that everyone may light his own fire. This was a war psychological strategy as from far away, those many fires would appear toto number in the hundreds of thousands thus the Quraish would be frightened into a quick surrender.

The Prophet gave the responsibility of guarding, to Umar.

On the other hand, Abu Sufyan Hakeem Ibni Hizam and Budail Ibni Warqa were informed that a big army had arrived in Marruz – Zahran. They came out to check. From far Abu Sufyan Ibni Harb said,

"I have never seen that many fires."

Nobody knows how big this army is. Budail said,

"This is the fire of the Khuza'a."

Abu Sufyan said,

"There are too few Khuza'a for this."

Budail meant that these fires were lit by the Khuza'a, as they asked the Prophet for help. But Abu Sufyan didn't understand.

Note: Hakim Ibni Hizam was the nephew of Khadija, the son of her brother. He was the cousin of Zubair Ibni Awwam, his paternal uncle's son. He was from the elites of Makkah. He was born thirteen years before the event of the Elephants.

Darrun Nadwah building was his property where the Quraish assembly was taking place. Later on, he sold it for 100,000 dirhams to Muawiya. He died in the time of Muawiya at the age of one hundred and twenty years. He spent 60 years in ignorance and disbelief and sixty years in Islam.

ABBAS GOT ABU SUFYAN

When Abu Sufyan was talking to Budail in the dark, Abbas was riding the mule of the Prophet to check on the surroundings. He says,

> *I recognized the voice of Abu Sufyan so I called him, "Abu Hanzalah!" He also recognized him and said, "Abul Fadl?" I said, "Yes, I am." He asked me, "Why you are here?" I said, "This is the messenger of Allah." He said, "Now what is the way out?" I said, "When he overtakes you people, he will kill you first. So come on! Sit behind me on this mule to take you to the Prophet and ask protection for you." He rode behind me and his other two colleagues went back.*

Abbas says,

> *Whenever I was passing by Muslims, they would ask who is this and they were seeing me, they said, "Oh the mule of the Prophet and his uncle is riding on it." But when I was passing by Umar, he came close to know who this is and when he saw Abu Sufyan behind me he said, "Oh! Abu Sufyan the enemy of Allah?" And said that Allah has given me this opportunity and thus he rushed towards the Prophet, so I made the mule run to approach the Prophet first and I entered to the Prophet followed by Umar. He said, "O the messenger of Allah! This is Abu Sufyan so allow me to cut his head." I said, "O the messenger of Allah, I have given him protection." I sat in front of the Prophet and held his head saying to him, "Tonight nobody will talk to you in secret except me," and Umar was repeating his request so I said "Umar! If he was from your tribe Banu Adi then you would have not said like this." He said, "Abbas! This is enough. I swear by Allah I was happy for your Islam more than that of my father because the Prophet was desiring for your Islam which means that they were giving priority to the will of the Prophet over*

their own will." The Prophet then said to Abbas take him with you for tonight and bring him tomorrow.

The next day I brought him back to the Prophet. The Prophet said to him, "Woe on you that until now you couldn't understand that there is no god but Allah alone." He said, "May my parents be sacrificed of you, for what a generous, mild, and kind man you are to your relatives. I understand if there had been other gods, they would have helped us."

Then the Prophet said, "Woe unto you, still you don't understand that I am the messenger of Allah." He said, "May my parents be sacrificed of you. How gentle, generous, and kind you are, still I have something in my heart [either doubt or resistance]." Abbas said to him, "Woe unto you, believe in, that there is no god but Allah and Mohammad is the messenger of Allah, before that your head is cut." So, he believed and said "Shahadah". Abbas said to the Prophet, "Abu Sufyan is the chief so if you can, kindly give him some prestige." The Prophet said, "Whoever enters the house of Allah is safe; whoever enters the house of Abu Sufyan, he is safe as well; and whoever will shut on himself the gate of his house, he is safe also." Abu Sufyan said, "What an honor he gave me!"

THE MARCH TO MAKKAH

The Prophet told Abbas to take Abu Sufyan to a narrow valley from which the Muslim army would proceed to Makkah. He took him there. On the 17th day of Ramadan, this march started from Marruz –

Zahran. Whenever a platoon was passing through the valley, Abu Sufyan was asking Abbas,

> "Who are these people?"

He was telling him one by one that this is Banu Sulaim, this is Muzainah and so and so on. With every tribe he was saying,

> "I have nothing to do with this,"

But when the Prophet was passing with a big platoon of Ansar and Muhajireen wearing armored coats, he asked Abbas,

> "Who are these people?"

Abbas said,

> "This is the Prophet with the group of Ansar and Muhajireen."

He said,

> "Abbas! The government of your nephew has been established."

Abbas said,

> "This is not government, this is Prophethood."

Abbas said,

> "Now you go and make the Quraish understand,"

So, he went and announced,

> "O Quraish! This is Mohammad with a big army. You cannot face him, so whoever will enter to the house of Abu Sufyan he will be safe."

His own wife, who had hatred and anger for the Prophet not only because of *Deen* but also because her father, brother, uncle, and son were killed in Badr, said to Abu Sufyan,

> "Just kill this man having the fat legs,"

Referring to the Prophet. Abu Sufyan said,

> "Woe unto you, deceive not yourself, you cannot face such a big army."

Also, it was announced that whoever will go enter the house of Allah means go to its vicinity he is safe and whoever will close the gate of his own house, he is safe also. So, people rushed to the house of Allah, to the house of Abu Sufyan and some of them to their own houses also.

Musa Ibni Oqbah narrated that Abbas said to the Prophet that he had given shelter to Hakeem Ibni Hizam and Budail Ibni Warqa also and they want to come to Islam. The Prophet said they could come so they came and accepted Islam as well.

In a narration it is said that the Prophet said to Abu Sufyan,

> "Has not the time come for you to say there is no God but Allah alone?"

Abu Sufyan said,

> "But what shall I do with Lat and Uzza?"

Umar was standing outside, he said, do excrement on them. Also, he said,

> "If you had been outside the tent, then I would not have said this."

Abu Sufyan said,

"Umar! Just let me talk to my cousin."

Sa'd Ibni Obadah was holding the flag of Ansar. When he was passing Abu Sufyan, he said,

"Today is the day of slaughtering and today the unlawful will be made lawful near Kaba. Today Allah has put the Quraish down."

Then when the Prophet was passing by Abu Sufyan, he said,

"O the messenger of Allah! Did you hear what Sa'd said?"

The Prophet asked him,

"What did he say?"

Abu Sufyan told him. Uthman and Abdur Rahman Ibni Auf said,

"O the messenger of Allah! we fear of the attack of Quraish on Sa'd."

The Prophet said to Abu Sufyan and others,

"Today is the day of mercy and today the holy Kaba would be given a Hullah [Ghilaf and cover] and today Allah has given the Quraish an honor."

Then the Prophet called Sa'd over, took the flag from him, and gave it to his son Qais Ibni Sa'd. In one narration it is said that it was given to Zubair but the first one is more authentic, as this was the flag for Ansar and also by giving it to his son the prophet kept him from being heartbroken. So, at once he cooled down Abu Sufyan and Quraish's anger and he kept the honor of flag in the family of Sa'd. Such actions are symbolic but have a heavy weight.

THE PROPHET'S ENTRANCE TO MAKKAH

When the Prophet entered the Zee – Tuwa zone, to show his humility he bowed his head so low that his beard was touching the standing wood of the she-camel's saddle.

The Prophet ordered Khalid to enter from the lower side of Makkah. He was on the Maimanah of the army having Banu Sulaim, Aslam, Ghifar, Juhainah and Muzainah and other tribes with him. He told him not to get involved in any battle, meaning not to attack, but if he did get attacked, then he was to cut them down. The Prophet himself entered from the upper side of Makkah. He ordered Zubair to take his flag and to erect it there in Hajun and wait for him there. It is worth noting that this flag was the flag of the head. Abu Ubaidah was with the infantry. The Prophet was on his she-camel and Osamah Ibni Zaid was riding on the same she-camel behind him.

At the time of entrance, the big flag was black, made of Sayyidah Aaisha's shawl while the small flag was a white.

KHALID WAS ATTACKED

When Khalid was entering to Makkah there some people from Banu Harith Ibni Abd Manaf and Banu Bakr were sitting with Ikramah Ibni Abu Jahl, Safwan Ibni Umayyah and Suhail Ibni Amr. They shot arrows on Khalid so Khalid retaliated. This had started at Khandamah and spread up to the Kharurah Bazar. So, some people went up to the hilltops and some others retreated to their houses. The Muslims followed them. Abu Sufyan and Hakeem Ibni Hizam shouted to them,

> "O Quraish, why do you offer yourselves to be slaughtered?"

Khalid put these people on run and killed fourteen of the Banu Bakr and four from Huzail. Two Muslims were martyred as well when they were separated from their platoon. They were Kuraz Ibni Jabiral Fihri and Khalid Al Ash Qar Al Khuza'a or Khunais Ibni Khalid.

Ubaidah and his infantry did not have the armor coats or helmets so they took the Batn Ul Wadi path to arrive in Makkah safe before the Prophet.

In the battle with Khalid Hamas Ibni Qais ran away, entered his house, and went to hiding therein. He was arms manufacturer and used to tell his wife, I make it for Mohammad and his people. Now his wife said to him,

> "What about those arms you were making for Mohammad and his people?"

He said a few verses,

If you would have seen the event of Khandamah when Safwan fled away and Ikramah also.

And it welcomed us with Muslim swords which were cutting of every arm and throat. With hit and nothing was heard except Ghamghamah, Lahm, Naheet and Hamhamah behind us certain sounds of hits. Then you would not have said a single word of blame (on us).

Khalid was coming into different streets of Makkah to meet the Prophet at Safa. When he came there the Prophet asked him to explain why he got involved in fight which I had forbidden him. He said,

> "I only retaliated to defend."

The Prophet said,

"That was what Allah willed."

In Hajun where Zubair erected the flag as the Prophet had ordered him, in that place now there is Masjid Ul Fath. The Prophet entered Makkah on the 20th day of Ramadan, year 8.

On this occasion the Prophet had Ummi Salmah and Maimunah with him.

ENTERING MASJID UL HARAM AND BAITULLAH

The Prophet entered along with Muslims to the vicinity of "Bait Ullah", he kissed Hajar-I-Aswad, and did Tawaf and the Muslims did the same. He did Istilam of Rukni Yamani with his stick, and the Muslims said Takbeer with a louder voice. The Mushriks were looking at the scene from the hill tops.

Mohammad Ibni Maslamah was holding the rope of the she-camel of the Prophet during *tawaf*. The Prophet and the Muslims did this *tawaf* in their regular dress.

After *tawaf* he came down to the ground and prayed two *Rakat* Nafl near Maqami Ibrahim. Then he came to Zamzam and said if Banu Abdul Muttalib would not have the control of it he would have taken a full bucket of Zamzam. Then Abbas brought out a bucket of water. The Prophet drank from that and made *wudu* as well. The Muslims were taking his used water, putting it on their dress and bodies. The Mushrikeen were saying,

"We have never seen any king or kingdom like this."

THE PROPHET MOHAMMAD INSIDE KABAH

The Prophet then called Uthman Ibni Talha and asked him for the key of "Kaba". He opened the door and the prophet entered to the house of Allah. He saw images of Ibrahim and Ismail on the walls and auguries and omens drawn with arrows. He said,

> *"May these people perish; Ibrahim and Ismail have never done this practice."*

He saw some other images there also and ordered them to be erased.

He took Osamah and Bilal with him and entered the Kaba. He faced the wall opposite to the door of the Kaba. He was standing three yards from the wall with two pillars to his right side, one pillar to his left side, and three on his back, and prayed two *Rakat* according to Bilal, and this is also narrated by Ahmad and Bukhari. And Bilal said this when Ibni Umar asked him, while Ibni Abbas says that the Prophet did not pray there but said Takbeer only. Osamah also says,

> *"I didn't see him that he prayed there."*

Now here are two narration one is affirmative and the second one is negative, then the affirmative one is given priority specially in practices and Ikhbar according to Abu Hanifa, Malik, and Ahmad. Here the Hadith of Ibni Umar says that the Prophet did pray inside the Kaba. But the Hanafites and Shafiites said that praying inside Kaba is allowed, maybe a Fard prayer or a Nafl one, while the Malakites and Hambalites did not allow Fard prayer inside Kaba. As for as the saying of Osamah is concerned so he says, I didn't see him praying. So it may be that Bilal entered along with the Prophet and Osamah entered later on.

THE PROPHET'S ADDRESS

The Prophet then addressed the people from the door of Kaba and said,

> There is no god but Allah alone who has no associate. He made his promise true and helped his slave. He defeated all the allies alone. Beware! Every type of pride, wealth, and blood is under my feet (means gone and demolished). Except the *Sadanah* [the key to the house of Allah] and the *Siqayah* [distribution of Zamzam], which means these two will remain in the hands of those it was in before. O Quraish! Allah has demolished your pride of ignorance and your boasting about your forefathers [lineage].

Then he recited,

> *"O mankind! Indeed we have created you from one man and one woman [Adam and Eve or your own father and mother are also one] and we made you tribes and sub-tribes so you may know one another. Indeed the most honorable of you with Allah is the most pious of you. Verily Allah is all knowing well acquainted." (49:13)*

The Prophet then sat in the vicinity of Bait Ullah. Ali was holding the key to the house of Allah asking the Prophet to give the *Hijabah* also to Banu Abdul Muttalib like *Siqayah*. In another narration it is said that Abbas said this. The Prophet said,

"Where is Uthman Ibni Talha al Hajabi?"

He came. The Prophet gave him the key and said,

> "Keep it forever. Allah has made you people the door keeper of his house so eat whatever you will get of it in a good way."

Then he ordered Bilal to go to the rooftop of Bait Ullah and give *azan*. When Bilal was giving *azan*, Abu Sufyan, Harith Ibni Hisham and Attab Ibni Aseed were sitting in the vicinity.

Attab said,

> "Allah saved the honor of Aseed,"

Referring to his father, that he didn't hear this *azan*. Harith said,

> "By God, if I had known that this Deen is right, I would have accepted it."

Abu Sufyan said,

> "I don't want to say anything. Because if I do"

And here he gestured to some pebbles on the ground—

> "These very pebbles will take my words to the Prophet."

Then the Prophet came to them and told everyone what he said. So Attab and Harith both said,

> "We testify that you are the messenger of Allah as nobody else was there when we said what we said."

The Prophet then went to the house of his cousin, the sister of Ali Ummi Hani. There he bathed and he prayed eight *Rakat*. The Hanafites call it *Salat – Ul – Duha* and that is a recommended prayer, while other scholars call it *Salat Ul–Fath*. And we say that before this when the Prophet entered the house of Allah, he prayed two *Rakat* there and then another two *Rakat* outside so that was *Salat – Ul – Fath* or *Salat – Ul – Shukr*.

When the Prophet was entering Makkah, this Ummi Hani called on him,

> *"O the messenger of Allah! I have sheltered two persons from my in-laws but my brother Ali is standing on my door with his sword in hand saying that I am going to kill them."*

So, the Prophet said,

> *"We shelter whom you have sheltered."*

And thus, Ali came back. These two were Harith-Ibni Hisham Makhzoomi, and Zubair Ibni Umayyah al Makhzoomi or Abdullah Ibni Abi Rabee'a. This means that shelter by a Muslim woman in battle is also accepted, as Islam is not eager for killing.

GENERAL AMNESTY ANNOUNCED

The Prophet in his address asked,

> *"Quraish, what do you think I am going to do with you?"*

They said,

> *"You are our noble brother and nephew so we expect of you only good,"*

So, he said to them and recited what Yusuf had said to his brothers.

> *"No reproach on you this day. Go, you are free."* (12:92)

THE WANTED PEOPLE

After announcing the general amnesty, the Prophet exempted a few people and declared that wherever they are found, they may be killed, because they had either committed war crimes or they were wanted for murder or they had denounced Islam. They are:

ABDULLAH IBNI ABI SARAH AL AAMIR

He was the foster brother of Uthman Ibni Affan. He accepted Islam but then denounced it and he was speaking out against the Prophet. Uthman hid him somewhere until he could find him a way to get him pardoned. So, when the situation had cooled a bit, he brought him to the Prophet and requested to pardon him and to accept his Bai'at. The Prophet turned his face from them more than once and ignored the request at first, but eventually he accepted. Abdullah Ibni Abi Sarah repented from his apostasy and took "Shahadah". Then he became an exemplary Muslim in obedience, loyalty, practicing accordingly and bravery. He made a *Dua*:

> "O Allah! If you have accepted my repentance then make my last action and deed the one you like the most."

He died in Jerusalem in *sajdah* during *Fajr* prayer.

Note: Amr Ibn Ul Aas is the one who conquered Misr (Egypt) and then Abdullah Ibni Abi Sarah is the one who conquered a major part of Africa.

ABDULLAH IBNI KHATAL

His name was Abdul Uzza. He came to Madina. The Prophet changed his name to Abdullah. The Prophet sent him as a collector of *zakat* to some areas. He also gave him an Ansari man to serve him. On their way they stopped for rest. He ordered the Ansari to slaughter a goat and cook it, but Ansari was also tired so he fell asleep. When Abdullah woke up, he saw that Ansari was sleeping and had not made the food so he killed him, denounced Islam, and went back to Makkah. He was a poet so he started saying bad about the Prophet. He had two slave girls. He was reciting his poetry to them and they were singing that.

This time when the Prophet was coming to Makkah, Abdullah mounted his horse with a spear in his hand saying,

"I will never allow Mohammad to enter Makkah by force,"

But when he saw the Muslim army, he lost his courage and rushed to the *Ghilaf* (cover) of the Kaba for shelter as announced by the Prophet. The Prophet saw him after *Tawaf*, so he ordered Sahabah to kill him.

FARTANA

QAREEBAH OR FAREEBAH

These were those two singing girls of Abdullah Ibni Khatal. In some narratives their names are mentioned as Arnab and Ummi Sa'd. Fartanah was pardoned but Qareebah was killed.

IKRAMAH IBNI ABU JAHL

He was an arch enemy of the Prophet, like his father. He was in Khandamah and attacked Khalid Ibn Ul Waleed. When he came to know that the Prophet declared him as wanted, he fled, thinking to throw himself in a well or starve himself. Some historians say that he was to go to the Roman Empire and to seek political asylum. His wife Ummi Hakeem, who was the cousin of Harith Ibni Hisham, accepted Islam and asked the Prophet a pardon for Ikramah. And the Prophet offered it to him if he would accept Islam. So, she after that went to find him. he accepted Islam and became a very good Muslim and a fighter as well. He was martyred in the battle of Yarmouk in the time of Umar Ibn Ul Khattab.

HUWAIRITH IBNI NAQEEZ

HABBAR IBNUL ASWAD

Huwairith was reciting bad poetry cursing the Prophet. He and Habbar both goaded the she-camel of Zainab, the daughter of the Prophet into a run when she was going to Madina. She fell off and as she was pregnant at that time, she suffered a stillbirth. She got a chronic disease from that and later on died of it. The Prophet declared Huwairith and Habbar to be killed, wherever they were. So, Ali found Huwairith and killed him, while Habbar went to hiding and after some time he came to the Prophet admitted his crime and asked forgiveness, saying Kalimah of Tawheed. The Prophet forgave him.

MIQYAS IBNI DUBABAH

Miqyas had accepted Islam but later on he killed an Ansari as Miqyas's brother was mistakenly killed by the hands of this Ansari in Ghazwa – I - Ziqirad as the Ansari thought he was an enemy. Miqyas had received the blood money also but he had still killed Ansari. He denounced Islam and fled to Makkah so the Prophet declared that he should be killed wherever someone found him, so Numailah Ibni Abdullah Allaithi from his own tribe killed him.

HARITH IBNI HISHAM

He was from Bani Makhzoom and was related to the in-laws of Ummi Hani the cousin of the Prophet. He was also the brother of Abu Jahl. He was declared as wanted but Ummi Hani sheltered him and asked the Prophet to forgive him and he did. Then he accepted Islam.

ZUBAIR IBNI UMAYYAH

He was also from the declared criminals but he was also sheltered by Ummi Hani as he was from her in-laws and the Prophet endorsed her shelter as we have mentioned before. He also accepted Islam.

KA'B IBNI ZUHAIR

This family was known for poetry and their poetry is considered "Deewan – Ul - Arab," which is the authenticity of Arabic language and literature. Kab's father Zuhair, Kab's brother Buhair, Kab's son Oqbah and Oqbah's son Awwam all were poets. Buhair Ibni Zuhair accepted Islam and wrote to his brother Ka'b about it as well but Ka'b reproached him for deserting the religion of his forefathers. As Ka'b cursed the Prophet and Islam in his verses so the Prophet declared him "Mubah Ud Dam," meaning he should be killed, no questions asked. So, he ran away and hid.

When the Prophet returned to Madina, Ka'b also came there praising the Prophet in his verses. Of that there is a verse,

"Indeed the messenger is a light wherefrom the light is to be taken and he is an Indian sword of the swords of Allah out of its case."

The Prophet gave him his cloak. He accepted Islam. Muawiya offered him 10,000 dirhams for that cloak but Ka'b refused. When Ka'b died, his family gave it to Muawiya for 20,000. He used to put it on his shoulders at Eid and other special occasions. Other Khulafa after him were also doing the same. But when the Tatars attacked the Muslim area, there the cloak was lost.

SAFWAN IBNI UMAYYAH

Safwan was an archenemy of the Prophet. He spared no opportunity to harm the Prophet. He was also declared "Mubah Ud-Dam". When he heard that he said,

"I should go and drown myself somewhere."

His cousin Omair Ibni Wahab al Jumahi came to the Prophet and asked the Prophet to forgive Safwan because he is the chief of his tribe and is planning to drown himself. The Prophet said,

"I have pardoned him so go and bring him."

He said,

"He is afraid and very smart as well. He will not believe me, so please give me a sign to assure him that the Prophet has forgiven you."

The Prophet gave him the turban he was wearing when he entered Makkah. When Omair went after Safwan, he had already boarded a ship in the sea. Omair told him to disembark.

> "I have got you pardoned by the Prophet,"

He said,

Safwan didn't believe it at first, so Omair showed him the turban of the Prophet as a proof of the pardon. Now he believed it was not a trick by Omair so he came with him to the Prophet and asked him to give him a time of two months to think about Islam. The Prophet gave him four months.

When the Prophet was leaving for Hawazin mission he asked Safwan to give him the armor coats he had and also 40,000 dirhams. He asked if it an extortion. The Prophet said it was merely a loan. So Safwan gave the Prophet what he asked for. He also went with the Prophet. In this mission the Prophet got lot of spoils. The Prophet separated for him one hundred camel three times. He was looking at that eagerly. The Prophet said,

> "Do you like all this?"

He said,

> "I love it."

The Prophet said,

> "Then it is yours."

He jumped and said,

> "By God! Kings do not give gifts like this. You are truly the messenger of Allah,"

and thus, he took *Shahadah*.

WAHSHI IBNI HARB

We have related his story in the battle of Uhud that how he was trained by his masters with a promise and the reward of freedom if he would kill Hamzah and mutilate his body. That was a war crime and general amnesty is not applied to war criminals so he was also declared "Mubah Ud Dam". He fled to Taif but when the people of Taif later came to the Prophet and accepted Islam, he also came with them and accepted Islam. The dialogue he did with the Prophet at that time, we have written about in the battle of Uhud.

He says,

> *"After accepting Islam, I was looking for an opportunity to do as much good as the bad I did in Uhud to atone for that heinous crime of mine."*

So, in the time of Abu Bakr, he joined the battle of Banu Hanifa with the intention to kill Musailamah al Kazzab and he did it with his spear as he was a trained archer and sniper. In the field he was shouting with joy,

> *"Maybe this will be an atonement for that crime of mine."*

SARAH

This lady was a slave of Banu Hashim at Makkah who came to Madina and asked the Prophet for help and he asked Banu Hashim to help her and they did. Later on, Hatib gave her a letter in the name of the Quraish. She used to sing the poetry of Abdullah Ibni Khatal. The Prophet declared her "Mubah Ud Dam" as well, but he was asked by some people to forgive her and he did. She accepted Islam and became a very good Muslim. She died in the time of Abu Bakr.

HIND BINT-I-OTBAH

She was the wife of Abu Sufyan and the mother of Muawiya and also of Ummi Habiba. She had hired Wahshi Ibni Harb to kill Hamzah and dismember his body. This is a war crime so she was declared "Mubah Ud Dam". She entered the same line of women who were taking *Shahadah* and giving Bai'at of Islam. When the Prophet said to the women to say I will never commit *zina* (adultery/ fornication), she said,

> "A noble woman can think of it."

The Prophet recognized her from her voice, so he said,

> "Hind!"

she said,

> "Yes, it is I."

But she had already said in Bai'at that she believed in the oneness of Allah and shall not make partners with him and thus she had saved herself. Then when the Prophet said to them to say that they shall not kill anyone then she recalled her mind and said,

> "We delivered and you people killed them."

As her son Hanzalah was killed in Badr. When the Prophet asked them to say they would not commit theft, she withdrew her hand from the fabric or rope they were holding for Bai'at and said,

> "I cannot give this word as my husband is a miser at home so sometimes, I take his money secretly."

The Prophet said,

> "Just give the Bai'at and take his money for your needs and your children's needs."

Then she completed her Bai'at and became Muslim. She was a smart and brave lady. She joined the battle of Yarmouk in the time of Umar and she encouraged and inspired Muslims in the battlefield.

All these who were declared "Mubah Ud Dam" were fifteen people but only four of them were killed: three men, Ibni Khatal, Huwairith, and Miqyas; and one woman, Qareebah. Two sons of Abu Lahab, Utbah and Mutab, had also gone underground because of fear but later on they came and accepted Islam. Suhail Ibni Amr also had gone underground but later on he came and met the Prophet at Ji'irranah, a well between Makkah and Taif, and accepted Islam.

The Prophet was in a tent in Hajun. He was asked whether he will go to stay in his own house in Makkah. He said,

> "Has Aqeel [his cousin and the brother of Ali] left for us any place to live therein?"

which means that he had sold all these houses.

Regarding the conquest of Makkah Shafi and Ahmad said, it was conquered without a battle, while Abu Hanifa said there was battle because the Prophet was very much ready to fight and as we said, a battle happened there in Khandamah area when Khalid got attacked. But yes, the Prophet himself did not involve himself in battle. Also, he told Sahabah,

> "We are in Haram and Allah has allowed me for a while if a fight is needed but you people may not start it. But if you are attacked, then fight,"

and that is what happened to Khalid.

THE IDOLS AND STATUES

When the Prophet entered into the vicinity of Bait Ullah, there were three hundred sixty statues the people worshipped. The Prophet pointed at them one by one with his stick and they fell down. He was reciting at that time,

> "The truth has come and the falsehood is vanished. Verily falsehood is bound to vanish." (71:81)

Also, it was announced by the Prophet that everyone may throw away the statue they have at home and they did it. Hind threw her statue to the ground, giving it kicks and saying,

> "Until today we were wallowing in deception because of you."

Hind also said to the Prophet,

> "You people were the utmost lowest to me but now you are the utmost honored people to me."

These idols were falling down, a worshipper from Banu Sulaim said a few verses,

> "The idols told me to come to us, I said no as Allah and Islam reject you. If I had not seen Mohammad and his army on the day of conquest when the idols were still being broken, I would have seen the light of Allah spreading and the darkness has covered the face of the shirkers."

The Prophet asked him his name and he said it was Ghadi Ibni Zalim. The Prophet said,

> "Now your name is Rashid Ibni Abdullah."

Now Ansar was concerned that now that the Prophet had recaptured his city, he might stay here, but when the Prophet came to know this concern, he said to them, "My life and death both are with you people." The Prophet stayed in Makkah for nineteen days but he was praying Qasr prayer as he was planning to go toward Hawazin. In these days he was teaching them *Deen*.

ABU QUHAFAH ACCEPTED ISLAM

Abu Bakr's father Abu Quhafah was a blind old man. Abu Bakr brought him to the Prophet. The Prophet said,

"I would have gone to him."

Abu Bakr said,

"But he had to come."

The Prophet made him sit in front of him, touched his chest with his hand and said,

"Accept Islam,"

So, he did. The Prophet congratulated Abu Bakr for the Islam of his father. He died in the time of Umar. At that time, he was ninety-nine years old.

MISSIONS AFTER THE CONQUEST OF MAKKAH

MISSION OF KHALID

On the 25th day of Ramadan, The Prophet sent Khalid Ibn Ul Waleed in thirty horsemen to demolish Uzza, the big deity of the Quraish and the Banu Kinanah. The Banu Shaiban were its custodians. This deity was a date palm tree in a garden. People used to come to it, worshipping it and asking their needs from it. They used to do its *tawaf* also. Khalid went there, cut the tree, and came back. The Prophet asked him,

> *"Have you seen anything there?"*

He said, I didn't see anything there.

The Prophet said,

> *"Then you have not destroyed the actual deity- you only cut down the tree."*

So, he went back with his sword in his hand. He saw there a black woman having disheveled hair. Khalid hit her and cut her in two. The custodian shouted at Khalid. When he came back, The Prophet told him,

> *"This was Uzza and she totally had given up hope that she would be worshipped again."*

MISSION OF AMR IBNUL AAS

In the same month of Ramadan, the Prophet sent Amr Ibn Ul Aas to the "Suwa" idol. That was the idol of Huzail tribe, three miles from Makkah. This was a date-palm grove in Rabat Village. The Banu Lahyan tribe was its custodian. When Amr arrived there, a custodian asked him,

> *"What you want to do?"*

He said,

"I want to demolish this idol."

He said,

"But you will be stopped."

Amr said,

"Woe unto you, still you think this is God?"

So, he broke it and then asked the custodian,

"What you want to do now?"

He said,

"I believe in Allah and His Messenger."

Amr said to his fellows,

"Check the room, see what is there,"

but they couldn't find anything there.

IDOL MANAT

This was one of the famous, most respected god of Arabia. This was the idol of Aus, Khazraj, and Anan tribes. The Arabs used to do its Hajj as well. The Prophet sent Sa'd Ibni Zaid Al-Ash'hali with twenty horsemen. When they arrived, the custodian asked him,

"What is your mission?"

He said,

"To demolish Manat."

When Sa'd was destroying it, a naked black woman came in front of him crying and mourning. Sa'd cut her first and then he demolished the idol. This is the story narrated in "Mawahib" and in "Tabaqat", but Ibni Hisham says the mission was led by Ali, so maybe both of them were there in the mission and one of them was the viceroy.

This Sa'd Ibni Zaid is the one to whom The Prophet had given some of the captives of Banu Quraizah to sell them in the Bazar of Najd and to buy horses and weapons with the money.

KHALID TOWARDS BANU JUZAIMAH

In Shawwal-Ul-Mukarram in the 8th year, the Prophet sent Khalid with 300 Sahabah from Muhajireen, Ansar, and Banu Sulaim to call Banu Juzaimah to Islam. The Banu Juzaimah were living one day from Makkah towards Yalamlam. Khalid called them to Islam, so, they started saying, "Sabana, Sabana" instead of "Aslamna," which means "We became *Sabi*," which were actually those who had left their Divine *Deen* and started worshipping stars. But later on, in the time of Jahiliya, a man from Makkah, named Abu Kabshah was not in favor of worshipping the idols. He was a trader. He saw some people in Sham worshipping stars, so he thought it was better to worship stars that God had made instead of man-made idols. He brought this idea and called people towards it, but people had been worshipping idols for centuries and it was a part of their culture so they resisted. Later on, Abu Kabsha's name became a title for one who brought a new idea or a new Deen and that's why the Quraish regarding The Prophet used to say "Ibni Abi Kabshah", the son of Abu Kabshah, as they were of the view that he brought a new thing like Abu Kabshah had done. It is also said that Abu Kabshah was from the ancestors of The Prophet on his mother's side and to put someone down they used to attribute him to his mother's side and not to his father's side. And the star worshippers were called *Sabi*. So, people used to call anyone who followed Abu Kabsha's idea at his time *Sabi*. They also referred to someone who accepted Islam, so the term became famous. So, the newcomers to Islam called themselves *Sabi* also, but because they were not aware of the actual concept of *Sabi*, they used to say *Sabatu* or *Sabana*, which means,

"*I [or we] became Sabi,*"

which means one has left one's religion and accepted this new one. That was what the Banu Juzaimah meant when they said *Sabana*, but Khalid took it otherwise, that they refused, so he started killing them or taking them prisoner. It is narrated that the Banu Sulaim killed their prisoners while the Muhajireen and the Ansar did not do that. Ibni Umar refused to kill.

Then, the Prophet sent Ali to pay blood money to the families of all those who had been killed.

The Prophet said,

"*O Allah! I declare immunity from this action of Khalid.*"

He said this twice.

Khalid and Abdur Rahman Ibni Awf also exchanged some hard words with one another. Abdur Rahman said to Khalid,

"*In Islam, you have practiced an action of the time of Jahiliyat.*"

Khalid said,

"*I have taken the revenge of your father.*"

Abdur Rahman said,

"But you have taken the revenge of your uncle Fakih Ibni Mughirah."

The Prophet ordered Khalid to stop the altercation.

"If you will spend gold equal to the weight or volume of Uhud, it cannot be equal to one morning or one evening efforts of these companions of mine."

<u>Note:</u> The Pact of Hudaibiyah opened the paths for Islam to spread in every direction, in some places with *dawah* and in others with *jihad* and with the conquest of Makkah, the whole scene changed and now there was no one to stop Islam from spreading.

THE BATTLE OF HUNAIN

On way to Ta'if from Makkah, there is a valley called Hunain. This battle is called also the battle of Hawazin. There is another valley close to Hunain called Awtas, and that is why sometimes historians also mention this name. This Hawazin tribe was big and strong. They were watching the Prophet to see what he was planning to do. When he was proceeding to Makkah, they were ready to fight but when he conquered Makkah, they decided to step in. All the branches and subtribes of Hawazin except the Kab and the Kilab were part of this plan. These tribes worried that now Mohammad would come for them. The head of the Jashm, tribe Dareed Ibnus Shammah, who was one hundred years old, told them not to fight, but nobody listened to him.

The Hawazin gave their command to a thirty-year-old man, Malik Ibni Awf of Banu Nadr. Dareed asked them,

"Why have you brought your women and children?"

Malik said,

"So no one will run away."

Dareed said,

"If someone wants to run away, nothing can stop him, but when defeat happens then, he will be too low in the eyes of his family."

The Chief of the Thaqeef tribe, Kinanah Ibni Abd Yaleel, was also there and he later accepted Islam.

THE PROPHET MARCHED

The Prophet sent Abu Hadrad Al-Aslami to inquire from inside the Hawazin and he did it. He came back and told the Prophet.

Malik put the horsemen in the front, then he put the women on camels behind them. Then, there were more camels, the goats, and the sheep behind them. He told people,

"When you see that I attacked, follow me as one man."

There were 4,000 Banu Sa'd and Banu Thaqeef, supported by Arabs from their back.

As we mentioned before, 10,000 people came with the Prophet from Madina, but then 2,000 more joined them, along with those who accepted Islam at the conquest of Makkah.

The Prophet departed from Makkah on 6th Shawwal Ul Mukarram. He appointed Attab Ibni Aseed at Makkah and ordered Muaz Ibni Jabal to teach *Deen* to people.

The Prophet asked Safwan Ibni Umayyah for 40,000 dirhams and some armor coats. He got 10,000 dirhams from Abdullah Ibni Rabee'a and borrowed 3,000 spears from his cousin Naufal Ibni Harith. He said to Naufal,

> "These spears will cleave the chests of Mushriks."

At Asr time, a rider came and said,

> "I climbed a hilltop, and I saw that the Hawazin have brought their women, children, and cattle with them."

The Prophet smiled and said,

> "This will be a booty for Muslims."

The Prophet appointed Anan Ibni Abu Marthad as night guard.

On their way towards Hunain, they saw a tree called "Zat Anwat". The Arab used to hang their weapons on it and slaughter cattle which was a kind of *ibadah*, so some people said,

> "We will have a "Zat Anwat" like this."

The Prophet said,

> "By one in whose possession is my soul, you people asked what the Jews asked Musa that make for us a God like as these people have gods [material and physical]. So Musa said, 'You are a people practicing ignorance.'"

The Prophet said,

> "You will ride [follow] the deeds of those who passed. (Tirmizi)"

The Prophet was riding his mule named Duldul. The Army, which was proceeding in front of The Prophet, Khalid was appointed as its commander, till the Prophet arrived in "Ji'irranah."

Malik Ibni Awf said to his people,

> "Mohammad has never faced as fierce a people as he is going to face today. So, you should organize your women and children behind you and then organize yourselves and you have to attack first, as those who attack first get the victory."

The Prophet was wearing two armor coats and one helmet.

Malik Ibni Awf according to the advice of Dareed Ibnus Shammah put his people in hidden points in the valley.

So, when the Prophet, was entering in Hunain Valley on the morning of the 20th day of Shawwal Ul Mukarram, these people attacked them from these hidden points so the Muslims couldn't stay together. Abu Sufyan, who had accepted Islam a few days ago, said that now they could not stop, but can only flee to the Red Sea, and Jibillah or Kaldah Ibni Junaid said, "The magic didn't work today." The Hawazin were expert archers, so, the Muslims were defeated at the very beginning.

THE PROPHET WAS STABLE

In this situation, the Prophet went to the right side and called to the people,

> "Come towards me, I am the Messenger of Allah, Mohammad the son of Abdullah."

Some Sahaba stood still with him, but they were fewer than one hundred people. Abu Bakr, Umar, Uthman, Ali, Abbas, his son Fazl, Uammah Ibni Zaid, Rabee'a Ibn Ul, Harith Ibni Abdul, Muttalib, Abu Sufyan Ibn Ul Harith, Utbah, and Mutab son of Abu Lahab and Aiman

Ibni Ummi Aiman were among these people. Abu Sufyan Ibn Ul Harith was holding the rope of the Prophet's mule and Abbas was holding its saddle so it could not run away.

The disbelievers surrounded the Prophet to frighten him, so he came down off his mule and started saying,

> "I am The Prophet and this is not a lie and I am the son of Abdul Muttalib."

By saying so, he was giving them a message that if you want to do this to me to put me on run or to denounce my prophethood, then, that is undoable. I am The Prophet and you know well that the blood of Abdul Muttalib does not run away.

THE PROPHET MADE A DUA

> "O Allah! Send your help."

He said to Abbas to call people. So, Abbas said, with his louder voice,

> "Where are the companions of the tree?"

Referring to Hudaibiyah, where they had given the Prophet a pledge unto death under the tree. He was reminding them of their pledge and thus when he called them like this, they came back. Then, The Prophet addressed them group by group and tribe by tribe and a face-to-face battle started and he said, now the oven is hot.

Thus, the Mushrikeen tried to run away and the Muslims were capturing them as prisoners. The Prophet picked up some pebbles and sand in his hand and threw it toward the disbelievers and said,

> "May their faces be disfigured."

And thus, as a miracle, a particle touched the face or the eye of everyone and they were captured. Dareed Ibnus Shammah got killed in this Battle. Rabee Ibni Rafee'a Sullami killed him. Khalid suffered a few injuries. The Prophet put his saliva on the wounds and they healed. From Thaqeef, some 70 people got killed.

In the beginning, when the Muslims saw the enemy, they were around four thousand in number, so, the Muslims said, we were three times less than their number in Badr, we defeated them and today we are three times more in number so we shall put them on the run and teach give them a lesson. Now, apparently this was right, but Allah didn't like this boasting because Muslims must look at Allah and not at their number, means and sources. To correct them, Allah caused them a defeat and ran them off the battlefield.

Allah said,

> "Indeed Allah had helped you in many battlefields, and on the day of Hunain when you rejoiced your great number, so it gained you nothing and the earth was straitened for you even if it was vast and you turned back in flight." (9:25)

> "Then, Allah sent down His tranquility on His Messenger and on the believers and he sent down forces you did not see and He punished those who had disbelieved and such is the recompense of the disbelievers." (9:26)

MUSLIMS FOLLOWED THE ENEMY

When the Mushrikeen were defeated, some of them fled towards Makkah and some others towards Ta'if and still others towards the Awtas Valley. The Prophet sent Abu Aamir Al-Ash'ari with a group towards Awtas.

There some fighting happened and ultimately the Mushrikeen were defeated, but Abu Aamir was martyred. Abu Aamir was the uncle of Abu Musa Al-Ash'ari. He was hit by Ala and Awfa, sons of Harith Ibni Jashm. The Prophet then appointed Abu Musa Al-Ash'ari. He was in the same group, when Abu Aamir was in his last moment he said to Abu Musa,

> "Say my Salam to The Prophet and ask him to make Dua for me."

The Prophet then made *Dua* and said,

> "O Allah! Forgive Obaid Abu Aamir. O Allah! Put him on the Day of Judgment over lot of your creatures and humans."

When Abu Musa heard it, he said, and make a *Dua* for me also, so, The Prophet said,

> "O Allah! Forgive Abdullah Ibni Qais's his sin and honor him with a noble entrance on the Day of Judgment."

Abu Musa fought the enemy and defeated them and got booty and captives therefrom. Umar had given the advice to The Prophet to appoint Abu Musa as Amir of that group after the martyrdom of his uncle.

The Prophet sent Rabee'a Ibni Rafiee with another group towards "Nakhleh". There he killed Dareed Ibnus Shammah.

The Prophet had told these groups to gather the booty and captives at Ji'irranah.

THE PROPHET PROCEEDED TOWARDS TA'IF

Malik Ibni Awf had run away with a good number of his army to Ta'if. He repaired and fixed an old fort there and stocked it with enough supplies for almost one year. The Prophet himself followed him. He had sent before himself one thousand people with Khalid there.

On his way to Ta'if, The Prophet saw a fort of Malik so he ordered the Sahabah to demolish it. Then, he proceeded to Ta'if. The Prophet stayed there for fifteen, eighteen, or twenty days while Anas Ibni Malik says he stayed there for forty days, so maybe he is including all the time that the Prophet was traveling to Makkah.

THE PROPHET ESTABLISHED A CATAPULT

As the enemy were there in the fort, so they shot arrows at Muslims and so many Muslims were injured while twelve of them were martyred as well, so, the Muslims came to an elevated place. Later on, a masjid was built there.

The Prophet established a catapult there and the Muslims started throwing big burning rocks at the fort. Under this fire cover, some Muslims succeeded in approaching the fort, but they were hit with fire rods and that catapult also got burnt.

The Prophet ordered the cutting and burning of their grape orchards and burn it, in the hopes that they would surrender, but then, Thaqeef requested The Prophet not to destroy the gardens, so the Prophet left them.

A caller of The Prophet announced that whoever will come out of the fort, would be free and 23 people came down. Among them was Nufay Ibn Ul Harith via a pulley. Pulley is called *Bakrah* in Arabic. So, The Prophet titled him as Abu Bakrah. The Prophet handed over these people to Muslims to take care of them and to teach them *Deen*, so each of them was paired with a Muslim.

As this siege dragged on asked the Prophet, Nawfal Ibni Muawiya for his opinion. He said, the fox is in its burrow; if you stay, you can catch it and if you will leave it, it cannot harm you. Then, The Prophet ordered Umar to announce that we are leaving tomorrow, but when he announced, then, some people said, without *getting* the fort open. So, The Prophet said, then fight. The next day so many people were injured. Then, once again, The Prophet announced that we are leaving tomorrow. This time the people got happy. The Prophet was smiling.

He told them to say,

> *"Going back and returning, worshipping and praising our Lord."*

The people asked The Prophet to curse,

> *"Thaqeef."*

He said,

> *"O Allah! Guide Thaqeef and bring them to me."*

THE BOOTY (SPOILS OF WAR) AND ITS DISTRIBUTION

The details of the booty are given by the historians as under: This is the booty of Hunain and Awtas:

- Prisoners: 6,000 people
- Camels: 24,000 camels
- Sheep and goats: 40,000+

- Silver: 4,000 *Awqiah* (equal to 10,000 tolas)

The Prophet has ordered that this will be in the custody of Masud Ibni Amr Al-Ghifari in Ji'irranah.

Among these captives was Shaima, the foster sister of the Prophet. She was the daughter of Halima, the foster mother of the Prophet. She said to the Prophet,

> "I am your sister."

The Prophet didn't recognize her, so he said,

> "Please give me some kind of proof or sign."

She said,

> "I was carrying you as a baby on my back and you bit me. I still have the scar."

The Prophet said,

> "Yes, I remember that."

Then, The Prophet spread his cloak on the ground for her and bade her sit on it. Before this, when his fostering mother had once come to him, he gave her a lot of respect as well.

The Prophet said to Shaima,

> "Whatever you ask for, you will be given."

Her own people said to her,

> "Go with us and ask for the prisoners to be released."

So, a delegation of 14 people under the leadership of Zuhair Ibni Surad came. Among them was the foster uncle of the Prophet, Abu

Barqan or Abu Qarwan Ibni Abdul Uzza. They accepted Islam. Zuhair said,

> O Messenger of Allah! All these women who are sitting here, they are your aunties and caretakers. They nourished you in your childhood. If we had suckled Harith Ibni Abi Shimr Al-Ghassani (the ruler in Sham) or Noman Ibn Ul Munzir (The ruler of Iraq) and then such a tragedy had befallen us, we would have expected kindness from them, but we do expect more than that from you as you are known for kindness and grace everywhere.

And Abu Qarwan said,

> O Messenger of Allah! Here your sisters and your aunties are sitting. They nourished you in their laps. They suckled you. I saw you sucking. I have never seen such a nice and lovely baby like you, then, I saw you weaning from milk and have not seen such a good weaning baby. Later on, I saw you young and I have not seen any young better than you. You have the perfect virtues and with all that we are your family, so, be kind to us, Allah is and will be kind to you more.

Then he recited two verses:

> "Do us a favor O The Messenger of Allah of your generosity as you are a man we expect from and waiting for.
>
> Do a favor to the women you used to suck (breast fed), when she was filling up your mouth with her milk drops like pearls."

The Prophet said,

> "I waited you people for six days, but when no one showed up then I distributed the captives. Now you may choose one of the two, the captives or the spoils of war."

They said,

> "We ask you for the prisoners."

The Prophet said,

> "Those in the hands of my family I can give it back, but those who I have given to others, I must make a request for them."

So, The Prophet spoke to the people after *Zuhr* prayer:

> "Your brothers have accepted Islam. So, my opinion is to give them their captives back so those who want to do the same for free, he should do that and the one who wants a compensation for that, then, I will compensate him from the first booty we will get."

All the Sahabah gave their prisoners to them. Oyainah Ibni Hisn was a villager of strong character. He had gotten an old lady and at first, he said,

> "I will not do this,"

but later on, he agreed. Likewise, Abbas Ibni Mirdas and Mohsin Ibni Fazarah agreed after some resistance.

Awf Ibni Malik, the chief of Hawazin also came. He accepted Islam. The Prophet gave him all his belongings back and an extra hundred camels.

The Prophet gave his sister, Shaima, a slave by the name of Mak'hul along with another slave girl and a herd of sheep and goats. The Prophet asked for her if she would like to go with the Prophet and stay in Madina, but she said she wanted to stay in her own area.

THE NEWCOMERS TO THE FOLD OF ISLAM

The newcomers to Islam are called "Mu'llafat Ul - Quloob". The Prophet used to give such like people from the booty and from *zakat* so their heart may warm to Islam.

The Prophet gave Abu Sufyan Ibni Harb forty *Awqiah* of silver and 100 camels. He gave the same each to his two sons Muaa'wiyah and Yazid. When The Prophet gave Hakeem Ibni Hizam 100 camels, he asked for another hundred and The Prophet gave them to him. The Prophet gave Nadr Ibni Harith Ibni Kaldah, Aseer Ibni Jaria Ath 'Thaqafi, Harith Ibni Hisham, Safwan Ibni Umayyah, Qais Ibni Adi, Suhail Ibni Amr, Huwaitib Ibni Abdul-Uzza, Aqra Ibni Habis At-Tameemi and Oyainah Ibni Hisn 100 camels each. But when he gave Abbas Ibni Mirdas only forty camels, he became upset and said some slanderous verse. The Prophet said to Ali,

"Cut his tongue."

Ali caught Abbas. When Ali was holding onto him, Abbas thought that Ali would actually cut his tongue, but he gave him 60 more camels and thus brought the number to a hundred like everyone else. Thus, he came to know that "cut his tongue" means to make him happy so he would not use his tongue to disparage the Prophet anymore. The Prophet gave Makhrama Ibni Nawfal, Ala Ibni Haritha, Saeed Ibni Yarboo, Uthman Ibni Wahab, and Hisham Ibni Amr Al-a Miri, 50 camels each. Altogether that makes 14,850 and all this was the one-fifth of the booty which was The Prophet's due right and share according to The Holy Quran.

Then, The Prophet ordered Zaid Ibni Thabit to count the Mujahidin and the goats. Then, He gave every Mujahid four camels and forty goats. Those on infantry side while the cavalry he gave 12 camels and 120 goats each.

Imam Malik, Imam Shafi, and Imam Ahmed said that every horse may be given double of the share of a Mujahid and thus every cavalryman received triple of an infantryman's share. As for the distribution in Khyber, there the number of Mujahideen was 1400, but we mentioned there it was 1600 and 200 horses and that is why the shares were 1800.

But Abu Hanifa said,

> *That Ibni Abbas relates from The Prophet that for a Mujahid on foot is one share and for a horseman are two shares (Ibni Maja). Also, Majma Ibni Jaria says the same (Abu Dawud, Dari Qutri, Ahmad, Bayhaqi, Hakim, Tabrani, and Ibni Abi Shaibah)*

Now these two Ahadith are sayings of the Prophet, while the aforesaid distribution is the practice of the Prophet and saying is preferred as regarding the Prophet's practice, we say that was his discretionary power and special case. In the Hadith of Ibni Abbas there is a narrator, Yaqoob Ibni Majma. He is known as "Mastoor Ul Hal," which mean to Muhaditheen his authenticity or otherwise position is not known, but we say that the Hadith of Majma Ibni Jaria is authentic, so that's why the Hadith of Yaqoob also got the authenticity as its subject is supported by the Hadith of Majma.

Also, it is not looking reasonable that the horse, which is an animal and a tool be given priority over humans.

THE PROPHET AND THE ANSAR

When Ansar said what was given to "Mu'llafat Ul Quloob", maybe you O The Messenger of Allah! Give more attention to your tribe?

The Prophet said,

> *"O the group of Ansar! Have I not found you lost, then Allah guided you through me, and you were disputing among yourselves then Allah joined you to one another through me; and you were poor, then Allah made you rich through me?"*

With every sentence of The Prophet, the Ansar used to say,

> *"Yes the favor of Allah and His Messenger to us is more than that."*

The Prophet said,

> *"Why you do not answer me?"*

They said,

> *"But what can we say?"*

The Prophet said, you could have said,

> *"You come to us as a belied one, but we believed in you. You came to us unaided so we helped you. You came to us driven out so we provided you resort and you came to us source less so we sympathized you."*

Then the Prophet said,

> *"I showed kindness to these newcomers to attract them furthermore to Islam so you O Ansar! Don't you like*

that the people will take camels and goats and you will take the Messenger of Allah with you?"

To console them more he said,

"If the immigration had not been there I would have liked to be one of the Ansar. And if the people will enter one valley and the Ansar to another one, Then I will enter to the valley the Ansar entered."

They broke down in tears and said,

"We are happy to have the prophet of Allah with us."

Then he made a *Dua*,

"O Allah! Have your mercy on Ansar, have your mercy to their children and have your mercy on the children of their children."

THE UMRAH

After distribution of the spoils the Prophet put on Ihram for Umrah from Ji'irranah.

He appointed Attab Ibni Aseed as Amir of Makkah and then he left for Madina and arrived there on 24th of "Dhul Qadah" in the 8th year.

THE MISSION OF TUFAIL IBNI AMR ADDAUSI

When the Prophet was leaving for Ta'if, he sent Tufail Ibni Amr Addausi towards Zul Kaffain, a wooden idol made by Amr Ibni Humamah Addausi, to destroy it. He told him to get the support of his people from the Daus tribe, and after the mission is completed, to join him in Ta'if. He went and lit a fire in the belly of that idol. At that time, he was saying this verse,

> "O Zul Kaffain! I am not of your worshippers. Our birth was before your birth. I have lit a fire in your heart."

After that he joined the Prophet along with 400 people.

THE MISSION OF QAIS IBNI SA'D

In *Yemen* there is a tribe by the name of *"Sudaa."* Hamawi said, *Sudaa* is the name of a valley there. So it may be that valley is named after the name of this tribe. The Prophet sent *Qais Ibni Sa'd* to fight this tribe. He gave him an army of 400 people. *Ziyad Ibni Harith As Sudaa'e* When heard about this mission, he came to The Prophet and asked him about the purpose of the mission. The Prophet told him it was for Islam. He said,

> "Then just ask the army to come back and I will bring these people to you."

The Prophet said to him,

> 'Then just go and tell the army to come back."

He said,

> "But my mount is too tired."

So, the Prophet sent another person and thus the army came back.

Then fifteen days later, Ziyad brought all his people and they accepted Islam.

The Prophet said to him,

> *"You are the respected person in your people, but actually Allah guided them."*

Then he said,

> *"But please do not appoint me Amir."*

The Prophet said,

> *"To be an Amir is not bad for a believer,"*

and he changed his mind.

Then the Prophet ordered him to give *azan*. This was Fajr time so he gave *azan*. Then at Jama'at time, Bilal got ready to give *Iqamah*, but The Prophet told him, as Sudaa'e has given *azan*, so, let him give the *Iqamah*.

Note: It is all right for one person to give *azan* and another one the *Iqamah*, but the recommended practice is that one person should give both.

THE MISSION OF OYAINAH IBNI HISN

The Prophet gave 50 horsemen to Oyainah Ibni Hisn. All were Arab, but there was no one from Muhajireen or Ansar. The Prophet sent them to Banu Tameem. They traveled at night and went underground during the day as a strategy to attack them by surprise. The Banu

Tameem were grazing the cattle in a desert when Oyainah attacked them. They ran away but he caught 11 men, 21 women, and 30 children and brought them to Madina. The Prophet put these captives in the house of Ramlah Bint Ul Haritha. Then 10 elites from the Banu Tameem came to the Prophet and it is also said that there were 70 or 80 people who came so maybe they were under the leadership of these 10 elites. When the children and women saw them, they cried.

These people were not well-mannered so they started calling to the Prophet from behind the apartments,

"O Mohammad! Come out!"

Allah said,

"Verily Those who call you from behind the dwellings, most of them do not understand. And if they had shown patience till you come out to them, it would have been better for them. And Allah is Oft-Forgiving, Most Merciful." (49:4,5)

The story of this mission is as follows: Banu Ka'b Ibni Khuza'a accepted Islam. Then, The Prophet sent Bishr Ibni Sufyan Al-Adawi Al Kalbi to them to collect Zakat therefrom. This tribe was a partner of the Banu Tameem, sharing a water well with them. The Banu Tameem asked Banu Ka'b,

"Why are you giving him this?"

They brought out their weapons and swore that they would never allow a single camel to go to Mohammad. They also stopped Bishr from taking anything. Banu Ka'b even told them,

"This is not an extortion, but we have accepted Islam and this is worship and we are bound to do that,"

but the Banu Tameem took a stand. Bishr came Back and told the Prophet what had happened. So, the Prophet sent this platoon under the leadership of Oyainah.

Now when the Prophet came out, they rushed to him in an uncultured way. The Prophet stood up close to them and started *Zuhr* prayer. Then he sat with them in the yard of the Masjid. He started to talk to them. They brought forth their orator, Attar Ibni Hajib. He started boasting and bragging. The Prophet brought forth his Sahabi, Thabit Ibni Qais Ibni Shammas. He had a commanding voice and was a poetic orator. He answered their orator. Then, they brought forth their other orator, Zabarqan Ibni Badr. Hassan Ibni Thabit answered him and they became speechless. Then their leader, Aqra Ibni Habis said,

> *"Your orator Is far better than ours and your poet is far better as well. Also, their voices are excellent,"*

So, they accepted Islam. The Prophet gave them their prisoners back. He also gave them gifts.

Note: Aqra Ibni Habis accepted Islam in Hunain as we have mentioned.

THE MISSION OF WALEED IBNI OQBAH

Banu Mustalaq had accepted Islam. The Prophet sent to them Waleed Ibni Oqbah to collect *zakat* from him. The family of Waleed and Banu Mustalaq had feud and enmity in the time of *Jahiliya* (ignorance). When they got the news that the collector of the Prophet was coming, 20 people came to welcome Waleed, along with the goats and sheep they were to give as *zakat*. And as they used to keep their swords with them as a part of their culture, so, when Waleed saw them that they are coming towards him, then because of the feud during Jahiliyat time, he thought that maybe they were coming to kill him. Therefore, he made a U-turn and went back to Madina and informed the Prophet. Now, to kill an ambassador of The Prophet is an apostasy and treason so The Prophet arranged an army under the leadership of Khalid Ibn Ul Waleed and sent it towards them. He stayed outside their area and sent a few people to inquire about them. When they came back, they told Khalid that they are Muslims as they were praying in their Masjid. In the morning, they also heard the *azan* from their Masajid so these people now planned to go back. In a narration, it is said that when these people of the Banu Mustalaq waited for the collector of the people but they didn't see him, then, they themselves planned to take the *zakat* to Madina. On their way they met this army of Khalid. They asked Khalid,

> *"Where are you going with your army?"*

He said,

> *"Towards you people."*

They said,

> *"But why?"*

Khalid told him the whole story.

They said,

> *"But we have not seen any collector or representative and that's why we are coming to you."*

So, they came with Khalid to Madina. The prophet asked the chief Harith Ibni Zarar (who was the father of Sayyidah Jawaria),

> *"Have you refused to pay zakat and plot to kill my collector?"*

He said,

> *"By Allah! We have not seen any collector."*

They spoke with The Prophet from Zuhr to Asr. When the *azan* for Asr was done, at that Time this verse came to The Prophet:

> *"O you, who believed! If there came to you a Fasiq [wrong doer] with a news, then inquire [about the news] lest you should harm people in ignorance and then you will become ashamed of [reproaching yourselves]." (49:6)*

The aforementioned Waleed was the brother of Uthman Ibni Affan from Mother's side. He and his brother Khalid both accepted Islam at the time of the conquest of Makkah. Waleed was a very good poet and was very generous man, but here he misunderstood what he saw of Banu Mustalaq and this misconception was because of that feud in the time of ignorance, and he is called *Fasiq* in the "Ayah" not because of that he had knowingly done some wrong but as a misconception.

In the time of Uthman, he was the governor at Kufa. Once he had taken wine and led the Fajr prayer 4 *Rakat* in the time of Uthman. The people of Kufa complained to Uthman and Waleed admitted so Uthman gave him the *Hudd* [punishment] and deposed him.

THE MISSION OF QUTBAH IBNI AAMIR

In the month of Safar during the 9th year, the Prophet sent Utbah Ibni Aamir to Tabalah, a city in "Tihamah" in Yemen with 20 people. These 20 people had ten camels so they were taking turns riding them. They caught one man in the area and interrogated him, but he was so frightened he couldn't say anything so they killed him. Then they waited until the people in the city slept. Then as the Prophet directed them, they attacked the city from all around. A few people from both sides were injured. Qutbah killed many of the enemies and he captured their women, goats, and camels. When he left for Madina, the people came after him but suddenly a flood flowed between those people and Qutbah, so, he came safe. From that booty after Khums. (1/5 of the treasury) every Mujahid Received either four camels or 40 goats, 10 goats for one camel.

THE MISSION OF ZAHHAK IBNI SUFYAN

In the month of Rabee-Ul-Awwal during the 9th year, the Prophet sent Zahhak Ibni Sufyan, Osaid Ibni Salamah, and some others to Qarta to call them to Islam. They met with in Zajlawah, but the people there refused so a fight happened. The father of Osaid, named Salamah, was riding his horse in a pool of water. Osaid asked him nicely to accept Islam. Instead of accepting he started cursing Islam, so, Osaid hit his horse's legs and the horse fell down. Salamah erected his lance in the pool and stood there with that. Another Muslim went ahead and killed him.

THE MISSION OF ALQAMAH

In Rabee – Ul - Aakhir of the 9th year, the Prophet came to know that the people of Jeddah had convinced Ahbash to join them in attacking Makkah. So, the prophet gave 300 horsemen to Alqama Ibni Mujaazzaz Al- Mudlaji to counter them. They arrived on the island. The river was flowing towards the enemy so they ran away. After that some Muslims wanted to go back to Madina. So, Alqama Ibni Mujaazzaz appointed Abdullah Ibni Huzafah As-Sahami as their Amir. He was a jolly man. On their way back when they were taking a rest and they lit a fire to warm themselves and to cook, he said to his fellows,

> "Am I not your Amir?"

They said,

> "Yes, you are."

He said,

> "Will you not follow my every order?"

They said,

> "Yes, we are bound to."

He said,

> "So jump in the fire."

Some of them got ready to do that. Abdullah said,

> "I was only joking."

These people then told this to the Prophet, so he said that obedience is required for lawful things so when there is an order for such a thing which is not allowed then there is no obedience necessary.

This Abdullah was from Muhajireen and joined at Badr. He died in Egypt in the time of Uthman while Alqama was sent by Umar with a group to Abyssinia and they all died there.

SARIYYAH OF ALI TO "QALS"

Qals was the name of an idol in Najd. The Banu Tai tribe used to worship it. In Rabee-Ul-Awwal year 9th, The Prophet gave a platoon of 150 people from Ansar to Ali Ibni Abi Talib. They had 100 camels and 50 horses with them. Ali was carrying one big black flag and one small white flag with him. He attacked in the morning and destroyed the idol and captured some people along with some cattle and some silver. Among these captives there was Safanah, the daughter of Hatim – at - Taa'i. Her brother Adi fled to Sham. Ali received Qals' treasure: three swords named Resub, Makhzum, and Saif Yamani, and three armor-coats as well. He appointed Abu Qatada as a guard on the prisoners and Abdullah Ibni Attik on the cattle.

When they arrived Rakak, a place there, they distributed the booty but kept the three swords for The Prophet. They kept the 1/5 of the booty and also what they got from the Banu Tai.

When they arrived in Madina along with the captives, Safanah said to the Prophet that her father had died and her guardian disappeared.

> *"And I am too old to render any service so do me a favor."*

The Prophet asked her,

> *"Who was your father?"*

She said,

> *"Hatim".*

The Prophet said,

> *"Hatim At-Taa'i?"*

She said,

> *"Yes."*

Now Hatim was a generous and hospitable man in the time of ignorance known for his generosity not only in Arabia, but all over the world and his name was a symbol and a title for generosity. The Prophet asked her,

> "And who was your guardian?" She said, "Adi Ibni Hatim."

The Prophet said,

> "The one who fled from Allah and His messenger."

Then, the Prophet went. The next day and the day after the same like dialogue took place so the Prophet did her a favor. He ordered Ali to arrange a mount and supplies for her. Then this lady went after her brother Adi Ibni Hatim and told him not to run away from this great man.

> "By God!"

She said,

> "He did what your generous father even never did. So go to him maybe because of fear or because of hope. Think! If he is a Prophet then the sooner you join Him is better and if he is a king still a man like you from a dignified family will never be a deprived one there."

So, Adi came and accepted Islam.

Imam Bukhari narrated from Adi:

> I was sitting at that time with the Prophet, A man came and complained of poverty and hunger. Then another one came and complained of robbers and robbery in his area. The Prophet asked me you are aware of Heerah, an area in Sham? If you were still alive, you would see that a woman could travel from there to Makkah with

> *no fear of anyone in anything except Allah; and if you were alive then you would see that you the Muslims will get the treasures of Kisra, the Persian emperor; and if you will be alive still then you would see that someone will be offering a handful of gold or silver as zakat but nobody would hold out his hand to accept it.*

In the end of this Hadith, Adi said when he was relating it,

> *"I saw women traveling alone from Heerah with no fear for their honor or their wealth, and I was among those who took over the treasures of Kisra in the time of Uthman. As for the third prophecy, maybe you people will see it."*

The scholars said the first thing was there in the time of Umar, the second one in the time of Uthman and then the third one happened in the time of Umar Ibni Abdul Aziz when no one was accepting *zakat* money as Umar Ibni Abdul Aziz had distributed the treasure among people and everyone had enough.

Besides these missions there were other missions and expeditions as well.

THE PROPHET SENT THESE MISSIONS AS FOLLOWS

1) Yazid Ibn Ul Husain to Aslam and Ghifar.

2) Abbas Ibni Bishr to Sulaim and Muzainah.

3) Rafi Ibni Mukaith to Juhainah

4) Bishr Ibni Sufyan to Banu Ka'b

5) Ibn Ul Lutaibah Al-Azdi to Banu Zubyan

6) He sent Muhajir Ibni Abi Umayyah to San'aa. Aswad al Anasi came to face him.

7) Ziyad Ibni Labeed he sent him to Hadramut Moot.

8) Adi Ibni Hatim to Tai and Banu Asad.

9) Malik Ibni Nuwairah to Banu Adi.

10) Qais Ibni Asim to Banu Sa'd

11) Ala Ibn Ul Hadhrami to Bahrain

12) Ali to Najran

Most of these missions went in the month of Muharram, while a few of them after Muharram.

BATTLE OF TABUK

As we mentioned before, the Amir of Busra Harith Ibni Abi Shemmar-Al-Ghassani killed the ambassador of The Prophet, Harith Ibni Umair Al-Azdi, who was carrying a letter from the Prophet to him, but he killed him when he was staying there in Muta. This was a heinous act in violation of the nearly universal rules and customs of diplomatic immunity. This Amir was a subject of Rome but he and the Romans didn't care due to the pride they had and thus the Battle of Muta happened, where 12 Muslims were martyred. Among them there were Zaid Ibni Haritha, Jafar, and Abdullah Ibni Rawaha, and as the Romans were greater in number, Khalid Ibn Ul Waleed brought the Muslim Army back safely through a strategy he adopted. But as this small number of only 3000 Sahaba strategically faced 100,000 Roman army, so Caesar was worried and his worry increased when the Muslims conquered

Makkah and defeated their enemies in Hunain, Hawazin and Ta'if. So, Caesar was preparing himself after Muta to fight a decisive battle with Muslims. This Battle of Tabuk is also known as Battle of "Osrah" (Distress) as Allah said,

> *"And those Who follow him [The Prophet] in the time of distress." (9:117)*

Tabuk is the name of a valley in between Wadil-Qura and Sham.

This was a hard time as the distance was great, supplies were low, and the weather was very hot. The Muslims used to slaughter a camel and to drink the water in its belly. This mission the Prophet disclosed it when he made the intention to go and did not keep it secret as he used to do for some Mission, like one of Makkah.

THE TENSION

This mission took place during the 9th year in Rajab Al Murajjab and was the last mission led by the Prophet. As the news was coming to Madina that Romans were getting ready for a battle, the situation was very tense. Imam Bukhari narrated from Umar that the wives of the Prophet asked him for certain things, which he did not like, so he had temporarily disconnected himself. Umar says that he and An Ansari agreed for turns that one-day Umar would do some other work and Ansari would join the Prophet, and whatever knowledge or news one received, he would tell the other. One day when Ansari came to Umar saying,

> *"Open the door, open the door!"*

Umar asked,

> *"Has Ghassani attacked?"*

Ansari said,

> "No, I have even bigger news than that, and that is that The Prophet separated himself from his wives."

This means that all of them were concerned about that attack.

Here, the Munafiqeen had given up all their hopes except if the Ghassani king attacked. Later in the book we will talk about Masjid-Darrar, the hypocrites built in Qaba as a conspiracy center for Abu Aamir Ar Rahib, who was an agent of Romans.

The traders came from Sham with the news that Caesar had gathered some 40,000 soldiers joined by, the Lakhm, the Jizam, and other tribes. Their first platoon arrived at Balqa. But the Prophet had decided to keep the positive effects of the conquest before facing the Romans and therefore he ordered the people of Makkah and Arab tribes to be prepared to face the Romans.

DONATION AND CONTRIBUTION

The Prophet used to distribute the booty and spoils of war and *zakat*, as well so in wartime they were making contributions as wars need money. This was a big war with a superpower of the time in a very remote area so the Prophet asked the Sahabah to donate and they did it.

Umar said that on every occasion, Abu Bakr would surpass the rest in generosity so this time I divided all my belongings in half and brought one half of it to the Prophet.

The Prophet asked me.

> *"What did you do?"*

I told him I had brought him half of my belongings. He made *Dua* for me.

Abbas Also donated a lot, as did Talha, Sa'd Ibni Obadah and Mohammad Ibni Maslamah. Asim Ibni Adi brought 90 *Wasaq* of dates.

Abdur Rahman Ibni Awf donated 200 *Awqiah* of silver and 400 *Awqiah* of gold. Uthman brought 200 camel which were ready for Sham on a business trip. He also gave 200 *Awqiah* of silver. Then he gave another 100 camels and 1000 dinars. The Prophet said,

"Nothing will harm Uthman after this day."

Altogether he brought 900 camels, 100 horses, and a large amount of gold and silver. He fulfilled the needs of almost a third of the whole army. Regarding this mission, Allah said as the hypocrites and some weak people were showing their weakness.

"O you who believed! What Is the matter with you, that when you are asked to go forth in the cause of Allah, then, you cling heavily to the earth? Are you pleased with the life of this world rather than the other world? But the enjoyment of the life of this world is too little in comparison to the other one." (9:38)

"If you do not go out, He will punish you with a painful torment and will replace you by another people and you cannot harm him a little even. And Allah has the power on everything." (9:39)

"If you do not help him [the Prophet] [so don't do it as he doesn't need you] as Allah has helped him [at that time] When the disbelievers drove him out the second of the two, when they both were in the cave, when he [the Prophet] was saying to his companion [Abu Bakr], 'Be not grieved! Verily, Allah is with us.' So, Allah sent down his tranquility upon him [Abu Bakr] and

strengthen him with forces [angels] which you saw not and he made the word of those who disbelieved utmost down and the word of Allah is the utmost high. And Allah is All-Mighty, All-Wise." (9:40)

"Go out [in the cause of Allah]. Whether you are light or you are heavy and strive hard with your wealth and yourselves [lives] in the path of Allah. That is better for you if you, but know." (9:41)

"Had it been an easy gain or an easy journey then for sure they would have followed you, but the hardship (of distance) Became too long [difficult] on them and they will swear by Allah. If we only could, For sure we would have gone out with you. They destroy their own selves [by these false oaths]. And Allah knows that they are liars." (9:42)

"May Allah forgive you, why did you grant them leave [you should have not done that] until those who told the truth would have become clear to you and you would have known the liars." (9:43)

Abu Aqeel, an ally of Banu Amr Ibni Awf, did worked all night carrying water on his back and watering the garden of a Jew. He was paid two Saa' dates as his entire wages. He brought one to the Prophet as donation, so the hypocrites mocked his donation. So, Allah said, 9:79,

"Those who taunt at the believers who give charity regarding their charity and on those also who couldn't find but their labor only so they mock at them. Allah will throw back their mocking at them and for them there is a painful torment."

Salim Ibni Omair from Banu Amr Ibni Awf, Harmi Ibni Amr from Banu Waqif, Abdur Rahman Ibni Ka' b from Banu Mazin, Salman Ibni

Sakhar from Banu Mu'alla, Amr Ibni Ghamam from Banu Salamah, Abdullah Ibni Amr al Muzani, Mohammad Ibn Us Samman, Olayya Ibni Zaid, Amr Ibn Ul Hammam Ibn Ul Jamooh, Abdullah Ibn Ul Mughaffal al Muzani Harmi Ibni Abdullah, and Ayad Ibni Saria al Fazari asked the prophet for mounts to join the *Ghazwa*, but the prophet said,

> "We don't have any so they were crying."

Allah said 9:92,

> "Nor [is any blame] on those who came to you to mount them, you said, 'I don't have any mount for you,' they turned back and their eyes were overflowing tears because of grief that they do not find anything they can spend in the path of Allah)."

The prophet was making *Dua* for everyone who gave charity.

THE DEPARTURE

The prophet appointed Mohammad Ibni Maslamah or Siba Ibni Urfuta as Ameer in Madina, while he left Ali in Madina to take care of the prophet's family. The hypocrites started spreading propaganda that the prophet didn't like Ali anymore so he did not take him with him. So, Ali came after the prophet and met him in a place by the name of Jaraf and said,

> "You are leaving me back with the women while the hypocrites say these terrible things."

The prophet said,

> "Why aren't you happy for me like Harun [Aaron] was for Musa [Moses] when he was going to Tur. He left Harun to take care of Bani Israel [the Jews], and you are to me like Harun was to Musa but there is no prophet after me,"

So, he came back to Madina.

When the prophet arrived at Thani Atul Wada, he made a few flags. He gave a big flag to Zubair and a small one to Abu Bakr, the same way he gave the flag of Aws to Osaid Ibni Hudair and the flag of Khazraj to Khabbab Ibn Ul Munzir. Also, he gave flags to different tribes. This army was 30,000 people. As the mounts were few in number, eighteen people used took turns riding one camel. They were eating leaves to conserve their flour so their mouths swelled and they slaughtered a camel to drink the water from its, belly. They came over the valley of Hijr, the valley of the Thamud tribe the people of Saleh whom Allah had destroyed. The prophet said,

> "Drink not from their well, nor make wudu with it. And if you have mixed flour with that water, give it to the camels."

He told them to use water from the well where the she-camel of Saleh used to drink

Imam Bukhari and Imam Muslim narrated from Ibni Umar that the prophet forbade them to enter their houses in the mountain. He himself covered his head there and walked out swiftly. On their way they became short of water so they complained to the Prophet. He made a *Dua* and a cloud came and a lot of rain fell, so they filled up their skin bags.

The prophet said to the Sahabah,

> "Tomorrow you will be passing by a water fountain in Tabuk no one should touch that water until I come,"

But two people touched it (although they were not supposed to). The Prophet came and asked if anyone had touched the water. The two people who had done so, confessed. The Prophet told them what Allah told him. Then the Prophet washed his hands and face and he put that water in the fountain so it gushed forth with a lot of water. The Prophet told Muaz,

> "If you are still alive, you will see a lot of gardens here thanks to this water's irrigation,"

And it happened later on.

The Prophet also told them that tonight a wind will blow so no one may stand up alone. But two men from the Banu Sa'idah stood up at night, one to answer the call of nature and the other one to look for his camel. The first one was choked and lost his senses, and the other one the wind lifted him and threw him over a mountain of the Tai tribe. The prophet then made *Dua* for them both, so the first one came back on his own while the "Tai" people brought the second one back.

In the same way the prophet's she-camel also got lost. There was a man by the name of Zaib Ibni Laseet from the Banu Qanuqa. He was sharing camel carriage with Ammarah Ibni Hazm Ansari. He jeered that Mohammad could tell them the news from heaven but can't find his she camel. The Prophet told Ammarah what Zaid said.

The Prophet also said,

> "When Allah tells me, then I convey the news."

And then he said,

> "My-she camel's rope got stuck in a tree in such and such valley,"

So, some people went there and they brought his she camel. Ammarah came and said to people that the Prophet had told them that someone said this. His brother Amr said that Zaid had said it, so Ammarah jumped on him and beat him, telling him to leave. It is narrated that later on that he repented sincerely.

Abu Zar was riding a lean camel. It was going slowly so he lagged behind. The Sahabah told the Prophet that they were concerned about Abu Zar. The Prophet said,

> "If there is good in him, Allah will bring him and if not, you can get rid of him."

Seeing that his camel could go no farther, Abu Zar left it and started walking. One day from a distance a person was seen walking but couldn't be known because he was covered in dust. The Sahabah said,

> "Someone is coming."

The Prophet said,

> "It should be Abu Zar,"

And it was. The Prophet said,

> "May Allah have his mercy on Abu Zar! He travels alone, he will die alone, and would be resurrected alone."

In the time of Uthman when the lifestyle of people changed thanks of wealth, it was against Abu Zar's nature to live in luxury and he was critic to people, so in order not to have problems, Uthman asked him to live in Rabazah, a suburban area. When he was dying, he was attended by his wife and servant. His wife said,

> "We don't know how we will do your Janazah and burial."

He said not to worry because we were twelve people sitting with the Prophet when somebody brought some milk to the Prophet and he gave it to all of them to drink. Then he said,

> "One of you people will die in loneliness and a caravan will be coming from Iraq, they will pray his and do hi Janazah and burial."

Abu Zar's wife said,

> "But all the caravans have already gone for Hajj so no caravan will come."

Abu Zar replied,

> "But all the other eleven people have died already and none in loneliness. Only I am remaining so for sure the caravan will come as the Prophet has foretold it. So when I die, you the man gave me a ghusl [shroud] and a coffin and put my body in an elevated place on the roadside and when a caravan is passing by, tell them, "The companion of the Prophet Abu Zar has died.""

So, they did so, and soon they saw a caravan coming that was late for the Hajj. They told the caravan what Abu Zar had told them to say. In the caravan was Abdullah Ibni Masud. He said,

> "The prophet said, 'May Allah have his mercy on Abu Zar, he travels alone, he will die alone, and would be resurrected alone."

He also told the caravan people the story of Tabuk. Ibni Masud led his funeral prayer and they buried him. He died in year 32 after Hijrah. His name is Jundub Ibni Junadah.

THE PROPHET WROTE A DOCUMENT FOR THE PEOPLE OF AILAH

In the name of Allah, the Beneficent, the Merciful. This is a guarantee of protection from Allah and Mohammad, the messenger of Allah, for Yahnah and the people of Aila. Their ships, their caravans, land, and sea are in the custody of Allah and Mohammad the messenger of Allah for him and anyone with him from the Sham people and those of the sea. If anyone contravenes this treaty, his wealth will not save him. It will be fair for one who will take it. It shall not be lawful to stop people from traveling by water nor from any path they travel on the land or sea.

THE MISSION OF KHALID IBNI WALEED

The prophet gave four hundred and twenty horsemen to Khalid Ibni Waleed and send him towards Ukaider Ibni Abdul Malik in Dum Atul Jundal. This was a sub-tribe of Kindah on a distance of fifteen days from Madina. Ukaider was a Christian and was a subject of Hercules. He came out of their fort along with his brother Hassan. The moon was full so the horseman attacked them. Ukaider surrendered but his brother started fighting and was killed. A third person was also with them, so he ran and entered the fort. Ukaider was given surety that he would come to the prophet and to open the gate of the fort. He did so and Khalid received from them 2,000 camels, 800 horses, 4000 armor coats, and 400 lances. He also agreed to pay *Jizyah*. He was ordered to collect this *Jizyah* from Dumah, Tabuk, Aila, and Taima.

Thanks to this, the boundaries of the Islamic State extended to the Roman border.

COMING BACK TO MADINA

The authentic narration is that the prophet spent twenty days in Tabuk, although this trip was fifty days long altogether. After that he departed for Madina. On his way back to Madina some twelve hypocrites had plotted to attack the prophet. They were hiding there in Aqabah. Ammar Ibni Yair was holding the rope of the Prophet's she-camel and Huzaifah Ibn Ul Yaman was behind the she-camel. The prophet heard some movements in the dark. He sent Huzaifah towards them. Huzaifah hit the faces of their mounts so they ran away. The prophet told Huzaifah their names but ordered him not to tell anybody, and he kept it a secret and never disclosed it to anybody. He is called "Sahib us - sir," the secret keeper. In his time Umar asked him about his officials that if there is any one of them? He said yes, there is one but I will not disclose his name. Later on, Umar inquired and he himself found that guy that he is doing hypocrisy so he deposed him. Allah said, 9:74,

> "And they resolved such a thing which they couldn't carry out."

Then when the prophet saw Madina from some distance, he said this is a beautiful scene and he said,

> "That is Uhud, a mountain that loves us and we love it."

And when he approached Madina, the women and the children welcomed him with song:

"The moon is risen on us from the traits of Al Wada.

Thanks are due on us as long as a caller calls to Allah.

O the one sent to us you have brought such a mission which must be obeyed.

You have come and honored Madina so well come O the best caller."

THE STAYED BEHIND AND THEIR CASE

The prophet came to his Masjid, prayed two *Rakat* and then he sat there. In this Ghazwa those who had excuses they stayed behind or the hypocrites stayed behind. Some of them made some excuses and asked permission to stay while some others stayed behind without permission.

Waqidi says there were 80 hypocrites from Madina and more than 80 from Banu Ghifar. Also, the followers of Ibni Obai stayed behind. These people started coming to the prophet, presenting their excuses. The prophet was leaving it to Allah.

There were three sincere Muslims named Ka'b Ibni Malik, Mura rah Ibni Rabe, and Hilal Ibni Umayyah. They also remained behind. They didn't offer any excuses. They said they would only delay one or two days and then leave to join the prophet. One of them said,

"My horse delayed me so I stayed longer."

The prophet ordered them to be socially boycotted and even their own wives boycotted them, but later on their repentance was accepted by Allah.

Allah says,

> 9:117,
>
> *"Allah has accepted the repentance of the prophet (for his followers) Muhajireen and Ansar, who followed him in the time of difficulty after that the hearts of a group of them were to deviate but he accepted their repentance [and gave them stability]. Verily he is compassionate and merciful unto them."*
>
> 9:118,
>
> *"And [he also accepted the repentance] of the three whose case was deferred till the earth got straitened on them along with its vastness and they perceived that there is no refuge from Allah but with him. Then he returned to them so they may repent. Verily Allah is the one who accept the repentance and he is the merciful."*

These three Sahabah did not present any excuse and admitted that they did wrong. But there were some people who had real excuses. The prophet said,

> *"Verily in Madina there are men who have not traveled a destination nor you crossed over a valley but they were with you (by hearts and Duas) they got seized by excuse."*

There were some other Muslims who were neither hypocrites nor had any excuse but were simply lazy, so Allah said 9:112,

> *"And there are others who have admitted their sins [mistakes] they have mixed a good deed and a bad one.*

May be Allah will accept their repentance. Verily Allah is off-forgiving, and merciful."

These people tied themselves to the pillars in Masjid to show their contrition. They said they would remain until Allah accepted their repentance and the Prophet untie them, and then when their repentance was accepted, the Prophet untied them.

THE BATTLE OF TABUK AS MENTIONED IN QURAN

"O those who believe! What is the matter with you when it is said to you to go out in the path of Allah [for jihad], you cling heavily to the earth? Are you pleased with the life of this world instead of the hereafter? So, the enjoyment of the life of this world compared to the hereafter is very little." (9:38)

"If you do not go out, he will punish you with a painful torment and he will replace you with another people and you cannot harm him even a little, and Allah has the power to do anything." (9:39)

"If you do not go out [then it does not matter at all) because Allah had helped him at the time when the disbelievers drove him out, the second of the two, when they were both in the cave, when he was saying to his companion [Abu Bakr] grieve not indeed, Allah is with us. So Allah sent down his tranquility upon him and he strengthened him with forces [angels] that you have not seen. And he made the word of those who disbelieved

the lowest and the word of Allah is the utmost high. And Allah is all-mighty all-wise." (9:40)

"Go out light you are or heavy, and strive hard with your wealth and with your lives in the cause of Allah. That is better for you if you do understand." (9:41)

"Had it been an easy gain and an easy journey they would have followed you. But the travel's hardship was long for them. And they will swear by Allah if we would have the power then for sure we would have gone out with you. They destroy their own selves and Allah knows that they are liars." (9:42)

"May Allah forgive you, why did you have granted them leave (you should not have done so) until those who told you the truth would have become clear to you and you would have known the liars." (9:43)

"Those who believe in Allah and in the last day would not ask you leave from striving hard with their wealth and their own selves [lives]. And Allah is the all-knower of the pious people." (9:44)

"This is only those who believe not in Allah and in the last day and whose hearts doubted so they are wavering in their doubts." (9:45)

"And if they had intended to go out [in the cause of Allah] they would have made some preparation [or weapon] for that, but Allah did not like their rising up [for that] so he withheld them, and it was said to them, sit with those who sit [at home, because they are sick or disabled and therefore excused; or like women, as they are exempted]." (9:46)

"If they had gone out with you, they would have added nothing but disorder and they would have put [created] discord amidst you, seeking a fitnah [sedition, chaos, and dissent] for you, and there are among you listeners to them, and Allah is all-knower of the wrong doers." (9:47)

"Verily they had plotted a fitnah [sedition] for you before and they had upset matters for you until the truth came and the Amr [Deen or decree] of Allah became manifest [or prevailed] and they were hating it." (9:48)

"And among them is the one who says grant me a leave and put me not in fitnah [test or trial]. Beware they have fallen into fitnah [sedition]. And verily hell is going to encompass the disbelievers." (9:49)

"If good befalls you it grieves them and if a calamity befalls you, they say, 'We took our precautions before' and they turn away rejoicing." (9:50)

"Say! Nothing shall even happen to us except what Allah has ordained for us. He is our maula [helper, protector] and in Allah let the believers put their trust." (9:51)

"Say! Do you want for us [anything] except one of the two goods [victory or martyrdom], while we are waiting for you that Allah will afflict you with a punishment from himself or by our hands. So wait, we too are waiting with you." (9:52)

'Say! Spend willingly or unwillingly [in the path of Allah], it will never be accepted from you, [as] you are rebellious people." (9:53)

"And nothing prevented their contributions from being accepted from them except that they disbelieved in Allah and in his messenger and that they do not come to prayer but in a lazy form and they contribute not but unwillingly." (9:54)

"So let not their wealth or their children amaze you [O Mohammad]; verily, Allah is going to punish them with it in the life of this world and that their souls may depart while they are disbelievers." (9:55)

"And they swear by Allah that they are for sure from you, while they are not from you, but they are a people who differ [in their words and actions]." (9:56)

"If they found a refuge, or caves or tunnels, they would have for sure gone to it with rushing to it swiftly." (9:57)

"And of them is one who accuses [blames] you in charity [distribution] so if they are given it, they are happy and if they are not given anything then they are enraged." (9:58)

"And if they had been content with what Allah and his messenger had given them and would have said, sufficient for us is Allah, soon Allah will give us of his bounty and his messenger, verily we are turning to Allah [looking towards him]." (9:59)

"Verily, Sadaqat [mandatory charity] are for "Fuqara" and "Masakin" [the poor not having enough for their basic needs, or having nothing at all] and those employed for it and for people inclined towards Islam, and for those whose necks are stuck in slavery [who agreed with his master to pay him to get freedom], and for those who are in debt and in the cause of Allah [the volunteer fighters], and for the wayfarer as a Fard

[mandatory charity] from Allah. And Allah is all-knowing, all-wise." (9:60)

"And among them there are those who annoy the Prophet and say, 'He is a hearer.' Say, he is a hearer of good for you, he believes in Allah and he believes in the believers [having trust in them] and a mercy for those who believed among you. And for those who tease the messenger of Allah there will be a painful torment." (9:61)

"They swear by Allah to you to please you, but Allah and his messenger are more deserving; they may please him if they are believers." (9:62)

"Did they not understand that whoever deviates from Allah and his messenger [in enmity] then surely for him is the fire of hell to abide therein? That is an extreme disgrace." (9:63)

"The hypocrites fear that maybe a surah [chapter of the Quran] will be revealed on them [about them] informing that what is in their hearts. Say, [go] mock! Verily Allah will bring out all that you avoid with fear." (9:64)

"And if you ask them, they will say 'Oh! We were only talking and joking idly.' Say, 'Were you mocking Allah, his messenger and at his verse (rules and laws)?'" (9:65)

"Make no excuse, you disbelieved after you had believed if we pardon a group of you will punish another group because they were criminals." (9:66)

"Male and female hypocrites are from one another [means alike]. They enjoin Munkar [prohibited things] and prevent good things and they hold their hands [from *doing good and charity]. They have forgotten Allah so he has forgotten them [left them without guidance]. Verily the hypocrites are the rebellious." (9:67)*

"Allah has promised [threatened] the hypocrites' men and hypocrite women and the disbelievers of the fire of hell, therein they shall abide, that is enough [suitable] for them and Allah has cursed them. And for them there is a painful torment." (9:68)

"Like those before you, they were mightier than you in power and more abundant in wealth and children. They had enjoyed their portion and you enjoyed [or enjoy] your portion like those who enjoy their portion and you indulged [and play and past time] as they indulged [in play]. They are those whose deeds are vanished in this world and in the hereafter and they are the losers." (9:69)

Then Allah said,

"Those who taunt those who give in charity voluntarily and they are from the believers [taunting them] in charity and [those also] who do not have but only their hard laborer's wage, they taunt them so Allah will throw back on them their taunting and for them there is a painful torment." (9:79)

"Those who stayed behind, became happy with their staying behind from The Messenger of Allah and they hated to strive hard [to fight] with their properties and their lives in the cause of Allah and said, 'Go not forth in the heat. Say, 'The fire of hell is more intense in heat,' if they could understand." (9:81)

"So let them laugh a little and cry a lot as a recompense of what they used to do." (9:82)

So if Allah will bring you back to a group of them and they ask your permission to go out [to fight], then say, 'You can never go out with me nor fight with me an enemy. You were pleased to sit [stay behind] on the first occasion, so sit with those who lag behind i.e., with the women, children and disabled]." (9:83)

"*And never pray [the funeral prayer] of anyone who dies, nor stand at his grave. Certainly, they have disbelieved in Allah and in His Messenger and died while they were Fasiq [outlaws]."* (9:84)

"*And let not their wealth nor their children amaze you. Allah wills to punish them with it in this world and that their souls came out of their bodies while they are disbelievers."* (9:85)

"*And when a "Surah" [chapter of the Quran] is revealed [saying] To believe in Allah and fight along with His Messenger, the capable among them asked your leave [to exempt them] and they said, 'Leave us to be with those who sit [stay behind].'"* (9:86)

"*They are happy to be with those who sit [stay] behind [with the women]. Their hearts are sealed up so they understand not."* (9:87)

"*But the Messenger and those who believed with him have striven hard and fought with their wealth and with their lives they are the people for them there are good things and it is they who are successful."* (9:88)

"*Allah has prepared gardens for them beneath which the rivers flow to abide therein forever. That is the great success."* (9:89)

"And those who made excuses from the Bedouins came to be exempted and those who lied to Allah and His Messenger sat at home [without asking exemption]. So those who disbelieved amongst them, a painful torment will seize them." (9:90)

"There is no blame on those who are weak or ill or who find no resources to spend [for the cause of Allah] when they are sincerely true to Allah and His Messenger. There is no way against the do-gooders [to be blamed]. And Allah is Oft-Forgiving, Merciful." (9:91)

"Nor on those who when came to you to give them a mount [so they may go] and you said to them, 'I can't find any mount for you,' they turned back and their eyes were overflowing with tears of grief because they could not find anything to spend." (9:92)

"The way [to blame] is against those who ask you permission [to be exempted)]and they are rich. They got happy to be with those who sit behind [the sick, the disabled, and the women]. And Allah has sealed up their hearts so they do not understand." (9:93)

"They [the hypocrites] will bring forth excuses to you when you will return to them. Say, 'Bring forth no excuse for we shall never believe you as Allah has already informed us of your news, so, Allah and His Messenger will watch your deeds then you would be taken back to the knower of unseen and seen then he will inform you of what you used to do.'" (9:94)

"They will swear by Allah to you when you will return to them that you may turn away from them [and not ask them why]. So turn away from them. Verily, they are filth and their abode is hell as a recompense for what they used to do." (9:95)

"They will swear to you so you may be pleased with them but if you are even pleased with them, then, even for sure Allah will not be pleased with people who are Fasiq [rebellious]." (9:96)

MASJID-I-ZIRAR

As we mentioned before, at the time of "Hijrah" the Prophet stayed for a few days in Quba, a village in the suburbs of Madina. He appointed a place there for prayers that later on became Masjid known as Masjid-I-Quba. The first cousin of the host of the Prophet, Kulthum Ibn Ul Haddam gave the land for it. Her name was Leena.

From day one, the hypocrites had been plotting to break the Muslims' unity. So, they plotted a structure at Quba in the shape of a Masjid. They told another nearby tribe, the Banu Amr Ibn Awf, that their cousin tribe got the name and fame because of the Masjid-I-Quba, so they should build one as well and the hypocrites would help them financially. These hypocrites were inspired by Abu Aamir Ar Rahib. This Abu Aamir was from Khazraj tribe of Madina who converted to Christianity before the Hijrah of The Prophet. People were giving him respect when the Prophet came and Aws and Khazraj tribes accepted Islam, he said to the Prophet,

"I already follow the religion of Ibrahim so I don't need yours."

The Prophet told him,

"My religion is the only religion representing Ibrahim's religion, while the previous forms of it are perverted and abrogated."

Abu Aamir showed his attitude and said,

"Whichever of us is a liar, may he die far from home in a humiliating way,"

And maybe the Prophet said,

"Amin."

Later on, Abu Aamir died in "Qinsrain" in a very humiliating way.

It is noteworthy that after this he lost his status and honor in Madina and when in Badr, the Muslims won, he fled to Makkah and started instigating Quraish to attack Madina. He also told them I will join you and when I will call on my people Khazraj, the big tribe in Madina,

"They will leave Mohammad and will join us."

He had planned the small trenches in Uhud and then covered it with grass so the Muslims would fall in, which did happen to the Prophet himself later on.

In Uhud, he called on Ansar to leave Mohammad and to join him and he said,

"I am Abu Aamir Ar Rahib."

His own people retorted,

"You are Abu Aamir Al Fasiq now."

He said,

"You people have gone astray."

Then he said,

"O Mohammad! After this anyone who will stand against you! I will join him."

Then up to the Battle of Hunain he joined every mission against the Prophet. After Hunain, he fled to Sham as no place remained for him to stay there. From there he sent a message to the hypocrites in Madina that soon he would bring a big army from Caesar that Mohammad would not be able to stand against it, and he repeated his suggestion that they may build a masjid in Quba and ask Mohammad to come to it for opening, so the Muslims will be divided.

When the structure was completed, these people came to the Prophet and asked him if he can come to start it. They also said,

> "By God we have not built up this Masjid with any bad intention, but at night and in rain it is difficult for old and sick people to go to Masjid-I-Quba as it is so far."

The Prophet didn't agree or decline, but merely said,

> "I am going to Tabuk."

On his way back from Tabuk, they were waiting for him, but these verses came to the Prophet when he was in a place called Arwan.

> "And those who put up a Masjid to harm (the Muslims) And for disbelief and to divide the believers and to outpost for those who warred against Allah and His Messenger before. And for sure they will swear that we have not intended but only good. And Allah testifies [or swears] that they are liars for sure." (9:107)

> "So never stand you therein; indeed, the Masjid whose foundation is laid on piety from the very first day is worthy that you stand therein. In it there are the men who love to purify [themselves] and Allah loves those who purify [themselves]." (9:108)

> "Is it then he who laid the foundation of his structure on piety to Allah and his good pleasure better or the one who laid the foundation of his building, on a brink of

precipice close to crumble down and it crumbled down with him into the fire of hell? And Allah guides not the wrongdoers." (9:109)

"Their building which they have built will remain a cause of doubt [confusion for people] unless their hearts are cut. And Allah is All-Knowing, All-Wise." (9:110)

The Prophet sent *Malik Ibni Dakhsham, Ma'n Ibni Adi* and *Wahshi Ibni Harb* to demolish that building, to burn it and to ask the people to throw their trash there in that place so no one may think of its sanctity after this.

The place for this building was given by *Khizam Ibni Khalid* and *Mutab Ibni Qushair, Abu Habiba Ibni Azar, Ayad Ibni Haneef, Nabtal Ibni Harith, Bakhzaj, Bijad Ibni Uthman, Wadee'a Ibni Thabit, Jariyah Ibni Aamir* and his two sons *Majma* and *Zaid* were the people who built it. But as we said that the Prophet sent the same *Malik Ibni Dakhsham* with *Sahabah* To demolish and burn it. *Itban Ibni Malik* once said to the Prophet that *Malik* is a hypocrite. The Prophet said,

"Does he recite the Kalimah?"

He said,

"Yes, he does, but not sincerely."

The Prophet asked him,

"Does he pray the prayer?"

He said,

"Yes, he does."

Then the Prophet said,

"That Allah had forbidden the killing of such people."

Maybe Itban was asking permission of his killing but we say that it is sufficient evidence that he was not a hypocrite that he went with Sahabah to burn that building. But he was misled in the name of Masjid, and even if he was before so he repented for that by destroying that building.

THE VERSE OF QURAN CLEARLY MENTIONED FOUR REASONS FOR THAT BUILDING

1) They built it to harm Muslims.

2) By way of disbelief.

3) To divide Muslims and disunite them.

4) To make it a station for one who fought Allah and His Messenger and that was Abu Aamir.

THE DEATH OF ABDULLAH IBNI OBAI

Abdullah Ibni Obai, the head of the hypocrisy who plotted conspiracies since the day the Prophet came to Madina, died in Zul-Qadah in the 9th year after "Hijrah." The Prophet visited him when he was sick on his deathbed. So, he requested the Prophet to perform his *Janazah* (funerary prayer). Later on, he also sent his son, whose name was also Abdullah, to the Prophet requesting one of his shirts as a shroud for his father. The Prophet gave him his upper *Abaya*, but Ibni Obai sent it back and asked for one touched the Prophet's blessed body, so the prophet gave him one of those. Umar said,

> *"Such a blessed shirt should not be given to such a dirty man."*

The Prophet said,

> *"But it cannot protect him from the punishment of Allah, but with this a thousand people will accept Islam,"*

And thus, it happened when his followers came to know that he put us on the path of enmity with the Prophet, while he himself asked for his shirt as a blessing. So, most of them accepted Islam.

Ibni Obai also asked his son to bring the Prophet for his *Janazah*. The Prophet told the boy to recite the *Janazah*, but he said,

> *"O Messenger of Allah! If you do not recite his Janazah no Muslim will."*

When the Prophet came to pray his *Janazah*, Umar came forward and asked the Prophet not to pray his *Janazah*, but The Prophet recited it.

After the burial, Umar came once again and asked the Prophet not to stand on his grave as the Prophet used to do so after burial and thus the verse came,

> *"And never pray on anyone of them who died nor stand on his grave, verily, they disbelieved in Allah and His Messenger and died while they were Fasiq [rebellious]." (9:84)*

The Prophet led his prayer as apparently, he was Muslim and that is Shariah. Also, his son Abdullah was a sincere Muslim so the Prophet didn't want to let him down.

THE HAJJ OF ABU BAKR

Hajj is Fard in Islam, but according to Hanafites and Malakites it is Fard immediately when the pre-requisites are fulfilled. And it is Fard once in a lifetime, so if someone performs it later on, it confers no sin on him.

The Shafiites, Hambalites, and Mohammad Ibn Ul Hasan from the Hanafites said that is Fard whenever he wants to perform it, and when one does it then there is no sin unless one dies without doing it. They said Hajj became Fard in the 6th year as that is mentioned in Surat Ul Ma'ida. And that is revealed in the 6th year, and the Prophet delayed his Hajj to the 10th year. But we say that Hajj is mentioned in Surat Ul Baqarah also and most of it was revealed in the second and third years. So, we say all that is related to its procedure, but Allah did not order its performing until the ninth year, when he sent Muslims to Hajj under the leadership of Abu Bakr. But why did he himself not go that very first year because the people of Makkah had disturbed the natural calendar to their own desires, that year's Hajj did not fall in "Zul Hijjah". So, he sent Muslims to perform that in order to send a message to people that now the Hajj was mandatory for Muslims. At that year the "Mushrikeen" were coming also and they used to be naked during Hajj, expressing "shirk" and also whistling and clapping in "Tawaf", so the Prophet didn't want to mingle with them.

Abu Bakr was taking a group of 300 people. The Prophet gave 20 sacrificial animals from his side to be slaughtered on his behalf. The Prophet garlanded them with his own hand. Abu Bakr was taking his five animals.

When the *Ayat* (verses) of Surah-I-Taubah regarding treaties with non-Muslims and rules about Harams came to the Prophet, he sent Ali After him to recite them in Hajj. The Prophet gave him his own she-camel, Qaswa for a ride. Ali Joined him in Araj or Dajnan. Abu Bakr asked him whether he was joining him as Amir or as a follower. Ali said,

"As a follower."

Then on 10th of Zul Hijjah, when the Hujjaj were there in Jamrat Ul-Aqabah, he recited those verses there. As the Prophet had ordered Abu Bakr to announce that,

"No Mushrik is allowed to come to Haram after this year for Hajj nor anyone is allowed to make a naked Tawaf."

THE PROPHET HAD TWO TYPES OF TREATIES WITH THE NON-MUSLIMS

1) A general treaty that no one who is coming to the house of Allah be interrupted and no harassment of the enemy is even allowed in the sacred months (Zul-Qadah, Zul Hijjah, Muharram, and Rajab).

2) Special treaties: These were the treaties with different Arab tribes. The custom for renouncing these treaties was that the nearest relative of the person who made the treaty could repeal it by telling the other side on behalf of that other party, and that is why the Prophet sent Ali, his first cousin, and gave him his own mount so there would be no doubt.

The four months mentioned in verse number two of Surah-I-Taubah are not the sacred months but the remaining 20 days of Zul-Hijjah, and then, the following three months, Muharram, Safar, and Rabi-Ul-Awwal and then the 10 days of Rabi Uth-Thani.

It is also narrated that these verses of Surat Ul Taubah had come to The Prophet before Abu Bakr's departure and he told him to recite the first ten verses there in Hajj and Abu Bakr had already ordered Abu Hurairah to recite these but then, the Prophet sent Ali to recite all 29 or 33 verses.

Ibni Jareer narrated that Abu Bakr gave his *khutbah* at Arafat. He ordered Ali to recite those verses, but all people were not present there, so, he asked Ali to recite it again at Jamrat Ul Aqabah the next day.

It is also narrated that Ali used to go to the tents later on reciting these verses there.

In verse number three the words "Yaumal – Hajjil - Akbar" The day of the great Hajj means the day of Arafat and some scholars say it is the day of Nah'r, which is the next day, the 10th of "Zul-Hijjah".

Now this was a clear message that after this there is no room for Shirk and Mushrik in Haram and they are not allowed to live in Haram and if a Mushrik wishes to come to the limits of Haram, he may only come with permission and for a limited time. And no relation with polytheists is allowed; at least, only to the extent of Shariah's permission. Also, these verses urged on *jihad* for these issues as well.

Allah said,

> *"Those who have broken treaties before or tried to are not trustworthy, so give them four months and then after this time there is no treaty."*

This is a clear message. Then, there is the issue that they are serving the Hujjaj and take care of Haram, so Allah made it clear that practice cannot compete or compare with "Aqeedah", so this job is now the duty of Muslims.

CAN NON-MUSLIM ENTER HARAM?

Allah said,

> "*Verily Mushrikeen are filth so they may not come close to Masjid-al-Haram.*" (9:28)

The Malakites said, they can enter the limits of Haram, but cannot enter to Masjid-al-Haram, but with permission. While Imam Abu Hanifa says,

> "*They can enter any Masjid with permission including Masjid Ul Haram as the filth mentioned in the verse is that of Aqeedah.*"

That is not a physical filth and the announcement of Abu Bakr made it clear that the prohibition is for Hajj and Umrah that they cannot come for that. Shafiites and Hambalites said, they cannot come inside the limits of Haram for any reason, permission means nothing as the text forbade them.

Then all of them said they can enter to other Masajid as the text is regarding Haram. There is one saying of Shafi that they cannot enter any Masjid.

The verses recited by Ali:

Surat Ul Taubah

1. *[This is a declaration of] disassociation [immunity from Allah and his messenger) and his messenger to those of the polytheists, with whom you made a treaty.*

2. *[Telling them to] travel freely for four months throughout the land, but know that you cannot weaken Allah [to escape from] and that Allah is the humiliator of the disbelievers.*

3. *And is a declaration from Allah and his messenger to mankind on the day Hajj the great [worship]. Verily Allah and his messenger is free from the polytheists [their treaties obligation]. Then if you the polytheists repent, it is better for you; and if you turn away then know that you cannot defeat Allah [to escape from him] and give news to those who disbelieved of a painful torment.*

4. *Except those polytheists with whom you have a treaty; they have not subsequently failed you nor they have supported anyone against you. So, fulfill to them their treaty up to the end of the term. Verily Allah loves the pious people.*

5. *Then when the sacred [or the granted] months have passed, then kill the polytheists wherever you find them, and catch and besiege them and sit [wait] for them in each and every lurking place [or point]. Then if they repent [by accepting Islam], leave their way. Verily Allah is all-forgiving, all-merciful.*

6. *And if anyone of the polytheists seek your protection then give it to them so he may they hear the word of Allah [the Quran] and then take him to where he is safe. That is because they are people who know not [do not understand].*

7. *How will be a covenant for the polytheists with Allah and his messenger except those whom with, you made a covenant near Masjid Ul Haram. So as long as they stand true to it for you, stand you true to them. Verily Allah loves the pious people.*

8. *How? And if they overpowered you, they will regard not either a kinship or a covenant with you. They will try to*

please you with their mouths [words] while their hearts are averse to you and most of them are Fasiq [rebellious].

9. *They have purchased [chosen] against the verses of Allah a little gain so they stopped themselves from his path [or kindred others from his path]. Evil indeed is that which they used to do.*

10. *They regard not [or they fear not] a kinship or a covenant with a believer. And they are the transgressors.*

11. *But if they repented [from disbelief], prayed the prayer and gave zakat, then they are your brethren in Deen. And we explain the Ayat [verses, rules, laws] in detail for a people to understand.*

12. *And if they break their oath [pledge] after their covenant and defame your faith, then fight the leaders of disbelief. Verily for them there are no oaths [pledges, meaning they and their oaths are not to be trusted], so that they may stop [from doing such treachery].*

13. *Why do you not fight a people who have broken their oaths [pledges] and they had planned to expel the prophet [from Makkah] and they have attacked first? Do you fear them? Allah has more right that you should fear him if you are believers.*

14. *Fight them, Allah will punish them by your hands, and he will humiliate them, he will help you against them and he will heal the hearts of the believing people.*

15. *And he will take away the anger of their hearts, and Allah will accept the repentance of whom he wills, and Allah is all-knowing all-wise.*

16. *Have you thought that you would be spared while Allah would not have known those amongst you who have*

striven hard [or fought] and have not taken against Allah, his messenger, and the believers, Waleejah [intruders as advisors and friends]. And Allah is well acquainted with what you do.

17. It is not for the polytheists to maintain the Mosques of Allah [to look after it] while they admit themselves of disbelief. They are people whose deeds are in vain. And in fire they shall abide.

18. Indeed that one [really] maintains the Mosques of Allah who believed in Allah. In the last day and performed the prayer, paid the zakat, and feared none but Allah, so it is they to be of those who got guidance.

19. Have you considered the providing of drinking water to the pilgrims and the maintenance of Masjid Ul Haram as equal to the worth of those who believed in Allah and the last day and strived hard [and fought] in the path of Allah? They will not be equal before Allah. And Allah guides not the wrong doers.

20. Those who believed, emigrated, and strove hard [fought] in the path of Allah with their wealth and their selves [lives] are of a far higher degree with Allah. And they are the successful.

21. Their lord gives them glad tidings of mercy from his side and his pleasure and gardens, for them there are everlasting delights.

22. They will dwell therein forever, and verily with Allah is a great reward.

23. O you who believe! Take not your fathers, your brothers as Auliya [protectors, friends, secret keepers, regarding

Deen] if they preferred disbelief to belief. And whoever of you will do so, then they are the wrong doers.

24. Say [O Mohammad] if your fathers, your sons, your spouses, your kinsfolk, or your associates, the wealth which you have gained, the business in which you fear a decline, the dwelling you love a lot are more dearer to you than Allah, his messenger, and jihad [striving hard for a fight] in his cause, then wait until Allah brings about his decision. And Allah does not guide the rebellious people.

25. Indeed Allah has helped you in many battlefields, and on the day of Hunain, you rejoiced at your great number, but it gained you nothing. And the earth was straitened on you along with its vastness, then you turned back [From the field or to the field as afterwards when the prophet called them and they came back.]

26. Then Allah sent Sakina [tranquility] on his messenger and on the believers and he sent down forces [angels] which you saw not and he punished the disbelievers. And such is the recompense of the disbelievers.

27. Then after that Allah will accept the repentance of whom he wills. And Allah is off-forgiving, most merciful.

28. O you who believe! Indeed the polytheists are Najas [filth] so they may not come close to Al – Masjid Ul - Haram after this year of them. And if you fear poverty then Allah will enrich you out of his bounty if he wills. Verily Allah is all-knowing, all-wise.

29. Fight those who believe not in Allah nor in the last day, nor they consider unlawful what Allah and his messenger has forbidden and they do not adopt the Deen of truth [or

the true Deen] among those who were given scripture until they pay Jizyah with willing submission and believe themselves subdued.

30. The Jews said Uzair [Ezra] is the son of Allah and the Christians said, Maseeh [Messiah] is the son of Allah. That is their saying with their mouths [having no base in reality], resembling the saying of those who disbelieved before them. May Allah curse [or punish] them, how deluded they are from truth.

31. They have taken their rabbis and their monks as their lords besides Allah and have taken Maseeh [Messiah] son of Maryam [Mary], while they have not been commanded but to worship only one God. There is no God but only He. Glory is to him high is he from all that they associate [with him].

32. They want to extinguish Allah's light with their mouths, while Allah denies but only to complete his light even though the disbelievers hate [this completion].

33. He is the one who has sent his messenger with guidance and with Deen of truth [or the true Deen] to make it prevail over every religion [or over all religions or over all systems or every affair]. Even the polytheists hate it.

34. O you who believe! Indeed many of the rabbis and monks eat up the wealth of people falsely and they hinder people from the path of Allah. And those who hoard gold and silver and spend it not in the cause of Allah, then inform them of a painful torment.

35. The day when it will be heated in the fire of hell and with it will be branded their foreheads, their flanks and their backs, that this is what you treasured for yourselves so taste what you used to treasure.

36. *Verily the number of months with Allah is twelve months in the book [system] of Allah, since the day he created the heavens and the earth, of them four [months)] are sacred. This is the right Deen [established system]. So wrong not yourselves therein. And fight the disbelievers all together as they fight you altogether. And know that Allah is with the pious people.*

37. *The transposing [of the sacred months with other months] is an addition to disbelief. Thereby the disbelievers are led astray, as they make it lawful one year and unlawful in another year, in order to adjust the number of months forbidden (been made sacred) by Allah so that they may make what Allah has forbidden, lawful. Their evil deeds are made fair seeming to them. And Allah does not guide the disbelieving people.*

THE ATTACK OF KHALID IBN UL WALEED ON THE BANU KA'B

Najran is a territory between Yemen and Najd. The Banu Harith Ibni Ka'b were living there. The prophet gave an army of 400 people to Khalid Ibn Ul Waleed to attack the area. He ordered them to ask them to accept Islam, for three days and attack them if they refuse. These people were Christians and they accepted Islam. Khalid then wrote a letter to the prophet.

> *In the name of Allah, the Beneficent, the Merciful. From Khalid Ibn Ul Waleed to Mohammad the Messenger of Allah. Peace be upon you O the Messenger of Allah, his mercy and blessings as well. I praise to you that Allah besides him there is no other God, and after*

that O the Messenger of Allah! You had sent me to Banu Harith Ibni Ka'b and ordered me to give them three days to accept Islam. If they accepted I was to teach them the book of Allah and the Sunnah of his prophet, and if they refused Islam, I should fight them. I gave them three days to accept Islam. I sent them horsemen from all around and asked them to accept Islam and they did. Now I am staying amongst them and teaching them the laws of Allah and telling them to abstain from what Allah has forbidden until a new order comes from your side. Wassalam.

When the prophet received the letter, he wrote back to Khaled:

In the name of Allah, the Beneficent, the Merciful. From Mohammad the prophet and the messenger of Allah to Khalid Ibn Ul Waleed. Peace be upon you. I praise to you Allah the one who besides him there is no other God. After that by the hand of your messenger I received your letter from Najran wherein you had written that Banu Harith accepted Islam without any fight. And the invitation which you had given them towards Islam and Kalimah, they accepted that and Allah guided them to the right path with his grace. So, you may give them a glad tiding of the good pleasure of Allah and also warn them of his torment if they disobey him. Then you should come back and bring a delegation of them with you. Wassalam Alaik wa Rahmatullahi wa Barakatuhu.

Then a delegation of these undermentioned people came with Khalid to Madina.

    1- Qais Ibni Hisn

    2- Yazid Ibni Abdul Muddan

3- Abdullah Ibni Quraiz Ziyadi

4- Yazid Ibni Muhajjad

5- Shaddad Ibni Abdullah Qanati

6- Amr Ibni Abdullah Sabbani.

When these people came the prophet said,

"They seem like Indians."

He was told they are Banu Ka'b. They came forward and said, "*Kalimah.*" The prophet also said it.

The prophet then said to them,

"Are you the people who, when prevented from fighting, were proceeding ahead?"

Nobody answered. The prophet repeated this four times then Yazid Ibni Abdul Maddan said,

"Yes, we were the people who, when prevented from war, were going ahead."

He also repeated this four times. The prophet said,

"If Khalid had not written to me that you people accepted Islam I would have cut your throats"

Yazid said,

"O the messenger of Allah! we do not praise you nor Khalid."

The prophet said,

"Then who do you praise?"

He said,

> "Allah! Who guided us to the right path through you."

The prophet said,

> "You said right."

The prophet then asked them,

> "In Jahiliyat [the time of ignorance] you overtook anyone who ever fought you. How did you do it?"

They said,

> "We never overtook anyone."

The prophet said,

> "You were overtaking your rivals."

They said,

> "Yes that is right. We the Banu Obaid used to be united and not dispersed, nor were we initiating any wrong against anyone."

The prophet said,

> "You said right."

Then the prophet appointed Qais Ibni Hussain as their Amir and they went back to Najran.

THE DEATH OF IBRAHIM, THE SON OF THE PROPHET

In the month of Rabi Ul-Awwal during the 10th year, Ibrahim, the son of the prophet from Maria al-Qibtiyya, passed away. He was nine months old. The prophet wept even though he had forbidden mourning of the dead, Abdur Rahman Ibni Auf said,

> *"And you also O the messenger of Allah?"*

He said,

> *"I have stopped you people from mourning, otherwise the heart grieves and the eyes drown in tears."*

He also said,

> *"O Ibrahim! We are grieved because you are gone from us."*

On that day a solar eclipse happened, so to quell superstitious rumors, the Prophet said,

> *"The sun and moon are two big signs of the signs of Allah; they do not eclipse for the death of someone, or for his life."*

THE MISSIONS AND THE DELEGATES

ABU MUSA AND MU'AAZ WERE SENT TO YEMEN AREA

Abu Musa al Ash'ari was from the Yemeni tribe Banu Ash'ar. His name was Abdullah Ibni Qais. The prophet sent him as Amir to Zubaid and Ad'n. Later on, Khulafa – I - Rashidden gave him certain duties in their time as well.

Muaz Ibni Jabal accepted Islam in the time of Aqaba - Thania at Mina when the Prophet was at Makkah, and he used to visit Hujjaj in Mina at the time of Hajj to call them to Islam. At that time, he was eighteen years of age. The prophet said,

> *"Learn Quran from Ibni Masud, Obai Ibni Ka'b, Saalim the liberated slave of Abu Huzaifah and from Muaz Ibni Jabal."*

Anas narrated a hadith that the prophet said,

> *In my ummah, Muaz Ibni Jabal is the most knower of Halal and Haram [lawful and unlawful]. When the prophet was sending him to Yemen, he said to him not to take their high-quality type of wealth in zakat and avoid bad supplication of a wronged one [meaning, never do any wrong to anyone otherwise he will invoke Allah against you]. The prophet was walking with him giving him advice but when he told him that maybe he would not meet him again, he wept.*

Later on, he came to Madina in the time of Abu Bakr. Then he migrated to Sham and passed away there.

THE MISSION OF ALI

In Ramadan year 10th the Prophet sent Ali with three hundred horsemen towards Yemen. There he got a lot of camels and goats. He called the people of the area to Islam, but they refused and started shooting arrows at Muslims. One man from the Mazhaj tribe came out and challenged the Muslims to a fight, one on one. Aswad Ibni Khuza'a came out for him and killed him. Then Ali arranged his horsemen in rows to fight. He gave the flag to Masud Ibni Sinan. Some twenty enemies were killed and then the others accepted Islam.

Note: Ali had attacked Yemen in the 8th year, also where the Hamdan tribe accepted Islam. At that time when the Prophet received the letter that Hamdan tribe accepted Islam, he made *sajdah* and then made *Dua* for Hamdan.

THE DELEGATES

When Allah gave such victories to the prophet and especially after the conquest of Makkah, the tribes started coming to the Prophet one after the other and accepting Islam. Amr Ibni Salamah says,

> *People used to pass by our area and talking about this Prophet but after the conquest of Makkah a lot of these people and tribes came and accepted Islam. My father also visited the Prophet in* Madina *and when he came back, he told us he had come to us from this Messenger. He orders for prayers in such and such time. He orders for azan and Iqamah in these times, so all of you may accept it.*

The scholars have mentioned some seventy delegations came to the prophet, even some of these delegations came before the conquest of Makkah and most of them after that. At the time of the conquest the Muslim army was 10,000 or 12,000 strong but when the prophet was heading for Tabuk, then their number was 30,000. It grew threefold in a brief time as he went to Makkah in Ramadan in the 8th year while to Tabuk in Rajab of the 9th year, barely ten months.

So here we will mention details of a few delegations.

ABDUL QAIS DELEGATIONS

One delegation of Abdul Qais had come in the 5th year; among them was Munqiz Ibni Hayyan. He used to come for business to Madina. When the Prophet came to Madina, Munqiz accepted Islam. He took a letter from the Prophet for his people so thirteen or fourteen people came to the Prophet. They asked about Iman and also about certain drinks they used to drink. Their leader Al Ashajj Alasri was amongst them. When he spoke to the Prophet the prophet praised him for having two qualities Allah likes, patience and clemency.

This second delegate came now in this year of delegation. They were forty in number. Jarud Ibni Ala Alabdi was among them.

DAUS DELEGATION

From Daus tribe Tufail Ibni Amr ad Dausi accepted Islam when the Prophet was at Makkah. Then he went back to his people and used to call them to Islam until he lost his hope in them so then he came to the prophet and asked him to have a bad supplication on Daus.

The Prophet said,

"O Allah! Guide Daus."

Later on, Tufail brought seventy to eighty people of Daus to Madina. The Prophet was in Khyber at that time.

FARWAH IBNI AMR AL JUZAMI

Farwah was the ruler of Ma'aan and its surrounding area under Roman Empire. When he saw the bravery of Muslims, especially in Muta, he accepted Islam. He sent his ambassador to the Prophet with a white mule as a gift. When the Romans got the news of his Islam, they put him to prison either to denounce Islam or to be ready for death. He opted for death. They crucified him in a place called Afra and then killed his group also.

SADA DELEGATION

When the Prophet was in Ji'irranah at the time of the conquest of Makkah and Ghazwa-I-Hunain, he sent four hundred people towards this tribe, but Ziyad Ibni Harith as Sudaa'e came and asked the Prophet to bring the army back. So, he brought fifteen of them, they accepted Islam and went back to their people to convince them so in Hajjat Ul Wada, some one hundred people joined the Prophet.

THE DELEGATION OF UZARAH

This delegation came to the Prophet in Safar al Muzaffar in the 10th year. They were twelve people. Hamzah Ibni Noman was one of them. When asked who they were, they said,

> *"We are the siblings of Qusai Ibni Kilab from his mother's side. Our elders helped Qusai to drive out Banu Bakr and Khuza'a from Makkah and to give the custody of holy Kabah to Qusai."*

The Prophet gave them the glad tidings about the conquest of Sham. He told them not to eat un-slaughtered animals. They accepted Islam, stayed in Madina for a few days and then left for their homes.

THE DELEGATION OF BALI

These people came in Rabee-Ul Awwal in the 9th year and stayed in Madina for three days. Their chief Abud Dabib asked the Prophet if there is any reward for hospitality.

The Prophet said,

> *"There is a reward for every good deed, whether you have done it for a poor person or a rich one."*

Abud Dabib also asked,

> *"If someone sees a lost sheep, should he take it to protect it?"*

The Prophet said,

> *"It could be either yours or of your brother or be for a wild dog."*

Then he asked about a lost camel.

The Prophet said,

> *"What you do with it? Leave it, his owner will find him."*

But now we should not leave a lost camel so, it must be kept by a God-fearing person for its owner, otherwise some thief might take it away.

THE DELEGATE OF THAQEEF

The chief of Thaqeef had come to the Prophet a little before the battle of Ta'if and accepted Islam. Then he went back to call his people to Islam, but they shot him with arrows and killed him. But after one month they consulted among themselves that most Arabs have accepted Islam, and it would be impractical to try to fight all of them. They asked Abd-I-Yaleel Ibni Amr if he can go to the Prophet to talk to him, but he said,

"I will not go alone."

So, they gave him two people and the Banu Malik also gave three. Then six people came to the Prophet. The youngest of them was Uthman Ibni Abul Aas Thaqafi.

They stayed in Masjid and listening to the Prophet. They said to the Prophet to give them a peace letter and allow them to drink wine, practice *zina* [adultery], and do usury, and to protect their god, Lat. They also asked for exemption from prayer and not to have to break their gods with their own hands. The prophet refused all that. Then they accepted Islam but requested not to have to break Lat with their own hands. They asked the prophet to do it himself. The prophet wrote a letter for them and appointed Uthman Ibni Abil Aas as their leader. For days when they were there in masjid, they used to leave Uthman with their belongings and they come and sit with the Prophet, and when they were done then they guarded their things and Uthman would come and to learn Quran and *Deen* from the Prophet. If the prophet was not there, then he was hearing from Abu Bakr. After the death of the Prophet when some tribes denounced Islam and Thaqeef also intended to do the same, this young man was telling them,

"You are the one who accepted Islam the last, so denounce it not in the first,"

And thus, Allah saved them.

When they went back to their people, they concealed their acceptance of Islam from them and told them that they asked the Prophet for all those concessions, but he refused it and warned them he would fight. First, they tried to persuade their fellows that they were not ready for Islam but after two or three days they became afraid of the fight and asked this delegate to go to the Prophet again and accept what he says, so then the delegates disclosed their Islam.

The Prophet then sent a few people with Khalid to destroy Lat. A nephew of Urwah who is a famous Sahabi, Mughirah Ibni Shobah, said to these Muslims,

> *"Leave me to make you laugh at them.: He hit Lat and then he intentionally threw himself on the ground. They said, "Look! Lat threw him on the ground." He jumped up and laughed at them, saying that their god was but a bunch of stones and mud and the Muslims have demolished it (Zad Ul, Ma'ad)*

THE HAMDAN DELEGATION

We have already mentioned this story.

THE DELEGATION OF BANU FAZARAH

This delegation of ten people came to the prophet after Tabuk. They accepted Islam and asked the prophet to make a *Dua* for rain as their area was suffering from drought.

THE KINGS OF YEMEN

The prophet received a letter from the kings of Yemen named Harith Ibni Abdi - Kalal, Nuaim Ibni – Abd – I - Kalal and Noman Ibni Qail zi - Ra'ain.

Their messenger from Ma'aafir and Hamdan named Malik Ibni Murrah Ar Rahavi came to say that they have accepted Islam and disconnected themselves from shirk and Mushrikeen. The prophet of Allah wrote them a letter wherein he mentioned what is for Muslims and what is upon Muslims. He mentioned therein the rights and duties of Ahl Uz Zimmah, i.e., non-Muslims living in a Muslim state. He also sent his men to them under the leadership of Muaz Ibni Jabal. He gave Muaz the responsibility of the Sukoon and Sakasak areas, which are near Aden. He was an imam, a commander, and a judge there. The prophet had given Abu Musa the areas Zubaid Ma'aarib, Zama, and Sahil. The prophet said to them both, "Be soft, not hard, keep people happy and coordinate with each other, differ not from one another. Then Abu Musa joined the prophet in Hajjat Ul Wada, while Muaz came to Madina after the death of the prophet.

THE DELEGATION OF NAJRAN

In the 9th year some sixty people from Najran came to the Prophet. Among them, twenty were their chiefs and three of them were the chiefs of the whole Najran area. One of these three was called Al-

Aaqib. He was their ruler. His name was Abdul Massee. The second one was called As-Sayyid. He was in charge of cultural and political affairs. His name was Aiham or Sharabeel. The third one was called Al Usquf. He was their religious and spiritual leader. His name was Abu Haritha Ibni Alqama.

These people stayed in Masjid having a sitting with the Prophet. The prophet recited verses 33-63 of Surat Ul Aal Imran to them:

> *3:13 – Verily Allah has chosen Adam, Nuh [Noah], the family of Ibrahim and the family of Imran above all Aalameen [the worlds].*
>
> *34 – Offspring of one another. And Allah is all hearing, all-knower.*
>
> *35 – When the wife of Imran said, O my lord! I have vowed to you what [the child] is in my belly [womb] dedicated [for the services of Baitul Maqdis), so accept [this) from me. Verily you are the all-hearer, the all-knower.*
>
> *36 – Then when she delivered it, she said "O, my Lord! I have delivered a girl and Allah knows this, and I have named it Maryam [Mary] and I seek refuge with you for her and for her offspring from Satan the outcast.*
>
> *37 – So her Lord accepted her with goodly acceptance, and he made her grow in a good way and put her in the care of Zakaria. Whenever Zakaria entered Al Mihrab [the room she was living in] to visit her, he found with her [out-of-season] provisions. He said, "O Maryam! Where did you get all this?" she said, "This is from Allah." Verily Allah provides whom he wills without limits.*

38 – There [at that place and time] Zakaria invoked his lord. He said, "O my Lord! Grant me from your side a good offspring. You are the all-hearer of invocations."

39 – So the angels called on him, while he was standing in Al Mihrab [a worship room] that Allah gives you a glad tiding of Yahya [John] confirming the word of Allah [and that is "Be"] and that is noble, chaste, and prophet from among the righteous.

40 – He said, "O My Lord! "How can it be a son for me while the old age has overtaken me?" He said, "Thus Allah does what he wills."

41 – He said, "O my Lord! Make a sign for me." He said, "Your sign is that you shall be only able to speak to people for three days in signals [sign language]. And remember your lord a lot in the afternoon and in the morning.

42 – And when the angels said O Maryam [Mary]! Verily Allah has chosen you, purified you and he has preferred you over the women of the worlds [of your time].

43 – O Maryam! Obey you Lord and prostrate and bow down with those who are bowing down.

44 – this is of the news of Ghaib [unknown to you] we reveal to you. And you were not with them when they were casting lots with their pens as which of them will be taking charge of Maryam's care, and you were not with them when they were disputing.

45 – When the angels said, O Maryam! Verily Allah gives you the glad tidings of a word from his side, his name is Maseeh [Messiah]. Isa [Jesus] son of Maryam

[Mary] will be of those who have been made near [to Allah].

46 – And he will be speaking to people from the cradle and in manhood [also] and will be of the righteous.

47 – She said, O my Lord! How there will be a son for me while no man has touched me? He said, "The same way Allah creates what he wills when he decrees a thing then he says to it, Be! And that is."

48 – And he will teach him the book and the wisdom and "Taurat" [Torah] and "Injeel".

49 – [And he will send him] as a messenger to the children of "Israel" [saying to them] I have come to you with a sign from your lord, that I will design for you out of clay the figure of a bird and I will breathe into it and it will become [a flying] bird with the leave of Allah. And I will heal one who is born blind, and the leper, and I will bring the dead to life [and all that] with the leave of Allah. And I will inform you of what you eat and what you store in your houses. Surely in this there is a sign for you if you are believers.

50 – [And he will send me] as one who will be confirming what was before me [news] the Taurat [Torah] and to make lawful to you some of what was forbidden to you and I have come to you with a sign from your lord. So, fear Allah and obey me.

51 – Then when Isa felt from them the disbelief, he said who will be my helpers [going] towards Allah? The "Hawariyyun" (helpers) said we are the helpers of [the Deen of] Allah, we believed in Allah and bear witness that we are Muslims [who submit to Allah].

53 – O our Lord! We believe in what you have sent down and we followed the messenger, so write us down with those who bear witness (Admit).

54 – And they [the disbelievers among the Jews] plotted [to crucify Isa] while Allah planned [to save him]. And Allah is the best planner.

55 – When Allah said, O Isa [Jesus] I will take you [intact] and lift you up to myself and clear you [save you or take you far] from those who disbelieved and I will make those who followed you over those who disbelieved till the day of judgment. Then to me is your return [or with me is your return place] then I will judge between you in what you used to dispute [differ each other].

56 – Then as for those who disbelieved, I will punish them with a sever torment in this world and in the hereafter, and for them there will be no helper.

57 – And as for those who believed and practiced righteous good deeds, so he [Allah] will pay their rewards in full, and Allah does not like the wrongdoers.

58 – This is what we recite to you of the verses and the wise (or established) admonition.

59 – Indeed, the likeness of Isa [Jesus] before Allah is the likeness of Adam. He created him from dust, then said to him, "Be!" And he was.

60 – The truth is from your Lord, so be not of those who doubt.

61 – Then whoever disputes with you regarding him [Jesus] after all that come to you, i.e., the knowledge [about him], then say to them come, let us call our sons and your sons, our women and your women, ourselves and yourselves, then we invoke the curse of Allah upon liars.

62 – Verily this is the true story and there is no God but Allah. And verily Allah is the all-mighty, all-wise.

63 – And if they turn away then Allah is the all-knower of those who spread mischief [disorder].

THE MUBAHALAH

After this the Prophet brought with him Fatima, Hasan, and Husain for Mubahalah (the invocation), so these people were afraid. The Aaqib and the Sayyid said to them,

> *"If he is a prophet and we will join him in Mubahalah, we will be ruined along with our offspring."*

So, they came and asked for peace and agreed to pay *Jizyah*. They agreed to pay one thousand dresses in Rajab and another one thousand in Safar every year. And with every dress they will give one gold *Aquia*. The Prophet wrote a peace treaty for them. They asked the Prophet to send to them a trustworthy man to collect the *Jizyah*. The prophet appointed Abu Ubaidah Ibn Ul Jarrah for that but it is narrated that when they went back then the Aaqib and the Sayyid accepted Islam and so many people followed them so there is no such narration that any Jizyah was taken from them. Then the prophet sent Ali to collect *zakat* from them as Ibni Hajar narrated.

BANU HANEEFAH DELEGATION

The people of the Banu Hanifah tribe from Yamamah came to Madina in the 9th year. There were seventeen people. One of them was Musailamah Ibni Thumamah Ibni Kabeer Ibn Ul Habib Ibn Ul Harith who later on claimed to be a prophet and received the title of Musailamat Ul Kazzab by the Prophet and was killed in Ghazwat Ul Yamamah in the time of Abu Bakr.

It is narrated that they stayed with an Ansari Sahabi. Then all of them came to the prophet except Musailamah, who stayed away out of pride, as he wanted to be appointed as a leader. The prophet tried to convince him but when he felt pride and stubbornness in him, so he said,

"This man will create a Fitnah [intrigue]."

The prophet saw a dream that he was given all the treasures of the earth but then he saw that two golden bracelets came into his hands. This grieved the prophet. He interpreted it that two falsifiers will claim prophethood falsely, but they will vanish.

Musailamah said,

"If Mohammad declares that I will be the ruler after him then I will follow him."

Then the Prophet himself came to him holding a tree branch in his hand. At that time Thabit Ibni Qais, the famous orator, was with the Prophet. Musailamah said,

"If you announce me as your successor, then we will not counter you."

The prophet said,

"If you will ask me for even this small branch, I will never give it to you, your fate is destruction."

After that when Musailamah went back he announced his prophet hood. He started making some rhyming sentences, calling it *Wahi* (revelation). He announced that wine, adultery, and fornication were allowed. At the same time, he used to say that Mohammad is also a prophet. The people followed him calling him the Rahman of Yamamah. He wrote to the Prophet,

> *"I have been made your partner in this matter, so we share the rule evenly."*

The Prophet wrote to him:

> *"This land belongs to Allah; he gives it to whom he wills of his slaves and the good end is for the pious people."*

Imam Ahmad narrated from Ibni Masud that when Ibn un Nawakhah and Ibni Athal, the two ambassadors of Musailamah, came to the Prophet, he asked them,

> *"Do you testify that I am the messenger of Allah?"*

They said, we testify that Musailamah is the messenger of Allah.

Musailamah made his claim in the 10th year, and as we mentioned he was killed in the time of Abu Bakr in the month of Rabee Ul-Awwal of the 12th year. Wahshi, the one who had killed Hamzah in the battle of Uhud, was the one who killed Musailamah and said maybe this will be the expiation of that sin of mine for killing Hamzah.

The other one who claimed to be the prophet was Aswad al Anasi. Firoz killed him and cut off his head. This was one or two nights before the death of the Prophet and the Prophet was informed via *Wahi* and he told that to Sahabah.

THE DELEGATION OF BANU AAMIR IBNI SA'SAA

In this delegation was Aamir Ibni Tufail, who cheated the Sahabah at Beeri - Ma'oonah; Arbad Ibni Qais, the sibling of Labeed from his mother's side; Khalid Ibni Jafar; and Jabbar Ibni Aslam. All of them were chiefs and villains. Aamir and Arbad plotted to kill the Prophet, so Aamir tried to distract the prophet by talking to him and Arbad went behind the Prophet with his sword out, but Allah seized his hand. Allah informed the Prophet about their plot, so the Prophet made a bad *Dua* for them both. Then Arbad was hit by a thunderbolt and killed, and when Aamir was staying with a woman from Banu Salol, he got a tumor on his neck and died of it.

THE DELEGATION OF TUJEEB

This delegation was thirteen people. They brought their *zakat* and *Sadaqat* to Madina. They stayed in Madina for some time learning Quran and *Deen*. They also asked about certain things. The Prophet wrote them down for them. When they were leaving, a boy came to the prophet. He asked the prophet to make a *Dua* of mercy, stability, and forgiveness for him, and also a *Dua* to be content. The prophet did make a *Dua* for him. This man was a very stable and content person in his life ever after. When the Prophet died and certain tribes denounced Islam, this man was in constant contact with his people, giving them the courage to be stable in Islam and thus his people were saved from apostasy thanks to his faith.

THE TA'I DELEGATION

This delegation of Taa'i tribe came to the prophet. In these people there was a famous man in Arabia. He was known as Zaid al Khail as he had great skill in horseback riding in the field. When he talked to the Prophet, the Prophet said,

> *"You have two qualities Allah likes: patience and clemency."*

He also said,

> *"The Arabs mostly overestimate people when they praise him, I heard from them about you, but they underestimated you as well. Your eulogy has surpassed your reality."*

The prophet named him Zaid al Khair,

> *"Zaid the bounteous."*

The historians have mentioned a few other delegations from Yemen in the 9th year. They are Azd, Banu Sa'd, Hazeem, Banu Aamir Ibni Qais, Banu Harith Ibni Ka'b, Banu Asad, Muharib, Khaulan, Bahraa, Ghamid, Bani al Muntafiq, Bani Abas, Muzainah, Salaman, Zubaid, Kindah, Murad, Zee Murrah, Nakh'a, Banu Aish, and Ghassan. Some of them came in the 10th and 11th years. Thus, Islam spread to many areas of Arabia and mankind gained freedom and broke the clutches of slavery of a different type.

HAJJATUL WIDA

Hajj is the fifth pillar in Islam. It is compulsory for all Muslims (both men and women) who have the means after fulfilling their social obligations to travel to the holy city of Makkah and back. It is performed in the holy city and the nearby valleys of Mina, Arafat and Muzdalafah.

This ritual was made obligatory for the believers in the ninth year after *Hijra* (the prophet's migration from Makkah to Madina). As the historical record and religious literature testify, this very year he commissioned his friend, Abu Bakr, to lead 300 Muslims to perform the *hajj*. The next year it was announced that the prophet himself was going to undertake a journey for the observance of the sacred duty. Thus, the people in and around Madina started preparing themselves to join him in the noble expedition, which in many ways had an everlasting effect on Muslim thought and conduct.

On the 26th of Dhul Qadah in the 10th year after Hijra, about 90,000 pilgrims accompanying the Prophet left Madina, and by the time they reach the vicinity of the holy *haram* in Makkah, the number was even greater. The Prophet moved and stayed with his people as one of them, practicing and imparting the tenets and manners of Islamic life, without any show of greatness or importance.

At a place called Dhul Hulaifa, a short distance from Madina, the prophet put on the *ihram* (a pair of unsewn white shrouds worn while performing *haj* or *umrah*). After praying the two *Rakats* of "Niyyah" intention he recited the Talbiyah and kept on repeating it, with some breaks, right up to the time he reached Makkah. The words of the Talbiyah are,

> "Here I am in your presence! O Allah! Here I am. You are without a partner! You are without a partner! Here I am! Verily praise is for you O Allah, and from you are all blessings! to you belongs the authority and rule! (indeed) you are without a partner."

On the fifth of Dhul Hijjah, the Prophet entered Makkah to perform *tawaf*, i.e., circumbulating the Ka'ba, and the *Sa'i*, marching and running between the hill rocks of Safa and Marwah, which is near the Ka'ba. On the hill of Safar where the Prophet stayed, he prayed to God.

> "There is no Lord except Allah. Every dominion and every praise is his. It is He who is the sustainer. There is no Lord except him. He has fulfilled his promises and helped his servants, and he has defeated all his Enemies."

On the 8th day of Dhul Hijjah, he went to Mina, a valley near Makkah, where he had stayed on the eighth, and on 9th he went to Arafat. He offered a sermon there.

ARAFAT'S SERMON

Arafat is a bigger valley situated a few miles away from Mina in which Jabal Al - Rahmah is located (the mount of Mercy), where the prophet delivered the most moving and inspiring sermon ever given to mankind. This sermon's wisdom and validity have never been and will never be eroded with the passage of time. It covers all important aspects of life. It is indeed the best charter of guidance for social justice, racial harmony, and international peace. A most radical command enjoining virtue, piety, and fraternity. It marks a turning point in the history of the world.

Islam, the apostle of Allah, showed the way to amity and civilized behavior establishing an ideal, eternal, and universal system of values and a pattern of conduct on the basis of the divine will and injunctions. His prophetic words in the sermon were:

> *O men! Listen to my words so that I may make things clear to you. I do not know, but it is quite probable that*

I should not meet you in this place again after this year. O people! Verily your blood and your property are sacrosanct until the day you meet your Lord – as sacrosanct as this day, this month, and this place (a reference to the prohibition of fighting within during the four Haram months of peace (or in Haram).

All usury is abolished, but you have your capital. Wrong not and nor should be wronged. God has declared that there is to be no usury and the usury of Abbas bin Abdul Muttalib is abolished, all of it.

All bloodshed in the pagan period is to be left unavenged. The first claim on blood I abolish is that of Ibni Rabia bin Al-Harith bin Abdul Muttalib [who was fostered among the Bani Laith and whom Hudhayl killed]. O men! No doubt your God is one, and your father is one. All of you sprang from Adam, and Adam sprang from dust. The most noble of you in God's sight is the most pious. Verily, Allah is all-knowing and well acquainted. No Arab has any privilege over a non-Arab, or a non-Arab over an Arab. Nor a non-colored one over a black or a black over a red, except based on piety.

O men! The Muslims are but brethren. It is not lawful for a Muslim to take from the belongings of his brother except that which he parts with willingly.

Every claim of privilege [especially in authority] of blood or property are quashed by me, except the custody of the mosque and the watering of the pilgrims. O Quraish! God has taken from you the naughtiness of paganism and its veneration of ancestors. Man, springs from Adam and Adam sprang from dust.

O men! We created you from one male and one female and made you into tribes and sub-tribes that you may know one another. Of a truth, the most noble of you in God's sight is the most Pious. 49:13, "Do not turn to kufr after me, striking the necks of each other. Understand my words, o men, for I have told you. I have left with you something which you will hold fast to, you will never fall into error a plain indication, the book of Allah and the Sunnah of the prophet.

O men! You have rights over your wife, and they have rights over you. You have the rights that they should not defile your bed, that they should not let any undesirable person into your house except with your permission, and additionally, that they should not behave with open unseemliness. If they do, God allows you to put them in separate rooms and beat them, but not with severity. If they refrain from these things and obey you then they have right to their food and clothing with kindness. Lay injunctions on women kindly, for they are your wards, having no control of their persons. You have taken them only as a trust from God, and you have the enjoyment of their persons by the word of God, so be fearful of Allah in regard to woman and enjoin that they be treated well.

O men! Postponement of a sacred month is only an excess of disbelief and misled. They allow it one year and forbid it another year that they may make up the number of the months which God has hollowed. Time has completed its cycle and is as it was the day that God created the heavens and the earth. The number of months with God is 12, four of them are sacred, three consecutive and one single. Dhul Qadda, Dhul Hijjah, Muharram, and Rajab, which is in between Jumada and Shaban.

O men! Satan despairs of ever being worshiped in your land, but if he can be obeyed in anything short of worship, he will be pleasing matters that you may be disposed to think of little account. O People! No message of God or prophet will come after me and no new religious community will appear. Listen carefully! You should worship your Allah, say prayers five times a day, fast once a year in the holy month of Ramadan, perform the haj [pilgrimage] to Ka'ba, which is the house of God, and obey your superiors. The reward of performing all these duties will be your admission to the best paradise.

O Allah! Have I delivered [the message]? the Prophet asked. And on hearing from the audience,

Yes, he said,

"O Allah, bear witness to what your servants are saying."

Then turning to the people, the Prophet said,

"Those of you who are present here should pass on my message to those who are not here. It is possible that those who are not here may understand my teachings better than those who are present."

After the prophet finished the sermon, almighty Allah sent these words in the form of the last revelation, to some scholars.

5:3 - "Today I have completed your religion for you and perfected on you my grace and I have chosen for you the religion of Islam." (Sahih Bukhari)

After this, the Prophet prayed the *Zuhr* and *Asr* prayers in *Zuhr* time. Bilal gave one *azan* for both prayers but separate *Iqamah* for each prayer. After that the prophet mounted his she-camel Qaswa facing the Qiblah until sunset.

Note: Jumhur says that *Zuhr* and *Asr* may be prayed together at *Zuhr* time anyway, but Hanafites say this is only if someone prays behind the Imam of Hajj who gave the Khutbah of Hajj, otherwise they should pray *Zuhr* prayer in *Zuhr* time and *Asr* prayer in *Asr* time.

After sunset the Prophet left for Muzdalafah. Osamah was riding behind the prophet on the Prophet's she camel. He prayed both *maghrib* and *Isha* prayers in *Isha* time in Muzdalafah, then he slept.

10TH OF ZUL HIJJAH

This day is called Yaumun Nah'r, the sacrifice day, as the Hujjaj are sacrificing animals on that day. On that day the Prophet prayed Fajr prayer at the very beginning. He came to Al-Mash-Arul-Haram in Muzdalafah, faced Qiblah and made *Dua*. After that he left for Mina. This time Fazl Ibni Abbas was riding behind the Prophet. The Prophet made his she-camel run swiftly in Muhassar valley. He came to Jamrat Ul Uqba and threw seven pebbles at it.

After that he came to the slaughter place. Ali put a hundred camels in two rows facing each other for the Prophet. The prophet slaughtered 63 of them with his own hand, then he ordered Ali to slaughter the remaining thirty-seven. The prophet ordered Ali to pick one piece from all these camels. They cooked them. The prophet ate the meat and drank the soup.

Then the Prophet after that mounted his camel and rode to Makkah. He prayed *Zuhr* prayer. He saw his family members, who were serving Hujjaj with Zamzam water. He also took water from them and drank it. Then he made Tawaf and Sa'i.

KHUTBAH AT MINA

The Prophet, at the time of Duha, gave a sermon in Mina after throwing pebbles at Jamrah. This was the 10th of Zul-Hijjah, as we mentioned.

This *khutbah* as Bukhari and Muslim narrated was.

> *The time has rotated like its state and form on the day when Allah created the heavens and the earth. A year is of twelve months, four out of that are sacred months. Three of these four are successive i.e., Zul-Qadah, Zul-Hijjah, and Muharram, and then the Rajab of Mudar tribe which is in between Jumada-al-Thania, and Shaban.*

The Prophet asked us,

> *"What month is this month?" We said, "Allah and his messenger know best. Then he kept quiet for a while. We thought maybe he will give it a different name. then he asked is this not Zul Hijjah? We said "Yes, it is."*

> *Then he asked, and what city is this? We said, "Allah and his messenger know best. Then he kept silent for some time. We thought, maybe he will name it with a different name. he said is this not the secure city Makkah? We said, "Yes this is." Then he asked us, "And what day is this?" We said, "Allah and his messenger know best." He kept silent for a while, and we thought maybe he will give a different name. Then he said is this not the day of Nah'r [sacrificing]? We said "Yes, it is. [now the month is sacred, the city is sacred, and the day is sacred, and for all three it is unlawful to be unsacred]. So, he said, then your bloods (lives) your*

wealth [properties] and your honors are haram [inviolable] for you like the inviolability of this day, this city, and this month.

And you will meet your lord then he will ask you about your deeds. So be aware! Go not astray cutting the necks (throats) of each other (killing one another). And then he said, have I not delivered the message? They said, yes (you have done). He said, O Allah! Bear witness. So, the one who is present, convey it to the one who is absent, as mostly the one who has been conveyed the message to, is better preserver than the one who got it directly (Bukhari).

The prophet stayed the 11th, 12th, and 13th of Zul Hijjah in Mina performing the Manasik and teaching it to the people.

It is narrated that the prophet gave a sermon on the 8th of Zul Hijjah at Makkah when he was leaving for Mina, and also on the 12th and 13th at Mina. On the 13th he came to Kheef Bani Kinanah. He stayed there till *Zuhr* then he did *Jamarat*, then he also prayed *Asr*, *maghrib*, and *Isha* prayers there. He slept for a while after *Isha* prayer, and then left for Makkah.

After the completion of Hajj, he did Tawaf Ul Wada and then left for Madina.

SARIYAH OF OSAMAH AND THE NUMBER OF GHAZAWAT AND SARAYA

SARIYAH USAMA IBNI ZAID

As we mentioned before, Farwah Ibni Amr al Jazami, the Amir of Ma'aan, accepted Islam, so Caesar killed him. So, after Hajj the prophet mustered a big army under the leadership of Osamah Ibni Zaid, a young man who was called the beloved of the prophet in the 11th year of Safar, so the horses of Muslims may tread on the land bordering Al - Barqa and Ad - Darawim in Palestine, so the Romans and others may know that the Muslims are alert and ready to face any situation. This was a strategic expedition.

Osama was a young man, so some people talked about it. When he heard the gossip, the Prophet said,

> *"If you contest his leadership, it is no wonder as you contested the leadership of his father before. By Allah, he was efficient for leadership, and he was beloved to me and his men is the beloved one to me after him."*

Then the people were inclined to stay with Osama and joined his army. They departed and were staying in Jaraf on some distance from Madina when they heard about the sickness of the Prophet.

The Prophet died and they were there. They asked Abu Bakr if they could come back. He said,

> *"Absolutely not, the Prophet has ordered me to send that army and I will send you on your mission."*

This was the last mission launched by the prophet and the first one sent by Abu Bakr and thus the succession of Abu Bakr was linked to the mission of the Prophet. When some people said to Abu Bakr that this mission should be delayed until the uprisings in the surroundings of Madina calm down. He said, "No, even if the birds [or other animals] tear me apart I will not stop sending this army."

THE NUMBER OF GHAZAWAT AND SARAYA

Ghazwa refers to missions the Prophet led himself while *Sariya* is the term for mission sent by him under one of his Sahabah. According to Ibni Ishaq the number of *Ghazwat* is twenty-seven and the number of *Sariya* is thirty-eight; while according to Tabari, there are twenty-six *Ghazwat* as he counted Ghazwa - I - Khyber and Ghazwa-I-Wadil-Qira as one, because the prophet had not come back to Madina from Khyber and went to Wadil-Qira.

THE SICKNESS AND DEATH OF THE PROPHET

In the 10th year during Ramadan the Prophet made *Itikaf* of twenty days while he used to do *Itikaf* for ten days every year. In the same way, Jibril (Gabriel) used to repeat the holy Quran to the Prophet once in Ramadan, but this year he repeated it twice. These were the indications that this would be the Prophet's last Ramadan. Also, he said in his Khutbah in Arafat,

> "Maybe I will not meet you here again in my life."

He repeated the same words at *Jamrat Ul Aqabah* as well. *Surat An Nasr* came to the prophet and was told that people would enter Islam in groups, one after another, and the Prophet was ordered to glorify Allah and praise him. All this means that the mission was accomplished and that was what Ibni Abbas said when *Surat An Nasr* came to the prophet.

In the beginning of Safar, he went to Uhud to visit the graves of Shuhada there. Then on the pulpit in Masjid he said,

"O mankind! I am to precede you [to Paradise] and I am a witness on you, and I look at my fountain. I have been given the treasures of land. By Allah! I don't have any fear for you – that you will go back to shirk. But have a fear that you will compete with one another in accumulating the wealth."

One night he went to the Baqee graveyard and made *Dua* for the buried there.

THE PROPHET'S SICKNESS AND DEATH

THE PROPHET FELL SICK

On the 28th or 29th of Safar the Prophet got sick. He attended a *Janazah*. He had a fever and a headache, but he still led the prayers for eleven days. He remained sick for thirteen or fourteen days. When he was too sick, he asked his wives,

"Where I shall be tomorrow?"

They understood what he wanted. They said,

"Wherever you want to be."

So, he was moved to Aaisha's house. At that time, he was leaning on Ali and Fazl Ibn Ul Abbas's shoulders, and he was dragging his feet. He spent the last one week in the house of Aaisha. He came there from the house of Maimunah. He said,

> *"I still feel the pain of the one morsel or piece of poisonous food I ate in Khyber."*

Aaisha said,

> *"The prophet of Allah used to recite the last two Surahs of Quran, blowing on his both palms and then touching his whole body, but now he was too weak, so he ordered me to do that for him.*

In the last few days his sickness became severe that he fainted. His temperature went up, so he said,

> *"Pour a skin bag of water on me,"*

And they did that. He felt a lightheaded, so he said,

> *"Take me to the masjid."*

They helped him sit in the pulpit. He addressed the people, saying,

> *The curse of Allah may be on Jews and Christians, they made the graves of their prophets as Masajid [worshipping that]. Make not my grave an idol to be worshipped. Anyone whose back I have lashed, this is my back he should avenge. One whom I have ever blasphemed his honor he should avenge. I admonish you to be nice to Ansar. They are my family. They have fulfilled their responsibilities but they still have their rights due, so do good to their do-gooder and forgive their wrongdoings. The number of the believers increases but the number of Ansar decreases, so they will be like salt in flour.*

Then he said,

> "Allah gave an option to a slave of his, to choose from the glamor of this world what he wills or to choose what is there with Allah, so he chose what is with Allah."

Abu Bakr cried and said,

> "We sacrificed our parents for you."

So, some people said the prophet said about a slave of Allah and Abu Bakr cried. But Abu Bakr knew what the prophet meant by *"that slave."*

The prophet said,

> "I feel secure in the company of Abu Bakr, and if I was to take a cordial friend, I would have taken Abu Bakr, but the prophethood of Islam and affection [I prefer]. Every gate to Masjid should be closed except the door of Abu Bakr."

Four days before his death it was Thursday when he said,

> "I will write something for you so you may not fall in error,"

But he was feverish and in pain so the people could not agree whether to give him something to write or not. Umar said,

> "No, as he is in acute pain, and you have the Quran with you."

Some others said,

> "We should give him something,"

And they argued loudly so the Prophet said,

> 'Just go, you people."

The Prophet still came to Masjid and lead the prayers; even four days before his death, he led the maghrib prayer and recited Surah al Mursalat. At *Isha* time, he asked if the people have prayed *Isha*. They said that people were waiting for him. He said,

"*Put some water in that big pot.*"

He put water on his body and tried to stand up but fainted. He repeated this three times, but he fainted every time. Then he said,

"*Tell Abu Bakr to lead the prayer.*"

Aaisha asked him three or four times to order someone else to lead the prayer as she was feeling that her father could not bear this pain and then to lead the prayer, but the prophet said tell him to lead the prayer. Abu Bakr led this prayer of *Isha*, then in the following three days he led all the prayers and also the next in the 4th day he led *Fajr* prayer and thus he led seventeen prayers during the life of the Prophet.

One or two days before his death, the Prophet felt lightheaded, so he came to the masjid leaning on Ali and Abbas, Abu Bakr had already started the prayer. When he saw the Prophet, he tried to go back to the *Suff* (rows of the faithful) and to leave the place for the Prophet, but the Prophet indicated that he should stay. He came and sat to his left side and started leading the prayer from the same place Abu Bakr ended with.

One day before his death, the Prophet freed his slaves. He had six or seven dinars, which he ordered to be given in charity.

The next night Aaisha borrowed some lamp oil from a lady. The prophet's armor coat was with someone as surety for thirty *Sa* of barley.

On Monday, which was then the last day of his life, Abu Bakr was leading *Fajr* prayer. The prophet opened the curtain of the door of his house a little. He saw them praying. Abu Bakr felt it so he tried to come to the *Suff*, but the prophet indicated to him to complete the prayer.

At *Duha* time he called Fatimah to him. He said something to her secretly and she cried. Then he said something to her again and she smiled.

Aaisha said,

> *"Sometime later I asked Fatimah about it. She said first he informed her about his death so she cried and then he told her she was the first one in my family who will join me, so she smiled. He called Hasan and Husain and kissed them. Also, he said about them that everyone must be kind to them. He also gave advice to his wives."*
>
> *The prophet's head was in Aaisha's lap. Abdur Rahman so Abu Bakr came. A miswak (tooth-cleaning stick) was in his hand. The prophet was looking at it and she was aware of how much the prophet valued cleanliness, especially clean teeth. She asked the prophet, "Should I take it for you?" He waved his head, and she got it from her brother and gave it to the Prophet, but it was difficult for him. She asked if she could soften it for him. He waved his head again. Then he used it. There was water in a pot near the prophet. He wet his hand, touching his face with, and saying, "La Ilaha Illallah, death has agonies." Then the prophet said a few times "prayer and your slaves" (meaning, be committed to prayer and kind to your slaves) (Bukhari).*

After using *miswak* the prophet raised his index finger, looking at the ceiling moving his lips, so Aaisha went close to him to listen to what he was saying, which was,

> *"With those whom upon you bestowed your grace [favor], means the prophets, the people of truth, the martyred and the righteous.*

> "O Allah! Forgive me, have your mercy on me and annex me with the companion [Allah], O Allah! The exalted companion."

The last words *("O Allah! The exalted companion")* he repeated three times and then he said,

> "Indeed, we belong to Allah and to him we are going back."

This was Monday, the 12th or 10th or 9th of Rabi Ul Awwal in the 11th year after Hijrah. The Prophet was sixty-three years and four days upon his death.

SAHABAH AND THEIR FEELINGS

The Prophet of Allah was more important to his companions that anything else, even their own selves. Most of them, upon when hearing of his death, lost their senses. Uthman was coming to masjid, and he fell down a few times. Umar brought out his sword and said,

> "Whoever say that the prophet died, I will cut his neck. He has gone to Allah like Musa [Moses] and will come back."

Abdullah Ibni Onais fell sick with this news. When Abdullah Ibni Zaid Ibni Abd Rabbihi heard the news from his son he stood up, looked at the heaven and said,

> "O Allah! Take away my eyes when I cannot see the prophet with them anymore."

THE PROPHET'S DEATH AND ABU BAKR

At that time Abu Bakr was at his house in Sanah. When he received the news, he came from there, riding his horse. He entered the house of Aaisha. The prophet was covered with a cloth. Abu Bakr lifted the cloth and kissed him, and said,

> "My father and mother be sacrificed of you; you were pure in life, and you are pure after death."

He also said that the prophethood is completed and now that process is stopped forever with your death.

Then he came out and saw Umar talking to people. He made him sit and then he gave a Khutbah, which brought people back to sense. He said,

> I bear witness that there is no God, but Allah and I bear witness that Mohammad is his slave and his messenger. I bear witness that the book of Allah is as is (true). The Deen of Allah is as is. And the Hadith is as he said. Allah is real truth. O People! Whoever was worshipping Mohammad, so he has died and whoever was worshipping Allah, so Allah is everlasting and never dies.

After that he recited verse 144 of Surah Aal-I-Imran,

> "And Mohammad is but a messenger of Allah. Indeed, messengers passed before him. If he died or got martyred, then you will turn around on your heels? And whoever will turn around on his heels so he cannot

harm Allah even a bit. And Allah shall recompense the grateful people."

Ibni Abbas says this verse came at the time of Uhud when the prophet was severely injured and fell down in a trench and it was said that the prophet was martyred and the Sahabah couldn't afford this sad news, so they lost both their sense and courage and started running off the battlefield, but when Abu Bakr recited it, people felt as if it was revealed now.

Umar said,

> "When Abu Bakr recited the verse, my legs were not holding me standing as I believed now that the Prophet died."

SAQEEFAH BANU-SA'IDAH

After the death of the prophet the Ansar gathered together in Saqeefa Banu Sa'idah, a porch-type place for their social gatherings. They said,

> "As we are the natural inhabitants of Madina, the new leader should be from Ansar,"

But later on, Umar brought Abu Bakr there so the situation could be controlled. Abu Bakr listened to them very attentively and then he stood up, praised Allah, and said *salat* and *Salam* on the Prophet. Then he said that Allah sent his prophet and Allah guided us through him. The Muhajireen suffered a lot for this Deen of Allah in Makkah till they got turned out therefrom and then the Ansar not only sheltered the Muslims but made them as brothers and shared us their own properties. Their support for this Deen for the prophet of Allah and for Muslims is exemplary and historical. Now as for as the leadership is concerned the Prophet said,

> "Leaders after me will be from Quraish."

Hearing that the Ansar said,

> "Now we are here, so select someone from Quraish and we will give him our pledge,"

And thus, Abu Bakr became the Khalifa of the Prophet.

THE BURIAL OF THE PROPHET

Imam Malik narrates that people had differences regarding Prophet's burial place. Some said he should be buried at Makkah, his birthplace; others said he should be buried in Jannat Ul Baqee, the cemetery of the Madinites. Abu Bakr said I heard from the prophet that a prophet should be buried in the same place where he died and thus Talha dug the grave of the prophet at his bed place. On Tuesday his body was bathed while still clothed. Ali bathed him. Abbas and his son Qutham were moving his body, Osamah Ibni Zaid as he came from his army in Jur'f with the permission of Abu Bakr, and Shaqram, a slave of the prophet, was pouring water. Fazl Ibni Abbas and Aws Ibni Khaulah were also there to help. Aws was holding his holy body to his chest. The water was brought from the well of Sa'd Ibni Khaithamah in Quba.

Crushed leaves were put in the water. His body was washed three times. For his *Janazah* people used to enter in groups and then at night between Tuesday and Wednesday he was buried. Peace be upon him.

WHAT WAS THE PROPHET'S PERSONALITY?

Allah has not created anyone like the Prophet neither in feature nor in nature. He was unique as he was chosen by Allah for his last, final, and perfect message, and this needed perfection and he was the utmost perfect human being and a perfect role model for human being and thus he was this last and final prophet of Allah. In his personality he was the final, also not only that he was sent after all the prophets but as an utmost perfect. The Muhaditheen have written specific chapters on his stature, features, nature and character, and Imam Tirmizi has written a book in this regard by the name of Shama'il.

Here we will mention a few narrations in this regard.

Ummi Ma'bad was a noble lady who was living on a roadside from Makkah to Madina and providing food to the travelers. When the Prophet was migrating to Madina he stayed there as well. Abu Bakr asked her if she had anything, but she said,

> "Unfortunately, today I don't have anything, not even milk, as my husband has taken the herd to the mountains for grazing."

The Prophet saw a lean goat on the ground and asked if they could milk it. Ummi Ma'bad said the goat had no milk and was so weak that she could not walk, which was why she was at home. The Prophet said,

> "Will you allow me to try?"

And she said,

> "Okay, go ahead."

The prophet helped the goat to her feet, touched her udder and said,

"Bismillahi Rahmaanir Raheem,"

And the udder swelled with milk. He milked her once and gave the milk to his companions. He milked her a second time and drank the milk. Then he milked her a third time and gave the full pot to *Ummi Ma'bad*. When her husband came back, she told him the whole story. He said,

"He may be the companion of the Quraish, the who says, 'I am the messenger of Allah.'"

He asked his wife to describe him and thus she described the prophet in a beautiful way:

"He was innocently bright. He had a broad face, good manners, and his belly was not bulging out, nor was his head bald. His eyes were black and attractive, arched by continuous eyebrows, glossy black hair inclined to curl, worn long. A commanding voice and a large head, well-formed and set on a slender neck. His expression was pensive and contemplative, serene and sublime. The stranger was fascinated from the distance, but no sooner did he become intimate with him then this fascination was changed to attachment and respect. His expression sweet and distinct. His speech was eloquent, like a rosary of beads, and free from the use of superfluous words. He was neither too tall nor too short His companions listened with rapt attention to everything he said. They vied with each other to carry out his orders. He was a master and commander. His words were marked with truth and sincerity, free from all kinds of lies and falsehood." (Zad Ul Ma'ad)

Ali said he was neither excessively tall nor excessively short, but of medium height amongst his friends. His hair nor curly nor straight but in between (a combination). His face was not swollen, meaty-compact. It was fairly round, and his mouth was wide. He had large black eyes with long lashes. His limbs and shoulders joints were rather big. He had a rod like little hair extending from his chest down to his navel. The rest of his body was almost hairless. He had thick palms, fingers, and toes. When walking he lifted his feet off the grounds as if he as walking in muddy water. When he turned a seal was between his shoulders. He is the seal of the prophets, the most glorious and the bravest of all.

His speech was the most reliable. He was the keenest and the most attractive to people's trust and careful to pay the people's due. He was the most tractable and the most yielding companion. Seeing him unexpectedly, you fear him. He who describes him says,

> *"I have not seen anyone like him before or since."*

Jabir Ibni Sammurah said,

> *"His was broad face with reddish/wide eyes and lean heels [Muslim]. Abu-t-Tufail said he was fair-skinned and good looking, neither fat nor thin, neither tall nor short."*

Anas said,

> *His hands were unlined and pink, neither white nor brown, but was rather whitish. On his head and beard were as many as 20 gray hairs, and some gray at his temples.*

Abu Juhaifa said,

> *"I saw some grey under his lower lip."*

Bara says,

he was of medium height, with broad shoulders and hair to his earlobes. He was dressed in red garments.

"I have never seen one more handsome. As first he used to let his hair loose so as to be in compliance with people of the book, but later on he used to part it."

Bara also said,

The most handsome face and the best character. He was asked, was his face sword-like?

He said,

"No, it was moon like."

Rubayi Binti Maaw'wiz says,

"Had you seen him, you would have felt a shining sun."

Jabir bin Sammurah said,

"I saw him under a full moon one night. He was dressed in red. He was brighter than the moon."

THE NOBLE CHARACTER OF THE PROPHET

As we mentioned he is the final prophet of Allah and his finality requires not only that, but it requires that he was the utmost perfect personality, neither before him Allah has created such a personality nor after him, he will create even the like of him. Allah himself says (68:14,)

> "And indeed, you are on an exalted character."

The prophet said,

> "Verily I have been sent to complete the best [noble] character."

And Allah also says [33:21],

> "Indeed, for you people there in the messenger of Allah is a best role model for one who expects Allah and the last day and remembers Allah a lot."

And Qatada narrated from Aaisha when she was asked about the character of the prophet, she said,

> "His character was the holy Quran."

The Holy Quran is the word of Allah and that is the utmost best word and is the attribute of Allah and the prophet was its practical shape and model. Now Quran is the utmost perfect word so the prophet as its practice shape for sure is the perfect human being.

Allah says [21:107],

> "And we have not sent you but a mercy for all the worlds." "A mercy and for all the worlds and all the times."

Means utmost perfection in character. So, he is the final perfect in person and as prophet.

THE FAMILY OF THE PROPHET

THE WIVES OF THE PROPHET

KHADIJA BINTI KHUWALID

She was a noble lady in Makkah known for her status, wealth, and cleverness. She was married before to Attiq Ibni Aa'iz al Makhzoomi. After his death she married Abu Hallah Nabbash Ibni Zurarah and after his death she was living as a widow taking care of her business and giving her wealth to someone on Muzarabat. He also once sent the prophet as her Muzarabah partner to Sham with her slave Maisarah and was impressed by the honesty of the Prophet when Masarah told her about him. She had a daughter from Attiq named Hindah. She had another daughter who was also named As Hindah, and one son, Halah Ibni Abi Halah from Abu Halah. She herself proposed herself to the Prophet through her cousin and friend Nafeesah. The Prophet said,

"I have to ask my uncle Abu Talib."

And Abu Talib said,

"She is a noble lady."

She was proposed by the elites of the area before but she refused. Abu Sufyan was one of them. And then the Prophet agreed as well. At the time of marriage, she was 40 and the Prophet was 25. Her nickname was "Tahira," "purity," due to her noble character. Her daughter from Attiq was married to her cousin Saifi Ibni Umayyah Ibni Aa'iz al Makhzoomi. Hind had a son with him by the name of Mohammad. His offspring are called the Bani Tahira. Khadijah was the first one who accepted Islam when the prophet told her about *Wahi*. As the prophet used to take care of the offspring of Khadijah a lot, Aaisha asked him,

"Why are you still in love with Khadija so many years after her death."

He said,

> "She believed in me when people denied me. She consoled me when people rejected me. She handed me over all her wealth when she married me and Allah gave me children with her as well."

She was the one who took the prophet to Waraqah Ibni Nawfal her cousin who was known for his knowledge and practice as Christian, as he had deserted shirk and converted to Christianity in the time of Jahiliyat. And he told the prophet,

> "The stranger came to you is the archangel Jibril [Gabriel] who used to come to the prophet Moses."

Then he told the Prophet,

> "I wish to be with you when these people will drive you out."

He believed in the prophet before he received the message.

The prophet had two sons with Khadijah:

1. Qasim. The Prophet is called Abul Qasim because of him.
2. Abdullah, who was called Tahir and/ Tayyib.

He had four daughters with Khadija as well:

1) Ruqayyah,
2) Ummi Kulthum (these two were engaged to two sons of Abu Lahab, Utbah and Otaibah, but when the prophet conveyed the message of *Tauheed* and Abu Lahab became his arch enemy, he ordered his sons to disown these daughters of the prophet and they did. Later on, these both daughters of the prophet got married to Uthman, i.e., Ruqayyah got married to him and when she died the prophet married Ummi Kulthum to Uthman.
3) Zainab was married to the nephew of Khadija, Abul Aas. When marriage between Muslims and *Mushrik* was forbidden

then Zainab came to Madina but later when Abu Abul Aas accepted Islam, then the prophet sent her back to Abul Aas either with new *Nikah* or with the old one. She had a daughter, Omaimah, from Abul Aas. Ali married her after the death of Fatima as Fatima had told Ali to do that. Khadija narrated one hadith.

4) Fatima: she was married to Ali and got from her 3 sons, Hasan, Hussain, Mohsin (Mohsin died in babyhood). She had three daughters Zainab, Ruqayya, and Ummi Kulthum. Ummi Kulthum was married to Umar. The prophet was in a great love with Fatima.

SAWDAH BINT-I-ZAMA'AAH

She was from among the early Muslims. She was married to her cousin Sakran Ibni Abmr Ibni Abd-Shams. They both migrated to Abyssinia (Ethiopia). Later on, they came back to Makkah where Sakran died. They had one son, Abdur Rahman who was martyred in the battle of Jalulaa in the 16th year after "Hijrah". When Khadija passed away, then Khawlah Bint-I-Hakeem the wife of Uthman Ibni Maz'oon the foster brother of the prophet told the Prophet to marry either Aaisha or Sawdah, as he was in grief after the death of Khadija. The prophet married Sawdah. When her brother got the news, he felt sorry for that and put some dust on his head. But later on, when Allah blessed him with Islam, he was feeling very sorry for that act of him. Sawdah was a very pious lady. Once Umar sent some money to her in a bag. She asked,

"What is this?"

The one who brought it said,

"It is money."

She said,

"O my Allah! Like dates in a bag,"

So, she immediately took it out and distributed it to the poor. When the Prophet performed his Hajj along with all his wives, he said it was a mandatory Hajj. After this, it would be good for them to stay at home. Other wives of the prophet used to go for Hajj after that but Sawdah and Zainab Binti Jahsh had got this advice of the Prophet as binding so they never mounted any ride to go anywhere. In the lifetime of Khadijah, the prophet never married any other woman. Sawdah was his first wife after Khadijah's death.

AAISHA THE DAUGHTER OF ABU BAKR

Aaisha got engaged to the Prophet at Makkah before Hijrah in 10th year of the prophethood, while the marriage took place in the 2nd year after Hijrah in Madina, but was it before the battle of Badr or after? As it is narrated that the prophet made a flag of Aaisha's scarf, but it is also narrated that the marriage took place in the month of Shawwal in the 2nd year after Hijrah while the said battle took place in the month of Ramadan before that, so maybe the Prophet had arranged a dress for the wedding and he used a scarf she already owned as a flag. Even though in narrations it is mentioned that her age at the time of engagement was seven years and it was nine years at the time of her marriage, but to the best of our research this is looking *Naskh* in writing s it is written *Sab'a* and *Tis'aa* (seven and nine) instead of *Sab'ata Ashara* and *tis'ata Ashara* (seventeen and eighteen). Arabs used to write numbers like this when the "added to" digit was mentioned already.

In this regard our book *"THE AGE AND MARRIAGE OF AAISHA"* will be beneficial *Insha'Allah*.

Asma, her sister, had a few sons. Of them, Abdullah Ibni Zubair, is the first one born in Quba in the time of Hijrah. Aaisha used to take care of him. That's why she was called Ummi Abdullah, the mother of Abdullah. Aaisha was a great scholar of the Quran and Sunnah and she narrated two thousand two hundred and ten Ahadith. She was a jurist as well. The prophet said, *"After me, ask this 'Humaira,'"* which means *"the red lady"* as her complexion was red.

Urwah Ibni Zubair was the brother of Abdullah Ibni Zubair. He was a committed student of Aaisha. He is the "Tabi'ee" and one of the seven known jurists of Madina. He is considered the treasurer or preserver of the knowledge of Aaisha. Abu Musa al Ash'ari said,

> *"Whenever there was a difficult issue in Deen, the solution and answer was with Aaisha."*

Mahmood Ibni Labeed says,

> *"All the wives of the prophet were great scholars but Aaisha and Ummi Salamah were excellent."*

Ummud Darda says,

> *"One day Aaisha was fasting. She had 1000,000 dirhams and she distributed it to the poor, while she did her iftar (post-fasting feast) with only dates and water.*
>
> *"I said, 'If you would have kept one dirham, you could have brought meat and cooked it.' She said, 'You should have reminded me.'"*

HAFSAH BINTI-I-UMAR

Hafsah was married to Khunais Ibni Huzafah Sahami. The prophet had sent him as an envoy to Kisra, the king of Faris. He took the prophet's letter with him. He had been injured in Badr and later on he died of those injuries. After his death Umar had already talked to Abu Bakr and Uthman about her marriage if anyone of them wanted to marry her, but they had not given any answer. Umar became a little upset with this. He talked to the prophet about Uthman that he did not give him an answer. The prophet said to him,

> "Should I not advise you towards a better person than Uthman for you and your daughter; and should I not advice Uthman towards a better one than you and your daughter?"

Umar said,

> "Who is that?"

The prophet said,

> "I will marry Hafsah and I will marry my daughter Ummi Kulthum to Uthman."

This is also possible that prophet had said something to Abu Bakr and Uthman in this regard and that's why they had not given any answer to Umar, and Abu Bakr later on said it to Umar that the prophet had told me about his intention.

The prophet married Hafsah in Shaban during the 3rd year after Hijrah. She narrated sixty *Ahadith*. She passed away in the 45th after Hijrah in the time of Muawiya. Marwan Ibn Ul Hakam, the governor of Madina, led her *Janazah* prayer. He carried the *Janazah* from the house of Banu Hazm to the house of Mughirah. And from there Abu Huraira carried it.

ZAINAB BINT-I-KHUZAIMAH

She was from Banu Hilal Ibni Aamir. She was married to Abdullah Ibni Jahsh, a cousin of the Prophet who got martyred in Uhud. The Prophet married her in the 4th year after Hijrah. She passed away three or four months after her marriage at the age of thirty. She used to take care of the poor and that is why she was called Umm Ul Masakin, *"the mother of the poor."*

UMMI SALMAH

Her name was "Hind," though she is named Ummi Salmah after the name of her son Salmah. Her husband, Abu Salmah, was the first one who migrated to Madina, but her family did not let her go with him. Her son was in her lap. Both families started pulling him, dislocated one of his hands. Abu Salma's family took him. For almost a year she used to come out of the house crying for the baby. The elders of the tribe said to her family,

"Fear God and let her go."

So, then she came out having no ride and nothing to travel, nor did she know the direction towards Madina. When she arrived in "Tan'eem" there a God-fearing man arranged a ride for her and took her to Quba where Abu Salma was staying. He told her,

"This is the village where your husband stays."

This couple was among those who had accepted Islam in the very beginning. Abu Salmah had two sons, Salmah, and Umar, and two daughters, Zainab, and Durrah, with her. This couple had migrated before to Abyssinia as well. Abu Salmah was the foster brother of the prophet and he was the cousin of Ummi Salmah. He joined in both the Badr and Uhud. He was injured in Uhud but recovered. In Muharram year 4th the prophet gave him one hundred and fifty people to go towards Banu Asad as they were getting ready for a war. When he arrived, they fled and he caught their animals and took them to Madina. But then his old wound reopened and on the 8th of Jumada al Ukhra in the 4th year he passed away. The Prophet sent Ummi Salmah a proposal of marriage and she accepted, but she said,

> "I am aged, I have children with no guardian here to marry me to you and I am a decent woman."

The Prophet said,

> "Everything will be all right."

She said, that in his sickness Abu Salamah made Dua in her favor that may Allah give you a better one than me after me, so she was thinking, who can be better than him, but when the prophet proposed to her, she said,

> "Allah accepted his Dua."

In Hudaiba when the treaty was done, one or two articles of the treaty were not acceptable apparently, but the Prophet accepting that looking at it in a long run or broad sense that this is the actual victory. So, when he told the Sahabah,

> "Slaughter the animals, shave your hair, take off ihram and bathe,"

They didn't even move. He came to Ummi Salmah and said,

> "These Sahabah used to consider my wish like an order but now I ordered and they didn't move."

She said,

> "They still love with you but to them some of the articles should not have been accepted because it gave an upper hand to Makkans even though actually that is not so. So,

they are little bit desperate and in such a situation sometimes the words do not work, action is needed so shave your head, bathe, and put on your regular clothes. Then you will see what they do. "The Prophet did that and when they saw him, they did the same."

She has narrated thirteen hundred and seventy-eight hadith.

It is known that she was the last one of the wives of the Prophet to die. But Waqidi says she passed away in the 59th year after Hijrah and Ibni Hiban said, she died in the 61st year after Hijrah after the martyrdom of Hussain in Karbala. There is one hadith narrated in Muslim Sharif, that Harith Ibni Abdullah and Abdullah Ibni Safwan asked her about that army that will be gutted in the earth and this they asked when Yazid Ibni Muawiya sent an army to Muslim Ibni Oqbah to attack Madina and thus the tragedy of Harrah occurred. It was in the 63rd after Hijrah but any how it is proven that she died at 84.

ZAINAB BINT-I-JAHSH AL ASADIA

Zainab was the sister of Abdullah Ibni Jahsh and the cousin of the prophet. As we have mentioned before that since the time of Jahiliyat, this culture considered that an adopted son to be like a real son in each and every aspect. The Prophet was ordered to reject that concept and he did but still they had something in their mind in this regard so it needed strong rejection, meaning an action and practice. So, Allah ordered him to marry Zainab to his adopted son Zaid Ibni Haritha and through *Wahi* the prophet was aware that this would not work as Zainab was from noble families on both her mother and her father's sides, while Zaid, even though had been made slave by wrongfully and force, was of lower status. He was sold to Khadija and when she handed over all her property and belongings to the prophet, Zaid was among it. The prophet freed him and adopted him as a son and he was called Zaid Ibni

Mohammad. So, when the relationship did not work, he would divorce her and she will get married to you O Mohammad and thus this wrong and unnatural concept will be rejected practically as to them she will be considered as your daughter in law while actually she is not, which ultimately means that an adopted son is not exactly like a real son.

The whole story we have related before. So, Zainab got married to the prophet. This marriage took place in 5th year after Hijrah. At that time, she was thirty-five. Aaisha says,

> "She was equal to me [in beauty']."

And when the hypocrites put false charges against Aaisha the prophet asked Zainab about that so she said,

> "By Allah I don't know but good only,"

meaning regarding Aaisha. And Aaisha said,

> "About Zainab, in truthfulness, fear of Allah, taking care of kin and in charity, I have not seen anyone like her."

Umar had fixed her stipend at 12,000 dirhams annually. She used to give it to the relatives and the poor. In the 19th or in 20th year after Hijra when he sent it, she distributed that and said,

> "O Allah! I don't want to see this again,"

So, she passed away before the next date of stipend.

When he was sick, the Prophet said to his grieving wives,

> "The one who has the long hand among you will join me first."

So, after the death of the prophet, they started measuring their hands, but the first to die was Zainab. So, they came to know that the prophet meant the one who was the most generous. She died in year

20th in the rule of Umar. She was 50 or 53 years old. Umar led her *Salati Janazah*. She narrated eleven Ahadith.

At the time of her death she said,

> *"I have made my shroud but Umar will also send one, so give one of them to charity."*

Her name was Barrah but the prophet changed it to Zainab. Her *Nikah* took place in Shaban year five. It is also narrated that her *Nikah* took place in the heavens as expressed in Quran.

> *"We married her to you."*

JAWARIA BINTUL HARITHA

Jawaria was the daughter of the chief of Banu Mustalaq, Harith Ibni Darrar. She was among the captives of war with the Banu Mustalaq. She was given to Thabit Ibni Qais Ibni Shammas. She did a contract of *Kitabat* with Thabit for nine *Auqia* gold in exchange for her freedom. Then she came to the Prophet and said,

"I had heard of your generosity so I did that contract."

The Prophet said,

"I will pay that to free you and then I will marry you."

Then when the Prophet married her and the Sahabah heard about it, they set free all their slaves as this tribe became the Prophet's in-laws. They were in hundreds.

Aaisha said, I have not seen such a lady who brought that many blessings to her people. This *Nikah* took place in Shaban year 6th. She was twenty at the time. Her name was Barrah, but the prophet changed her name to Jawaria. She narrated seven hadith. She died in Rabi-al-Awwal year 20th.

UMMI HABEEBAH RAMLAH BINTI ABU SUFYAN

She was married to Obaidullah Ibni Jahsh and they migrated to Abyssinia but unfortunately Obaidullah denounced Islam there and converted to Christianity as he had not accepted Islam with sincerity. When the Prophet sent the letter to Negus, the king of Abyssinia by the hand of Amr Ibni Umayyah Ad Damari, his envoy, he proposed to Ummi-Habiba also and she accepted. Negus paid 400 dirhams in *mahr* (bride price) for the *Nikah*. He sent Ummi Habiba with Sharabeel Ibni Hasanah. This happened in Muharram year 7$^{th.}$ When Abu Sufyan heard it, he became angry and said,

> *"This girl could not be controlled."*

Later on, when the Banu Bakr attacked Khuza'a the allies of the Prophet and they complained to the Prophet and this caused the breakage of the pact of Hudaibiyah, then the Makkans sent Abu Sufyan to use his good offices to avoid that breakage as they were afraid that they could not face the Muslims. He went straight to the house of his daughter Ummi Habiba. She welcomed him but when he proceeded to sit on a bed that was the sitting place of the Prophet, Ummi Habiba rushed forth and folded it to put another one there. He said,

> *"I don't know which you value more, me or the bed."*

She said,

> *"The bed belongs to the Prophet and you are a polytheist, so you cannot sit there."*

This resonated in his heart and later on it brought him to the fold of Islam. She narrated sixty-five Ahadith. She passed away in year 44 and was buried in Jannat Ul Baqee in Madina.

SAFIYA BINTI HUYAY IBNI AKTAB

She was the daughter of the chief of the Banu Nadeer. When the Banu Nadeer Jews were turned out because of their conspiracies to kill the prophet, they settled in Khaybar. They were part of every conspiracy against Muslims and their state until the prophet attacked Khyber and conquered it. Safiya was among the captives of Khyber. It is said that she was given to Dihyah al Kalbi but when he found out that she was the daughter of the king he came to the Prophet to let him have her. The Prophet had the right to choose and pick anything from the spoils of war, including captives. So, he chose her and that's why she was named Safiya, meaning *"the chosen one."* Before that she was married to Sallam Ibni Mishkam and after his death to Kinanah Ibni Abul Huqaiq. Kinanah was killed in Khaybar and she was captured. Once the prophet saw a scar on her face and asked her about it. She said,

> *"I saw in a dream that the moon fell into my lap. I told Kinanah about it and he slapped me as hard has he could and this is the mark from that. He said at that time that I wanted to marry that king of Arabs,"*

Meaning Prophet Mohammad.

She also told the Prophet that one day when her father and uncle both visited him in Quba at night they were talking to one another and she was listening to them from my bedroom, which was adjacent to their room. Her uncle asked Her father,

> *"Is he the same one whom prophet Musa told us about?"*

He said,

> *"Yes."*

Her uncle said,

> *"Then we should believe him."*

Her father said,

> *"Never ever; as long as I am alive, I will oppose him. I cannot desert my chieftainship and kingship, nor can I accept Banu Ismail to be the leaders."*

As she was from the offspring of the prophet Haroon [Aaron] she used to take pride in saying that her father was a prophet, her uncle was a prophet, and her husband is a prophet as well.

MAIMUNAH BINTUL HARITH

She was the sister of Umm Ul Fazl Lubabah al-Kubra, the wife of Abbas. She was the aunt of Abdullah Ibni Abbas and also Khalid Ibn Ul Waleed. She was the wife of Masud Ibni Omair Thaqafi. He divorced her and then she married Abu Rahm Ibni Abdul Uzza. He died, then Abbas arranged her marriage to the prophet. When the prophet was in Umraht Ul Qadah in the 7th year after Hijrah. Then this *Nikah* took place in a place named Sarif. She passed away in the 51st year after Hijrah. Ibn Ul Abbas led her *Salati Janazah*. She narrated seventy-six Ahadith.

MARIA QIBTIA

This was a culture in the area that whenever they wanted to give an utmost respect to someone, they tried to establish a relationship with them. For the said purpose they used to propose their daughter or niece or at least a slave girl. Muqawqas, the king of the Copts, received the letter of the Prophet by the hand of Hatib Ibni Abi Balta'a. He gave him his due respect and then he sent with him the gift and also two young girls, Maria and Sirin. It is unclear whether the Prophet kept her as a slave girl, or set her free and then married her, or she was a free woman to begin with. So, it is said she was either the daughter of the king or his niece or even a slave but the king kept her as his daughter. Then the prophet had a son with her named Ibrahim, who passed away when he was only 9 months old.

So, all together the Prophet married twelve women, or if Maria is considered a slave, eleven women and one slave. Two of his wives, Khadija, and Zainab binti Khuzaimah, passed away during his lifetime and the rest out lived him.

THE WISDOM BEHIND IN THESE MANY MARRIAGES IS

1: This was Arab's custom that whenever a woman from their tribe was married to a man from another tribe, they used to defend their son-in-law or brother-in-law or at least not to harm him, and this was a support from various tribes for Islam even though mostly it was a silent support. For example, we see that Abu Sufyan never came to the front lines against the Prophet after the battle of Ahzab as in seventh year after Hijrah his daughter married the Prophet. The same was the case of Banu Mustalaq after the Prophet's marriage to the daughter of their chief, Jawairiyah, and from the Banu Nadeer after the Prophet married Safiya, the daughter of their chief. And when the Prophet married Maimunah then this was the cause that brought Khaled Ibni Waleed to the fold of Islam, as she was his aunt. Also, another reason was Ummi Salmah as she was from the tribe of Khalid Ibni Waleed.

The Prophet married Aaisha, the daughter of Abu Bakr and Hafsah the daughter of Umar as they both were his closest associates, so that was a great honor for both of them.

The Prophet married Ummi Habiba as a solace to her when her husband denounced Islam. Ummi Salma's husband was the first one who migrated to Madina and then he was martyred in Uhud so marrying her was a condolence for her. The same was true in the case of Sawdah. She along with her husband migrated to Abyssinia and when they came back to Makkah her husband died. The Prophet married her to acknowledge her sacrifice. His marriage to Zainab binti Jahsh was to nullify a bad custom of "Jahiliyat". Zainab binti Khuzaimah married the Prophet as she had remained widow. Her husband Abdullah Ibni Jahsh was martyred in Uhud.

Another wisdom is that prophet of Allah was a prophet, a teacher, and a role model for Ummah in every aspect of life, so it was needed that his every word and action may be preserved. He had thousands of Sahabah who did it properly and perfectly. But a good part of his life is there inside the house and especially the marital side and that could be known to the wives only, so for the said purpose he needed a group to preserve that part of his life and his wives did it perfectly. Allah said to them (33:34),

> "And remember that which is recited in your houses meaning the verses of Allah [the holy Quran] and the "Hikmah" [wisdom meaning the Sunnah of the prophet]. "Besides that, all that was in accordance with the order of Allah."

So, the Ayah (4:3),

> "Then marry women of your choice, two or three or four."

This did not apply to him as Allah said, (33:38:39),

> "There is no blame on the prophet in that which Allah has made lawful for him. That had been Allah's way with those who have passed away before [him]. And the order of Allah is a decree determined. Those [before him means] who used to convey the messages of Allah and used to fear him and not to fear from any one besides Allah."

It means that for some people Allah relaxed his own rules for a greater purpose, which is to carry on his message.

THE CHILDREN OF THE PROPHET

As we mentioned before, Khadijah was the first wife of the Prophet. He married her before receiving the message and prophethood and she was the first who believed in his message. The prophet begot four daughters and two sons from Khadijah as follows:

1- RUQAYYAH

2- UMMI KULTHUM

3- ZAINAB

4- FATIMAH

5- QASIM

6- ABDULLAH

His son Qasim was born before prophethood. The prophet is named Abul Qasim after him. Abdullah was born after his prophethood. He was called Tayyab and Tahir as well.

Ruqayyah was engaged to Utbah, son of Abu Lahab, and Ummi Kulthum was engaged to his brother Otaibah. When the prophet received the message and Abu Lahab became his archenemy, he ordered his sons to break off their engagements and disrespect the Prophet. They both broke off their engagements, but Otaibah openly disrespected the prophet as well, while Utbah kept quiet. Later on, he accepted Islam. The prophet made a *Dua* on Otaibah and said,

> "O Allah, put a dog from your dogs on him."

When they came and told the whole story to their father, he was worried about Otaibah because of this *Dua*. Once Otaibah was going on a business trip with a caravan to Sham. Abu Lahab insisted that the caravan keep his son in the middle. So, once they were taking rest and they put him in their middle. A wolf came sniffing the people sleeping there and when he came to Otaibah, he picked him up in his mouth and threw him with a full strength on ground or on a tree and he was crushed.

Later on, Ruqayyah married Uthman and when she died the Prophet married him his other daughter Ummi Kulthum.

Zainab was married to a nephew of Khadijah named Abul Aas. When the prophet started *Dawat* Quraish said to Abu Aas,

> *"You may desert Zainab like the sons of Abu Lahab did."*

But he refused. Close to Badr or in Badr Abul Aas was captured by the Muslims. Zainab sent a golden necklace she was given by Khadijah at the time of her marriage to get Abul Aas released. When the Prophet saw it, it brought him the memories of Khadijah and tears came to his eyes. He told Muslims about that necklace and asked them if they would send it back to Zainab and release Abul Aas. They agreed and thus Abu Aas was released. This necklace was brought by Abul Aas's brother Amr so he took back both Abul Aas and the necklace. The Prophet told Abul Aas to let Zainab to come to Madina and he did it. Zaid Ibni Haritha and an Ansari Sahabi went and they brought her. In Batni Yajaj Habbar Ibn Ul Aswad and Huwarith Ibni Naqeez made her camel run and she fell on rock on her belly. Because of this she miscarried. Also, she got a chronic illness from that delivery and later on she died of that as well. At the conquest of Makkah, the prophet declared them criminals to be killed wherever they were found, but Habbar secretly approached the Prophet and before his saying anything he took Shahadah and became Muslim, while Huwarith was killed by Ali.

In Jumada al Oola in the 6th year Abul Aas was captured again when he was in a caravan in a place "Eas" by Zaid Ibni Harith's expedition. In Madina, Zainab sheltered him and after Fajr prayer she came and said,

> "I have sheltered Abul Aas, and the Prophet has said, 'Shelter by a common Muslim is binding also.'"

The prophet gave him his assets. He went back to Makkah. He gave people's assets to them. Then he asked in a louder voice if anybody had any claim on him? They said no. Then he said Shahadah and became Muslim. He said,

> "I was to accept Islam there when I was in Madina but that the people cannot say I did it to grab your wealth."

He came to Madina and the prophet sent Zainab to him either with a new *Nikah* as a long time had passed, and this is what the Hanafites said or based on the old *Nikah* as other jurists say, but we say that this was a special case of the Prophet and he is the source of Shariah and an authority as well.

Zainab passed away eight years after Hijra. Saudah Ummi Salmah and Ummi Aiman bathed her and Abul Aas put her in the grave himself.

She had one son, Ali, and one daughter, Omaimah, from Abul Aas. It is said that Ali passed away in the life of his mother but in another narration, it is stated that he was martyred in the battle of Yarmouk in the time of Umar. In the gifts sent by Negus there was a golden ring the prophet gave that to Omaimah. Also, Aaisha says,

> "A necklace came to the Prophet. He said, 'I will give it to a beloved of mine amongst you.' Omaimah was playing in a corner and he gave it to her."

Once Abul Aas said to Zubair that when the time will come then marry Omaimah while Fatima at the time of her death said to Ali to marry Omaimah. When Zubair came to know that he said to Ali to do what Fatimah said. After the death of Ali, Mughirah married her. He had a son named Yahya with her.

Fatima was the beloved of the Prophet. She was also known as Bat Ul and Zohra. When the prophet was marrying her to Ali, he asked him,

"Have you anything for mahr?"

He said,

"Yes, I have one horse and one coat."

The prophet said,

"Keep the horse jihad but sell the coat."

Uthman bought it for 480 dirhams. He took the money to the prophet. The prophet gave some to Bilal to bring some fragrance and some to Ummi Salmah to arrange some dowry and thus the marriage was done.

Once some differences arose between the couple. The prophet came and saw that Fatima was alone. He asked,

"Where is Ali, my cousin?"

Fatima said,

"We had a fight."

The Prophet said,

"Where is he?"

She said,

"He is in the Masjid."

The prophet went there and found Ali lying on the ground. Due to hot weather, he had taken off his shirt. The prophet said,

"Ali!"

He stood up. His body was dusty. The Prophet said,

"Abu Turab!" (Which means "the father of dust".)

Sahl Ibni Sa'd says then this name Ali used to consider a pride for himself.

When the Prophet was in his last days, Fatima came. The Prophet called her to come close. He said something to her and she cried. Then after a while he called her again and this time when he said something to her, she laughed. After the burial of the Prophet, Aaisha asked her about that. She said that the prophet told her about his death so she cried, then he told her that she would be the first one in her family to join him. Six months later she passed away. Abbas led her *Janazah* prayer. Ali, Abbas, and Fazl put her in her grave. She had three sons Hasan, Hussain, and Mohsin and three daughter Ruqayyah, Zainab, and Ummi Kulthum. Mohsin and Ruqayyah passed away in their childhood. Zainab was married to Abdullah Ibni Jafar and Ummi Kulthum married Umar.

The prophet got one son, Ibrahim, from Maria al-Qibtiyya. He passed away at nine months of age. The prophet wept. Abdur Rahman Ibni Awf said,

"And you O the messenger of Allah!"

He said,

"The hearts grieves and the eyes fill with tears."

And then he said,

"I have not forbidden this; I have forbidden from mourning."

On that day a solar eclipse happened. In order to quell superstitious rumors, the Prophet said,

"The sun and the moon are two signs from the signs of Allah; they do not eclipse because of the life or death of anyone."

Maria was living in Awali of Madina. Ummi Saif, the wife of a blacksmith, used to take care of Ibrahim. The prophet used to visit Maria and Ibrahim there. Once when he came, the whole house was full of smoke. The prophet picked up Ibrahim and kissed him. Anas says then after that he used to go a little before the Prophet to tell Abu Saif to stop his fires because the Prophet was on his way.

Ibrahim passed away in Abu-Saif house. The prophet prayed his Janazah. Fazl Ibni Abbas and Osamah put him in the grave. The prophet dug his grave close to the grave of Uthman Ibni Maz'oon, the prophet's fostering brother. May Allah bless all of them.

JIHAD AND THE PROPHET

In Islam Muslims have two duties. One is *dawah*, meaning to convey the message of Allah and to convince people to convert them to Islam as there is no room for coercion to convert someone by force in Islam. The other is *jihad*, which literally means striving hard for a lawful purpose and aim. So, it includes every struggle that is lawful and is for a lawful aim, especially when it is regarding an aim that is incumbent upon Muslims.

To promote virtue and prevent vice is also a *jihad*, and to counter and stop wrong, cruelty and brutality is also *jihad*, and thus to fight those who are doing wrong to others brutalizing them and do cruelty to them is *jihad* as well. Allah says (22:78),

> "And strive hard in Allah's [cause] as he deserves [or as the striving hard requires means with any lawful means.)"

This is the way Allah is controlling people by people as he said, (2:251_,

> "And if Allah was not to check people by [means of] another people then the earth would have filled up with disorder."

> "And if Allah did not check one people by another then for sure the monasteries, the churches, the synagogues and the mosques would have been destroyed." (22:402)

Now the cause to fight is the wrong doings and cruelties. These cruelties are sometimes against people because of their faith and sometimes against a Muslim state. This is the opinion of Abu Hanifa, Malik, Shafi and Ahmad. Even though there is another saying of Shafi that the *Illat* (reason) for *jihad* is the disbelief, if that is the case then there will be no break and stop of fighting but it will be an ongoing practice every time, while Islam has given the concept of *Zimmah*, which is a protection for non-Muslims who subjugate themselves to the Islamic state. They either became its citizens or its subjects. Also, Islam gave the concept of peace treaties with non-Muslims; they may still be disbelievers but there is no quarrel with them anymore. The prophet himself did this many times. Allah says, (8:61),

> "And if they are inclined to peace then you incline to peace also."

And not only that but Allah ordered implicitly to be just and kind to non-Muslims if they are not miscreants.

> "Allah does not stop you from those who have not fought against you on account of Deen nor they have driven you out of your houses, to do good to and justice to them. Verily Allah loves those who do justice." (60:8)

> "Allah forbids you from those who fought against you on account of Deen, drove you out of your houses and helped in your turn out [of your houses] to befriend them. And whoever among you will befriend them, then they are the wrong doers." (60:9)

So, the fight is not over some people's lack of belief in Islam but because of their wrongdoings. And wrongdoings must be stopped in the easiest possible way. And that is why sometimes even Muslims are to be fought if they have done wrong.

> "And if two groups of the believers begin to fight then make peace between them. But if one of them outrages against the other, then fight the perpetrator until it complies with the command of Allah." (49:9)

Here the outraged one is Muslim but Allah orders to fight against them. Now this is reasonable and logical to counter the cruelty and to stop it and that is not a simple right of someone but his duty.

Allah says, (22:39),

> "Permission [to fight] is given to those who are fought because they have been wronged. And verily Allah is able to help them. Those who have been turned out of their houses unjustly only because they said our lord is Allah."

> "And fight in the path of Allah against those who fight you and transgress not, verily Allah does not like the transgressors." (2:190)

> "And fight them until no fitnah [intrigue] remains and Deen is for Allah." (2:193)

Also, Allah said, (4:74),

> "And what is the matter with you that you do not fight in the cause of Allah while there are oppressed men, women, and children? Those who say, 'O our lord, take us out from this town whose people are cruel and give us from your side a protector and give us from your side a helper.'"

Also, Allah said (2:216),

> "The fight is ordained for you and that is disliked to you and it may be that you will be disliking a thing and that will be good for you. And it may be that you will be in love with something and that will be bad for you. And Allah knows and you do not know."

So, this means that Islam is a *Deen* that likes peace, but situations arise where fight is inevitable, then Islam insists upon fighting. The prophet of Allah was an apostle of mercy.

Allah says (21:107),

> "And we have not sent you but a mercy for all the world's [creatures]."

Then Allah said, (8:60),

> "And make ready for them whatever you can of power and of steads of war to threaten with that the enemy of Allah and your enemy and others besides them."

So, to have weapons is a must as nobody knows when the enemy is going to wage war on them. Now to have weapons ready as a deterrence. That is why the Prophet used to have the weapons ready. Here are some details of the weapons of the Prophet.

THE PROPHET'S SWORDS

ZUL FIQAR

This was sword belonged to Aas Ibni Wa'il Sahami, who was an enemy of the prophet, and it was in the spoils of Badr. Its hilt was silver. Later on, the Prophet gave it to Ali and now it is in the Turkish Museum.

MAATHUR

The Prophet inherited it from his father. Its hilt was gold. Its length is 99 centimeters. The Prophet brought it to Madina. Later this one he also gave it to Ali. This is also in the Turkish Museum.

AS SAMSAMAH

This belonged to Amr Ibni Madi Karab. When the prophet appointed Khalid Ibni Saeed Ibn Ul Aas as governor in Madina, he gifted him this sword.

AL QAL'E

This sword is named "Al Qal'E" either for a place named Burj-I-Qila, or to a shining white metal aluminum it was burnished with. It is

100 centimeters long. This is also in the same Turkish Museum. This came to the prophet from the Fay spoils of Banu Qanuqa. In another narration it is said that when the Jurhum tribe turned out Khuza'a from Makkah, they filled up the well of Zamzam with mud, stones, and other things, including two golden deer and this sword, and later on when Abdul Muttalib dug that well again, he found these things and thus it came to the hands of the Prophet. It is also said that the Prophet received it from a fort in between Madina and Helwan.

AL-ADB

Its name literally means "cut." In Badr or Uhud, Sa'd Ibni Obadah gifted it to the Prophet. This was the sword the Prophet raised in Uhud asking,

"Who can fulfill its right?"

Ali, Zubair, Umar and few others came forward but the Prophet gave it to Abu Dujanah, as he asked the prophet,

"What is its right?"

The prophet said,

"To hit the faces of Mushrikeen with it and disfigure them."

Abu Dujanah said then,

"I will take it."

Then he tied his head with the strip of red fabric he was known for. The Sahabah used to say,

"Now he will fight until death."

He then started walking with pride. The Prophet said,

"This is a walk Allah doesn't like except on the battlefield."

Now this sword is preserved in Cairo in Masjid Hussain Ibni Ali.

HAT'F

This sword's name means to die naturally as a sign. The Prophet received it in Banu Qanuqa's assets. It is said that prophet Dawud (David) made this sword. It was 112 centimeters long and 8 centimeters wide. This sword is also in the Turkish Museum. This was a beautiful sword amongst. Some scholars called it Heef, but others said Heef is another sword of the Prophet.

QAZEEB

This name means "cut" or "cutter" and is also used to refer to an untrained she-camel. This was a thin sword where upon "La Ilaha Illallahu Mohammadur Rasulullah" was written in silver. Also, the name of the Prophet was written upon with silver separately as Mohammad Ibni Abdullah Ibni Abdul Muttalib. It was never used in war. It was 100 centimeters long. Its scabbard was made of leather. The prophet wore it hanging at his side. It is also said that it was used in war in the time of the Fatimaiyun. It is also in the Turkish Museum.

AL MUHZIM

This name means "the cutter." It is said that this used to be hanging at the shoulder of the Banu Tai's idol, Ghalas. But the preferred narration is that Ali won it in a battle with people in Sham along with other spoils. Also, it is said that first it came to the prophet, then he gave it to Ali. Later on, it was inherited in his offspring. The name of Zain Ul Abadeen is inscribed upon it. It is 97 centimeters long and preserved in Turkish Museum.

GHALAS

This was hanging on the shoulder of idol Ghalas.

RASOOB

This name means "the penetrating one," like water. This was gifted by Queen Bilqees of Saba (Balkis, Queen of Sheba) to prophet Suleiman. That is 140 centimeters long. It was getting inherited by the Prophets and thus came to Prophet Mohammad. The name of Jafar Sadiq is written upon it. This is also there in Turkish Museum.

AL BATTAR

It means the utmost cutter. Its hold was of silver. This was the sword of Goliath who got killed by prophet Dawud (David) under the leadership of Talut (Saul). Later on, Talut married his daughter to Dawud and he also became king after him as promised and got this sword. There is an image on this sword that shows that Dawud cutting off the head of Jalut (Goliath). Also, the Petra mountains city's image is also mapped there upon. This sword is called the sword of the prophets as the names of Dawud, Suleiman, (Solomon) Harun (Aaron), Al Yasa (Elisha), Zakaria, Yahya (John), Isa (Jesus) and Mohammad are written on it. It is also said that Isa will counter *Dajjal* (the imposter) with this sword. The prophet received it in the spoils of Banu Qanuqa. Its length is 101 centimeters. It is also in the Turkish Museum.

AL-URJUN

It means "curved one," and this sword is called this for the dried curved branch of date palm tree. It is narrated that the sword of Abdullah Ibni Jahsh was broken in Uhud so the prophet picked up a dried branch and gave it to him, and it turned to a sword in his hand.

AL FAQR UL HADR

This was another sword of the prophet. This sword, al Mathur, and Hatf were inherited by the Prophet from his father. Three of them he won as spoils of war and others were gifted to him.

THE BOWS OF THE PROPHET

AS SAFRAA

This was a bow made of *Naba* tree wood. Its arrows were also from the same tree branch. It got broken in Uhud.

AL BAIDAA

This was made of a mountainous tree. The prophet got it in the spoils of Banu Qanuqa. Due to its name, it seems that the color of the first one was yellowish and the second one was whitish.

AZ ZORA

This bow was also known as "al Katum". When an arrow was shot with this one its sound was going down. The Prophet got it in the spoils of Banu Qanuqa along with other bows like Al Bauta and Ar Rauha. He had a Sadad bow as well.

THE SPEARS AND LANCES OF THE PROPHET

In war two types of spears are used: a long one, called a Lance, and a shorter or smaller one, which is called a spear. The spear is used more often. The prophet had two famous lances:

AL MATHWA

This means "place" or 'taking a place," so anyone was hit with this one this was stuck therein and took a place, or the hit one was stuck in his place and was unable to take it out.

AL MUTHANNA

The prophet of Allah had a few famous short spears and these were called *Al Ghazah, Al Baida, An Nab'a, Al Mahr,* and *An Namr. Al Ghazah* was actually king *Negus'* spear. Once *Zubair* killed an enemy of Negus with this spear in front of Negus, then *Negus* gave it to him as gift. *Zubair* took it with him in *Badr, Uhud* and *Khyber*. After that the prophet got it from *Zubair*. The prophet used it as a stick when he was walking. Also in *Eid* prayer, *Bilal* used to take it and erect it as a *Sutrah* in front of the *Prophet*. Also, it was used as a *Sutrah* when the Prophet was praying while traveling.

THE SHIELDS OF THE PROPHET

At that time the war was mostly face to face with swords, so there was the need of as shield as well to protect oneself from the hit of the enemy. For this purpose, the shields are used. The prophet had a few shields and two of them are.

FANAQ

AZ ZALUQ

Which means causing to slip as it was causing the hit to slip off.

THE ARMOR COATS OF THE PROPHET

These are called coats of nail as well. The Prophet's coats were.

ZATUL FUZUL

This means "extra" or "having an extra," as mostly these types of coats covered all the way down to the thighs or knees, but this one was extra-long, covering to the ankles. At Badr time Sa'd Ibni Obadah gifted it to the prophet with a sword Al Adb. This was the same one the prophet had put it as a security for thirty *Sa* barley when he was on his deathbed.

ZATUL WISHAH

It is so named called as it was embroidered with flowers on its side.

ZATUL HAWASHI

This coat was embroidered as well.

AS SAFRIA

This coat is also called "Saghdia". It was made in a place called Safr. This was Dawud's coat, which he was wearing at his battle against Goliath. It was received by the Prophet in the spoils of Banu Qanuqa.

AL BATRA

Which means "the tail [is] cut," as it was short, covering only the chest.

AL HAZEEQ

This was made of soft iron.

THE HELMETS OF THE PROPHET:

To cover head in war there is the need of a helmet. The prophet had

AL MUWASHSHAH

AL SABOO

THE MOUNTS OF THE PROPHET

The prophet used to ride different mounts on different occasions.

THE CAMELS OF THE PROPHET

AL QASWAA

CAMELS

At the time of "Hijrah" Abu Bakr brought forth two she-camels to choose one of them for himself. The prophet chose one but he asked Abu Bakr,

"How much?"

He said,

"It is a gift."

The prophet said,

"For this journey of mine I want to spend my own money."

This she-camel was named Al Qaswa.

JAD'AA

Its nose was cut so it was known as Jad'aa.

ADBAA

She was that swift that she had never been overtaken by any other camel or she-camel. She was so sad for the prophet when he passed away that water flowed out of its mouth, nose, and eyes, and she weakened and died.

HORSES OF THE PROPHET

AL MURTAJIZ

This was a horse with a melodious neigh. His color was white.

AS SAKB

Sakb literally means "flow of water. Because of its speed it was named Sakb. This was the first horse the prophet owned. He named it "Ad Dars," but due to its speed he got the title of "As Sakb." It was dark brown with white on its forehead and three legs. Only its right foreleg was brown.

YAASUB

The queen bee was called "Yaa'sub." This was his best horse.

AZ ZARF

AL LAHEEF

Farwah Ibni Amr sent it to the prophet as a gift.

SAB'HA

It means "the swimming one." His gait was very smooth.

AL WARD

Tameem Ad Dari had gifted it to the prophet. After some time, the prophet gifted it to Umar.

AL LAZAZ

This was the gift of Muqawqas the king of Misr.

THE MULES OF THE PROPHET

DULDUL

Muqawqas sent this mule to the prophet. It was blackish and white. This was the first mule used in Islam for riding and the Prophet used it in Madina. It lived so long that even Uthman and Ali mounted it, he used it when a fight was going on with Khawarij. Hasan, Hussain, and Mohammad Ibn Ul Hanafia also mounted it.

FIDDAH

Its name means "silver" because of its color. It was gifted to the prophet by Amr Ibni Amr Al-Juzami. Later on, the prophet gave it to Abu Bakr. The prophet brought a mule from Dum Atul Jundal as well. Kisra of Faris and Negus both also sent him one mule each. In the battle of Hunain, it is narrated that the prophet was on a white mule. Also, the prophet had a donkey by the name of Yafur.

THE GUARDS OF THE PROPHET

When the prophet came to Madina, the Sahabah used to guard his house at night. More than once people were captured on their way to assassinate the prophet. Even Ali used to be with a pillar in Masjid keeping an eye on every strange person coming. That pillar is called a guard pillar.

In Badr Sa'd Ibni Muaz was guarding the prophet's tent at night and Abu Bakr was doing the same during the day. In Uhud, Mohammad Ibni Maslamah was guarding him. In the battle of confederates, Zubair performed this duty. In Hudaibiyah Mughirah Ibni Shoba was guarding the prophet. When the prophet was coming back from Khyber and he was in the tent, Abu Ayyub al Ansari was guarding the tent. In Ghazwat Wadil Qura, Bilal, Sa'd Ibni Abi Waqas and Zakwan Ibni Abdul Qais were guarding him. In Hunain the prophet asked who the guard for night will be. So Marthad Ibni Abi Marthad al Ghanawi came forward. The prophet made *Dua* for him.

The prophet of *Allah (Mohammad PBUH)* was given the greatest ever mission and he fulfilled his obligation and performed his duty properly and perfectly. His *Seerah* is the way of life in every aspect. *Muslims* succeeded when they followed it and they stumbled when they forgot it. So, we make *Dua* that *O Allah*! As you have made your Prophet a perfect role model for us so give us the *Taufeeq* (strength and courage) to follow his *Seerah* and *Sunnah* in the proper way.

BOOKS BY *QAZI FAZL ULLAH*

Qazi Fazl Ullah has written other books. Below is a brief list with summaries.

FIQH KEE TAREEKH WA IRTIQA (URDU)

Islam is *Deen* (religion) and is a complete code of life. Its laws are of two types, textual and deduced, but how the text is interpreted and how laws are deduced therefrom is called *"Jurisprudence"* and the laws are called *Fiqh,* and how this *Fiqh* got developed and compiled. This book gives the details about its stages of development.

MOHAMMADUR RASOOLULLAH (URDU)

The biography of the *Prophet Mohammad* was preserved from day one by his blessed companions. Then scholars and historians have written books in this regard in various times, both concise and detailed. This book on the biography of *Prophet Mohammad* is an excellent balance of concise and detailed, as a concise a book sometimes misses things, and people do not have time to read and understand too detailed a book. Another important feature of this book is that almost with every important part of the *Prophet's* biography, the relevant part of the *Holy*

Quran has been quoted, which illustrates that the *Prophet's* life was the practical shape of the *Holy Book*.

SARMAYA DARANA NIZAM ISHTIRAKIYAT AUR ISLAM (URDU)

Humans, throughout their history, have thought ahead and planned their economics and economical needs. They created systems for these purposes. The three systems most widely practiced in history are capitalism, communism, and *Islam*. This book is a comparative study of these 3 economical systems, and it proves that the *Islamic* system bestowed upon us by the Creator is the best one with regard to justice and no room for exploitation.

DAWAT O JIHAD (URDU)

The basic duty of every *Prophet* and his followers was and is to call the people towards *Allah* in a peaceful, attractive, and convincing way, and wherever and whenever they encounter resistance and hindrances in this regard, they must remove these hindrances. At times, this leads to fights, as when the conspiracy is big and the opponents try to take away their fundamental rights, so they have the right to defend it but how, when, and where? In this book, it is mentioned that *Islam* teaches us to convey, convince, and convert, but not to coerce. This book is an answer to anti-*Islamic* propaganda, especially about the concept of *Jihad* in *Islam*.

ISLAM AUR SIYASAT (URDU)

Islam and Politics—as it is known from the title that this book discusses *Islamic* political system, because *Islam* is *Deen*, meaning a complete code of life and not a set of a few rituals. It has its own system for state and government. So, wherever *Muslims* are in power, if they will implement this system, they meet the needs of everyone, regardless of color, caste, or religion. *Islam* covers the details, such as how to elect a government, and how to run the state to provide peace and justice to all.

RIYASATI ISLAMI KA TASWWAR (URDU)

The title means the concept of an *Islamic* state, and *"concept"* means its conduct. In this book, it is mentioned how and why a state and government is needed, and how that state and government may be and should be run. The Creator *Allah* the Almighty knows all our needs, necessities, qualities, and shortcomings, so the system he has given is the only system that can ensure people's security and safety and can provide them peace and justice, making the state a welfare state.

USOOLUT - TAFSEER (ARABIC)

Every branch of science has its own rules, principles, and methodologies, which provide guidelines for explaining it and how to interpret it, so this methodology is a circle or limits one may keep himself confines to, so he will not get lost or go astray.

This book covers the explanation of the *Holy Quran*, the last and final book of *Allah*. The book of *Allah* is the basic source of *Islam* and *Islamic* law, so its explanation requires certain rules to be followed in its explanation, so one may not be unbridled and without restraint, otherwise he will put his faith in danger.

DIRAYATUR RIWAYAH (ARABIC)

Hadith (sayings, actions, and sanctions) of *Prophet Mohammad* is the second fundamental source of *Islam* and *Islamic* laws and also it is the interpretation of the *Holy Quran*. The companions of the *Prophet Mohammad* have preserved them in their memories and in their scriptures and the second and third generation took it from them and preserved them as well. Later on, when there was a fear of perversion, then these *Ahadith* were compiled officially and later on, the authentic scholars gathered them together in various books. Furthermore, critics compiled a biography of all these narrators and put certain rules about how a *Hadith* could be accepted. This book includes all these details.

HUJJIYATI HADITH (URDU)

This book is regarding the authenticity of *Hadith* of the *Prophet*, as there is a baseless propaganda that *Hadith* were not written in the time of the *Prophet*, but later on, making them unreliable. This is wrong, as *Sahaba* used to write *Ahadith* and sometimes the *Prophet* himself used to order them to write. But they trusted their memory more than writing. Official compilation took place later on, when *Muslim* rulers became aware of the weakness of people's memories and the loss of those individuals writing. This book provides all these details and makes it clear that *Hadith* is *Wahi* (Revelation) and source of *Islamic Shariah* (Law).

FUNDAMENTALISM, SECULARISM AUR ISLAM (URDU)

Propaganda is being spread either because of ignorance or with mala fide intention that *Islam* is fundamentalism.

Fundamentalism was a term used for Christianity when it blocked the ways of scientific research, invention and development, and some people wanted to adopt it as a basic guideline for states and government. So those who were with research and development branded that as fundamentalism. But *Islam* does not stop or block progress and research; rather, it encourages it and even orders scholars to go ahead and do research, as discussed in this book.

AL IJTIHADU WAT TAQLEED (URDU)

Humans are social and intellectual animals. They have all the same needs as animals, but they are distinct from them because of their intellect as they are looking for their ease, to do a little and get a lot. For this purpose, some intellectuals invent things and others follow them. Then as they are bound to obey the *Deen* of *Allah*, there are other intellectuals who deduce laws from its fundamental sources: the *Quran* and the *Sunnah*, and the less intellectuals follow them, as they should. This is the only intellectual and reasonable way. This book explains this issue and its importance.

MUSALMAN AURAT (URDU)

Allah created the world. He created humans and made them men and women. He gave different qualities to both genders for the smooth running of this life to depend upon each other, but as humans they are equal. Some women made history and they did memorable work that many men could not have done. This small book mentions some of the great work of some great women, particularly *Muslim* women, to make it clear that *Islam* deeply respects women and appreciates their contributions to society.

ASMATI RASOOL OR ZAWAJI AAISHA (URDU)

This world is a combination of opposites and some people have been given a great status. The messengers of *Allah* are the chosen and beloved of *Allah*. He made them and built them up for himself and his work. They are the most respected and honored people, and they must be given respect, as any disgrace to them can harm the feelings and sentiments of their followers, which can cause trouble. In this book this issue is discussed, as well as a misconception about the *Prophet's* marriage to *Aaisha*; namely, that she was minor at that time. Academically and research fully, this book corrects this misconception.

AL FARA'ID FIL AQA'ID (ARABIC)

Aqeedah and *Aqa'id* means faith and beliefs, respectively, and they are the base of *Deen*. Certain beliefs are the contents of *Iman*. What is important for a *Muslim* to believe? These are detailed in this concise book. Some *Muslim* sects have misconstrued some of these beliefs, so the book mentions that as well and makes the right faith clear.

QAWA'IDUT - TAJWEED (ARABIC)

One of the basic duties of the *Prophet* was to teach his followers how to recite the holy book properly. His *Sahabah* learnt it from him and then this became a specific science in future generations. They not only taught their students the proper way of recitation, they also wrote books about it. This science is called *Tajweed*, which literally means to make good, but in this science, it means to recite good. This book prescribes the basic rules for *Tajweed* as proper pronunciation not only makes the words and sounds good but also helps in giving the proper meaning of the word.

AL QAWA'IDUL FIQHIYAH (ARABIC)

Islam is *Deen* and a complete system and code of life. For each and every aspect of life there are rules and laws in *Islam*. Some of these rules are in text of the *Quran* and the *Sunnah*, while some others are deduced therefrom. For deduction, the authentic jurists have laid down rules of deduction and the qualities required for themselves. Then, after deduction, they have found some commonalities in different laws in different chapters, so they laid down a common rule for that and these rules called *Al Qawa'idul - Fiqhiyah*, or legal maxims, which make the study of *Fiqh* easy and understandable. This book includes some known and famous legal maxims in all four schools of jurisprudence.

AL JIHAD FIL ISLAM (ARABIC)

Jihad is a very important issue in *Islam*; to defend life, property, honor, and faith is not only a well-known right in each and every culture but also a duty in *Islam*, but how and when? This book is written on this subject; and as this issue is quite controversial, this is a reasonable answer to these questions in the light of the *Quran* and *Sunnah*.

MAULANA UBAIDULLAH SINDHI (URDU)

Maulana Ubaid Ullah Sindhi, originally from a *Sikh* family, accepted *Islam* when he was a teenager. He studied *Deen* in the proper and traditional way, then joined the freedom movement. He went through a lot of difficulties and lived in exile for 24 years. As a revolutionary leader, he is controversial, and many people wrote against him as well as for him. This book describes his personality, struggle, and thoughts to know who he was and how he was.

ASMATI RASOOL AND KHATMI NUBUWWAT (URDU)

Asmati Rasool and *Khatmi Nubuwwat* are reasonable and logical. This book consists of two parts. The defense of the *Prophet* and that of him being the last and final *Prophet* of *Allah* is a reasonable and logical thing, as *Allah* sent messengers in different times to different areas and different nations, and when they worked in their respected times in those areas, *Allah* sent the *Prophet Mohammad* to the entire world to combine their work and bring humanity together on the same theme, subject and faith that all those earlier messengers were sent for. This book is a concise, detailed, and logical interpretation of this finality.

SAYYIDAH AAISHA'S AGE AT MARRIAGE (ENGLISH)

Islam is a Natural *Deen* or *Deen* of Nature. This is a balanced *Deen* providing a comprehensive justice system, and the *Holy Prophet* is the perfect role model as a perfect human. His words, actions, and sanctions are the proper interpretation of the *Holy Quran* and the second fundamental source of laws in *Islam*. There is a commonly held belief, especially among critics of *Islam*, that the *Prophet* married *Aaisha* when she was only nine years of age. In this book, all the details about this issue are given that how this word *Tis'aa* (which means nine) happened there and what the real story is to counter the false accounts and correct the record.

JIHAD IN ISLAM: WHY, HOW, AND WHEN? (ENGLISH)

Jihad as a word in *Arabic* means struggle or striving hard, especially for a noble cause, while as a term in *Islam*, it specifically means to fight in the path/cause of *Allah*. But when does this fight happen? When it is inevitable and unavoidable as the very integrity of a state, the lives of its citizens or the very ideology is facing a big danger. But a very baseless smear campaign is going on against *Jihad* and it is branded as a synonym to terrorism, so this book is a must to make the true concept of *Jihad* clear and counter the propaganda.

SHARIA AND POLITICS (ENGLISH)

Islam is *Deen* and *Deen* means a complete system and a perfect code of life as this is given by the very creator of the worlds, who knows all about his creatures, their qualities, and their shortcomings, and can provide a perfect solution to their problems. But unfortunately, some people have been doing wrong in the name of *Khalafat* and presenting their wrong idea as the *Islamic* political system, so there was great need of a book that can present the proper shape of an *Islamic* state and *Islamic* political system given by the Creator; when executed properly, it is actually a mercy and blessing for the creatures. This book explains this concept clearly.

HAJJ & UMRAH IN ALL FOUR SCHOOLS OF JURISPRUDENCE (ENGLISH)

Hajj (pilgrimage to *Mecca*) is one of the Five Pillars of *Islam* and an especially important but a complicated type of *Ibadah* (worship) as *Muslims* from all around the world get together to perform it together. They follow the interpretation of their *Imams* (jurists), sometimes they look at others when they do not perform a specific virtue the way they do, then they think they are doing wrong, which is not so, but all of them are performing correctly according to the interpretation of their *Imams*. This book gives all these details in sequence according to all four *Imams* the *Muslim Ummah* follows.

MOON SIGHTING, SALATUL TARAWEEH AND SALATUL WITR (ENGLISH)

The *Islamic* Calendar is lunar based. It's different *Ibadaat* time is based on moonsighting; the lunar month starts with the new moon. Even though astronomy tells us what day the moon will be born (i.e., new) with perfect accuracy, discerning on which day it will be visible in a specific area is still not accurate. That is why differences in opinion happen all over the world, and should we to go by the calendar or by a sighting?

Also, at *Ramadan*, which is the most important month in *Islam* as a mandatory *Ibadah*, fasting is mandatory as well, but there is an extra, highly recommended *Ibadah,* the *Taraweeh*, but how many *Rakat* should we pray? *Muslims* differ about this. Another important *Ibadah* is *Salat Ul Witr*. We use this prayer all year, but during *Ramadan* this is prayed in *Jama'at,* and different *Imams* have different opinions regarding the number of *Rakats* and its procedure. So, this book gives all the details about these three prominent issues.

SCIENCE OF HADITH (ENGLISH)

Hadith is the second fundamental source of *Islamic* law. They are the words, actions, and sanctions of the *Holy Prophet*. To record all these in memory and writing, to compile it and to record the biography of those narrators who did this great job, and this is considered as a miracle of the *Prophet*. But the enemies of *Islam* used to create doubts in this regard. This book is written on this subject, and it is enough an answer to all the objections that people made from different angles.

HAJJ & UMRAH IN ALL FOUR SCHOOLS OF JURISPRUDENCE (URDU)

Hajj (pilgrimage to *Mecca*) is one of the Five Pillars of *Islam* and an especially important but a complicated type of *Ibadah* (worship) as *Muslims* from all around the world get together to perform it together. They follow the interpretation of their *Imams* (jurists), sometimes they look at others when they do not perform a specific virtue the way they do, then they think they are doing wrong, which is not so, but all of them are performing correctly according to the interpretation of their *Imams*. This book gives all these details in sequence according to all four *Imams* the *Muslim Ummah* follows.

USOOL AT - TAFSEER (PASHTO)

Every branch of science has its own rules, principles, and methodologies, which provide guidelines for explaining it and how to interpret it, so this methodology is a circle or limits one may keep himself confines to, so he will not get lost or go astray.

This book covers the explanation of the *Holy Quran*, the last and final book of *Allah*. The book of *Allah* is the basic source of *Islam* and *Islamic* law, so its explanation requires certain rules to be followed in its explanation, so one may not be unbridled and without restraint, otherwise he will put his faith in danger.

BIDAYATUL FI ILMIL USOOL (ARABIC)

Islamic Fiqh is "shariah" or laws of Islam. Laws are of two types substantive and procedural and all of these laws are based upon jurisprudence. "Ilmul Usool" which is called "Ilmul Fiqh" also is the jurisprudence of "shariah." As we know that in Islam there are four famous schools of jurisprudence. i.e. Hanafi, Maliki, Shafi, Hanbali. In this book the jurisprudence of all these schools are explained which can be useful for those who are interested in it. It will help them know how imams differ on certain issues.

KHUDA KAHA HAY? (URDU)

Allah placed his concept in human nature. Throughout human history people believed in Allah in one way or the other. Even agnostics as they bewilder like one who is looking for something. The atheists deny him but their denial is actually an admission that something exists but deny it. Muslims believe in Allah but there are certain issues they differ in. Its proper interpretation as to whether Allah is on the throne or is everywhere. In this book we tried to bring forth both concepts along with its proper expression as to what they meant by both.

USOOL AT - TAFSEER (URDU)

Every branch of science has its own rules, principles, and methodologies, which provide guidelines for explaining it and how to interpret it, so this methodology is a circle or limits one may keep himself confines to, so he will not get lost or go astray.

This book covers the explanation of the *Holy Quran*, the last and final book of *Allah*. The book of *Allah* is the basic source of *Islam* and *Islamic* law, so its explanation requires certain rules to be followed in its explanation, so one may not be unbridled and without restraint, otherwise he will put his faith in danger.

MOHAMMAD THE APOSTLE OF MERCY (ENGLISH)

The biography of the *Prophet Mohammad* was preserved from day one by his blessed companions. Then scholars and historians have written books in this regard in various times, both concise and detailed. This book on the biography of *Prophet Mohammad* is an excellent balance of concise and detailed, as a concise a book sometimes misses things, and people do not have time to read and understand too detailed a book. Another important feature of this book is that almost with every important part of the *Prophet's* biography, the relevant part of the *Holy Quran* has been quoted, which illustrates that the *Prophet's* life was the practical shape of the *Holy Book*.

AHSANUL KALAM FIL A'IMMATIL AALAM (URDU)

IQNA-US SAAIL FI THALATHI MASA'IL (URDU)

BAHLOOL DANA AIK MU'AMMA SHAKHSIYAT (URDU)

KHULAFA E RASHIDEEN. (URDU)

ABOUT THE AUTHOR

Qazi Fazl Ullah is an American philosopher, linguist, and author. He is *Fazil Wafaqul Madaris* where he studied *Arabic* grammar, *Arabic* literature, *Fiqh*, jurisprudence, logic, philosophy, *Ilmul Kalam, Seerah, Tafseer, Hadith,* and *Islamic* history. He studied at *Peshawar University* and *Islamic University Islamabad* in *Pakistan* and specialized in law, economics, and political science. He has taught all these subjects in *Pakistan* and the United States at different institutions. He was elected as a *National Assembly Parliamentarian* in *Pakistan*. He worked in underserved areas to provide jobs, build infrastructure, schools, museums, public health facilities, and increase communication technologies as the chair of the *Social Action Board*. He has traveled extensively throughout the Middle East, North Africa, Europe, Southeast Asia, North and Central America. He has given seminars in various parts of the world in these subjects. He speaks and has given lectures and seminars in *Urdu, Pashto, Farsi,* English, and *Arabic*. He has published works in *Pashto, Urdu, Arabic,* and English internationally. He has given the complete *Tafsir Ul Quran* in *Pashto* multiple times in *Pakistan*. He has also given *Tafsir Ul Quran* in *Urdu, Pashto,* and English in the United States. It includes *Usul Ul Fiqh, Usul Ul Mirath, Hadith al Qudsi, Hadith an Nabawi* in English on multiple occasions. He considers himself a student to continue acquisition of knowledge. He is currently leading *Tafsir Ul Quran, Usual Al Fiqh, Seerat Un Nabi,* Science of Inheritance (*Mirath*) in English and *Al Mukhtar Lil Fatawa, Dirayat Ul Riwaya* in *Arabic* in Los Angeles, California.

www.ingramcontent.com/pod-product-compliance
Lightning Source LLC
Chambersburg PA
CBHW021347290426
44108CB00010B/148